Retail Strategy

Retail Strategy

The view from the bridge

Edited by
Jonathan Reynolds and Christine Cuthbertson

With contributions from
Richard Bell
Richard Cuthbertson
Ross Davies
Dmitry Dragun
Elizabeth Howard

ELSEVIER
BUTTERWORTH
HEINEMANN

AMSTERDAM BOSTON HEIDELBERG LONDON NEW YORK OXFORD
PARIS SAN DIEGO SAN FRANCISCO SINGAPORE SYDNEY TOKYO

Elsevier Butterworth-Heinemann
Linacre House, Jordan Hill, Oxford OX2 8DP
200 Wheeler Road, Burlington MA 01803

First published 2004

British Library Cataloguing in Publication Data
Retail strategy: the view from the bridge
    1.   Retail trade – Management
    I.   Reynolds, Jonathan   II.   Cuthbertson, Christine   III.   Bell, Richard
    658.8'7

Library of Congress Cataloguing in Publication Data
A catalogue record for this book is available from the Library of Congress

ISBN 0 7506 5696 4

For information on all Elsevier Butterworth-Heinemann publications
visit our website at www.bh.com

Typeset by Newgen Imaging Systems (P) Ltd, Chennai, India
Printed and bound in Great Britain

Contents

Contributors

Richard Bell joined the Boots Company after graduating from University College, London with a degree in economics. Richard later joined Pedigree Petfoods, the UK pet food division of Mars Incorporated, working initially in forecasting and planning, then purchasing, and latterly in marketing. He went on to run the international division of Mars Inc., later becoming MD in Belgium and finally assuming responsibility for Mars Inc.'s European sales strategy and their global consumer research. During this period he was a member of the CIES Marketing committee. He left Mars in 1996 and joined Templeton College as an associate fellow specializing in retailer–supplier relations.

Christine Cuthbertson began her career in marketing at Hymac Engineering and moved into publishing with Parrish-Rogers. Christine has also developed an information systems specialism, and has lectured at the universities of East London, Bournemouth, Cranfield and Southampton. Christine is completing a research methods MPhil at the University of Southampton. She is author of book chapters, journal and conference papers and is presently editor of the *European Retail Digest* and senior research associate at Templeton College, University of Oxford.

Richard Cuthbertson has a wide variety of professional experiences working both in industry and academia, in managerial, consulting, research and teaching positions. Richard has held managerial posts for the Unipart Group of Companies and British Gas in both marketing and supply chain management. Management consultancy work has typically involved the strategic modelling and analysis of retailer–supplier and retailer–consumer systems, operations and relationships. Before joining Templeton College as a senior research associate, Richard was a senior lecturer at Bournemouth University. His current research projects include: the strategic evaluation of consumer loyalty to European retailers, sponsored by KPMG; benchmarking international FMCG supply chains with the Boston Consulting Group for CIES (the World Food Business Forum); a European Union funded study on the effects of transport trends in retail logistics and supply chain management; and the development of a new approach to inventory replenishment systems. Richard has a degree in management science from Lancaster University, and is currently completing a PhD at

Southampton University. He is also a member of the Operational Research Society.

Ross Davies was a founder director of the Oxford Institute of Retail Management in 1985. Ross's research interests centre on the retail and shopping centre development process, location strategy, the internationalization of retailing and public policies towards the industry. He has held academic appointments at the universities of Massachusetts, Newcastle-upon-Tyne, Windsor (Canada) and New England (Australia). He has also been technical director of the Coca-Cola European Retail Research Group, a Specialist Adviser to the House of Commons Environment Committee's Enquiry into Shopping Centres and their Future, and remains chairman of the Oxford Retail Group, a consortium of companies concerned to improve retail planning policies within the UK. He is the author of numerous books and articles and has been a consultant to several UK and international retail and development companies, through his company Retailing and Planning Associates. He is presently Emeritus fellow at Templeton College and a visiting professor in retail management at the University of Surrey.

Dmitry Dragun. Prior to arriving in Oxford to study for an MBA, Dmitry worked at the National Bank of Belarus as director for foreign exchange operations and controls. In this capacity, he implemented the EBRD/WB credit line for small and medium companies ($30 million + facility, 1994/5); structured and executed the financing scheme for the viable export-oriented projects in the private sector of Belarus ($12 million + facility, 1996); and contributed to the development of the external debt management system for Belarus as a sovereign borrower. Dmitry's PhD thesis – and a corresponding degree conferred by the Belarusian Academy of Sciences – was a result of the five years of research into international finance and external debt management. As the senior research associate in finance at Templeton, Dmitry is responsible – at the request of the Templeton corporate clients – for equity analysis and risk assessment of the leading European companies such as Vodafone, AXA, RWE and Unilever. He has progressed the value creation line of executive research, related in particular to the patterns of risk and value recognition among the global regions and countries. Professional assignments include development of the risk management framework for Shell T&T, an analytical review of Tesco's risk and value comparative performance, and a number of the innovative data-mining finance products.

Current research interests include: development of the UK Retail Confidence Index ('Templeton RCI'), strategic and financial performance review of the top UK companies, value creation and convergence in global retailing.

Elizabeth Howard specializes in international retail development and environmental issues in business. After professional posts in town planning, Elizabeth began research work on retailing at the University of Newcastle and came to Templeton in 1986. Her work on public policies and the impact of out of town retail development, as part of the Oxford Institute of Retail Management at Templeton, is well known. Current research focuses on international retail development. She designs, directs and teaches executive programmes for a variety of international companies and is a tutor for the Oxford Strategic Leadership Programme. She has taught university degree courses in environment and business, established the business project scheme for the Oxford University MBA and is keenly interested in management learning through project work. Publications include many articles and monographs on retail development, an examination of concepts of partnership in shopping centre businesses, research for the CEC (DGXVII) on the retail response to energy labelling, *Business and the Natural Environment* (editor, with P. Bansal), and most recently *European Retailers' Approaches to Asian Markets.*

Jonathan Reynolds first joined Templeton to work with UK food retailer Tesco on the application of new information technology, following time spent at the University of Edinburgh, with Coca-Cola, and at the University of Newcastle-upon-Tyne. A geographer, urban planner and retailer by turn, Jonathan now teaches and researches in the areas of retailing and technology, retail and services marketing and retail planning and development. He has published and spoken widely on e-commerce, structural changes in retailing and in the fields of database, direct and local marketing. As director of the Oxford Institute of Retail Management, he is actively involved with Templeton's commercial clients in the retail, financial and leisure services sectors and, as a faculty member of Oxford University's Said Business School, teaches marketing and e-commerce on Oxford's undergraduate and MBA programmes.

Figures and tables

Figures

Tables

Part I

Introduction

Chapter 1

Introduction to retail strategy

Jonathan Reynolds

Introduction

Retail practitioners, historically, have been suspicious of strategy. Sir Ken Morrison, chairman of family-run Morrisons supermarkets in the UK, is on record as saying that running supermarkets is simple. Sir Ken reportedly has little time for fancy theories or clever marketing: 'It's just taking money off people, isn't it? And giving them something in return' (*Mail on Sunday*, 2002). Marketers and economists used to share this somewhat folksy view, in effect regarding retailers as mere ciphers in the distribution channel, working as intermediaries just to smooth the flow of goods and services between suppliers and consumers. Then it became clear that in practice, retailers were able to become much more active agents in their own right within the value chain than was sometimes suggested. Indeed, the flows of people, goods and money through the retail supply chain make the sector's businesses some of the most influential corporate players in the economies of developed countries. In 1999, for example, European retail trade generated sales of €1518 billion; created €292.5 billion in added value and employed 12.4 million people (European Commission, 2003).

From the point of view of the marketer, retailers are, by definition, closer to the consumer than supplier companies. This has two implications. First, retailers are in principle better placed to gather information on the behaviour of consumers and customers than organizations further back in the supply chain. Second, and as a consequence of this data-gathering activity, such companies are also therefore becoming better placed to communicate more effectively with consumers and to develop strategies that are more effectively market-oriented. And strategies are required, as Sam Walton once remarked: 'retailing is simple but it ain't easy' and such businesses – like Wal-Mart – are becoming increasingly complex animals: very large, widely spread organizations, managing multiple product supply lines, managing very large amounts of data, and above all, far from being

ciphers, are competing more and more with other large organizations rather than
small ones.

But strategy has come late to retailing. Business strategy text books have contained few references to the sector until relatively recently. Now retailing is the
domain of corporate strategy, format strategy, marketing strategy, international
strategy and so on. Strategy has arrived because of the most important of the structural trends we can identify: this is that large organizations now run most of the
retailing in western economies and are now coming to do so in transitional economies. In a strategic sense, retailers are concerned with growing larger and faster
than their competitors, being different from the competitors, attracting and keeping customers, and gaining efficiencies in systems and procedures. Bell describes
the way this has happened for food retailing as an 'inexorable logic' (Bell, 2000).
There are, he suggests, four stages:

- *The development of retail chains as retailers sought to increase their buying power.* The
  early exponents of this process were the consumer co-operatives and during this stage
  most chains, including the co-ops were organized on a regional basis within a country. This was followed by the emergence of national retail chains with large market
  shares.
- *The development of large retail formats.* The emergence of these formats across Europe
  coincided with increasingly lax planning regimes, initially in Belgium followed by France,
  Spain, Portugal, and then the UK. The large surface outlets resulted in a reduction in
  the number of small corner stores and the decline of town centre supermarkets. This
  process in itself contributed to the retail concentration of ownership characterized by
  stage 1.
- *The development of dedicated distribution systems by the large integrated retailers.* The development and application of scanning systems provided the necessary information for the
  supply chain to be reversed from 'producer push' to 'consumer pull'. A consequence of
  this process is the decline of traditional wholesalers and cash and carries that has the
  effect of further disadvantaging small retailers.
- *The emergence of retail chains as national brands in their own right.* The effect is to move
  away from head-to-head price competition to a differentiation strategy based on range,
  service, store format and location.

This book is about achieving a better understanding of the characteristics and
consequences of this process. In doing so, it seeks to bridge the gap between
retailing and strategy and between retailers and academics. It takes several of the
corporate themes of strategic interest to contemporary retailing and explores them
through the presentation of practitioner insight underpinned by rigorous academic
analysis. In particular, a series of case studies are developed based on interviews
with senior executives in some of the world's leading retailers. The book is an
attempt to communicate contemporary retail thought from the perspectives not
only of senior international retailers but also retail commentators and analysts.

Size and its consequences

Even as recently as 1990, there were no retailers in the Fortune 500 list of the largest global companies. Now there are over 50, and in 2002 Wal-Mart became the largest of all companies, judged by size of sales. (Wal-Mart alone employs over 1.3 million associates worldwide; 100 million customers a week visit the company's 4,300 stores.) In just two years – between 1996 and 1998 – retailers' share of the revenues of the Fortune top 500 grew by over 25 per cent, and their share of total assets doubled (Gestrin, 2000). Small shops, independent retailers and small firms have closed in their hundreds of thousands. Some large and medium sized companies have grown dramatically: Dutch retailer Ahold tripled in size between 1990 and 1998 and then added over 50 per cent in the following year. French retailer Carrefour is five times its size at the beginning of the last decade. Wal-Mart's compound annual growth rate throughout the 1990s was 19.5 per cent. Despite significant consolidation activity in the US, it is European countries that show the highest levels of concentration. For example, in France, the five largest retailers have increased their share of grocery retailing from 61 to 83 per cent in just six years (Bell, 2001). Maturing markets are also catching up: in Greece the top ten food retailers' market share grew from 18.5 per cent in 1990 to 72 per cent in 1999 (Bourlakis, 2001). Nor should we forget that large companies dominate many of the specialist non-food retail trades too – although by their nature levels of turnover are generally smaller. In the UK, three companies accounted for 26.4 per cent of clothing sales in 2001 and fully 82 per cent in DIY. Italy, so long a preserve of small firms and small retailers within the EU is changing too: the presence of Carrefour and Auchan in the country has helped increase the number of hypermarkets to over 400 in 2000 – a fourfold increase in ten years (Mintel Retail Intelligence, 2002). From negligible levels in 1989, large multiple firms have grown to take substantial proportions of a growing retail trade in the countries of central Europe. The trends are the same in Latin America and Asia Pacific countries. The degree to which large corporations dominate in the latter seems mainly related to the degree to which the countries are open to foreign direct investment. In China, for example, the reforms and changes of the last few years mean that, apart from the foreign entrants who see huge prospects for growth, indigenous multiple retailers are growing. Although they are responsible for only a small fraction of retailing at the moment, official policy is to encourage their growth, as a means to increasing the efficiency of distribution and encouraging growth in the consumer economy (Central Committee of the People's Republic of China, 2002).

The implications of size become significant when retailers affect consumer choice, obtain a relative competitive advantage and/or influence supplier profitability. This has brought retailing to the attention of the regulatory authorities. Market share reflects retailers' influence over consumers, competitors and suppliers. Absolute size is also important vis-à-vis suppliers. The potential impact of retailer size can be measured by their ability to extract non-cost-related discounts from suppliers. Size becomes important here when the potential lost volume to a supplier has a significant effect on profit. Businesses whose profit is highly sensitive to changes in sales volume are more likely to offer non-cost-related discounts and are more vulnerable to smaller sized accounts, e.g. with market shares of under, say, 10 per cent. Thus the exact level of size at which a retailer exercises power varies with financial structure of each supplier. Chapter 3 discusses the consequences that have emerged in terms of supply chain collaboration of such a situation.

The relevant measure of size with respect to influence over consumers, and relative competitive advantage is the level of concentration shown by the Herfindahl-Herschman Index. The HHI is determined by adding the squares of the market shares of each competitor within the relevant product and geographic market. For example, if there are four firms, with shares of 30 per cent, 30 per cent, 20 per cent, and 20 per cent, respectively, then the HHI equals 2,600 (900 + 900 + 400 + 400). If two or three retailers have a very large market share, this is reflected in a higher HHI than if five retailers have similar market shares, even though the aggregate share for the top five retailers is similar. The US regulatory authorities have used the HHI as a means of understanding and potentially challenging prospective post-merger outcomes in retailing (Miller, 1997):

> The guidelines under which the FTC and the Department of Justice operate are as follows: If the pre-merger HHI is between 1,000 and 1,800, the industry is moderately concentrated, and the merger will be challenged only if it increases the HHI by 100 points or more. If the HHI is greater than 1,800, the market is highly concentrated. In a highly concentrated market, a merger that produces an increase in the HHI between 50 and 100 points raises significant competitive concerns. Finally, mergers that produce an increase in the HHI of more than 100 points in a highly concentrated market are deemed likely to enhance market power.

Usually, levels of concentration are calculated nationally (see examples in Table 1.1) but there is a growing weight of evidence to suggest that influence over consumers is better measured by regional or local market share of each store type. Absolute turnover is also increasingly relevant as suppliers organize themselves at a European level and food retailers organize their procurement at a European (or global) level even though their operations may be national. Turnover enables a comparison to be made between retailers from different countries. The competition directorate within the European Commission has ruled on several cases during the 1990s of pan-European businesses making strategic acquisitions in different countries that have consequences in terms of buyer power and influence over consumer choice. For example, in the case of the French Promodès-Carrefour merger, the Commission referral followed concern that in three Spanish administrative regions, post-merger market shares were particularly high. In one region, six out of seven hypermarkets would have been run by the combined group.

Table 1.1 Grocery market concentration levels of the five largest retailers 1999–2000: selected European countries

Country	HHI
Denmark	2,502
Finland	2,529
France	1,619
Germany	1,216
Italy*	285
Norway	2,500
Spain	462
Sweden	1,811
Switzerland	2,535
UK**	1,506

* organized distribution.
** base is grocery stores referenced in Competition Commission Inquiry, 2000.
Source: OXIRM, ACNielsen, DCF, ICA

The terms of regulatory clearance in this case meant that in January 2003, a group of French financial institutions paid €242m (US$258.9m) to buy 59 Spanish supermarkets from Carrefour. The company will continue to operate the supermarkets under long-term leases. In the UK, the debate over the acquisition of supermarket chain Safeway during 2003 revolved around, amongst other things, the extent to which the competing would-be acquirers would be forced by the regulators to dispose of stores in local areas where their potential market share was regarded as excessive.

Increasing retailer size and power, especially buyer power, is now beginning to concern competition authorities worldwide. In a recent and little-publicized conference in New York, representatives from European, American and ASEAN competition agencies met specifically to exchange views on the topic (Fordham Corporate Law Institute, 2000). A number of governments, not least southern European ones, have expressed particular concern that failure to regulate the growth of large retail businesses will destroy the still large numbers of established small- and medium-sized businesses within those countries. At a European level, the Commission's Directorate-General XXIII, whilst unable to intervene in the planning policies of member states, funds training and technological assistance programmes for small businesses within those states considered most vulnerable to increased levels of retail concentration. This approach has been criticized as being unduly concerned with conserving historic patterns of change, rather than allowing retailers to operate more freely in an increasingly turbulent business environment (Dawson, 1996).

Strategic routes to growth

Growth of this kind by a small number of retail businesses has not been accidental. The success of a retailer can be seen as a consequence of the effectiveness of its strategy: its ability to create long-term superior financial performance through the cultivation of valuable *internal resources* and their matching to the set of most advantageous *external opportunities* as it grows. As Dawson and others have suggested (Dawson, 1996), the environment for strategic decisions in retailing has become considerably more complex. The ultimate drivers of retail change and the permissible range of external opportunities are generated by the demographic, political and economic forces in society, alterations in social values and behaviours, and in the communications and technological revolutions we are experiencing. Retailers respond to, and in some ways help create or facilitate these changes.

There are a number of conventional conceptual frameworks in strategic management that seek to organize the kinds of *external opportunities* available to businesses and it is not the intention of this chapter to provide an exhaustive review of alternatives. Ansoff's (1988) well-established matrix suggests four particular options for growth based upon any business's market and product with risk increasing as the business moves away its existing products and markets towards new ones (Figure 1.1). This is a very appealing distinction to draw. However, it is clear that in any business, let alone retailing, the options available to business are more than can be portrayed in a simple two-by-two matrix. Retailing additionally deals with

	Existing market/ mission	New market/ mission
Existing product	Market penetration	Market development
New product	Product development	Diversification

Figure 1.1 Ansoff's product-mission matrix
Source: After Ansoff (1988)

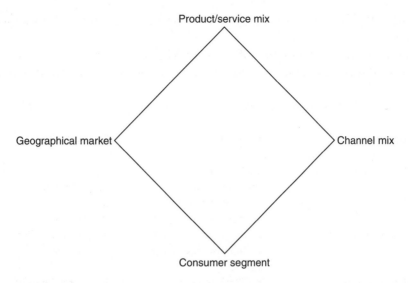

Figure 1.2 Opportunity diamond
Source: OXIRM

assortments of goods and services, rather than with *individual* products per se. Further, in retailing the channel formats through which the product selection is offered (whether they be stores, branches and web sites) may be significant and integral characteristics of the business and not simply downstream consequences of the strategic marketing process. We also need to consider that retailers operate both in geographical markets of different scales as well as in markets determined by their size and nature of their consumer base.

We argue that a more relevant way of representing the strategic options available to retailers is to talk of a 'diamond' of opportunities (Figure 1.2).

Put simply, the questions we need to have answered are: what are we selling, to whom, how and where? At the four apices therefore are:

■ *Product/service mix* The key choice of an appropriate assortment of products or services that defines what a retailer is in the eyes of its customer base.
■ *Consumer segment* To whom is the product/service mix targeted and what are their perceived needs?
■ *Channel mix* How is the product/service mix to be delivered in terms of formats or channels?
■ *Geographical market* Where is the product/service mix to be delivered in terms of site, location and geographical market?

These apices provide directions for growth. Following Ansoff's lead, retailers can choose to intensify their existing activity to optimize their *penetration* of one of these elements. They can seek to achieve dominance against one or more of the four opportunity criteria given in Table 1.2.

Alternatively (Table 1.3), they can choose to *develop* new opportunities along one of the axes.

For example, many larger retailers are seeking to diversify into services. Eagle *et al*. argue that this is not just for reasons of growth per se, but because retailers have

Table 1.2 Penetration strategies

Strategy	Description	Examples
Product/service mix	Seek to dominate a product/service category through specialization	IKEA Home Depot B&Q Toys 'R' Us
Consumer segment	Increase market share within primary target segment	Frequency marketing programmes
Channel mix	Proliferate stores to optimize store densities	Boots the Chemist McDonald's
Geographical market	Deliberate concentration of geographical penetration at local or national levels	Carrefour Wal-Mart

Table 1.3 Development strategies

Strategy	Description	Examples
Product/service mix	Diversification into related or totally new product/service mixes	Wal-Mart (financial services)
Consumer segment	Appealing to related or totally new groups of consumers	Lowes Hardware (women)
Channel mix	Diversification into new store formats or alternative distribution channels through the development of associated transactional web sites	Borders (online) Staples (Dover) Wal-Mart (Neighbourhood Markets)
Geographical market	Growth into new geographical markets	Carrefour Ahold Zara

actively identified a need amongst consumers for improvements in the efficiency and speed of handling of certain types of complex transaction. The best service diversification is characterized, they argue, in terms of packages of inter-related products, services and information (Eagle *et al.*, 2000, p. 108).

> Home Depot now offers design and installation services, home improvement financing, and tool rentals. Carrefour, the world's second-largest retailer, provides insurance, telecom, and travel services. Meanwhile, the US office supply retailer Staples, extending its products and services for small businesses and home offices, provides insurance, telecom services, copying, shipping, and payroll servicing.

Sometimes, the largest businesses are able to take advantage of all these routes to growth. Tesco, the UK's largest grocery retailer is an excellent case in point. With a packaged grocery market share of some 25 per cent within the UK, the majority delivered through large outlying superstores, sustaining profitability growth through pure penetration strategies in a slow-growing UK grocery market and within the regulatory constraints of the UK competition and planning authorities has been challenging. Whilst penetration strategies have been pursued, the company's long term route to growth in profitability is developmental. Its strategy is summed up below. We can recast these elements into the opportunities framework developed in Table 1.4.

Table 1.4 Growth opportunities for Tesco

Strategy	Description
Product/service mix	Diversification into clothing, health & beauty, electrical, entertainment and other non-food categories; joint ventures in financial services
Consumer segment	Appealing to broader groups of consumers
Channel mix	Diversification into Tesco Express, Metro and Extra formats and the development of Tesco.com, now accounting for some 5 per cent of the company's turnover; acquisition of 862 T&S convenience stores, of which 450 will be converted to the Tesco Express format
Geographical market	Growth in Eire, central Europe and south-east Asia, accounting in 2002 for 45 per cent of group floorspace and some 18 per cent of turnover

Our successful long-term growth strategy has four elements:

strong UK core business – continues to grow and to build market share

non-food – making excellent progress towards our goal of being as strong in non-food as food

retailing services – following the customer into new areas such as personal finance and on-line retailing

international – our long-term organic growth programme is progressing well and we are on track for 45% of Group space by 2002.

Tesco plc Annual Report and Accounts, 2001

We can note that in Tesco's case, this mix of strategies has been achieved through a mixture of organizational methods: independently, through organic growth; via merger or acquisition; or through a variety of joint ventures. Chapter 7 reviews the financial efficacy of such activity; Chapter 5 puts this into the context of international development.

Creative positioning: art or science?

The interaction between product/service mix and target consumer segment is an iterative one. Crafting an offer that meets shoppers' perceived needs, can be as much an art as a science. The offer conventionally requires positioning in relation to the offers of other retailers to establish a differential advantage. Retailers conventionally must choose from the list of store choice criteria seen by consumers as important to determine how they wish to compete. Hill (2000) suggests that we can distinguish between *order-winning* criteria and *order-qualifying* criteria. Qualifiers are those criteria that a company must meet for a consumer to even consider it as a possible choice. However providing or attaining these criteria does not win orders. Winners comprise the criterion, or criteria, against which consumers will make the final choice. Strength in both winning and qualifying criteria build switching barriers and generate loyal customers.

Chapter 2 discusses the relationship between business effectiveness and customer loyalty. An example is shown in Figure 1.3, which provides insights into grocery shopping behaviour and distinguishes between the most important factor in store selection and those factors which are important but not critical. In this context, more shoppers find the 'one-stop shop' criterion a winning one than price alone, although price is a significant qualifier and, for a smaller group of consumers, a key winning criterion in its own right. Convenience is the only other criterion to attract a greater than 10 per cent appeal as a main factor in store choice. This example suggests that there may be three key positioning dimensions in the market available to grocery retailers: a 'full service' range one-stop shop; a low price offer and a convenience offer, each relevant to certain customer segments at certain times; and of course, this maps very closely on to what we know about how this sector is presently structured in many developed economies. Further, the dominant 'one-stop' positioning criterion has the effect of raising barriers to store switching: the move to larger surface grocery stores, the shift in location to out-of-town for such stores, and the absence of competing stores at the same location will work to raise consumers' search costs and reduce consumer awareness of product price and availability elsewhere.

It is also necessary that such positioning solutions be sustainable over a reasonable period, since re-positioning can be expensive as well as being confusing to the customer. Such sustainability can be challenging to generate: the CEO of UK supermarket retailer Tesco, Sir Terry Leahy, once remarked that the lead time for the innovative grocery retailer was in the order of six weeks.

As Figure 1.3 suggests, one of the key trade-offs in developing compelling strategic positioning is that between price and a bundle of non-price factors. Identifying how competitors are positioned in relation to these two sets of factors can be a starting point in determining gaps in the existing market. For example, in the case of selection of a clothing retailer, consumer surveys have shown that non-price consumer choice differentiators include: a wide range of sizes, good stock availability, clothes that are 'a bit different', a wide range of colours and sizes, good changing areas and more helpful staff. Figure 1.4 shows a sample competitive map of retailers' positioning in relation to their aggregate score against a bundle of non-price factors, and a score on a price index as perceived by shoppers themselves. The size of the circles indicate market share.

Recently, and in line with increasingly professional and strategic thinking by the leading organizations in the sector worldwide, we have witnessed a move to

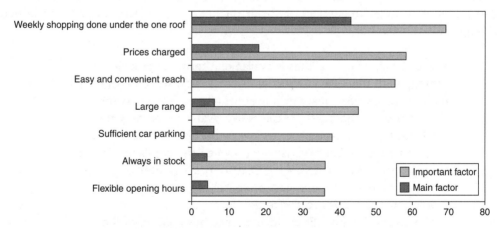

Figure 1.3 Determinants of store choice, UK grocery shoppers
Source: Competition Commission, 2000

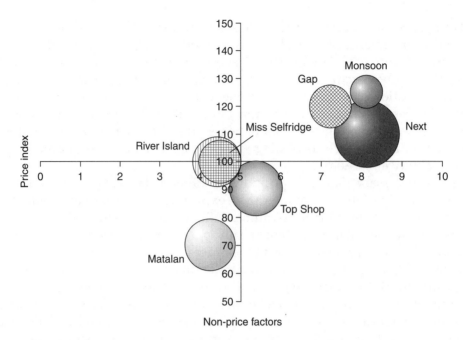

Figure 1.4 Retailers of speciality women's outerware – UK competitive map
Source: OXIRM

develop an 'image' of good price. So-called every day low pricing (EDLP), first developed by leading US retailers such as Wal-Mart and perpetuated, for example, in Europe not just through Wal-Mart subsidiaries such as Asda and Wertkauf, but also in Castorama (France), and the 'never knowingly undersold' claim of the John Lewis Partnership of the UK: all examples of attempts to develop a longer term belief in the price positioning of leading retailers. German retailer Aldi's brand is even more about lowest price at acceptable quality. The differences between the two main types of strategy in respect of supermarket price positioning are explained by Tang, Bell and Ho (2000):

> A wide range of possibilities is available in terms of pricing strategy, with the 'Every Day Low Price' (EDLP) store on one end and the store which offers promotional pricing, known as the HILO store, on the other. Retailers like Wal-Mart employ the EDLP strategy and typically offer low prices all the time. As a result, there is minimum variability between the regular price and discount price. In contrast, a HILO store has a greater disparity between the highest and lowest price, relying on sales and promotional strategies to entice the buyer.
>
> The 'Every Day Low Price' format generally appeals to the cost-conscious buyer. EDLP shoppers normally buy many things in one trip, they benefit from the small average cost savings on

> individual items. In contrast to the EDLP stores, the HILO store
> competes on service and assortment, not price. The consumers
> who like to make small and frequent shopping trips are more
> likely to go to the HILO store.

Tang, Bell and Ho make clear that supermarket companies cannot 'have their cake and eat it': that is, it is not considered generally viable for them to offer both extensive assortments and very low prices across their full assortments. Grocery multiple retailers therefore have choices available to them in terms of their positioning in terms of price and retail service. EDLP stores in general compensate for their small range of price fluctuations by offering limited product ranges in certain categories.

Branding and the development of retail brands

The use of branding has been a major historical source of supplier power. Whilst branding has come late to retailing, it is one of the most important elements of retail strategy today. The expression of the retailer as a brand serves as a means of articulating its strategic positioning choices. The traditional dominance of simplistic 'product-price' announcements once reinforced commentators' views that the sector was a relatively unprofessional proponent of marketing principles: 'Each store sings the same song . . . "here tomatoes are cheaper". The result is a poor attribution of advertising claims and some lack of credibility' (Kapferer, 1986).

Whilst there are still examples of isolated product-price claims, as retailers have come to control more of the supply chain, to be larger and more corporate enterprises, and to face more competition in maturing markets, they have come to develop increasingly coherent and professional marketing functions and expertise, made manifest in the brand. As we have already suggested, some retailers have even been able to project an image of 'good price' through 'every day low price' positioning, as well as to professionally package other, often intangible, 'non-price' factors. Branding serves to protect or increase product and price differentiation and thereby customer loyalty. As Whittington (2000) comments: 'good strategy rarely means doing exactly the same as everybody else'.

Whilst the most successful retailers are clearly focused on branding their offer and themselves, they have yet truly to make their impression on the global branding stage. By 2000 Interbrand's survey found only three conventional retail brands in the top 100 worldwide by value: Gap, Benetton and IKEA. A number of vertically integrated luxury goods manufacturers (Gucci, Louis Vuitton and Armani) were also represented. By 2002, there were still only three retailers in the top 100, but Benetton had been replaced by Amazon.com (*Business Week*, 2002). Yet branding is an important trend among grocers and general merchandisers as well as specialists like these. Our interview in Chapter 12 with the marketing director of Auchan (a grocery and hypermarket operator based in France, where price has traditionally dominated retail competition), suggests that the business is moving from a distribution focus to a brand focus.

What can retail brands be? Brands are much more than products: they are (using de Chernatony and McDonald's definition) identifiable clusters of functional and emotional values (de Chernatony and McDonald, 1998). Price can still be a part of the brand offer and positioning, as we have suggested above. Price is not everything however: Aldi is offering the customer the chance to be a 'clever' consumer, with a selected and low priced range. Strong brands create strong differentiation in consumers' minds and can only be created over time. The strength of the Marks & Spencer brand for instance, despite its recent difficulties, lies in a long history of familiarity for the British shopper.

Whale (2001) suggests that retail brands, as distinct from product brands, can offer to simplify our lives (Argos); help edit or filter the choices we make in our lives (Zara, Selfridges); or provide increased personalization (Amazon, Tesco.com). Retail brands can truly be said to be post-modern brands in the sense that they can seek to assist individual consumers manage their life goals. Our interview with Auchan suggests that the company wants to be 'the creator of solutions that improve the standard of living for the majority of people'. We can see elements of all three of Whale's possibilities in this, together with the engaging, emotional proposition that most people's lives can be improved by Auchan. Emotional branding is not just for Benetton!

Some of the strongest brands in retailing are built on product, format and staff. For example, Pilgaard (2001) cites the Danish BoConcept store: 'It's all about stores providing a total experience – from the moment a customer sees the store, to when he or she goes through the door, sees the product, experiences the service, perhaps gets a whiff of freshly made coffee in the café area, right through to the products being delivered problem free to the purchaser.'

Retail own-brand products can of course be an element of retail branding and are a most significant element of a branding strategy. Beginning generally with limited aims of increasing margins, own brand approaches are now far more complex and connected with overall strategic intent.

Own-label product can be the key to differentiation, as in the case of say Hennes and Mauritz (H&M), Marks & Spencer or Aldi, where own-label product accounts for all or virtually all products. Or they can be contributors to it, with interesting subsidiary benefits in terms of cost and control, for firms selling a mix of own and suppliers' labels. Doubts as to whether grocery own label products can work in emerging as well as mature markets are disappearing, as companies like Tesco and Delhaize use them as part of their growth strategies in international operations, as Howard suggests in Part II, Chapter 5.

But retail branding can also work without own-brand products. The success of grocers in developing their brands, with part own-label product, shows this. It is even clearer with branded retailers who sell only manufacturer branded product. Sephora, for example, bases much of its appeal on its offer of the widest range of proprietary products. Its own overall brand image has been strongly developed over the last few years however (though the company has existed for many years): 'The aim is to act as an umbrella for merchandising quality beauty product brands ... however at the same time the Sephora brand must not overwhelm the products' (Alpi, 1999).

There is however undoubtedly a trend in every sector – electricals, do-it-yourself, department stores, grocery, drugstores, all of them – for retailers to use more own-label products, and to develop more differentiated ranges, to be used for strategic ends. The tendency for some firms to differentiate themselves, as Sephora does, by emphasizing range of proprietary products is becoming rarer.

All retailers adapt their offer to some degree in new markets. Even McDonald's offers different menus in different countries. Tesco's products in Thailand are quite different from its stock in Poland. But can retailers be global brands? Can they expand by exploiting similar brand values (if different products) in similar market positions? Chapter 5 discusses these issues and concludes that there are a sufficient number of successful stories to suggest that the answer is yes, but both international expansion and sophisticated brand strategies are new enough in retailing for there to be no clear-cut prescriptions. Indeed, there are doubts as to whether the successes can really be extended globally in the ways that some consumer goods brands have been.

IKEA and H&M may be cited as successes. Yet they remain predominantly European firms – not truly global. Still, the strength of both is their brand, supported by efficient and effective supply chains which enable them to achieve the price and rapid stock turnover which support their brand propositions. H&M uses a single global brand, and own-label products within this. It offers fashionable but not trend setting clothing at affordable prices. Stores are recognizably the same everywhere: brand consistency is regarded as a key strategic task. 'Although the company emphasises the importance of maintaining a uniform concept throughout its market, it adapts a flexible attitude to local conditions. . .. There is room for some adjustments and decentralised stock control provided the character of the retail format remains intact and costs are controlled' (Helfferich and Hinfelaar, 1999). For retailers like H&M and BoConcept (above), the key is control with sufficient attention to the advice of local management. Human and organizational factors of decision making are important factors in success.

For others, particularly the general merchandisers and grocers, the problem is a different one. It is whether similar brand concepts and positions can be achieved with very different product ranges and possibly even different formats in different places. For a brand to be global, it must have a single identity, unified positioning and communications programmes, centralized development and there must be wide internal dissemination of best practice. Tesco is achieving a great deal, as Chapter 5 and our discussion above suggests. Their positioning is based on customer research, which has apparently demonstrated to them that consumers in many places want essentially the same things from: lower prices, wider selections of goods, more service and more non-food goods. Perhaps the convergence of consumer interests and globalization of taste which has been remarked upon in the context of Coca-Cola or McDonald's is indeed sufficient to allow successful global branding strategies for all kinds of retailers. Certainly the most interesting retailers are building strategies around customer values rather than baskets of goods.

The arrival of the Internet and of new, international formats in retailing challenges not so much the old rules of the game, or the essential role of the retailer (although other, newer, intermediaries may be able to perform the role more effectively than older incumbents) but has worked to increase the speed, efficiency and need for flexibility and responsiveness within many retail markets. The growth of 'fast fashion' operators such as Zara and H&M in relation to more traditional operators such as C&A and Marks & Spencer is a case in point. Emerging evidence online, discussed in Chapter 7, suggests that whilst the notion of the Internet as a frictionless, efficient marketplace has proved to be something of a myth – at least as far as the majority of consumers are concerned – its role in creating potentially new, if not profitable, models of intermediation and new channels to consumers with very different attributes from conventional ones, provides significant challenges to the hegemony of bricks and mortar retailers.

Internal capabilities

The final, balancing, component in an effective strategy revolves around *internal capability*. What are the retailer's key capabilities? We can identify desirable industry specific as well as more generic skills. The role of the retailer, as an intermediary, has always been to source an authoritative range of goods designed to appeal to consumers and which achieve an appropriate, but profitable, trade-off between price and quality. To do this, the retailer has conventionally required stores in convenient, accessible and sometimes attractive locations, buying power through expertise or scale, and an intimate knowledge of consumers' needs. These capabilities underlie the major thematic chapters in Part II. The execution of the role requires considerable skills in operations management and attention to detail. Increasingly, the most powerful and professional retailers have created, and cultivated specific brand positioning – over and above the branding of the products sold in store – that adds to their distinctive appeal to consumers. Increasingly professional retail businesses also need to demonstrate excellence in generic skills such as leadership, negotiation and team management.

In more and more countries, consumption may be regarded as a most important part of the every day life of most people, and retailers as key actors in both economic and cultural life. Retail companies have become big business. Their activities are very visible, to consumers, citizens and politicians and are subjected to increasing scrutiny. This book provides a further contribution to a better understanding of the retailing sector and its challenges and concerns.

Table 1.5 The evolution of own brands

	1st generation	2nd generation	3rd generation	4th generation
Type of brand	• generic • no name • brand free • unbranded	• 'quasi-brand' • own label	own brand	extended own brand, i.e. segmented own brands
Strategy	• generics	• cheapest price	• me-too	• value-added
Objective	• increase margins • provide choice in pricing	• increase margins • reduce manufacturers' power by setting the entry price • provide better-value product (quality/price)	• enhance category margins • expand product assortment, i.e. customer choice • build retailer's image among consumers	• increase and retain the client base • enhance category margins • improve image further • differentiation
Product	• basic and functional products	• one-off staple lines with a large volume	• big category products	• image-forming product groups • large number of products with small volume (niche)
Technology	• simple production process and basic technology lagging behind market leader	• technology still lagging behind market leaders	• close to the brand leader	• innovative technology
Quality / image	• lower quality and inferior image compared to the manufacturers' brands	• medium quality but still perceived as lower than leading manufacturers' brands • secondary brand alongside the leading manufacturer's brand	• comparable to the brand leaders	• same or better than brand leader • innovative and different products from brand leaders
Approximate pricing	• 20% or more below the brand leader	• 10–20% below	• 5–10% below	• equal or higher than known brand
Consumers' motivation to buy	• price is the main criterion for buying	• price is still important	• both quality and price, i.e. value for money	• better and unique products
Supplier	• national, not specialized	• national, partly specializing to own label manufacturing	• national, mostly specializing for own brand manufacturing	• international, manufacturing mostly own brands

Source: Laaksonen and Reynolds, 1994

Table 1.6 Making sense of the cases

Case (Chapters)	Chapter 2 Attracting and keeping customers	Chapter 3 Collaboration in the retail supply chain	Chapter 4 Planning policy for retailing	Chapter 5 Retail internationalization	Chapter 6 Prospects for e-commerce	Chapter 7 The financial implications of retail strategy
8. Migros		✓				
9. Ahold		✓				
10. Legoland	✓			✓		
11. Screwfix Direct	✓	✓		✓		
12. Auchan			✓		✓	
13. B&Q				✓		
14. Metro			✓	✓		
15. HMV	✓				✓	
16. Wellbeing	✓				✓	
17. Supermercats Pujol	✓					
18. Carrefour Belgium		✓		✓		
19. Safeway	✓					
20. Wal-Mart	✓			✓		
21. Shoppers' Stop	✓			✓		
22. Kingfisher	✓	✓		✓	✓	✓
23. KarstadtQuelle	✓					✓
24. Alfa-Beta	✓	✓				
25. Sainsbury's				✓		✓

Structure of the book

The book is not structured as so many other case study books are structured, with the introduction of a subject followed by a series of vignettes or real world examples focused firmly on the topic. *Retail Strategy: The view from the bridge* features some key, strategic themes in retailing in Part II and then in Part III presents the case studies. The case studies are not focused on a particular theme. However, this does not mean that the book is unstructured. Each key theme has two or three case studies that draw out the issues from a real world perspective, drawn from interviews with leading retailers from a wide range of retail companies. Table 1.6 summarizes this coverage. Part IV provides an integrative exercise that takes a more holistic view of the cases. In addition, Chapter 27 on 'portents' provides contrasting perspectives on the alternative strategic futures facing retailing. In this way, both the key themes and the present and likely future complexity of the retailing environment are explored in theory, in practice and then in student-based activity.

References

Alpi, J.-C. (1999) 'Sephora – A Shrine to Beauty'. *European Retail Digest*, Issue 24, p. 48.

Ansoff, H.I. (1988) *New Corporate Strategy: An Analytical Approach to Business Policy for Growth and Expansion*. Wiley, New York.

Bell, R. (1999) 'Food Retailing in the Nordics'. *European Retail Digest*, Issue 24, p. 19.

Bell, R. (2000) 'Food Retailing in Southern Europe'. *European Retail Digest*, Issue 25, p. 29.

Bell, R. (2001) 'Food Retailing in France'. *European Retail Digest*, Issue 30, p. 27.

Bourlakis, M. (2001) 'Greek Food Retailing at the Dawn of the 21st Century'. *European Retail Digest*, Issue 32, pp. 27–29.

Business Week (2002) *The 100 Top Brands*, 5th August, pp. 95–99, http://www.businessweek.com/pdfs/2002/0231-brands.pdf

Central Committee of the People's Republic of China (2002) 'Shi Guangsheng on Achievements of China's Foreign Trade and Economic Cooperation'. Press Statement by the Chinese Minister of Foreign Trade and Economic Cooperation at the 16th CPC National Congress, Beijing, November, http://www.16congress.org.cn/english/features/48710.htm

Competition Commission (2000) *Supermarkets. A Report on the Supply of Groceries from Multiple Stores in the United Kingdom*. London, TSO.

de Chernatony, L. and McDonald, M.H.B. (1998) *Creating Powerful Brands in Consumer, Service and Industrial Markets*, 2nd edition, Oxford, Butterworth-Heinemann.

Dawson, J.A. (1996) 'Retail change in the European Community', in Davies, R.L. (ed.), *Retail Planning Policies in Western Europe*. London, Routledge.

Eagle, J.S. *et al.* (2000) 'From products to ecosystems: Retail 2010'. *McKinsey Quarterly*, Issue 4, p. 108.

European Commission (2003) 'Economic overview of the commerce and distribution sector'. *Overview of the Retail Sector Seminar*, Department of Trade & Industry, London, 20th January.

Fordham Corporate Law Institute (2000) *Fordham Annual Conference on International Antitrust Law and Policy*, Fordham University, New York.

Gestrin, M. (2000) 'The globalisation of retail: on your marks . . .'. *European Retail Digest*, Issue 26, p. 6.

Hays, C.L. (2003) 'Big Retailers Start to Think Small'. *The New York Times*, January 22nd.

Helfferich, E. and Hinfelaar, M. (1999) 'Hennes & Mauritz: Swedish Fast Fashion'. *European Retail Digest*, Issue 24, p. 35.

Hill, T. (ed.) (2000) *Manufacturing Strategy*. Macmillan, London.

Kapferer, J-N. (1986) 'Beyond positioning: retailer's identity'. *Retail Strategies for Profit and Growth*, Amsterdam, ESOMAR.

Laaksonen, H. and Reynolds, J. (1994) 'Own brands in food retailing across Europe'. *The Journal of Brand Management*, **2**(1), pp. 37–46.

Mail on Sunday (2002) *The rich report 2002*, 24th February.

Miller, R.L. (1997) 'The Federal Trade Commission's New Definition of Relevant Market', *Economics Today Newsletter*, **9**(1), Fall, http://hepg.awl.com/miller/econtoday/Economics%20Today.html

Mintel Retail Intelligence (2002) *Food Retailing in Europe – Italy*, June.

Pilgaard, T. (2001) 'BoConcept: Buying dreams, lifestyle and total experience'. *European Retail Digest*, Issue 31, p. 24.

Rafiq, M. (2000) 'Global retailing and its implications for competition regulation'. *European Retail Digest*, Issue 26, p. 9.

Tang, C., Bell, D. and Ho, T.-H. (2000) 'Store Choice and Shopping Behaviour: How Price Format Works'. *Working Paper*, Andersen School, University of California at Los Angeles.

Whale, M. (2001) 'Same thing, only different: the retail pursuit of differentiation'. *European Retail Digest*, March, Issue 29, p. 7.

Whittington, R. (2000) *What is Strategy – And Does it Matter?* International Thomson.

Part II

Strategic issues in retailing

Chapter 2

Attracting and keeping customers

Richard Cuthbertson and Richard Bell

The attraction and retention of customers consistently tops the list of concerns on the retail CEO's agenda. This considers the management of retailer–customer relationships, which encompasses the often-quoted retailer objective of customer loyalty. The chapter discusses the role of loyalty in retailing and explores some key ways in which retailers seek to create customer loyalty, including the role of private label products, loyalty schemes and multiple channels. The varied factors affecting the outcome of a retailer–customer relationship are discussed, and the implications for retailer strategy and implementation are thus derived.

Customer loyalty

Loyalty is the state of 'being faithful' or 'steadfast in allegiance' to another party, according to the *Oxford English Dictionary* (1996). Therefore, customer loyalty to a retailer can be defined as existing when a customer chooses to shop in only one store or retail chain for a specific product or group of products. Sheth and Parvatiyar (1995) define relationship marketing as 'the ongoing process of engaging in co-operative and collaborative activities and programmes with immediate and end-user customers to create or enhance mutual economic value at a reduced cost'. The emphasis on a two-way economic relationship is supported by Woolf (1996) who states 'great success comes from a marketing strategy based primarily on understanding customer economics – and only secondarily on customer loyalty'. To the retailer, 'profitable' customers appear more important than 'loyal' customers. Hence, this chapter concentrates on the business effectiveness of loyalty

marketing rather than the customer loyalty created. Moreover, the focus is on the
retailer view rather than the customer view.

Customer priorities

Customers may be classified in many ways. One way is to consider them as
attribute- or attitude-based shoppers (Mantel and Kardes, 1999). An attribute-based
shopper makes a judgement based on knowledge of key product attributes. As long
as products are available in a store that meets the customer's key criteria, the customer is likely to be store loyal. Attitude-based purchasing is more intuitive and
based on lifestyle and marketing choices. If the chosen product brand is unavailable at a store, an attitude-based customer is prepared to search for it. A customer
may be an attribute-based shopper in some circumstances, for example, the usual
grocery shop or in a hurried lunch period, and an attitude-based shopper in other
circumstances, for example, buying sports clothes or on a restful Sunday morning.
Furthermore, this may change as circumstances change over time, for example,
due to salary increases or new family members. With increased access and information, customers are more able to become attribute-based shoppers rather than
attitude-based shoppers, reducing loyalty based on restricted choice.

Customer loyalty is not only difficult to gain; it is difficult to define. A customer
may be loyal to choices other than those defined by retailer or manufacturer brands
or product. For example, loyalty may be price-driven (high or low) or be based on
location rather than a specific brand. Dick and Basu (1994) divide consumers into
four loyalty segments, as shown in Figure 2.1 and further described below.

The difference between brand concept (relative attitude in Figure 2.1) and customer behaviour (repeat purchase in Figure 2.1) also emphasizes the importance

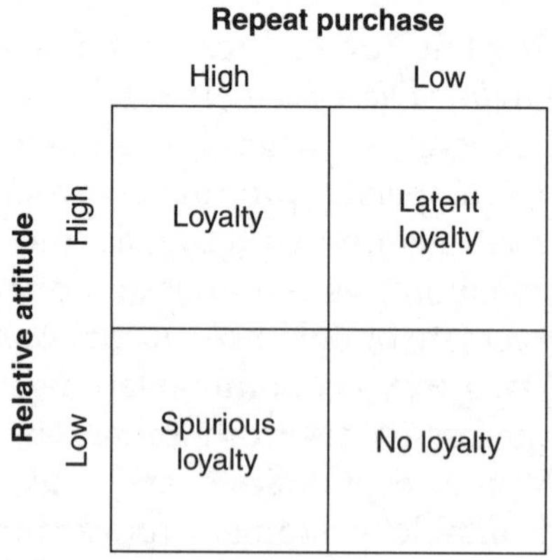

Figure 2.1 Loyalty segmentation
Source: Dick and Basu (1994)

of accessibility in determining loyal behaviour. Consumers who are latently loyal (in the top right quadrant of Figure 2.1) may value a particular brand (product or retailer) but may not purchase that brand because it is not easily accessible. Similarly, customers who are spuriously loyal (bottom left) may be so because they only have access to a particular brand. They may not value that particular brand highly at all.

Current and past research (Vanhoof *et al.*, 1997) shows that a customer disappointed by the retail experience may still continue to be loyal to the retailer if product attributes (price, quality, etc.) are most important. This may be true even if a particular product experience is also unsatisfactory, as long as there is a choice of products.

The loyalty marketing mix

Loyalty in retailing is difficult to achieve when customers have choice, and are empowered by information, such as price comparisons. Customers increasingly know more about services and products, and expect a great deal from their suppliers and retailers. The average customer today is more mobile and willing to travel long distances to shop, contributing to the success of large out-of-town centres, such as Bluewater in the UK, CentrO in Germany or Bay 2 in France. Competition for customer loyalty works on a number of levels. Retailers' private label products compete with manufacturers' branded products, while new e-tail offerings compete with established retailers' distribution channels. First-movers may be quickly imitated and the pace of change seems unrelenting. Customer loyalty may become even more difficult to gain in the future, when artificial loyalty (based on a lack of consumer choice and information) disappears in the face of better products and services. Shrinking brand loyalty is a constant threat to any business. In the highly developed automotive industry, for instance, where the retail brand and product brand are virtually indistinguishable, brand loyalty in Europe's five main car markets (Italy, France, Spain, Germany and the UK) has consistently reduced in recent years (*Business Times Singapore*, 1999). On the other hand, the time-constrained customer may be less willing to visit alternative stores and may be more willing to accept alternative brands, and so may be more loyal to a single retailer.

There is wide variation within customer loyalty trends. There is a need to differentiate between loyalty of necessity (low mobility or time-constrained customers) and loyalty through choice (highly mobile customers with time to spend shopping). Loyalty to a retailer is multi-dimensional and varies between sectors and the nature of the purchase, for example, grocery or clothing, frequent or infrequent purchases. The most important factor in keeping customers loyal according to a survey by Verdict (1999) is the introduction of the 'one-stop shop'. Retailers have provided more out-of-town, one-stop shopping, where petrol can be bought along with prescribed drugs and photographic services, with the result that customer loyalty may be heavily influenced by the structure of retailing. At the same time, loyalty through lack of product knowledge or choice is changing. A major area of competition policy concerns the potential existence of local monopolies where one or two retailers exist with little competition. This may be due to the 'natural' forces of economics, such as the limitations of a small marketplace, or 'artificial' barriers to entry, such as planning restrictions. As the retail sector becomes more concentrated, competition authorities are increasingly investigating the practical choices available to consumers. For example, the European Commission required both French-owned Carrefour and German retailer Rewe to divest stores in order to avoid excessive local market shares following acquisitions. The Competition Commission in the UK also raised important issues regarding potential local monopolies within the grocery sector (Morris, 2000).

Increasingly, competition authorities are considering the impact of retailers and manufacturers on consumers at an increasingly detailed level, moving the focus of inquiries from national to local markets, from basket to product pricing and from supplier dependency to supply terms and conditions (Office of Fair Trading, 1999). This focus on detail aims to reduce barriers to competition at a consumer level rather than a (national) market level and so increases the possibility of consumer fickleness. While this may be good news for the consumer, it has been argued that mini monopolies, and therefore imperfect competition, are sometimes necessary for efficient capitalism (Schumpeter, 1987). Mini monopolies, in any case, may find it difficult to exist in the new global, electronic markets. They require limited choices and imperfect consumer information, whereas e-commerce potentially widens choice and allows access to more information, though this depends upon the consumer taking advantage of such facilities. The information available to consumers via consumer organizations and the media also reduces the barriers to loyalty based on ignorance. It has been argued by Kuttner (1998):

> The Internet is a nearly perfect market because information is instantaneous and buyers can compare the offerings of sellers worldwide. The result is fierce price competition, dwindling product differentiation, and vanishing loyalty.

This harsh price competition is well illustrated where a third party, such as BestBookBuys.com and dooyoo.co.uk, provides competitive information at one access point.

Under this constant price pressure, many retailers have attempted to build a retail brand that the consumer perceives as uniquely satisfying, and even exceeding, their own requirements. This is a major reason for retailers to focus on the other aspects of the marketing mix (McCarthy, 1964). In particular, in the case of product, a retailer may develop a portfolio of private label products. In the case of place, a retailer may offer new distribution channels and in the case of promotion, a retailer may monitor and reward loyal customer behaviour. (For a broader text on retail marketing, see McGoldrick, 2002.)

Private label: strategic alignment

In building loyalty to the retailer brand, many retailers choose to use the store brand as an umbrella brand for their private label products. This creates marketing synergy between the store name and the product name. The retailer's name on the label can increase the trust towards the products and encourage the customer to buy. For example, Wal-Mart Asda in the UK include the Asda brand name on the 'smart price' range of products, to increase trust to the range and strengthen the Wal-Mart Asda price positioning. Retailers usually put heavy emphasis on the quality of their private label products, within the limits of their general strategy and price positioning. The aim is not to take the cheapest alternative available, but rather to choose products with the best combination of price and quality that fits the retailer's overall marketing strategy. Hence, even German hard discount grocery retailer Aldi, who have a very high proportion of private label products, stock selected lines of manufacturer branded product, such as Mars chocolate bars.

To maximize brand loyalty, it is important for a retailer to manage the quality of private label products throughout the range. This is especially true in the case of store brands, where there is a strong association between private label products and the retailer. If the retailer has different names for each product, as do Aldi, the ability to convey values of originality and consistency may be reduced but the consequences of poor product development, low sales and subsequent risk to brand loyalty are also reduced.

As retailers become more highly differentiated and focused, brand loyalty tends to increase, though the relevant potential market may decrease. What is important is to maximize brand loyalty within the overall marketing strategy adopted by the retailer. This can be illustrated in the private-label strategic alignment model (Cuthbertson *et al.*, 2000) as in Figure 2.2.

Using this analytical framework, it is possible to evaluate the consistency of a retailer's private-label strategy. A consistent strategy appears as a small area on the framework, while an inconsistent strategy covers a large area. For example, a retailer with an overall marketing strategy based on a highly differentiated product range (and hence offering limited customer choice) has a consistent private-label strategy if there is a high proportion of private-label product over which the retailer exerts a high level of design and manufacture control. This would be represented as in Figure 2.3.

An example of an inconsistent strategy for this retailer would be if the private label objectives did not align with the overall marketing strategy (see Figure 2.4). Inconsistency may occur through incorrect private label development and/or through a change in the overall marketing strategy.

Private-label strategies are implemented successfully by gaining the customer's trust both in the retailer and the private-label products themselves. Thus, private-label products may be used to create further trust in the retailer's ability to reliably meet consumer needs. Consequently, high standards of quality control (pre-transaction) and customer service (post-transaction) are vital. The leading UK

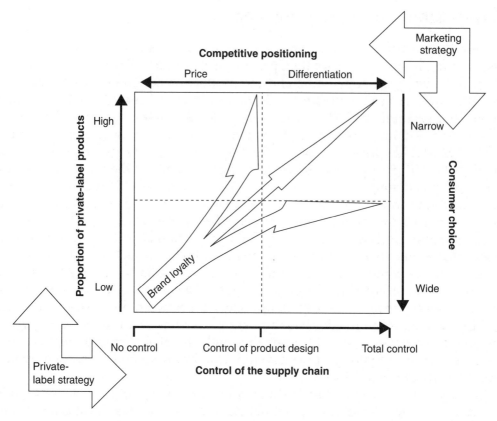

Figure 2.2 Private-label strategic alignment model

retailers, with high levels of private-label product, appear to enjoy a high level of consumer trust and this continues to increase, as Table 2.1 shows.

Similarly, retailers appear to be well trusted, even compared to many well-established manufacturer brands and to other institutions and professionals, as a comparison of Tables 2.1 and 2.2 shows.

Furthermore, retailers have several ways of reinforcing consumer trust and therefore loyalty towards their private-label products. Refund policies aimed at quality assurance are common. Examples of these are Marks & Spencer's 'No Questions Asked' refund policy and Aldi's 'No Quibble Guarantee'. Decathlon, French sports clothes and equipment retailer, offers a one-year (or more) warranty on all Decathlon private-label products. All UK health and beauty retailer Boots brand products are covered by a two-year guarantee. Tesco prints on its private label products that 'We are happy to refund or replace any Tesco product which falls below the high standard you expect. Just ask any member of staff.' Private-label product information, such as nutritional information, written on packaging or provided elsewhere in-store often exceeds legal requirements and may be more extensive when compared to manufacturer brands. Many retailers produce information leaflets, such

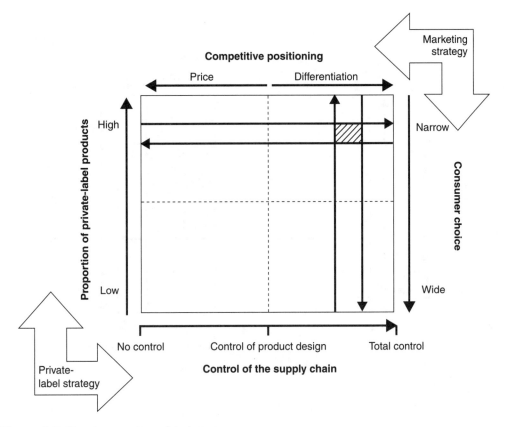

Figure 2.3 Consistent private-label strategy

as Tesco's healthy eating guide, featuring their private-label products, or Boots' medicine guides. Another potential advantage that private label has in increasing consumer trust is that it is often easier and quicker to alter the production of lower volume, private-label products, than higher volume, manufacturer branded products, in response to changing consumer preferences. For example, many food retailers in the UK were quicker than branded manufacturers to exclude genetically modified ingredients from their products, following consumer concern.

The unit price and retailer competence influences the amount of trust a customer needs when making a purchasing decision. This relates to the retailer's core competence. Where the unit price is low, the customer is more inclined to try a private-label product, since the consequences of the decision proving unsatisfactory are small. New private-label products are also more likely to be successful if they are considered close to the retailer's core competence. Therefore retailers can move transitionally into new product areas. For example, retailers may initially offer loyalty cards or credit before moving to a more comprehensive range of financial services, as we have seen with some leading retailers. For some products, it is not so much a question of trust in technical elements, but rather social credibility

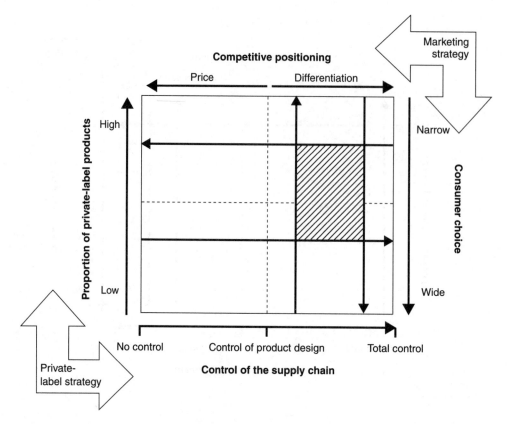

Figure 2.4 Inconsistent private-label strategy

Table 2.1 Trusting companies to be honest and fair in the UK

Company	1994	1997
Boots	78	83
Marks & Spencer	73	83
Sainsbury's	59	74
Tesco	52	71
Asda	46	67
Safeway	45	64

Source: Henley Centre (1998)

in these niche markets. This is particularly true in high fashion markets. In these and similar upmarket product categories, a generalist retailer's regular store brand may be regarded as being too easily available.

Finally, while some customers may only trust 'branded' products, this does not necessarily stop successful private-label development. According to consumer

Table 2.2 Trusted to be honest and fair

Institution/brand	% Trusted
Your GP (doctor)	85
Kellogg	84
Cadbury	83
Heinz	81
Nescafé	77
Rowntree	74
Your bank	72
Coca-Cola	65
Your church	64
The police	62
...	
Your member of parliament	28

Source: Croft (1998)

research, many customers of Marks & Spencer believe that they never purchase private-label products and that only branded ones will do (Mintel, 1998). This is despite the fact that Marks & Spencer sell almost only private-label products.

Multiple channels: e-loyalty

As consumer access to and usage of the Internet has grown, there has been a move towards multi-channel retailing by many major retailers. In this dynamic environment, the relative importance of retaining existing customers (loyalty) compared to the acquisition of new customers varies over time, though most multi-channel retailers would consider both acquisition and retention important. However, less established e-tail operations tend to agree that customer acquisition is the dominant focus at this point in their development. On the other hand, more established e-tail operations, with a large existing customer base, tend to be more focused on retention. So, the importance of loyalty marketing appears to be related to the development life cycle of the e-tail operations. At the start of an e-tail business, loyalty marketing is an important consideration though it requires less focus than the initial acquisition of customers. In the first year of operation, the need to grow the customer base then dominates. However, once established, the focus then tends to shift more towards retaining this customer base. This could be summarized as in Figure 2.5.

There are some important differences in loyalty marketing when comparing the e-tail and store-based shopping environments. These can be summarized according to the traditional marketing mix (McCarthy, 1964) of product, place, price and promotion.

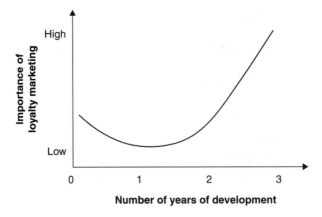

Figure 2.5 Importance of loyalty marketing over time

In product terms, many loyalty marketing techniques in an e-tail environment are the same as in a store environment. However, in a store environment, the customer is not required to place so much initial trust in the product characteristics, because they can test some attributes within the store, for example trying on clothes before purchase.

The place variable in the marketing mix is fundamentally different in an e-tail environment compared to a store-based environment. While the virtual market-place may be easier to manage, in that it may be a single point (website), the delivery points may be anywhere. Thus, delivery issues must be carefully and proactively managed by the e-tailer to ensure effective and efficient fulfilment to achieve customer satisfaction, and therefore retention. Moreover, it is easier to manage fulfilment if the customer base is more constant, i.e. loyal.

All retailers, online and offline, are reluctant to discuss pricing strategy in detail. However, there appears to be general agreement that e-tail product pricing needs to be competitive with store-based pricing, while delivery may represent an acceptable extra charge, though often not at the full commercial rate.

E-tail promotional strategies are very varied and include advertising, links from other websites and stores, conventional promotions and loyalty schemes. The virtual environment of e-tailing allows for the potential to personalize a website for loyal customers; it is impossible to personalize stores to the same extent. Many customer relationship management (CRM) techniques may be employed in a digital environment, where customer data, both transaction and browsing, may be captured at source. Of particular interest are the multi-channel retailers who treat their digital channel as an integral part of the retailer's overall offer. This enables the e-tail division to gain synergies in advertising and other promotional activities. Similarly, loyalty schemes for multi-channel retailers may be run across all channels. Pure-play e-tailers tend not to employ conventional loyalty schemes because of their ability to capture customer behaviour data without having to offer a reward. The management of existing customers tends to be an important activity for all e-tail businesses in improving repeat purchasing rates and increasing average expenditures.

Multi-channel retailers are able to compare online and store-based loyalty. Evidence suggests (Cuthbertson, 2002) that there appears to be less loyalty online, though this may be explained by the current growth in attracting new customers to digital channels. Future expectations for online retailing are varied. The key predictions for the future are a maturing marketplace experiencing fewer problems, with fewer but stronger competitors able to satisfy the increasing customer requirements, and thus increasing consumer loyalty.

Successful retailing in the future requires integration, communication and measurement as key ingredients. Successful multi-channel retailers, such as Tesco in the UK and Tchibo in Germany, integrate their digital channel into the overall retail brand, including loyalty marketing. This provides for a more cost-effective and complete retail offering. For multi-channel retailers, the digital channel is evolving as an important marketing channel, as well as a sales channel. Successful e-tailing consists of leveraging the advantages of the digital channel, such as communicating with the customer, via promotions and feedback, at a frequency appropriate to customer purchasing frequency. In particular, the frequency of such communication may be designed to increase an individual customer's purchasing frequency from its present level towards the level of the retailer's most frequent purchasers. Successful e-tailing also requires measuring and modelling customer sales, satisfaction, value and loyalty both in terms of absolute figures and trends. In an evolving environment, trends tend to be more important in this respect than current absolute figures. However, the time horizon of any forecasts should still be kept fairly short, as they may not be very reliable.

In conclusion, the successful retention of loyal customers in multi-channel retailing is based on the whole retail offering and experience, but offers huge potential for leveraging individual customer information. This may also be done in a store-based environment via a card-based loyalty scheme.

Loyalty schemes: the purchaser–purveyor matrix

Assuming that the product offer is relevant and accessible to the consumer, retailers may then offer a loyalty scheme to track and reward customer purchases, with the aim of increasing the retailer understanding of individual consumer demand. The combination of the purchaser (customer) and purveyor (retailer) viewpoints can be used to define the loyalty card strategy chosen by a retailer, and is summarized in Figure 2.6.

The purchaser–purveyor matrix (Cuthbertson and Bell, 2001) shows five major strategic classifications of loyalty card schemes: pure, push, pull, purchase and purge.

- **Pure loyalty schemes** are pure in the sense that both card use and customer benefits apply only to a specific retailer. A typical example might be purchasing product from

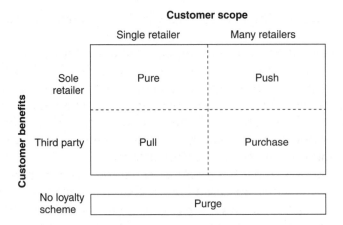

Figure 2.6 The purchaser–purveyor loyalty matrix

a specific retailer to gain a discount off future purchases from that same retailer. The Swedish retailer ICA has a Kundkort that provides an example of such a scheme. Pure retailers tend to focus on promoting the retail brand, in order to attract and retain a core group of high-spending and profitable customers.

■ **Push loyalty schemes** aim to push the customer towards a particular retailer by allowing spending at other retailers to accrue benefits provided by the target retailer. A typical example might be the result of the target retailer working together with a bank providing access to many retailers through the use of a common payment scheme, such as Visa or MasterCard. The GM MasterCard or Sainsbury's Visa card are examples of such schemes. Push retailers tend to focus on providing well-regarded or desirable products and services, in order to attract and retain a wide group of profitable customers.

■ **Pull loyalty schemes** aim to pull the customer towards the retailer by offering benefits. A typical example might be purchasing petrol in order to claim gifts from a catalogue provided by a third party. Shell's plusPoints loyalty scheme is an example of this. Pull retailers tend to focus on ensuring accessibility, and then increasing customer transactions by offering incentives provided by a third party.

■ **Purchase loyalty schemes** aim to encourage the customer to purchase in general, with many retailers and third parties involved. A typical example might be the use of general credit cards in order to claim gifts from a catalogue. American Express provides an example of such a scheme. Purchase retailers are interested in increasing transactions through the financial services provider, rather than creating loyalty to a retail store.

■ **Purge loyalty schemes** represent the antithesis of the other types of loyalty card schemes, which is to purge your loyalty card scheme if it exists at all. Wal-Mart Asda and Aldi are important examples of this approach. Purge retailers tend to focus on offering the lowest price to all consumers, and view loyalty schemes as an unnecessary cost.

The classification of loyalty schemes helps focus loyalty scheme strategy and management. This is dependent upon the retailer marketing mix and the customer reaction to the retail offer and competing offers. The different types of loyalty schemes are not exclusive. For example, the Tesco Clubcard Visa offers discount off future purchases (a pure scheme), may act as a payment card (a push scheme), offers benefits from third parties, such as Air Miles (a pull scheme), may be used at other retailers for financial transactions (a purchase scheme), and may not be used at all by some Tesco customers (a purge scheme).

The day-to-day operations and marketing tactics employed are then informed by the strategy defined. The results of any CRM activities can then be measured and evaluated against the strategic objectives.

The future development of loyalty schemes depends on many issues, such as legislation on the privacy of data, public attitudes towards personal data, competition authorities, the economic environment, and national and cultural issues. However, loyalty schemes have always occurred in some form throughout the history of retailing. It may be argued that technology is the driving force behind loyalty card-based schemes. Furthermore, it can be argued that it will be technology that will drive developments away from the current format of loyalty schemes. The magnetic strip and microchip of today will seem as basic as a book of Green Shield Stamps at some point in the future.

Switchability and substitutability

Switchability

According to recent studies in UK grocery retailing, customers often switch retailers when they move house or a new store opens (East and Hammond, 2000). This reflects the importance of location in retail brand loyalty. If a store is out of town, there may be little alternative without travelling a considerable extra distance. The propensity to switch stores depends upon the nature of the store and the shopping objective. Where stores are located close to alternative stores, the cost of switching is less. The importance of location is confirmed in a study by East and Hogg (1997) of the increase in market share by Tesco, UK in the 1990s. This study demonstrated that much of the increase in market share was due to the increase in the number of Tesco stores over the period, rather than through other factors. However, location is not likely to be so important to online shoppers, who can buy via their iDTV, PC or other web-enabled devices.

When a product is unavailable, customers may switch stores, substitute other products or defer purchases. Switching stores happens most frequently when there is easy access to competing stores. The nature of the purchase is also important. Customers may feel unable to defer purchases, especially where high frequency consumption products are unavailable, and so may feel obliged to substitute other products. For example, if a customer has Anchor butter on her shopping list but the store is out of her favourite brand on one occasion, she is unlikely to change stores but would substitute another brand such as Kerrygold or the retailer's private label.

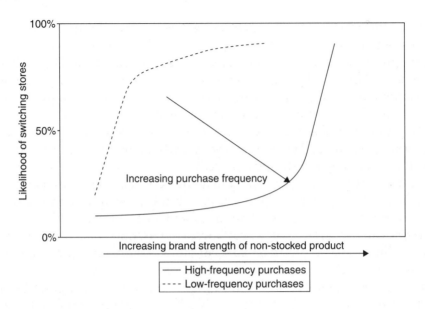

Figure 2.7 Store switchability

However, switchability is also dependent upon the strength of the product brand. Strong product brands deter customers from substituting another product, and so may lead to the customer spending more time and effort on switching stores, rather than substitute another product brand. For example, some customers will not accept Pepsi-Cola as a substitute for Coca-Cola, or vice versa. This is illustrated in Figure 2.7.

Substitutability

Branded products appear to be increasingly important to the consumer, but brand loyalty is reducing (Scase, 1999). This is because more people are content with *a* brand rather than *a particular* brand. If several well regarded branded products or retailers are available that can satisfy consumer expectations, then consumers may not care which particular brands they buy. For example, a customer may rate equally French Connection and Gap, or Mars and Snickers – all well-known and highly regarded brands. Some marketers would argue that these are not true brands, since differentiation is so weak. In any case, the substitutability of product brands is affected by the availability of competing products.

Retailers may have a major influence on product loyalty. As retailers increasingly stock private-label products, there is a potential conflict of interest between the retailer's dual roles, as an agent for manufacturers' brands and at the same time a provider of competing brands. The substitutability of manufacturer branded products with retailer private-label products depends upon a number of factors including: familiarity with store brands, extrinsic cues in product evaluation, perceived quality, perceived risk (which is heavily dependant upon the frequency of purchase), perceived value for money, as well as consumer income and family size (Richardson *et al.*, 1996).

Retail operations may also heavily impact the substitutability of branded and competing products, including private-label products. For example, the retailer may analyse the elasticity of implementing multiple facings of products or product placing according to shelf height. Based on such analyses, shelves may be stocked accordingly, perhaps in favour of the retailer's private label products. For example, multi-facing may produce a significant increase in sales (though with declining economies of scale), as Figure 2.8 illustrates.

Retailers may choose advantageous multi-facings for their own private-label product rather than branded manufacturer's product. The shelf height and position along fixture and in-store positioning also affect sales, and may be similarly set out in favour of the retailer's private-label products.

Product promotions can have a major impact on customer loyalty to branded products. There is evidence that non-price-focused promotions, such as free samples, appear to encourage brand loyalty, while price-focused promotions seem to attract more promiscuous shoppers (Gedenk and Neslin, 1999). This can cause conflict between a retailer and a manufacturer. Retailers may welcome constantly changing price promotions, as they may drive category sales. However, from the manufacturer's view, product sales may rise while a product is on promotion but may quickly fall away at the end of the promotion, especially if there is another

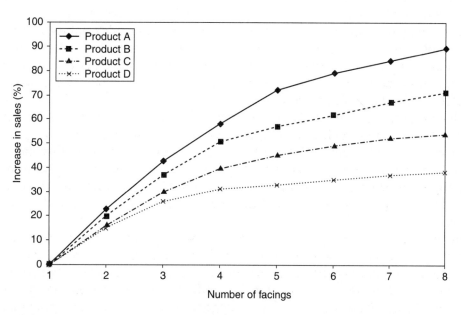

Figure 2.8 The effect of multi-facings in store

competing product being similarly promoted. Retailers may also stock one branded manufacturer's product rather than another, such as Rite Aid (US) did in 1998, stocking Pepsi-Cola at the expense of Coca-Cola.

So, retailers may have a major input into the level of substitutability likely to take place. The retailer's overall marketing strategy may also be very important here. For example, it can be argued that an every day low price (EDLP) strategy may encourage loyalty to the retailer through a consistent low price offering, but individual product loyalty may vary considerably.

Switchability versus substitutability

Research into branded product substitution tends to have been carried out separately from research into store switching and vice versa. In any case, there is no simple cause and effect relationship between product brands and retail brands. Successful product brands enhance the retailer brand, while successful retail brands enhance the product brands stocked. According to conventional marketing wisdom, brands build loyalty (Matthews, 1998) regardless of whether they are retail brands or product brands. This ability to build brand loyalty affects the initial product or service trial and repeat business. It is generally agreed that strong brand values are more easily created for a single product than for a retail store with its varied ranges of product and service.

The real test of whether a customer is more susceptible to switching stores (store loyal) or substituting competing products (product loyal) occurs when a previously available product in a retail store becomes unavailable. This may be temporary, due to problems with supply, or permanent, when an item is delisted by the retailer or withdrawn by the supplier. A customer may change purchasing habits if a product line is delisted. The retailer may not worry when a product is delisted if there is no impact upon the overall demand for the product category. This may imply that customers have substituted products, but not switched retailers. However, the delisted supplier may be far from happy.

Where a product is delisted, the customer has four choices: to no longer make such a purchase, to switch store, to switch brand or to substitute another product. Analysis (Cuthbertson *et al.*, 2001) of delisted grocery products in Germany and France, via retail audit and consumer panel data supplied by ACNielsen and delisting data provided by AIM, show the impact on product sales before and after delisting to be ambiguous. This may be due to cultural and economic influences.

For instance, in Germany the research findings indicate that the loss of sales from delisting a product was more than made up by a general increase in category sales. (Of the 16 cases analysed there is one exception to this where category sales plummeted below the loss of sales for the product delisted. This effect is discussed later when France is considered.) These category increases are much higher than the general rise in retail spending over the period. This could reflect the retailer's better category management, resulting in the delisting of a non-performing product, and perhaps related to a price-focused strategy, common in Germany.

In isolation, this suggests that, when a product is delisted, product substitution takes place rather than switching retail stores. However, in 11 of the 16 cases (69 per cent) researched in Germany, the manufacturer's total sales for the delisted product increased over the same period, suggesting store switching. This may be because the manufacturer switched promotional expenditure for the product to other retail stores. The effect of these 11 delistings appears to benefit both the retailer and the manufacturer.

In 5 of the 16 cases (31 per cent), manufacturers' overall sales plummeted below the loss expected from one retailer delisting. As the retailer did not suffer a similar loss of sales, this implies that customers substituted other products rather than switched stores.

In France, analysis of sales patterns for delisted products is quite different. In 11 of the 22 cases (50 per cent), the loss of sales from the delisted product does not appear to affect overall category sales, suggesting that customers are substituting other product brands.

In another three cases (14 per cent), the category loss was less than the delisted product sales suggesting a mixture of product substitution and store switching. In the other eight cases, there is evidence of retail store switching, because category sales plummeted more than the delisted product sales alone. And in six of these cases (28 per cent) it appears that the delisted product brand's strength is so influential that the strength of the whole category is undermined once the product is delisted.

In 50 per cent of cases, the manufacturer is also affected, losing sales not only to the delisting retailer but also to other retailers. So in France, both product substitution and some store switching are evident. This may be related to a combination of market share and brand value. Where products have high market share and brand value then the customer may switch stores. In all other cases the customer may be more likely to substitute other products.

This analysis illustrates the difficulties in clearly distinguishing between switchability and product substitutability. Retailers attracting the highest levels of customer loyalty tend to carry the products attracting the highest levels of loyalty, and so it is very difficult to differentiate between customer loyalty to the retail experience and customer loyalty to product brands.

Other research into the effects of delisting particular product brands has produced similarly mixed results. For example, Verbeke *et al.* (1997) carried out two such experiments by delisting five leading branded products from five different categories in two Dutch grocery stores (with and without nearby competition). The purchasing patterns of 590 customers were analysed. The results varied between categories as shown in Figure 2.9.

An average of 55 per cent of customers substituted other brands, 25 per cent switched stores and 20 per cent postponed the purchase. Interestingly the results

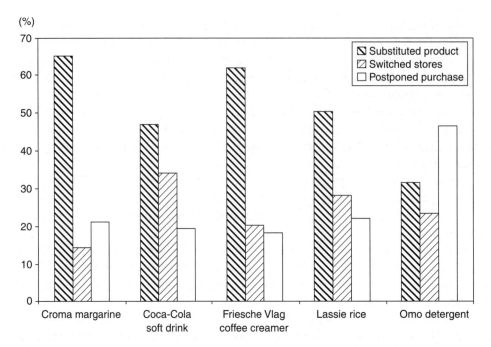

Figure 2.9 Customer response to out-of-stocks
Source: Vebeke (1997)

were similar, regardless of whether there was a nearby competitive store, suggesting that the competitive environment may not be very important in the two-week
period over which the experiment took place.

An important conclusion of this analysis is that delisting products appears to
have a major effect on the whole category, which may be negative or positive
depending upon the customer's attitude towards the delisted product brand. The
commercial implications of delisting products may be unclear but they are always
likely to affect the category as a whole. A clear and measurable rationale when
making such decisions therefore needs to be in place.

Options for brand loyalty

Product and retailer brand loyalty results from a complex combination of factors
relating to: pre-transaction consumer requirements; the marketing mix provided
by retailers and suppliers; and post-transaction customer experience of the retail
store and product bought.

The major factors are summarized in Figure 2.10. The relevance of factors affecting customer loyalty differs according to target customer groups. Four broad types
of customer groups may be identified on the basis of price and quality: budget,
value, quality and luxury.

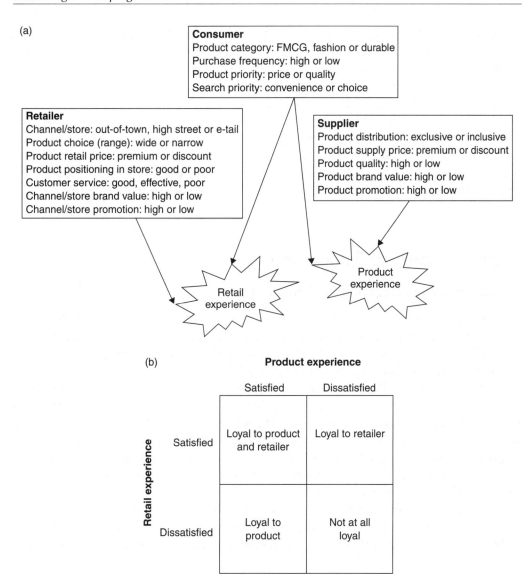

Figure 2.10 Major factors affecting switchability and substitutability

   Budget customers are price-focused. Retailers targeting these customers include German discount retailers such as Aldi, Netto and Lidl. Value customers focus on value for money, which implies a range of products to choose from at different price-quality points. Retailers targeting these customers include the big grocers and general merchandisers such as Tesco, Albert Heijn, Carrefour and Wal-Mart. Quality customers are focused on high-quality products and service. While price is not a prime issue to these customers, they will not pay 'excessive' prices. Retailers for these customers include the more niche retailers such as French retailer Sephora or even UK grocer Waitrose. The final category of luxury customers is focused on exceptionally high quality products and services. For these customers, price is not an issue and may even have a positive rather than negative correlation with loyalty. Typical retailers targeting these customers might include the more exclusive department stores, such as KaDeWe in Berlin or Harrods in London. These customers are summarized in Figure 2.11.

Based on the earlier discussion, Table 2.3 illustrates the key requirements for customer loyalty for each target group.

A dash (–) indicates a variable that may be appreciated by the customer but it is not generally key to gaining their loyalty. For example, budget customers may appreciate a good retail experience but it is not necessary to gain loyalty.

Loyalty strategy and implementation

Retailer loyalty strategy and implementation

Within the key requirements of customer loyalty, there are four critical elements: access, price, brand and assortment. The critical elements of a successful retailer loyalty strategy can be related to the traditional marketing mix of place, price, promotion and product, as shown in Figure 2.12.

Retailers directly influence customer loyalty to a store through a combination of the store location, brand marketing, product range and store environment. They can also directly influence product-brand loyalty, via variables, such as price, promotion, location on shelf and display. Customers will often choose to go to one retail location rather than several, allowing the retailers within that location to control many of the essential elements required to develop customer loyalty, both to the retailer and to branded products.

In summary, retailer-brand loyalty is the direct result of the retailer fulfilling customer needs. Indirectly, this may rely on the supplier's product being stocked. Retailers must be accessible and have a clear brand strategy that results in consistent

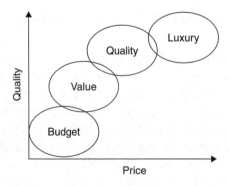

Figure 2.11 Target customers

marketing and operations, especially with respect to private label products and customer relationship programmes.

Retailers need to take different routes to achieve customer loyalty, depending upon their target customer group.

Budget retailers focus on price competitiveness and then accessibility, as shown in Figure 2.13. Quality retailers focus on both accessibility and their retail brand, illustrated in Figure 2.14. Figure 2.15 illustrates a luxury retailer's focus on their retail brand and then their category assortment.

Value retailers try to focus on all the critical issues at the same time, since they are attempting to offer 'everything to everyone'. Figure 2.16 shows the value retailer strategy. Arguably, the value retailers have the most difficult task, but also the largest potential markets.

All of these different routes to customer loyalty are summarized in Figure 2.17.

In the digital world, access may become less of an issue. As business-to-consumer e-commerce grows, particularly in mass-appeal broadband applications, such as digital television, retailers may be accessible from anywhere, and at any time. When customers choose to purchase through these digital channels, then physical location becomes less important.

Table 2.3 Key requirements for customer loyalty by customer group

	Customer type			
	Budget	**Value**	**Quality**	**Luxury**
Retail factors				
Channel/location	–	Out-of-town	–	High street
Range	–	Wide	Wide	Wide
Retail pricing	Discount	Mixed	–	–
In-store positioning	–	Good	Excellent	–
Customer service	–	Good	Effective	Excellent
Supply/product issues				
Distribution	Exclusive	Mixed	Inclusive	Exclusive
Manufacturer's product price	Low	Mixed	–	–
Product quality	–	Mixed	High	Excellent
Consumer view				
Retailer brand value	–	High	High	Superior
Retailer promotion	High	High	–	–
Product brand value	–	Mixed	High	Superior
Product promotion	–	Mixed	High	–
Product experience	–	–	Good	Excellent
Retail experience	–	Good	Effective	Excellent

Source: Oxford Institute of Retail Management

Summary

A loyal customer base is an asset for any company. However, marketing strategies must consider the overall commercial success of the business. Witness the recent

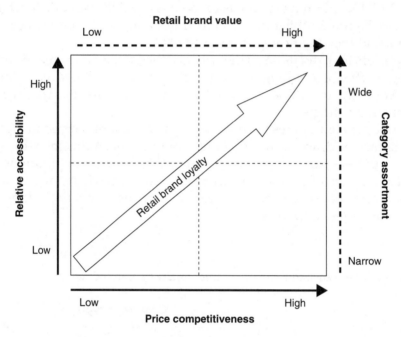

Figure 2.12 Retailer loyalty strategy

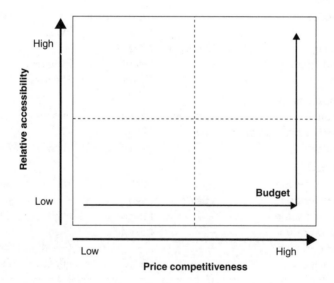

Figure 2.13 Retailer loyalty: budget customers

e-commerce retailers proclaiming customer attraction and retention without delivering profits. This is despite the fact that it has long been understood that, in commercial terms, *quality* of market share (loyalty) appears to be more important than *quantity* of market share. For example, Reichheld and Sasser (1990) estimated that a 5 per cent increase in customer loyalty can increase profits by between 25 and 85 per cent. However, it should be recognized that, in some markets, retailers may retain loyal customers without focusing a great deal of marketing expenditure on

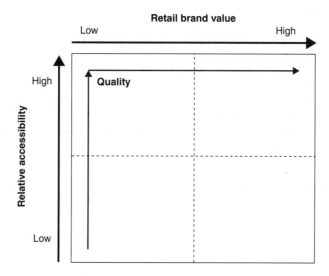

Figure 2.14 Retailer loyalty: quality customers

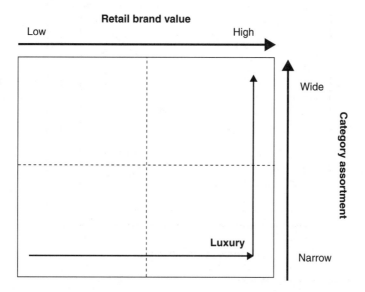

Figure 2.15 Retailer loyalty: luxury customers

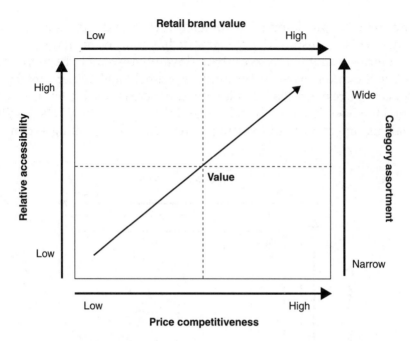

Figure 2.16 Retailer loyalty: value customers

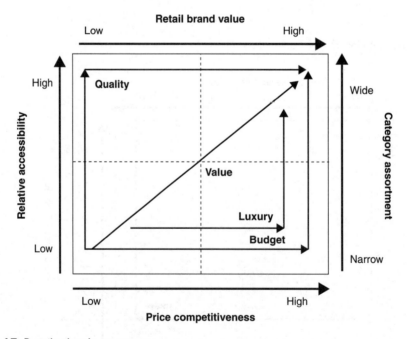

Figure 2.17 Retailer loyalty: summary

them. In this instance, it may be more cost-effective to focus marketing strategy and expenditure on non-loyal customers. For example, it has been demonstrated (Bolton, 1998) that when short-term and long-term customers experience poor service, the long-term customers are less likely to defect, because they may consider that this is not typical of the provider. Marketing strategy, in this situation, should be directed at new customers, who in turn may become loyal customers.

Each retail situation needs to be analysed individually to assess the relevant loyalty strategy. It is clear that retailers must have a clearly defined loyalty strategy and that increased customer loyalty should lead to increased profits. If this is not the case, then serious questions need to be asked. A key aim for retailers is to create a profitable long-term customer base.

Review questions

1 With reference to a retailer of your choice, identify, explain and evaluate the major factors affecting switchability and substitutability.
2 With reference to the Tesco case study and the purchaser–purveyor loyalty matrix, critically evaluate the CRM strategy of Tesco and two of its partner organizations.
3 Design (and carry out) some field research to identify and evaluate the private label strategy in relation to customer loyalty, of a retailer that sells both branded manufacturer's product and private-label product.

Discussion questions

1 Compare and contrast the marketing effectiveness of two retailers: one that operates through a range of channels and formats and one that operates through a single channel and/or format.
2 'Better informed customers lead to less loyal customers.' Discuss.

References

Bolton, R.N. (1998) 'A dynamic model of the duration of the customer's relationship with a continuous service provider: the role of satisfaction'. *Marketing Science*, **17**:1, pp. 45–65.

Business Times Singapore (1999) 'VW acts to combat shrinking brand loyalty'. September 30, Singapore Press Holdings Ltd.

Competition Commission (2000) *Supermarkets: A Report on the Supply of Groceries from Multiple Stores in the United Kingdom*. The Stationery Office.

Croft, M. (1998) 'Trusted to be Honest and Fair'. Brand Strategy, July 24.

Cuthbertson, R.W. (2002) *eLoyalty Retailer Strategies*. KPMG, London.

Cuthbertson, R.W. and Bell, R. (2001) 'The purchaser–purveyor loyalty scheme matrix'. *Proceedings of EAERCD*, Tilburg, The Netherlands, June 2001.

Cuthbertson R.W., Bell, R. and Howard, E. (2001) *Customers for Life: The Role of Retail Brands and Branded Products in Increasing Customer Loyalty.* KPMG Global Consumer Markets.

Cuthbertson, R.W., Bell, R. and Koskinen, S. (2000) *Customer Loyalty and Private Label Products.* KPMG, London.

Dick, A.S. and Basu, K. (1994) 'Customer loyalty: towards an integrated framework'. *Journal of the Academy of Marketing Science,* **22**:2, pp. 99–113.

East, R. and Hammond, K. (2000) 'First store loyalty and retention'. *Journal of Marketing Management,* **16**:4, p. 307.

East, R. and Hogg, A. (1997) 'The anatomy of conquest: Tesco versus Sainsbury'. *Journal of Brand Management,* **5**:1, pp. 53–60.

Gedenk, K. and Neslin, S.A. (1999) 'The role of retail promotion in determining future brand loyalty: its effects on purchase event feedback'. *Journal of Retailing,* **75**:4, pp. 433–59.

Henley Centre (1998) *Planning for Social Change.* London.

Kuttner, R. (1998) 'The Net: A Market Too Perfect for Profits'. *Business Week,* May 11, p. 20.

Mantel, S.P. and Kardes, F.R. (1999) 'The role of direction and comparison, attribute-based processing and attitude-based processing in consumer preference'. *Journal of Consumer Preference,* **3**, pp. 335–8.

Matthews, R. (1998) 'Introduction: Brands and beyond'. *Progressive Grocer,* July, p. 4.

McCarthy, J.E. (1964) *Basic Marketing: A Managerial Approach.* Homewood, Illinois: R.D. Irwin.

McGoldrick, P. (2002) *Retail Marketing.* McGraw-Hill.

Mintel (1998) *Own Label Food.* November. Mintel International Group Limited, London.

Morris (2000) *Annual Review and Accounts.* Competition Commission, London. Download at http://www.competition-commission.org.uk/review/cc2001.pdf

Office of Fair Trading (1999) *News release.* 11/99, 8th April 1999.

Reichheld, F.F. and Sasser, W.E. (1990) 'Zero defections: quality comes to services'. *Harvard Business Review,* Sep./Oct., pp. 105–11.

Richardson, P.S., Jain, A.K. and Dick, A. (1996) 'Household store brand proneness: a framework'. *Journal of Retailing,* **72**, pp. 159–85.

Scase, R. (1999) *Trends and Changes in Mobile Working.* Oracle.

Schumpeter, J.A. (1987) *Capitalism, Socialism and Democracy,* 6th edition. Unwin.

Sheth, J.N. and Parvatiyar, A. (1995) 'Relationship marketing in consumer markets: antecedents and consequences'. *Journal of the Academy of Marketing Sciences,* **23**:4, pp. 236–45.

Vanhoof, K., Bloemer, J. and Pauwels, K. (1997) 'A case study in loyalty and satisfaction research'. 9th *European Conference on Machine Learning,* April 23rd–25th, pp. 290–97.

Verbeke, W., Farris, P. and Thurik, R. (1997) 'The acid test of brand loyalty: Consumer response to out-of-stocks for their favourite brands'. *Journal of Brand Management,* **5**:1, pp. 43–52.

Verdict (1999) *Consumer Loyalty.* Verdict Research, London.

Woolf, B. (1996) *Customer Specific Marketing.* Teal Books, p. 44.

Further reading

Corstjens, J. and Corstjens, M. (1995) *Store Wars*. John Wiley & Sons.
Kotler, P., Armstrong, G., Saunders, J. and Wong, V. (2001) *Principles of Marketing: European Edition*, FT Prentice Hall.
McGoldrick, P. (2002) *Retail Marketing*. McGraw-Hill.

Acknowledgements

This chapter is based on research carried out for KPMG International. Further details may be found at www.loyalty4profit.com. The primary sources of information are company interviews, company documents (statistics, memorandum, annual reports, etc.), observation and data supplied by ACNielsen and AIM (average bimonthly sales over a six-month period). Due to the competitive nature of this research, most of this information remains anonymous. The focus of the study is on western European retailers and markets. Dr Emyr Williams, KPMG, Richard Bell, Templeton College and Elizabeth Howard, Templeton College provided valuable additional input.

Chapter 3

Collaboration in the retail supply chain

Richard Bell and Richard Cuthbertson

Vertically integrated retail chains are not new phenomena. UK retailer Boots the Chemist, for example, has operated as a vertical chain since the nineteenth century. However, the notion of collaboration within the supply chain has developed as a subject in its own right with the emergence of powerful retail chains that have changed the balance of power vis-à-vis producers. The nature of collaboration is influenced by a variety of factors. The type of retail store, the nature of the products sold and the ownership of the intellectual property of the products are amongst the more important determining factors. Information technology has allowed independent commercial entities to behave as if they are part of a vertically integrated chain. This chapter examines the contribution of those factors that shape the construction of individual supply chains. It begins by examining the principles of supply chain efficiency and identifying the requirements necessary to introduce a consumer-responsive supply chain. It goes on to address the operational and financial implications of introducing a 'consumer pull' chain, identify the industry-wide programmes of collaboration that exist and explain the relevance of collaboration in the context of increasing retail concentration. Finally, it discusses how the structure of the supply chain is shaped by the pattern of retail shops, the type of products involved and the requirement to also deliver direct to the consumer. The chapter argues that collaboration between suppliers and retailers is now essential if aggregate efficiency is to be achieved.

Principles of supply chain efficiency

Producer push

The traditional supply chain is based on the source of production. Manufacturers procure the raw materials necessary to manufacture a product that had been designed to meet a perceived consumer need. The driving force of manufacturing was production efficiency. Such factories are engineered for low-unit-cost production and usually embrace the concept of long production runs and minimal product changes. It is this philosophy that inspired Henry Ford to offer the Model 'T' in 'any colour, so long as it's black'. His goal was to simplify the product, maximize production efficiency, minimize the cost and stimulate consumer sales and profits. Such a philosophy focuses on the efficient use of fixed assets such as plant and equipment, and undervalues current assets such as inventory and other working capital. The philosophy also assumes that price rather than variety is the primary consumer motivation. As disposable incomes rise, consumers place an increasing value on variety and self-personalization, and although Ford's Model 'T' held a virtual monopoly in private motoring in the US for several years, eventually customers wanted greater choice.

In a production oriented supply chain, production determines availability and usually equals sales. Typically, the manufacturer sells to wholesalers, who in turn supply independent retailers. This is illustrated in Figure 3.1. The manufacturers base their production schedules on previous sales rates to the wholesaler. Manufacturers are unaware of the stock levels in the wholesaler, the sales rates of the wholesaler, the stock levels in the retailer and generally the level of consumer sales. In essence each component in the supply chain operates in isolation. Table 3.1 shows an example of the effect on stock and subsequently production volumes of a manufacturer attempting to increase output without understanding consumer sales. In this situation, retailers are unable to influence consumers to increase their purchases.

Table 3.1 examines the situation of just one product moving down the supply chain. However, retailers do not sell just one product; they sell a wide range of product lines, and stock availability at wholesalers across the product range will

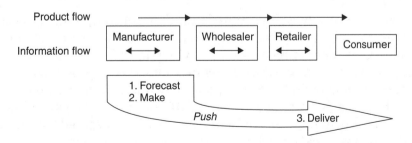

Figure 3.1 A push supply chain

54

Retail Strategy

Table 3.1 Example of an inventory replenishment in a push system

Manufacturer		Wholesaler		Retailer		Consumer	Overstock as a percentage of sales (%)
Production	Overstock	Received	Remaining	Ordered	Unsold	Bought	
500		500		500		500	
	0		0		0		0
550		550		550		500	
	0		0		50		10
650		650		500		500	
	0		150		50		40
800		350		450		500	
	450		50		0		100

influence total retailer sales. Variable product availability at the wholesaler will constrain retail sales on some lines while excess stock on other lines will not necessarily increase sales unless discounted in price. A retailer therefore seeks balanced stock availability across each of the product lines they choose to sell.

A push supply chain controlled by the manufacturer is often characterized by large fluctuations in stock levels, erratic changes to production schedules and the use of time as a buffer as consumers order product that is not available at the retailer and return at a later date to collect it. Production-led chains do not necessarily lead to production efficiency due to unplanned changes to production schedules. The cost of current assets is high as stock is often used to buffer each stage in the chain. Retailers often fail to maximize sales because of variable product availability, and consumer satisfaction may be low.

Consumer pull

The lessons from a producer push supply chain are that:

- retail sales can be maximized if there is available stock across the entire product range, production can be increased if consumer sales are maximized, and inventory can be reduced if production and deliveries are aligned to the level of retail sales.

The contemporary supply chain is thus focused on consumption, rather than production, with the volume of consumer purchases used as a surrogate measure of consumption. Consumer purchases equate with retail sales and these can be measured using store census data, which measures sales of each product line from each store for a given time period. Consumption may differ from consumer purchases since households carry some stock, particularly of grocery items, and household stock levels can fluctuate. Consumption can only be measured by sample data, which is usually insufficiently accurate to drive the supply chain. This is discussed in more detail later in this chapter. The chosen period of replenishment time will

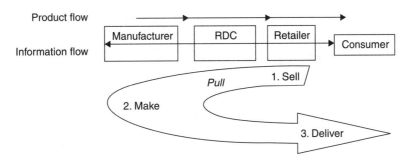

Figure 3.2 A pull supply chain

Table 3.2 Example of an inventory replenishment in a pull system

Manufacturer		Wholesaler		Retailer		Consumer	Overstock as a percentage of sales
Production	Overstock	Received	Remaining	Ordered	Unsold	Bought	
500		500		500		500	
	0		0		0		0%
550		550		550		500	
	0		0		50		10%
500		500		500		500	
	0		0		50		10%
500		500		450		500	
	0		50		0		10%

vary according to the type of products sold by the retail store and the most economic replenishment cycle. Supermarkets selling fast moving consumer goods (FMCG), such as grocery products, can be efficiently replenished on a daily basis. The short shelf life of some of the products sold necessitates frequent replenishment. Products where the rate of sale of each item is slower, and where there are no immediate shelf life concerns – such as electrical products – require a less frequent replenishment cycle. The measurement period of retail sales thus varies between types of retail store.

The consumer pull supply chain requires full visibility of consumer sales to all participants in the chain. In addition visibility is required for product movements and stock levels along the supply chain. In this way each independent entity can observe current demand and translate that into potential movements. The identification of product movements will then determine the production schedule. In the example shown in Table 3.2, consumer sales drop in Week 2 due to an unforeseen event such as unseasonable weather. Since both the regional distribution centre (RDC) and the factory can see the change in retail sales, they are able to adjust respectively their deliveries and production in the following week. Had the factory

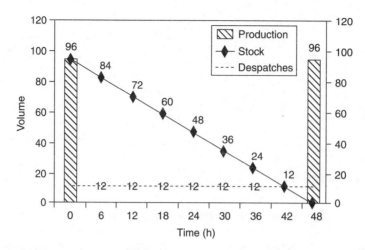

Figure 3.3 Production frequency and stock

waited until after the RDC had reduced deliveries to adjust their schedules, their build up of stock would have been greater and the eventual cut in production would also have been greater. An important principle of the consumer pull supply chain is cooperation between each stage and each commercial entity in the chain. In this respect it differs from the 'beggar thy neighbour' attitude prevalent in producer push chains (see Table 3.1). The concept of supply chain collaboration is therefore most relevant in consumer pull supply chains.

Algorithms based on optimum operating efficiency can be developed for each stage of the chain. Thus at the factory stage there is an optimum relationship between efficient production schedules and stock levels. If a factory produces 240 separate products on five production lines and the minimum efficient production run is one hour then on average each item is produced every 48 hours. If full vehicle loads can be efficiently despatched at hourly intervals to warehouses then it follows that 24 (48/2) hours of stock (plus safety stock) will be held at the factory. This is illustrated in Figure 3.3. Production quantity 96 is manufactured once every 48 hours and despatches are constant at 12 every 6 hours. Stock rises to 96 immediately following the production run and falls to zero over a 48-hour period. In this example, the appropriate algorithms for the factory are one hour run lengths and 24 hours of stock. The factory has calculated the optimum rate of exchange between production efficiency (utilization of fixed assets) and stock (current assets).

Important considerations

Consumer pull supply chains operate on the principle of 'just-in-time' (JIT). The concept is that product flows like water and that production is perfectly aligned to consumer purchases. In this situation there would never be a change in stock levels as there would be instant adjustment to a variation in sales. In practice, as the example illustrates, there is 'lumpiness' around each stage in the chain. Factories cannot instantly change schedules, because by doing so, they would not only lose efficiency but also stop manufacturing another product line creating other stock imbalances. Similarly efficient transportation requires vehicle utilization and it is usually impractical to ship one item at a time. Stock will always be required as a buffer but the goal of the consumer pull supply chain is rapid response to sales variations and the minimization of the 'lumpiness' of each stage. Successful minimization of 'lumpiness' leads to lower stock holding. In the longer term this requires a reassessment of the efficient operating parameters of each stage in the chain in turn leading to a re-engineering of the fixed assets (plant and capital equipment).

Sales variations can have important consequences for factory and vehicle utilization. Such variations can either be buffered by stock or lead to fluctuations in the utilization of fixed assets. Seasonality, weather and fashion, for example, may lead to variations in sales. To a large extent these may be predictable as winter, for example, occurs every year. The issue is that the precise timing of the onset of winter can vary. Stock can be used to act as a buffer, but in extreme situations lost sales may result. An important principle to support rapid response is to hold stock in one location *and* as close as possible to the point of sales. If stock is held only at the retail store, some stores may become out of stock while other stores have excess stock. The only way to balance this is to incur the added cost of transporting product between stores. An alternative is to hold stock in depots that service a number of stores and are capable of responding quickly to variations in retail stock. In many cases retail sales fluctuations are induced by promotional activity, including advertising. If this activity is pre-planned and advance notice given to all stages in the supply chain, then stock outs and sales losses can be minimized. Even if the activity is pre-planned it will create a surge in demand on production and transportation facilities, thereby reducing efficiency. Some retailers and their suppliers have adopted policies of constant pricing ('every day low price') to achieve maximum efficiency by excluding promotions. This may then be translated into lower prices.

Fundamental requirements

There are a number of fundamental requirements to achieve a pull supply chain. These are based on the provision of effective information systems throughout the supply chain.

Point-of-sale data

The fuel for consumer pull supply chains is data on retail sales. This data must be held at the lowest level, where possible. Each product line is referred to as a stock-keeping unit (SKU). Stock replenishment takes place at the product line level rather than the brand, or sub brand level. Coca-Cola as a brand comes in many varieties (diet, regular and so on), in many package types (glass bottles, plastic bottles, cans) in many container sizes (1 litre, 2 litre, 500 ml) and in many pack sizes (6, 12, 24, etc.). Retailers will list many combinations of a brand, and stock is held at the distinct product or SKU level (e.g. Coca-Cola regular 12×330 ml). Similarly, each SKU may be produced at a different time within the production schedule. The supply chain thus operates at this level. Large stores such as a grocery supermarket can list as many as 30,000 SKUs. Data on the sales rate of each SKU must be captured. Each SKU has a unique bar code and the sales data is captured at the electronic point of sale (EPOS), i.e. the cash desk. A further benefit of EPOS data is the frequency with which it can be accessed and the short time intervals, usually daily and in some cases hourly, in which consumer purchases can be tracked.

It has only been possible to capture this data since the introduction of scanning equipment, introduced by British retailers during the 1980s but only effective when all stores in the chain are equipped. It was not until the early 1990s that consumer pull supply chains were developed in the UK. Retailers' knowledge of rates of sale per item prior to the introduction of scanning was obtained from invoice data. This related to retailer purchases, not consumer sales and the difference between the two numbers was accounted for by changes in inventory levels. Such data applied to longer time intervals, usually monthly, and was inadequate to drive a consumer pull supply chain. Figure 3.4 shows the progress in adopting scanning across the European grocery industry.

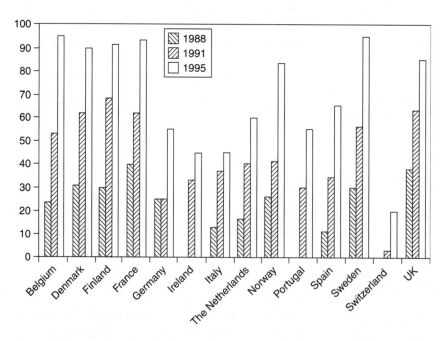

Figure 3.4 Percentage of grocery turnover scanned

The use of scanning and the emergence of large integrated retail chains have led to a situation where retail sales data are in effect census data. Each chain records sales per SKU for all of its stores and then calculates the aggregate. Thus actual aggregate sales data can be used to drive the supply chain. Retail concentration, whereby four or five retailers account for around 75 per cent of sales in each retail sector, enables actual data for product retail sales to be obtained for each sector. Manufacturers can therefore have access to actual retail sales of their products through all outlets. This contrasts with the accuracy of measures of domestic consumption. Such measures are obtained from a sample of consumer households. A panel with 20,000 households would be a sample size of one thousandth of the total households in a country the size of the UK. This relatively small sample will lead to grossing up errors in projecting national sales. This level of error is too large to drive a consumer pull supply chain, where the goal is stock minimization. Further, it is not practical for household panels to report more frequently than monthly, which is too long a time interval in which to replenish fast moving consumer goods such as grocery products.

Information technology integration of retail operations

The capture of EPOS data alone is not enough for retailers to develop a consumer pull supply chain. Such a supply chain embraces the retail functions of inventory control, depot management, marketing, category management, buying and finance. Planned marketing activities need to be communicated to retail branches and the required quantity of product ordered. Since invoices will not be paid without some form of purchase order, this information must be accessible to both the buying and finance functions. Integration of each of these retail operations is therefore necessary for a consumer pull supply chain to be introduced and is illustrated in Figure 3.5. The linking of individual processes of distribution is often referred to as connectivity and is achieved by the application of information technology.

The cost of investment in information technology is high. British retailers such as Sainsbury's and Marks & Spencer were estimated to have spent between 1.5 and 2 per cent of turnover on information technology in the early 1990s. At that time Marks & Spencer is estimated to have spent £500m on IT systems for its 285 UK stores dealing with 700 suppliers and 150,000 product lines. Such investment has to be justified on increased efficiencies and greater competitiveness. The efficiencies would be gained in lower operating costs, lower inventories and greater sales resulting from less out-of-stock situations in its branches. A study by Martec in 2002 showed that UK retail spend on IT had fallen to 1.1 per cent of sales as retailers adapted the mainframe-based systems installed in the 1990s to meet the needs of the next decade. This level of expenditure is 60 per cent of that of the US retail market.

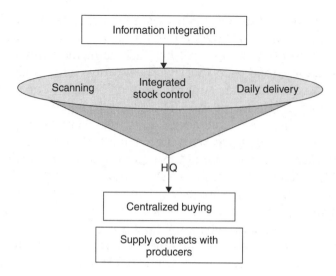

Figure 3.5 Integration upstream

Store control

Retail stores must operate within an agreed corporate framework for the consumer pull supply chain to operate efficiently. The framework will embrace product range, store layout and promotional policy. An aspect of integration is the incorporation of planned marketing activities so that forward surges of demand can be anticipated all the way up the supply chain. Precise implementation of marketing plans is essential at store level for the forward surges to be predicted with accuracy. Low accuracy leads to an imbalance of stocks (either too many or too few), which induces an unplanned surge up the supply chain. A necessary condition for accuracy is centralized control of store operations. Stores that order direct from suppliers, without communicating with head office, will be unable to supply sales data for re-ordering. More importantly such 'pirate' products will interfere with the planned marketing activities of products supplied through the centralized replenishment process. In the UK, most retail chains are centralized public limited companies whereas in mainland Europe, many stores are independently owned and operate under a franchise agreement.

Data synchronization

Since 'just-in-time' solutions are aimed at increased efficiency, it is important that different retailers (each of whom have many suppliers) and their suppliers (each of whom may supply many different retailers) communicate in a compatible manner. The use of separate complex communication systems would generate levels of administrative complexity that could negate the gains in operational efficiencies. The objective of data synchronization is to establish a common framework for product and party data, offering businesses a single, streamlined gateway for standardized and constantly synchronized product data to drive all supply chain applications. It has been estimated in a Global Commerce Initiative (2002) special report that 30 per cent of transactions contain inaccurate data and 3.4 per cent of sales are lost annually because of supply chain inefficiencies. The aim of data synchronization is to help everyone in the supply chain implement compatible processes thereby reducing opportunities for error and the costs of duplicate data entry.

Visibility

The level of retail sales drives the consumer pull supply chain. It follows that the level of retail sales should be available to all entities within the supply chain. The time period for retail sales will be influenced by the replenishment cycle. In the case of fast moving consumer goods, such as groceries, the time period could be daily. In the case of Japan, where shops are small in size, and velocity of sales is high, then the replenishment cycle could be as short as every four hours. This rate of sale needs to be available to both the wholesaler or regional distribution depot and to the manufacturer. Similarly the product flows between each link in the chain need to be visible to all parties. The replenishment cycle may vary between different links in the chain. Dutch grocery retailer Albert Heijn has a policy of guaranteed replenishment of its stores within eighteen hours and requires a six-hour response time from its suppliers to its depots. A large volume beverage supplier such as Heineken has full visibility of aggregate (all store) sales rates and has introduced a dedicated production line to service Albert Heijn. Such an integrated operation is only possible if Heineken can observe hourly aggregate sales rates and product movements between depots. The primary goal of a supplier such as Heineken is to ensure that there is neither out-of-stock nor excess stock at the Albert Heijn depots. The concept of visibility requires the retailer to supply sales data for specific products to each commercial entity up the supply chain. This integration of independent commercial entities (separate companies) contrasts with the producer push process where each company utilizes its own despatch data to determine replenishment of its own stocks in isolation.

Reconstruction of the supply chain

The physical supply chain has to be re-constructed to facilitate the implementation of a consumer pull supply chain. In the traditional producer push supply chain, it is necessary to hold stock in each link of the chain. This is because each stage does not know sales and stock levels at the next stage of the chain. Despatches fluctuate widely, and the fluctuations are likely to increase in intensity the further back each stage is from the consumer. Stock is held to buffer the sales fluctuations. Stock holding may be high at each stage of the chain and high in aggregate across the total supply chain. The producer push supply chain therefore often requires a high level of current assets (stock). It also often requires a high level of warehouse space (fixed assets) to hold the stock. In this situation, retail stores require a stock holding facility, retail and wholesale warehouses are primarily stock holding facilities, and manufacturers also usually require stock holding facilities.

The concept of 'just-in-time' is to align production to consumption, thereby minimizing the requirement to hold stock. The more perfect the alignment, the less stock holding is required throughout the supply chain. Further, the damping down of unplanned sales fluctuations at the consumer level by controlled marketing programmes also reduces the required stock buffer. The concept of smooth product flows changes the requirement for warehouses. Rapid replenishment at the store level allows retail stock rooms to be converted into selling space. Warehouses become 'flow through distribution depots'. Product is moved in, re-assembled into loads for stores and moved out. The primary focus shifts from holding stock to re-assembly. Space changes from volume, where height is needed for stacking, to surface area where floor area is required for product movement, detailed order picking for each store, and vehicle loading. Vehicles also have to be adapted to transport a wide range of products in small quantities. For example, grocery retailers adapt vehicles to transport ambient, frozen and chilled products on the same lorry. Importantly, each retailer develops their own flow-through distribution depots, thus reducing the role of the wholesaler. Retailers are faced with an increased capital expenditure on new regional distribution centres (RDCs), flexible vehicle specifications and computerized integration systems in order to achieve lower stocks and higher sales through less out-of-stock situations at the retail store.

Suppliers are required to schedule their vehicles to arrive at times determined by the retailer's distribution depots. Vehicle scheduling thus assumes greater importance to manufacturers than previously. The manufacturer is involved in a reassessment of factory efficiencies versus inventory levels. Shorter production runs and more frequent product changes are necessary to meet the 'little and often' demands of each retailer's RDC. Some manufacturers, as in the case of Heineken and Albert Heijn, are able to reorganize their production facilities. For others the cost of implementing this is greater than the saving in lower stock levels and they will buffer the more frequent replenishment required by retailers with high stock levels. Manufacturers are thus faced with an evaluation of increased capital expenditure in order to lower inventories to meet the demands for rapid replenishment.

Industry programmes of supply chain collaboration

A consumer pull supply chain aligns each participant within the chain to the common goal of maximizing product availability to consumers, while minimizing stock held within the chain. In the past, each commercial entity may have operated, largely in a vacuum, to maximize its own profit. Within a consumer pull supply chain, each entity must operate within a partnership to maximize consumer purchases. Maximized consumer purchases translate into increased sales for both retailer and manufacturer. Since profit for both participants is sensitive to changes in volume, then maximization of volume will result in profit maximization. Sharing of information between retailers, and their suppliers raises important issues of competition, since this may increase barriers to entry and dampen competition. If the supply chains are exclusive, so that some manufacturers supply only one retailer, then competition concerns may be heightened. The common goal of retailers and manufacturers is the development of an integrated consumer driven supply network. Such a network is common and accessible to all participants in the supply chain and avoids the risk of separate and exclusive supply chains. Industry-wide programmes such as ECR Europe and the Global Commerce Initiative, both discussed below, that foster a common communication language and operating standards, contribute to reduced complexity costs and so minimize the entry barriers for both retailers and manufacturers.

ECR Europe

The Efficient Consumer Response (ECR) movement began in the mid-1990s with the emergence of new principles of collaborative supply chain management. ECR developed along the principle that consumers could be served better, faster and at less cost if companies worked together.

ECR is a response to a business environment characterized by rapid advances in information technology, shifts in consumer demand and the increasing movements of goods across national boundaries made easier by government initiatives, such as the internal European market. New trading environments require a fundamental reconsideration of the most effective way of delivering the right products to consumers at the right price.

There are four focus areas of ECR. These areas are further broken down into core and advanced improvement concepts. They form the basis of the ECR Global Scorecard, which is illustrated in Figure 3.6. ECR Europe essentially addresses the grocery industry, which is characterized by the high frequency of consumer purchase and the presence of well-known manufacturer brands such as Coca-Cola, Nescafé, Whiskas and Pampers.

Demand management, as shown in Figure 3.6, is an important component of ECR, when manufacturer brands are an important component of total retailer sales and where the brand owner initiates promotional and marketing activities on their brands. It is important that these activities are co-ordinated between retailer and manufacturer if product is to flow smoothly from the production line to the point of sale.

The enablers of Figure 3.6, the common data and communication standards, and the measure of cost/profit and value, provide a common language of

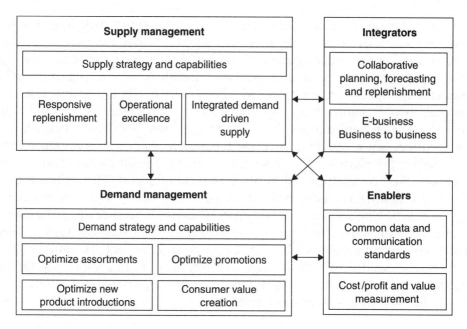

Figure 3.6 Footprint Global ECR Scorecard

communication and embrace such notions as data synchronization. Management of supply in Figure 3.6 embraces the concepts of consumer pull supply chains in responsive replenishment, operational excellence and integrated demand-driven supply. The integrators from Figure 3.6, such as collaborative planning, forecasting and replenishment (CPFR) are common tools that aim to facilitate smooth product flow by the accurate anticipation of future demand. This is particularly pertinent where marketing activities create fluctuations in sales volumes. The accurate prediction of future surges in demand enables production capacity to be planned to meet such surges.

Individually these concepts are well known and fully documented methods to improve effectiveness and efficiency. However, when applied under ECR they have two distinct differences: they are intended to be addressed as an integrated set, not individually, and they are assessed in terms of their impact across the entire supply chain, not just the business of individual trading partners.

Global Commerce Initiative

The Global Commerce Initiative (GCI) began in 1999 in response to the international development of retailers and the reorganization of manufacturing facilities for global brands. Retailers wished to adapt common methods of operation as they expanded their operations into other continents. Similarly, manufacturers of global brands were rearranging their manufacturing facilities to a global supply platform. The GCI is a voluntary platform to improve the performance of the international supply chain for consumer goods through the endorsement of recommended standards and key business processes. It builds on the foundations of the regional ECR initiatives and was set up to encourage the speedier development and consistent adoption of global trading standards. It is not in itself a standards body but endeavours to identify best practice in areas that will streamline global supply chain management.

The focus areas of GCI include:

- Product identification to ensure that there is a consistent global implementation of product identification numbering and bar codes, to enable a bar coded product from any company large or small to be scanned anywhere in the world.
- Intelligent tagging is a business application for radio frequency identification (RFI). Radio frequency tags (RFT), incorporated into packaging, could deliver more efficient shelf stocking in store, faster checkouts and improved security. These benefits result at the retail level, though the producer incurs the costs. The development of a common standard employed by retailers will facilitate a lower cost solution.
- Global data synchronization.
- Product classification aims to develop a system for product classification that can be adapted for consumer products industries worldwide, supporting global product search.
- Collaborative planning, forecasting and replenishment (CPFR) is a GCI-backed initiative to ensure compatible approaches between each continent.

Collaboration and concentration

The development of the consumer pull supply chain and the associated increase in retailer supplier collaboration should be seen in the context of a rise in retail concentration. Collaboration becomes an imperative when powerful retailers sell well-known manufacturers' brands. This situation is particularly prevalent in the food industry in both Europe and North America. Manufacturer concentration has existed since the 1980s at a national level and has developed during the 1990s with the emergence of global brands and international manufacturers. Companies such as Nestlé, Procter & Gamble, Unilever and Coca-Cola market their brands in many countries. Retailer concentration increased at the national level during the 1990s so that by 2000, the median market share of the top five grocery retailers in Europe was 83 per cent (see Figure 3.7). Since the mid-1990s there has been an acceleration of grocery retailers that have pursued international expansion. Retailers such as Wal-Mart of the US, Carrefour of France, Metro of Germany, Royal Ahold of The Netherlands and Tesco of the UK, each dominant in their domestic market, have substantially increased the number of countries where they have operations. Most of these participate

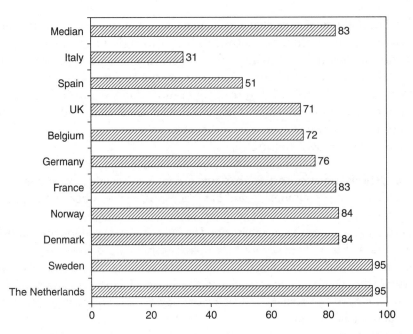

Figure 3.7 Grocery shares in Europe: top five retailers

in the GCI. At the start of the twenty-first century, the increase in retail concentration and power in distribution channels is fundamentally altering retailer–
manufacturing relations. The extent of further concentration will depend on
strategic moves by the world's leading food firms and by the attitude of competition
authorities.

Many of the recent initiatives in vertical co-operation, including ECR and
GCI, can be interpreted as a response to increasing concentration at all stages of
the supply chain. The channel may now have 'shared' monopoly, i.e. an oligopoly, at both manufacturing and retail stages. Vertical co-ordination is therefore
required to prevent double marginalization (higher margins at both the producer and retailer stage). Oligopoly leads to higher margins than would exist in a
situation of perfect competition. Cotterill (1999) demonstrates that co-ordination
reduces double marginalization increasing total channel profits and lowering
prices to consumers. The presence of industry-wide programmes, such as ECR,
provides a framework for co-ordination without the prospect of collusion, enabling
the elimination of double marginalization without breaking competition laws.
Industry-wide programmes are perceived to encourage competition by lowering the entry barriers to an industry where consumer pull supply chains are
prevalent.

In summary the drive to consumer pull supply chains is greatest when three
factors are present: the application of information technology to the retailing process; the presence of large producer brands; and high levels of retail
concentration.

Supply chains in practice

Supply chains by type of store

Size of store has an important bearing on the structure and operation of a consumer pull supply chain. Some outlets are so large and have a high rate of sale that they can receive full vehicle loads direct from the manufacturer without these generating high stock levels. Outlets with a slow rate of sale and selling a broad product range require their deliveries to be consolidated at an intermediate trans-shipment depot. Rate of sale per retail outlet and product range are key determinants of the structure of the supply chain.

'Large surface' outlets

Cash and carry outlets, such as Metro/Makro, are at one end of the spectrum. Their primary focus is to supply small retail and catering establishments. Unlike a retail outlet that sells direct to consumers, they sell multiple quantities of an item. For example, their customers might buy, on average, six cans of a particular SKU of cat food, such as 'Whiskas 400 gm Supermeat with Chicken'. The chain of cash and carry stores will seek the manufacturer's cooperation to supply packs of six. Each six-pack will then be packed into outer cases of 24 cans (4 × 6 packs) for transportation, and these outers stacked onto a pallet for ease of movement and storage. In this way the cash and carry will stock full pallet loads in its racks, and the customer will be asked to select their required quantity of six packs from the outer. The breakdown of cases into individual cans is thus avoided and the handling costs are minimized at the cash and carry outlet. The manufacturer generates economies of scale by supplying the optimum pack quantity of the SKU and outer size to all branches of the cash and carry, and ideally to all cash and carry chains. The supply chain to cash and carry is thus direct from the manufacturer to the outlet, obviating the need for an intermediate warehouse and avoiding the cost of double vehicle movements and handling. Such a supply chain can only be economically viable if all (or at least most) suppliers agree to supply packs and outers that are specific to the cash and carry trade. Transport costs can be minimized by the cash and carry taking full vehicle loads where each pallet contains only one SKU. If there are 20 pallets to a vehicle, the maximum number of SKUs delivered will be 20. The efficiency of such a supply chain is thus determined by the rate of sale of each outlet and the product range. A large range will inevitably include some smaller selling items that cannot be supplied on full pallets if excess stock is not to be carried.

Hypermarkets, large superstores and supercentres (as operated by Wal-Mart in the US) are examples of large surface outlets that sell to consumers. The aggregate volume of sales of each outlet may be very similar to a cash and carry outlet justifying delivery of full pallet loads of an SKU and hence incurring minimum transport costs when supplied direct from the manufacturer. However, consumers shopping at such a large surface outlet may require just one or two items of each SKU. The shipping containers (outers of 24 in the Whiskas example) will have to be unpacked by the staff of the hypermarket, and placed on the shelves of the store. This is an additional handling cost compared with the cash and carry but not additional to being supplied by an intermediate warehouse, since such warehouses will have to transport product in shipping containers (outers). It is therefore a cost effective solution to supply such large surface stores direct from the manufacturer. Again, the critical factor is rate of sale and product range. The product range of a hypermarket is so large that inevitably some SKUs are slow selling products and will be supplied by an intermediate depot to avoid excess stock at the store. A hypermarket may thus have more than one supply chain, of which one would be direct from the manufacturer. When Spain embraced the retail revolution in the mid 1980s and there was a rapid expansion of hypermarkets, the primary method of supply was direct from the manufacturer. Centralized distribution centres, with integrated information technology systems, could not be developed at a speed necessary to keep pace with the growth of hypermarkets. The economics of direct supply enabled the hypermarkets to be more competitive on both price and range than traditional retailers.

Supermarkets
The average store size of a supermarket is approximately one third that of a hypermarket, but their product range is around 80 per cent of the grocery SKUs carried by a hypermarket. The average rate of sale is correspondingly significantly lower than that of a hypermarket and only a few of the best selling SKUs can be delivered on full pallets. It follows that direct deliveries from manufacturers are not economically viable. They would result in higher stocks, increased out-of-stock situations and the conversion of selling space into product storage. The optimum structure of a supply chain for medium-sized stores is based on 'flow-through' distribution centres. Deliveries are received from manufacturers on full pallets of SKU for the fast moving products, thus minimizing manufacturer distribution costs. Full outers from different suppliers are combined onto one vehicle for efficient, frequent and rapid replenishment of each retail branch. Consolidated deliveries (of many different SKUs) to branches utilize effective material handling systems such as roll cages that can be unloaded at the retail store without recourse to cumbersome equipment such as fork lift trucks. The measure of efficiency of the distribution centre is the speed to receive, consolidate and despatch product such that stock moves in and out but is not stored. It is the hub or universal coupling between frequent deliveries from suppliers and rapid replenishment of retail stores.

Retailers of medium sized stores seeking geographical expansion of their chains, such as Delhaize in the Czech Republic, or Waitrose from the south of England, need to develop new distribution centres as the precursor to new store openings. Lengthy driving times from depot to store serve as a strong influence against rapid and frequent replenishment. However, a new distribution centre needs to service a cluster of retail stores to obtain the minimum product flow required for efficiency. Geographic expansion thus requires the parallel development of new retail stores and an RDC.

Discounters and smaller stores

Discounters and smaller stores also require the support of a flow-through distribution centre, to achieve efficient replenishment. They differ from supermarkets in terms of a lower rate of sale per retail outlet. This requires a greater density of stores per distribution centre if the centre is to operate efficiently. Discounters are able to achieve a high rate of sale per SKU by limiting their range to fast selling items only. This maximizes their replenishment efficiency and minimizes stock levels because stock sales ratios are invariably higher for low selling items. Leading discount food chains, such as Aldi and Lidl, differ from supermarkets by selling mainly own-brand products. Their commercial policy thus makes unnecessary one of the three essential criteria for supply chain collaboration discussed above.

The importance of store size in determining the optimum supply chain is illustrated in Figure 3.8.

Supply chains by type of product

Three types of product can be used to illustrate the contrasting influence product can have on the construction of a supply chain. These are ambient grocery products; perishable foods; and fashion clothing.

Ambient grocery products

These can be expected to include both manufacturers' brands and retailers' own brands. In the case of retailer brands, production schedules can be directly aligned to rate of retail sale. In the case of manufacturer brands, production schedules are determined by aggregate retail sales through all retailers listing the product.

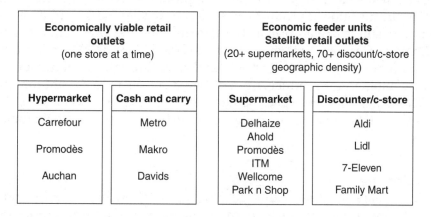

Figure 3.8 Formula for expansion

Production is therefore less perfectly aligned to the rate of sale in any one retailer. Since production schedules are less flexible for manufacturer brands, it follows that the manufacturer must buffer fluctuations in sales at individual retailers by holding higher stocks. The supply chain for ambient grocery products may differ between fast sellers and slow selling lines.

Fast selling lines will conform to the principle of full vehicle loads of pallets containing one SKU from the supplier, where such products move through an RDC. For example, in the case of supermarkets, the shipping unit (outer) remains intact.

In general, the Pareto principle applies, i.e. 80 per cent of the lines account for 20 per cent of the sales volume. Slow selling lines, therefore, generate much complexity and for this reason are often kept separate from the fast selling lines. For purposes of stock minimization, it is unlikely that full vehicle loads are delivered to the distribution centre. Secondly the shipping unit (carton) will have to be disaggregated at the RDC to allow small quantities to be sent to each retail branch. This is a labour intensive exercise and should be kept separate from the redirection and aggregation of fast sellers. Larger retail chains favour separated distribution centres for slow moving product lines, to achieve depot efficiency; others prefer a separate operation within the same depot to utilize the same roll cages and delivery vehicles as the fast sellers.

Perishable products

The distinguishing characteristic of these products is a very short shelf life. The products included are dairy products, flowers and chilled foods. Stock minimization is essential to maximize the time before the expiry date and therefore to avoid product wastage. Production therefore has to be very closely aligned to sales rate. Since sales rates will vary between retailers, production must be aligned to individual retailer sales rather than aggregate retail sales. It is for this reason that manufacturer brands are unusual in perishable products. Production must be flexible and will switch frequently between products according to fluctuations in sales. This classification of products most closely applies the 'just-in-time' concept. The supply chain is driven primarily by retail sales and production efficiency is subordinate to freshness (maximum time to best before date) at the retail outlet (Jones and Simons, 2000). Product will still flow through distribution centres as loads are combined for products from different suppliers to be sent to individual stores. The requirement for specialist temperature-controlled vehicles and depots often results in this supply chain being separate from the supply chain for ambient products.

Fashion clothing

The unique characteristics of this category are: a short life cycle for individual items; a stream of new products reaching the market; sales fluctuations between seasons of the year; and unpredictability of the exact start and finish of each season.

New products have to be available in store at the start of the new season and the current season's products have to be available right up until this time. In this way, sales are maximized. Stock cannot be used to buffer variations in timing and fluctuation of sales, since unsold stock cannot then be sold the following season. Excess stock has to be discounted in price (hence the concept of 'end-of-season sales') to a level where sales equal stock. Significant volume sales at a discounted price reduce the profit margins of retailers. The history of fashion retailing is littered with companies that have gone out of business because they could not match inventory to sales. More pertinently, they were unable to match production to sales without surges in inventory levels. Next in the UK is reported in the financial media to have suffered a downturn in sales in September 2002 because of an 'Indian summer' when summer conditions continued a month longer than had been expected. Consumers delayed purchasing the autumn range, but Next had run down its stocks of summer clothing by the end of August.

The fashion clothing industry is a major beneficiary from the introduction of a consumer pull supply chain and the origins of ECR were born out of the textile apparel industry. The stars of this industry in recent years have been those retailers that have succeeded in introducing consumer pull supply chains. The existence of such a chain is not a guarantee for success, products still have to be deemed fashionable by consumers, but without such a supply chain retailers cannot compete effectively. Retailers that have succeeded include Zara, Benetton, Gap and Marks & Spencer. Each of these retailers has succeeded by vertical integration, to varying degrees, up the supply chain. The supply chain includes not just the assembly and manufacturing processes, as with the grocery industry but also the manufacture of the clothing materials. Marks & Spencer have long been involved, with their suppliers, in the development of materials that resulted in a high quality finished article, so that products are shrink proof, colourfast, etc. Such materials may be manufactured in countries geographically remote from the major markets. Zara, for example, have a buying office in Beijing. In the section on the Principles of supply chain efficiency (earlier in the present chapter), we identified the importance of holding stock in one location and as close as possible to the market. This is particularly important for fashion clothing with its large range of items. Marks & Spencer has over 150,000 SKUs, five times the quantity of a grocery store. Zara handle 25,000 SKUs. The solution adopted by Spanish retailer Zara and the UK's Marks & Spencer is to manufacture the garments in countries geographically close to the consumer markets. Zara has its main production area in Galicia in Spain where products are cut, sewn, ironed, packed and ticketed. Marks & Spencer sources three-quarters of its turnover from UK manufacturers. Both retailers are able to control the production schedules, Zara through direct ownership of the factories, and Marks & Spencer through selection of suppliers that are dedicated to meeting its sales and quality requirements. Such integration is only possible across a wide range of SKUs because the retailer is responsible for the product design. Both Zara and Marks & Spencer have extensive specialist design teams, product developers and material technologists. They also exert tight influence on the operations of their retail stores. Zara test store designs centrally and recommendations for window dressing are sent to store managers from a centralized merchandising department. It is through the control of both the product and the retail store that fashion clothing retailers are able to develop consumer pull supply chains handling up to 150,000 SKUs, each having a high sales seasonality.

Centralized warehousing controlled by the retailer is the second part of the solution to holding stock in one location and close to the point of sale. Zara's central warehouse is one of the largest (400,000 square metres) and most automated worldwide. Store managers handle two deliveries per week and in each delivery they receive 12.5 per cent of the new products for the month. Thus all SKUs in the store are new every month. The final design to sales cycle time for any one item is 22–30 days (1 day for final design, 3–8 days for manufacturing, 1 day for shipping and 17–20 days for selling). US clothes retailer Gap operates along similar principles, the main difference being the greater number of countries in which Gap operates. Gap has a centralized distribution system based in the US. Information on sales by SKU is transmitted on a daily basis to the US, analysed and then optimum replenishment rates are transmitted to the European distribution depot in The Netherlands. This warehouse acts as a central platform for delivery to all Gap stores in Europe. Replenishment levels are based on daily inventory movements, by style and store location. Where stores are concentrated in one geographical area such as Paris, all delivery is direct from The Netherlands warehouse to store. In this way transport economies are achieved, as one vehicle will travel to Paris daily. Gap will serve to minimize deliveries from the central warehouse in The Netherlands by seeking to switch stock between stores in the Paris area. This can be done within hours and minimizes the duration of stock-outs since delivery from the central warehouse takes 48 hours. One distinguishing feature from grocery is that each clothing chain will have fewer retail stores per geographic area, so that inter shop movements are made less complex. Marks & Spencer in the UK has 300 stores compared with around three times as many Tesco stores.

Home delivery

Home delivery is, in many ways, just another supply chain. However, the changes in home delivery, particularly for fast moving consumer products, have been so significant within a short period of time that it requires separate consideration. Home delivery, of course, is not new. Mail order catalogues have been in existence for many decades. Grocery deliveries are not new. These were a common occurrence in the UK, particularly in rural areas, until the 1960s. The growth in car ownership, and the focus on price by the supermarket chains reduced the demand for home delivery. The late 1990s saw the convergence of two separate trends. First, there was the social phenomenon of a high level of working women with increasing disposable income for whom time was precious. The concept of 'money rich, time poor' was identified. Secondly, there was the explosive growth of the Internet and access to the Internet by consumers. With the Internet it became possible to explore the price and availability of items within different retail chains. Online shopping became not just feasible but easy and attractive, as solutions were introduced to overcome the risks and difficulty of making a financial transaction over the web. Here, we address the challenges that home delivery posed to the supply chain, particularly of grocery retailers, and the solutions that they have adopted.

A key difference between shopping in store and home delivery is that the responsibility for picking an order is transferred back to the retailer, introducing an additional labour intensive procedure. This in itself raises further questions; is it desirable to have a small army of supermarket employees moving around the store mingling, even competing, with customers undertaking their own shopping; and, should expensive retail space be used for order picking or could this be better undertaken in a warehouse? Another difference is the implication for optimum vehicle movements. Does it make sense to transport volume from warehouse to store and then transport again to the consumer's home or should product move directly from the warehouse to the home? Thirdly, picking orders from store increases the probability of an individual SKU being out-of-stock and therefore alienating customers. This conflicts with the theory that stock should be held in one location close to market.

The logical response to these issues is that orders for home delivery should be picked in a warehouse, not the retail store. Whilst this may be the eventual long-term solution, it is not the solution that is speedily implemented. Consumers buy in single units of each SKU but the existing RDCs of multiple grocers handle only full cartons. The cartons are not broken into single items until they reach the retail shelf. Furthermore, RDCs are designed as trans-shipment (or flow-through) centres, which are not stock-holding warehouses, so there is no product available for consumer order picking. Thus the optimum supply chain structure to supply retail stores is quite different to that required to supply consumers. Specialist consumer order picking warehouses that hold stock would need to be constructed, which takes time and money. This delays the implementation of home delivery providing an opportunity for others, perhaps the cash and carry outlets, to enter the market. Tesco, the current UK market leader in home delivery, concluded that speed of market entry was essential and could best be achieved by the picking and delivery of orders from store. Large surface retail outlets are best suited to in-store order picking and Tesco has a wider and more national portfolio of such units than its competitors. A national home delivery operation is likely to lead to better returns on the IT infrastructure necessary to enable customers to shop using the Internet.

Once a position of market leadership in home delivery has been achieved, Tesco can re-assess the benefits of building specialist order picking warehouses for consumers. These require a different form of supply chain collaboration. Production does not need to be perfectly synchronized with sales because the order picking warehouses hold stock. In any event, manufacturers may find it difficult to align their production processes to both a rapid response and flow-through principle of the existing RDC and to the stock-holding order picking warehouse for home delivery, where vehicle utilization is paramount. Only time will tell whether the long-term supply chain solution to home delivery of groceries is based on specialist order picking warehouses.

Producer brands and vertically integrated supply chains

The introduction of consumer pull supply chains requires collaboration where there are powerful producers and powerful retailers. Power derives from the influence that each has with consumers. Influence derives from the existence of brands and the esteem in which consumers hold the brands. In a situation where the retail brand is dominant and the products sold carry the retailer's name, the retailer selects suppliers to participate in their brand. The retailer selects both the suppliers of the basic material, and manufacturers of the product and the retailer designs the product. The intellectual property of the product resides with the retailer. Integration is required rather than collaboration. Collaboration, in terms of supply conditions, is one part of the supplier selection process. Suppliers are selected on the basis of their competence to produce and supply to the retailer's requirements. This tends to be the situation in fashion clothing.

Where powerful producer brands exist, then collaboration is essential when powerful, even oligopolistic, retailers introduce consumer pull supply chains. The grocery industry is characterized by such a relationship. The relationship is made more complex by the presence of retailer product brands alongside the producer brands. It is the existence of retailer product brands that is invariably the catalyst for retailers establishing consumer pull supply chains. Since retailers cannot simultaneously operate both producer push and consumer pull supply chains, it follows that collaboration is required from the owners of producer brands. The issue of supply chain collaboration is thus most relevant where producer and retail product brands co-exist and where short shelf life products exist. These conditions are most prevalent in grocery distribution. The first condition partially exists in electrical retailing with powerful retail chains and strong producer brands. However, retailer product brands are a small proportion of total retailer sales and the need to handle short shelf life is mostly absent. Of increasing importance is the frequency of new product introductions and associated product obsolescence, as with mobile telephones. Collaboration regarding new product introductions is of increasing importance if the retailer is not to be left with surplus stock, but this does not necessitate a consumer pull supply chain where production cycles flexibly respond to the level of retail sales. Electrical retailing thus has some of the challenges of both grocery retailing (supplier brands) and fashion retailing (short product life expectancy).

The contrasts between food retailing and fashion retailing are stark (see Table 3.3). There are important structural differences that explain why supply chain collaboration is primarily an issue for food retailing. Both channels of distribution benefit

Table 3.3 Supply chain contrasts between food, fashion and electrical retailers

Structural composition	Grocery retailer	Benetton	Zara	The Body Shop	Electrical retailer
Presence of producer brands	Yes	No	No	No	Yes
Control of production	No	Yes	Yes	Yes	No
Product design competence	No	Yes	Yes	Yes	No
Uniqueness of retail chain	No	Yes	Yes	Yes	No
Owned branches	Yes	No	Yes	Partially	Yes
Sale of perishables	Yes	No	No	No	No
Length of product life	>1 year	<1 year	<1 year	<1 year	1 year

from a consumer pull supply chain but collaboration is an issue for the grocery trade and this explains why programmes of industry wide collaboration have been largely confined to food retailing. There are seven structural components that are relevant to assessing the importance of supply chain collaboration:

1 The presence of strong producer brands
2 The control/ownership of production facilities
3 Competence in product design and development
4 The uniqueness of the retail chain
5 Ownership and control of retail outlets
6 The presence of perishable, short shelf life, products
7 Length of product life cycle.

Summary

The emergence of a consumer-oriented society has been the driver of the change from producer push supply chains to consumer pull supply chains. Advances in information technology that permits, at a lower cost, the linking of hitherto individual processes of distribution, have facilitated this change.

Consumer pull supply chains require a transparency of transactions between each constituent member of the chain. Movement of product between each stage and location of inventory must be visible to each member. The consumer pull supply chain is driven by consumer purchases, and the advent of scanning technology in the early 1990s enabled sales per store of each product line to be recorded on a daily basis.

The emergence of powerful retail chains provided the vehicle to implement consumer pull supply chains. The size of the retail chains enabled economies of scale to be achieved for both the application of information technology and the restructuring of warehouses and vehicle fleets. The economies of scale allowed a rate of return to be earned on the capital investment that was required.

The effect of a consumer pull supply chain is to respond rapidly to changing patterns of consumer purchases and demand for individual products. This faster speed of response is achieved whilst utilizing less inventory. Consumer pull supply chains are most beneficial for products with a short shelf life (perishable foods) and with a pronounced seasonality of sales (fashion clothing).

Collaboration is particularly important when there are two, or more, powerful members of a supply chain. Where the supply chain is dominated by a powerful retailer the other members of the chain respond to the requirements of the retailer, and the structure of the chain is determined by the retailer. Collaboration is necessary where there are powerful producer brands (e.g. Coca-Cola) being distributed by powerful retail chains that may also be selling their own brands. Where such retailers have developed consumer pull supply chains for the rapid replenishment of fast moving consumer goods, then collaboration is essential.

Industry wide programmes of co-ordination such as ECR best facilitate collaboration in a situation where powerful retailers have many suppliers of powerful producer brands. Grocery retailing uniquely combines the stimulus for consumer pull supply chains and the requirement for collaboration. It is characterized by: powerful retailers and powerful producer brands; fast moving consumer goods; and perishable products.

Fashion clothing with strong retail chains, high seasonality, and a long supply chain also benefits from a consumer pull supply chain, but lacks the need for collaboration when most products sold are retailer private labels.

Review questions

1 Using examples, compare and contrast a push supply chain and a pull supply chain.
2 With reference to an organization of your choice, explain and evaluate the role and value of information in managing the supply chain.
3 How do different product characteristics lead an individual retailer to construct separate supply chains?
4 How does the nature of retailer supplier collaboration differ between retailers selling mainly own-label brands and those selling a substantial proportion of manufacturer brands?

Discussion questions

1 'The Global Commerce Initiative increases the dominance of the global retailers and suppliers at the expense of smaller players.' Discuss.

2 Critically evaluate the extent to which different product lines sold by a hypermarket require different supply chains.

3 Using an appropriate framework, explain how the retail supply chain of the future may be managed.

4 Examine the paradox that a retailer can determine the structure of a supply chain and control the logistics *but* never own a delivery vehicle or a warehouse.

References

Cotterill, R. (1999) 'Continuing Concentration in the US'. In Ramsay, W. (ed.), *The Future of the Global Food Industry*. Financial Times, London.

Global Commerce Initiative (2002) *Special Report: Summer/Autumn 2002*.

Jones, D.T. and Simons, D. (2000) 'Future Directions for the Supply Side of ECR'. In *Academic Perspectives on the Future of the Consumer Goods Industry*. ECR Europe, Brussels.

Further reading

Harvard Business Review (2000) *Harvard Business Review on Managing the Value Chain*. Harvard Business School Press.

Hill, C.A. and Scudder, G.D. (2002) 'The Use of Data Interchange for Supply Chain Co-ordination in the Food Industry'. *Journal of Operations Management*, **20**:4, pp. 375–88.

Lambert, D., Stock, J.R. and Ellram, L. (1998) *Fundamentals of Logistics Management*. McGraw-Hill.

Levy, M. and Grewal, D. (2000) 'Supply Chain Management in a Networked Economy'. *Journal of Retailing*, **76**:4, pp. 415–30.

Lysons, K. and Gillingham, M. (2002) *Purchasing and Supply Chain Management*, 6th edition. FT Prentice Hall.

Myers, M.B., Daugherty, P.J. and Autry, C.W. (2000) 'The Effectiveness of Automatic Inventory Replenishment in Supply Chain Operations: Antecedents and Outcomes'. *Journal of Retailing*, **76**:4, pp. 455–81.

Patel, T. (2003) *Retail Logistics 2003*. IGD Business Publication.

Chapter 4

Planning policy for retailing

Ross Davies

Public planning policies are part of the process of promoting retail development in many countries of the world. However, they can also be part of the process of resisting retail development in many countries, often with the aim of defending a country's traditional small- and medium-sized retail sector against the inroads of contemporary large-scale retailing or non-domestic competition. A comprehensive review of public planning policies and retail development around the world within a single chapter is impractical. Instead, we make selective trawls of the impact or otherwise of retail planning policies in the major regions of the world, seeking to draw out a small number of different approaches to the regulation of retail locations worldwide. In particular, we can differentiate between conditions of restraint, those of leniency and those countries presently making a transition between the two states.

Definitions

Most commentators interpret retail planning policies to be merely a specialist by-product of general governmental land use planning regulations or advisory notes issued to the principal actors in the development process. In the case of retailing, these include retail companies, shopping centre developers, investment agencies, consultants and local authorities. Regulations, which are usually legally enforced documents, can range from zoning maps, which indicate where and where not certain types of retail development may take place in an area, to stipulations about how large new store or shopping centre proposals can be in an area. Advisory notes, in contrast, are not legally binding but often comprise central government guidelines dealing with what is expected from the retail development process and in the case of the European Union, consist of encouragements to governments about what might or might not be appropriate at a supra-national level.

Strongly related to these definitions of retail planning policies are two other areas of public policy making. The first is the legislation in some countries about trading hours. Historically, the predominantly catholic countries of western Europe and Latin America – and also as a unique case Germany – have had very strict laws on when stores can or cannot be open for trading but these are beginning to be eroded. They have largely focused on constraints on Sunday and evening trading. Secondly, restrictions in some countries have been placed on the price of goods and the product in stores. The US has long had retail price maintenance agreements set by manufacturers and suppliers whilst Japan effectively has the same although with convoluted wholesale agreements as well. The Scandinavian countries still have structures over product sales in stores, particularly over liquor (generally sold in state-controlled outlets) and some food and pharmaceutical products. These additional policies are, in effect, 'competition policies' and competition and planning have sometimes been seen as two faces of the same state interventionist cause. We will return to this issue at the end of the chapter.

Two other issues drive retail planning and related policies around the world. One is the impact of new corporate chains with large stores or powerful brands on the traditional structure of retailing in many countries, comprising independent businesses with very small stores. Government intervention has often been intended to protect the Davids from the Goliaths. The second issue has been the development, in the most advanced economies, of 'out-of-town' retailing (suburban developments of free-standing large stores and shopping centres) that may have an impact upon historic town and city centres and also other traditional centres within large urban areas.

Countries of restraint

The selection here of regions and countries is necessarily partial but includes countries that have recently tightened their controls over retail development. For example, western Europe and Japan have been consistently restrictive over many years.

Western Europe

The countries of western Europe have probably, over several decades, enacted the most sophisticated and stringent retail planning policies in the world. An historical interpretation of what has developed between them is instructive. The structure of retailing in west European countries was not very dissimilar 50 years ago to what we see in emerging markets today; the difference is that planning control then was almost autonomous. Throughout western Europe in the 1950s and 1960s, retailing was dominated by small shops and spatially configured in a rigid hierarchy of shopping centres: neighbourhood centres offering convenience goods; district centres offering a mix of convenience and low-level specialist goods; town and city centres providing a full range of convenience, specialist and service goods through both small and large stores including department stores.

This structure and pattern of retailing was purposely upheld by government policies that required local authorities to draw up maps displaying the hierarchy of shopping centres and either legislating or encouraging any new store proposals to fit with the existing scheme. This was effectively zoning planning.

The 1970s was a decade when the retail format of the hypermarket was born, initially in Belgium but widely adopted in France. At first, it led to a breakdown in planning controls in those two countries and a retail development 'free-for-all'. Reactive planning constraints were eventually introduced towards the middle of the decade as a result of concerns about the impact of these huge food and general merchandise stores on traditional, small independent businesses but precedents had been set. In France especially, planning control was often influenced by other political considerations that meant the hypermarket development programme continued largely unabated. However, elsewhere in western Europe, strict retail planning controls on new retail innovations were generally upheld.

The 1980s saw some other significant changes in the political/planning approaches to retail development across the region. The most spectacular change was in the UK where, under Prime Minister Margaret Thatcher, planning policies of all kinds were effectively abandoned in the name of the need for enterprise. In consequence, there was a proliferation of out-of-town shopping centres. This apparently enlightened attitude towards development also affected southern European countries. Spain, Portugal and Greece all opened up their borders to hypermarket development, principally from French companies, but the north and central countries of western Europe maintained a relatively strict retail planning regime.

The 1990s proved to be another volatile decade. The reunification of Germany and the opening up of the former Soviet bloc countries to western retail company investment saw huge expansion programmes, particularly by German retailers, against the background of minimal, indigenous planning policies. However, the decade generally was coloured by an almost complete *volte face* by several west European governments about how to deal with the pressures of modern retail development. Britain and southern Europe, experiencing new governments, decided to reject the previous laissez-faire approach to out-of-town development and concentrate on a future regeneration of traditional town and city centres (and protection for small, independent businesses). France and Belgium followed suit with some new harsh limits about the sizes at which new stores could be built. Germany, Austria and Switzerland had retained rather hard regulations on out-of-town development for almost four decades; and the Scandinavian countries broadly matched the German.

On entering the twenty-first century, the countries of western Europe are almost at one in seeing curbs taken by their governments to limit the further development of out-of-town retailing, in encouraging the renovation and improvement of traditional town and city centres and in supporting the small, independent retail sector.

A summary of these country planning policies towards new retail development is contained in Table 4.1, which also demonstrates the shift in government attitudes towards modern retail practices.

United Kingdom

The UK is interesting enough to warrant closer consideration not just because of changing government policies but also because of its experience in retail development in all kinds of locations. Also, unlike most other countries in western Europe that implement their retail planning policies through controls on the sizes of stores and shopping centres, the UK controls development through a series of guidance notes.

The most important guidance note is *Planning Policy Guidance Note 6* (PPG6), revised initially in England and Wales in 1993 under the title *Major Retail Development*. (A complementary set of guidelines was published for Scotland and Northern Ireland.) Issued by central government, it sought to persuade local authorities to turn back the tide of out-of-town development by recommending the refusal of planning applications for new stores and shopping centres in suburban areas and encouraged planning applications for town centre-based schemes. Whilst the new PPG6 signalled a major shift in government policy, however, it was followed in 1995 by a Parliamentary Inquiry into 'Shopping Centres and their Future' that ruled that the guidance note did not go far enough. It was replaced by a further PPG6 in 1996 called *Town Centres and Major Retail Development*.

The later PPG6 exhorts local authorities, particularly the County Councils through their countywide Structure Plans, to identify where new retail development may be appropriate in a map form. It therefore requires local authorities to take a plan-led approach, almost returning to the old system of zoning plans. Developers seeking new applications for shopping schemes outside the recommended areas must satisfy local authorities on three tests: that the schemes will not generate adverse traffic conditions; they will have a minimal adverse trading effect on a town centre or other traditional centres; and sites for the new schemes should ideally be first identified within a town centre or on the edge of it, and only in exceptional circumstances will an out-of-town site be countenanced.

This tougher planning stance has, by and large, been working well. There has been a significant reduction in out-of-town development and much regeneration of town and city centres. But some developers and other agencies involved in the development process have complained that the development tests, particularly the third one called the *sequential test*, are not clear enough. Central government has declared that in 2003 it will publish yet another PPG6. This will not mark any major

Table 4.1 Recent retail planning policies in western European countries

---

France
1996 Loi Royer: Planning permission required for any development proposal larger than 300 square metres net. Presumption against large development. Trading is not generally permitted on Sundays except in designated tourist areas.

Spain
1995 General Commerce Law: Special licences to be obtained for any retail development proposal of 2,500 square metres net or more. Trading hours generally limited to 72 hours per week and restricted on Sundays.

Portugal
1996 Commerce and Tourism Law: Planning permission required for development over 2,000 square metres in cities with a population over 30,000 and 1,000 square metres in towns of less than 30,000 population. Trading hours can be from 6 a.m. to midnight including Sundays because of the importance of tourism.

Belgium
1994 Royal Decree: Planning permission required for development over 1,500 square metres gross size in Zone 1 (most densely populated areas) or 600 square metres outside Zone 1; and 1,000 square metres sales space in Zone 1 or 400 square metres outside Zone 1. Trading hours are restricted to 8 p.m. except on Fridays and working days preceding legal holidays, when it is 9 p.m.

UK
1996 Planning Policy Guidance Note 6: Advocated local authorities to channel new retail development to traditional shopping centres and reduce out-of-town development. Trading hours are limited to 10 a.m. to 4 p.m. on Sundays but otherwise stores can be open for 24 hours.

The Netherlands
1990: Presumption that out-of-town development proposals should be located at public transport junctions. But in 1996, 13 of the largest municipalities allowed, as an experiment, to permit development over 1,500 square metres gross on a selective basis. Trading hours permitted are from 6 a.m. to 10 p.m. except on Sundays, although trading is allowed on eight Sundays per year.

Germany
1980: Planning permission generally granted for stores of less than 1,200 square metres sales in designated industrial areas. In 1995 the size limit was reduced to 800 square metres in most areas.

Trading hours have historically been very strict with stores closing at 6.30 p.m. on weekdays and at lunchtime on Saturdays except on the first Saturday of each month. Since 1996, stores can be open on weekdays until 8 p.m. and until 6 p.m. on Saturdays but closed on Sundays.

Scandinavia
Municipalities have taken over planning decision-making from central government in recent years but it remains difficult for developers to build out of town. In contrast, Sweden was the first country to allow virtually unlimited trading hours in 1972. Denmark and Norway continue to restrict trading on Sundays whilst stores in Finland can open from 9 a.m. to 8 p.m.

continued

Table 4.1 Recent retail planning policies in western European countries (*continued*)

Austria and Switzerland

Specific retail planning policy does not exist in either Austria or Switzerland but in 1994 a Trading Act in Austria made it difficult for retailers to develop either hypermarkets or retail warehouses, whilst in Switzerland, local political decision-making has for long been negative towards out-of-town development. Trading hours are generally restricted to 6 a.m. to 7 or 8 p.m. during weekdays, depending on municipalities or cantons, but stores, with exceptions, are closed on Sundays.

Ireland

2000: National guidelines for local authorities to impose a size cap of 3,500 square metres sales on food store proposals in Dublin and 3,000 square metres elsewhere in the country; and on retail warehouses of 6,000 square metres gross throughout the country. Stores can legally open for 24 hours on every day of the week but usually trade on limited hours during the daytime period.

Italy

1999 Bersani Decree: New land use planning regulations replace complicated commercial licensing procedures, which were dominated by the independent retail sector. Stores with a sales area up to 1,500/2,500 square metres (depending on a town's size) requires municipal authorization. Larger stores are referred to regional government. Retailers can trade for a maximum of 13 hours with Sunday trading permitted in tourist centres.

Sources: Davies (1995) and Jones Lang Wootton (1996)

shift in policy but apparently will clarify those procedures that seem to be causing confusion.

The revival of town and city centres in the UK in recent years, particularly the biggest ones, has also been aided by legislation assisting the general regeneration of urban areas. New legislation will shortly come into force to allow local authorities to designate Business Improvement Districts (BIDs), along the lines of those found in the USA. Within such BIDs, additional taxes will be imposed on businesses to be re-invested in cleaning up declining areas, improving security and increasing overall business and consumer confidence. There has also emerged in Great Britain in recent years a new body of professionals known as town centre managers. Such managers are mainly funded by local authorities but in some cases, with the help of retail companies. Town centre managers now exist in some 400 UK towns and cities. Their responsibilities are to co-ordinate cleaning, security and marketing of town and city centres.

Japan

For much of the last 30 years, retail development in Japan has been controlled by a similar mechanism to that used in most west European countries, i.e. a cap on the sizes at which stores (and shopping centres) can be built. In the case of Japan, until recently, there was a specific law called the Large Stores Law. It was introduced in 1974 as a result of pressure on the government by the large independent retail sector in Japan, which feared the decline of their businesses against the background of growing general merchandise and supermarket chains. Companies could no longer build stores of more than 3,000 square metres in the 11 largest cities in Japan and 1,500 square metres elsewhere. Initially this appeared relatively generous, but the policy was subject to political approval and independent retail interests were influential. The caps were reduced to 500 square metres nationally in 1979, holding back both indigenous modern retail development and western foreign investment for the next 15 years.

From 1994 onwards, however, the Large Store Laws were relaxed, primarily through pressure from the US government concerned at the overall trade imbalance between Japan and the US. A modern retail industry in Japan, with many more large stores, was seen as an ideal way for more US manufacturers and suppliers to export their goods. There were still local political barriers to getting planning permissions but the reaction was sufficient to encourage several American retail companies with very large stores to enter the market, such as Sports Authority, Office Depot and Costco. The opening of stores of 500–1,000 square metres was largely free from regulation, and a further benefit to such companies was the fact that they could trade through to 8 p.m. and the number of weekend and holiday closures was reduced to 24 per year. Whilst the hugely cumbersome procedures of the 1970s and 1980s were reduced, however, the decision-making process in the Large Store Laws of the second half of the 1990s was still relatively complex.

In June 2000, nevertheless, there was a more profound change in Japan's approach to regulating the retail industry. The onset of a major economic recession persuaded more politicians that the country's overly bureaucratic industries and archaic distribution systems needed to be more competitive and this was encouraged through further de-regulation. The Large Stores Laws were abolished and a new Large-Scale Retail Stores Location Act bought into being. Two years earlier, however, a revised City Planning Act and a Central District Vitalisation Act had also been passed. All three new measures shifted away from a simple cap method of controlling store (and related shopping centre) development to a more westernized land-use approach to planning.

The new City Planning Act replaced a traditional system of controls over spatial development with a simplified system that allows local authorities to determine the location of new large stores and shopping centres within preferred commercial areas. The Central District Vitalization Act was enacted to prevent traditional town and city centres from declining in overall health against the growing competition of large stores and new shopping centres in suburban areas. Whilst this is seen as a forward step in pure planning terms, there are sceptics who still see the independent retail sector continuing to be able to exercise influence in defence of its own interests. The Large-Scale Retail Store Location Act has introduced a national policy, interpreted by local authorities, whereby large store proposals have to be examined in the context of their traffic impacts and environmental intrusions. This applies to all store proposals of more than 1,000 square metres.

The new retail planning reforms of Japan clearly signal some kind of reduction in hitherto stringent regulations on the industry, and it is interesting to see that the new three spatial/land use approaches parallel, to a degree, those that operate within the UK. However, we will need to see some passage of time before being able to judge whether the new procedures have really been to the benefit of western investors.

Countries in transition

Whilst Japan has shown some movement towards more relaxed planning policies, there are other countries that have done more and over a relatively shorter time span. We review here the cases of Korea, China and Canada.

Korea

Until the late 1990s, the retail industry of Korea was dominated by small independent shops and almost completely insulated from foreign competition. A Market Act of 1960 had promised much assistance and protection for the independent sector but little financial and technological support materialized until the late 1980s when amendments to the Act supported indigenous retail companies' attempts to modernize. Over the same period, foreign acquisition of land for retail and services provision was prohibited although land acquisition could be obtained occasionally, with government consent, to buy land for factories, offices and warehouses.

This situation changed dramatically in the last few years of the 1990s. The trigger was the dramatic collapse of the Korean economy, which hitherto had been growing almost exponentially. Pressures to allow foreign retail investments into the country had also been rising, although not to the extent of those in Japan. Three enactments ushered in the change of retail planning policy. First, was the Distribution Industry Development Act of 1997, which stipulated that any proposals for new large store development, whether from indigenous or overseas companies, only required registration with the appropriate local authorities. Previously, in the early 1990s, special permission was required to open stores of more than 1,000 square metres.

Secondly, an amendment to the Foreigners' Land Acquisition and Management Act in 1998 made it possible for all types of potential developers to buy land without restriction but with notification to the appropriate local authority. Thirdly, again in 1998, an amendment to the Zoning Law, which particularly had strongly protected agricultural land and forest areas surrounding Korea's principal cities, meant that these areas were opened up for potential out-of-town store and shopping centre development.

The overall effect has been that, in the space of five years, the retail industry in Korea has gone from being one of the most highly regulated in the world to being one of the most open. However, this is set against a background of continuing economic difficulties and a slump in consumer demand, which has deflated much western retail interest to invest in the country over the same period of time.

China

There may be some readers of this chapter who are surprised to see China included in a section on retail planning policies in transition. The reason for China's inclusion is that, like Korea albeit not to the same extent, the country's political approach to retail development and especially its attitude to western investment has changed dramatically in the last seven years. Before the late 1990s, like Korea again, China had begun to embark on limited programmes opening up its markets to foreign companies (following the 1979 Law of the People's Republic on Joint Ventures with Chinese and Foreign Investment) but these were aimed almost exclusively at manufacturing and construction companies.

A change was signalled in 1992 with the publication of the State Council document 'An Official, Written Reply to the Questions on the use of Foreign Capital in the Retail Sector'. The document announced that one or two joint ventures with large foreign retailers would be allowed to operate on a trial basis in a number of selected cities and within the five established special economic zones (Shenzhen, Zhuahi, Shanton, Xiamen and Hainan). During the subsequent five years, this led to a fairly significant number of joint venture experiments, primarily by Japanese retailers with Chinese construction companies.

A further move towards greater openness was triggered in 1997 by a state enquiry into the fact that approximately 300 joint venture retail and related companies had been established by this time – many apparently outside of the official trial planning areas. This led to a decree that within any joint venture operation, 51 per cent of the ownership must be Chinese. A consequence of this was that some foreign retailers decided to withdraw from the market.

In 1999, following China's entry into the World Trade Organization, there were further relaxations of retail planning policies and related trade restrictions. The state published another document, 'The Methods on Foreign-Funded Commercial Businesses for Trial Implementation', that expanded the trial areas for joint ventures from a limited number of cities and the economic zones to all provincial and regional capital cities, municipalities directly under the Central Government and cities enjoying separate budgetary status. The seeds were sown for a national expansion of new chain stores and also shopping centres.

There remained two strict rules of engagement over the formation of joint venture companies, however. First, a foreign retailer seeking this arrangement needed to have a trading record of annual sales of US$2 billion for the three years prior to submitting an application to form the joint venture; and secondly, a Chinese partner had to be a distribution enterprise that displayed 'solid economic strength and management capacity', with assets valued at or above RMB50 million in the year prior to applying for joint venture status. Moreover, in cases where there are more than three branches of chain stores (except convenience stores, specialty stores and brand licence stores), over 51 per cent of the total investment must come from the Chinese joint venture partner.

Despite these constraints, there has been much foreign retail investment in China over the last few years, as Table 4.2 demonstrates. Indeed, in some municipalities, there has been concern over 'overheating' of both store and shopping centre development, with size caps being introduced of 5,000 square metres. The Chinese market is therefore by no means fully or even relatively de-regulated compared to many other developing countries; but its progress over the last seven years has been enormously impressive against the background of what could have been the case.

Canada

Until the beginning of the 1990s, Canada, like Australia and New Zealand (other former colonial territories) had adopted a UK-based land use planning approach to regulating retail and other commercial development. This was very much state-based, however, with variations reflecting those that might be found between England, Scotland, Wales and Northern Ireland. A further major difference had also emerged over the last 20 years: plan-making in Canada became very concentrated within just the largest metropolitan areas. (Large, metropolitan areas dominate the overall settlement pattern in Canada.)

Recently, however, the plans for the major metropolitan areas have ignored the challenges or issues raised by the retail development process. The new official plan for Toronto, for example, does not make any specific reference to retailing and the old hierarchy of shopping centres has been discarded. Retailing has become subsumed into a number of other general land use categories for the purposes of planning control: neighbourhoods (mainly residential areas); mixed use areas (small subsidiary downtown areas); employment areas (where some retailing facilities may service office or factory employees); avenues (strip developments); and centres (including both the main downtown area and other civic centres that might incorporate shopping malls). Retailing as a specific policy area has effectively been abandoned.

There are two specific contexts, however, in which retail issues might come to the fore: one is in secondary plans for specific metropolitan areas, such as Bloor West Village, Yorkville or The Beaches; and the other is in Business Improvement Areas which are about the re-vitalization of run-down mixed use areas where retail renovation can take an active part.

The general consequence of the overall demise of retail planning policies in metropolitan areas like Toronto, however, is that there has been an explosion of out-of-town development in the last decade or so, especially in terms of 'big box' stores. There is now in the order of 20 million square feet of such development

Table 4.2 Foreign retail investment in China, 1992–2000

Country of origin	Year of entry	Number of outlets	Store format
France			
Carrefour	1995	22	Hypermarket
Galeries-Lafayette	1997	2	Department store
Printemps	1995	1	Department store
Promodès	1999	1	Hypermarket
Auchan	1999	1	Hypermarket
USA			
Wal-Mart	1997	6	Super centre
Price Smart	1997	3	Warehouse store
The Netherlands			
Macro	1996	4	Warehouse store
Ahold (withdrawn)	1996	45	Supermarket
Germany			
Metro	1997	6	Warehouse store
Sweden			
IKEA	1998	2	Furniture store
UK			
B&Q	1999	1	DIY store
Japan			
Yaohan (withdrawn)	1992	7	Department store
Seibu	1993	1	Convenience store
Seiya	1996	5	Supermarket
Jusco	1996	3	General merchandise
Ito Yokado	1996	2	General merchandise
Niko Niko Do	1997	2	Department store
Sogo	1998	1	Department store
Mycal	1998	1	Department store
Heiwa Do	1998	1	General merchandise
Thailand			
Lotus	1994	4	Hypermarket
Korea			
E-Mart	1996	1	Hypermarket
Malaysia			
Parkson	1994	16	Department store
		2	Supermarket
Taiwan			
Pacific	1994	5	Department store
Trust Mart	1997	11	Warehouse store
Chung-Yo	1998	1	Department store

continued

Table 4.2 Foreign retail investment in China, 1992–2000 (*continued*)

Country of origin	Year of entry	Number of outlets	Store format
Hong Kong			
Wellcome (some closed)	1995	25	Supermarket
Park n Shop (some closed)	1995	18	Supermarket
Watsons	1995	27	Speciality shop
7-Eleven	1995	50	Convenience store

Source: Davies and Yahagi (2000)

in Toronto, led by Wal-Mart and Home Depot (which recently acquired the local DIY chain of Aikenhead) from the USA. This has had an effect upon all levels of traditional centres: the major arterial strip malls that radiate out from the city; older shopping malls the locations of which were formerly controlled by land use planning measures; and the major downtown area, which has seen retail sales fall by about 20 per cent in the last decade, albeit maintaining its overall health through commercial substitutions such as restaurants and other consumer service businesses. One particular casualty of out-of-town impact has been the famous Canadian department store chain of Eatons.

Countries of leniency

Having reviewed some countries with rather strict retail planning regimes, and others moving from this situation towards more openness, or vice versa, we come now to a selection of countries that have relatively few barriers to entry for foreign retail investors.

United States of America

The states, countries and municipalities of the United States of America do not generally identify the retail development process as a special feature of land use planning, which of itself is not seen as a very important consideration for government. In so far as land use planning is recognized as an ingredient of decentralized government responsibility, retail development is positioned as part of a wider raft of commercial activities alongside industry, transport and housing. Curiously, in those municipalities that have a 'planning' function, plans are drawn up in the form of rather restrictive zoning plans. However, these zoning plans have relatively little legal backing. The consequence is that, when retailers and developers seek to develop stores or shopping centres in areas not zoned for development, they go to the courts for remedial redress. The whole question of retail development approval in the USA comes down to court battles over when and where zoning boundaries on maps were approved and appropriated.

There has been one exception to this general state of affairs over the last several years, and that has been the state of Vermont. Some 20 years ago, the Vermont District Environmental Commission refused permission for an out-of-town regional shopping centre to be built on the outskirts of Burlington on the grounds that it would have a negative impact on the trading health of the city centre. A study in 1978 estimated that US$24.4 million of projected retail sales up to 1983 would be deflected from the downtown and job losses would outstrip those of new job opportunities. This state of affairs has continued and Burlington's city centre remains extremely vibrant and economically healthy. This is not the case in swathes of America's mid-west and south. The lax approach to retail planning policies across most of the USA has resulted in widespread bankruptcy, the exodus of small independent businesses, and the terminal decline of traditional town and city centres. Out-of-town regional shopping centres have been a major factor in the demise of even the biggest town and city centres; but within rural communities, Wal-Mart, the world's largest and most successful retailing company, has been accused of being the main culprit, allegedly destroying hundreds of thousands of small businesses through its aggressive general merchandising activities.

In recent years, however, there has been something of a backlash in some American communities, towards the apparent inexorable advance of out-of-town development. There is increasing objection to the development of out-of-town general merchandise supercentres, or regional shopping centres, especially in wealthy, white suburban areas, and community representatives have been using the courts to give their areas protection from these forms of retail development. However, it is possible that too little is happening too late. Table 4.3 gives some statistics about what happened to the spatial structure and retail performance of Atlanta city, three decades and more ago.

Table 4.3 Change in Atlanta city centre retail sales, 1954–77

Year	Sales as % of metropolitan sales	Sales as % of city sales
1954	28.9	39.1
1958	26.4	38.0
1963	19.3	31.2
1967	13.9	24.4
1972	7.4	18.6
1977	4.0	15.1

Source: Dent (1985)

Eastern Europe

Poland, Hungary and the Czech Republic have collectively become a major focus for western retail investment ever since the fall of the Berlin Wall and with most of the former communist states gaining their independence. With a combined population of 59 million and growing levels of disposable income, about one half of that of the UK at present, this is an attractive market for both food retailing companies and shopping centre developers. Until about 10 years ago, small, independent businesses and state outlets dominated the retail industry of these countries. Hence, with the onset of free market forces, there were huge gains to be made by western retailers and developers alike.

Nominally, Poland, Hungary and the Czech Republic, all have land use planning regulations to control new retail development. However, regulations are lax and open to considerable interpretation. In Poland, there is a two-stage planning process with outline consent granted to proposals that are in line with the statutory general plans of urban areas, which describe permitted uses and specifications. This is followed by a detailed application containing the architectural, engineering and infrastructure details of a proposal. Since 1995, local authorities have had wide discretion in interpreting retail-planning policies and have generally been generous in their decision-making, except where it affects agricultural land. In Hungary and the Czech Republic, land use planning controls are mainly administered in the capital cities of Budapest and Prague. They are little developed elsewhere. Budapest and Prague now have 'master plans' but these do not refer to retail development, and decision-making about retail development proposals is inconsistent and not seen as a priority in the wider scale of metropolitan advancement.

The overall net result is that western foreign retail and shopping centre development in Eastern Europe in the last 10 years has been explosive. Table 4.4 shows how many companies have made eastern European market entries over this time period. German retail companies, because of their proximity to the east, have led the charge, but Tesco from the UK is amongst the most aggressive.

Middle East

Most Middle Eastern countries, like those in eastern Europe, have been relaxing their general trading regulations over the last several years in order to attract western investment into all kinds of industries. With respect to retailing, there have been few planning regulations and some of the traditional retail structures and retail environments that we take for granted throughout Europe are not found in the Middle East. For example, the concept of the High Street does not exist; retailing, historically, has been dominated by markets (souks) and street traders. Extensive recent developments, however, comprise a mix of large shopping malls and stand-alone large stores, the former of which have been very successful in

Table 4.4 Western retail company investment in the Czech
Republic, Hungary and Poland, 1990–98

	Czech Republic	Hungary	Poland
Austria	7	10	3
Belgium	2	2	1
Canada	1	–	–
Denmark	4	2	8
France	9	9	28
Germany	27	22	30
Greece	1	–	–
Italy	7	3	4
The Netherlands	6	2	2
UK	6	4	5
Norway	–	1	2
Spain	–	1	–
Sweden	–	1	1
Switzerland	–	1	1
USA	–	2	2
Portugal	–	–	3
Total	**70**	**60**	**90**

Source: Retail Intelligence (1999)

meeting modern consumer requirements, whether these are driven by nationality, climate, disposable income or individual taste.

Rather similar to North America and in contrast with most of Europe, the Middle East has extensive territory with a scattered population. Ruling or distinguished local families usually own the land. The owner often donates or bequeaths land to local citizens; hence developable land is usually in the hands of a few people and has cost little or nothing at all. The development of shopping malls or freestanding large stores to obtain substantial or rental income is therefore highly attractive to the new landlords.

There are usually two 'local' regulations to satisfy: statutory requirements for a licence to construct a proposed development; and discussions based on trust and local influence with the 'government', i.e. the representatives of a ruling family that would agree (or otherwise) to the development. There are no guarantees for the latter, but the general lack of proper regulatory control has led to an over-supply of retail floorspace, which has become a serious problem in some countries.

In a similar way, the architectural design of new retail provisions are not subject to planning regulations as such, but depend on an owner's preference or local government permission. Certain local laws may apply in terms of the religious facilities of a building, e.g. prayer rooms or floors in a shopping mall for women only. Consequently, the absence of regulations for design provides for a mix of traditional and modern designs that comfortably co-exist.

In a part of the world that gained its independence only three decades ago, the hungry consumer demand for up-to-date brands and retail facilities contrasts markedly with the history and culture of the ownership and development of land for retailing with the Arab way of doing business – discussion, agreement and binding trust – and not yet the regulatory format of western Europe or parts of the Far East.

Brazil

Specific retail planning regulations are also scarce and, where they do exist, are highly variable in South America, represented here by Brazil. The variability within Brazil arises because any planning decisions directed at the retail industry are taken at the municipal level and there are close to 6,000 'municipals' in the 26 states of the country, each with differing interests and policies. However, the largest municipals often have a zoning plan, much like in the USA, which demarcates urban land allocated for residential, commercial, industrial and mixed-use development. Any developer seeking to build a new store or shopping centre must refer to the 'planning director'; but this is not often enforced and permissions are easily gained. There are no additional regulations that protect small businesses or traditional town centres from the impact of large new developments, nor are there usually regulations on potential visual intrusion, traffic congestion and social disruption. However, reminiscent of the US again, there have recently been cases of residential area representatives using the courts to prevent development, as in a highly publicized case in São Paulo, where a major shopping centre proposal was rejected.

Differing state and municipal taxes also influences variability in retail planning effectiveness in Brazil. For example, a municipal tax on services (the Imposto Sobre Services) can vary from 0.25 per cent of the turnover of a retail company in one city to 5 per cent in another, within the same state. This has an important bearing on where retail companies develop their stores and even locate their headquarters. Another tax on urban property (the Imposto Sobre Propriedade Territorial Urbana) has similar influence. By contrast, some states and municipalities provide subsidies in the form of tax mitigation or special prices for public services (such as electricity and water) to encourage investment.

In the background, nevertheless, is a federal government agency, the Administrative Council for Economic Defence (CADE) that is seeking to control the acquisition of smaller companies by larger ones, to preserve competition. So far, however, CADE has made little impact in controlling retail acquisitions within the country although the biggest inroads by foreign investors, namely Wal-Mart and Carrefour, have been by organic growth. These two companies have brought significant modernization to the retail industry of Brazil but also a considerable impact on indigenous independent businesses.

Summary

The level of stringency of policy-making equates to the experience of different societies with contemporary retailing and their geographical size. Thus, western Europe, together with Japan, exhibits the most stringent legal regulations or guidelines. The USA, Eastern Europe, South America and the Middle East are the most lenient. In between, we see a mixture of countries in terms of both society and size, which are going through periods of dramatic change.

Most countries around the world face three major conflicts about the accommodation of modern retail development, whether large stores or shopping centres. The first conflict is that, however developed their retail planning policies are in detail, there is concern at governmental level over the impact of large retail investment companies over small businesses. The second conflict is that, besides individual retail companies, major shopping centre companies can come in and, through out-of-town development, cause deterioration in traditional town and city centres. The third issue is the general question of competition – to what extent do you allow competition between large and small companies and between out-of-town and in-town-development – when there are conflicts over business interests but consumer preferences.

Review questions

1 With reference to the Legoland case study, identify and explain the major planning constraints that Legoland might face in developing standalone retail stores in three countries of your choice.
2 As retail planning policies in China continue to develop, compare and contrast the approaches of the Metro and B&Q case studies in China.

Discussion questions

1 'The big retailers will always have more influence than smaller retailers over retail planning decisions'. Discuss.
2 Critically evaluate the future of out-of-town retail development in a country of your choice.
3 To what extent should governments consider retail planning to be part of competition policy?

References

Davies, R.L. (ed.) (1995) *Retail Planning Policies in Western Europe*. Routledge, London.

Davies, R.L. and Yahagi, T. (eds) (2000) *Retail Investment in Asia Pacific: Local Responses and Public Policy Issues*. Oxford Institute of Retail Management, University of Oxford.

Dent, B.D. (1985) 'Atlanta and the Regional Shopping Mall: the Absence of Public Policy'. In Dawson, J.A. and Dennis Lord, J. (eds) *Shopping Centre Development: Policies and Prospects*. Croom Helm.

Findley, A. and Sparks, L. (1999) *A Bibliography of Retail Planning*. National Retail Planning Forum, London.

Jones Lang Wootton (1996) 'Retail Planning Policies: Their impact on European Retail Property Markets'. London.

Oxford Institute of Retail Management and Jones Long Wootton (1998) *Shopping for New Markets: Retail Opportunities in Central Europe*.

Retail Intelligence (1999) *Retail Sans Frontiers: The Internationalisation of European Retailing*. London.

Simmons, J. and Yeates, M. (1998) 'The Need for International Comparisons of Commercial Structure and Change'. *Progress in Planning*, **50**:4, pp. 291–313.

Yahagi, T. and Tsuruta, T. (2002) 'The Large Scale Retail Stores Act and its Erosion in the 1970s–80s'. In Miwa, Y. *et al.* (eds) *Distribution in Japan*. Oxford University Press, Oxford.

Acknowledgements

I am grateful for assistance in preparing this chapter from: Gareth Williams, formerly CEO of Al Fultaim & Sons, Dubai; Gleb Bylor and Professor Ken Jones of the Canadian Institute of Retail Studies, Ryerson Polytechnic, Toronto; Professors Jose Augusto Giebrecht da Silveira and Claudi Felisoni de Angelo of the University of São Paulo; and Dr Yong Gu Suh of the Women's University of Seoul.

Chapter 5

Retail internationalization: how to grow

Elizabeth Howard

Internationalization has become one of the most troublesome issues in retail strategy. Compared with other industries, retailing is far less international. There has been a surge of activity in the last few years and a great deal of attention is being paid to international operations. However, there have been many failures. Companies are taking a variety of approaches to extending their operations and this chapter looks at some of the differences. This chapter begins by discussing the activities that can be internationalized in retailing, and goes on to look at motives for international development. It then considers the strategic choices that retailers must make in setting up foreign operations. These decisions include those about timing, direction or destination, mode of entry, partner selection and how and how far to adapt to new markets. The chapter ends by identifying key competences required by international retailers.

What international activity?

Buying

Even if their stores are entirely domestic, many retailers have been buying goods from foreign countries for a long period, most often through agents and wholesalers of various kinds. Recently, more 'direct sourcing' operations have been set up. Companies are trying to apply the lessons they have learned domestically about the advantages of closer relations with suppliers and of control of their supply chains, to international buying. Chapter 3 on supplier relations has discussed these issues. In addition, as some large companies have developed store operations in several countries, there have recently been some interesting examples of attempts to extend the advantages of their large buying power, by sourcing some products centrally to supply several countries. The most notable example is Wal-Mart but there are others. For example, look in Part III (Chapter 13) at the interesting comments from Steve Gilman, international director for B&Q, about the way his organization is beginning to supply European stores from manufacturers in China. Tesco, similarly, is looking to supply European stores from its new Asian supply network. Roland Vaxelaire in Part III (Chapter 18) has some interesting comments about the pros and cons of this activity for the UK.

Ideas

Ideas and know-how have become international in retailing much more easily than companies themselves. It can be relatively easy to copy the essential ideas in a retail offer: the format, the merchandise supplied by manufacturers and the product mix. Formats especially are easily imitated and cannot be patented like say, the formula for a pharmaceutical product. Hypermarkets may have been developed first on any significant scale in France, but they appeared in other countries because domestic retailers imitated retailers such as Carrefour, without waiting for an international company to 'export' them. Ideas from self-service to the category killer format have regularly come eastwards to Europe from the USA. Interestingly, the transfer of ideas can sometimes be used strategically to block international activity. It seems clear for instance that Kingfisher's initiative to build very large format B&Q Warehouse stores from 1994, filled a market gap that the biggest DIY firm, Home Depot, might have considered invading. On the other hand, Asda's imitation of aspects of Wal-Mart's operation and format meant that it became an attractive acquisition for the latter. Seen to 'fit' the culture and the business model of Wal-Mart, it was bought by the latter in 1999, giving the American company an immediate, substantial share of the British market.

Store operations

The internationalization of store operations is the third kind of internationalization, and the rest of this chapter concentrates on this issue.

Cross-border retailing has accelerated dramatically through the last two decades, though of course it began much earlier. There were a few international retailers operating in the nineteenth century. C&A was expanding from The Netherlands by the 1920s, and there were some notable international retailers by the 1960s such as F.W. Woolworth, along with many smaller companies.

Carrefour began its international moves with openings in Spain and the UK, in 1973. Tengelmann from Germany acquired large interests in the USA in 1979, and made some smaller moves into Austria and The Netherlands. Vendex from The Netherlands was beginning to acquire the first of many operations in retailing and catering across Europe and the USA. Benetton, Stefanel and Laura Ashley, along with numbers of smaller luxury goods retailers, led fashion retailers at this time. Already, different strategies were apparent: from the 'conglomerate' development of Vendex and GIB, to the franchising processes of the speciality brands. The big waves of expansion date from the late 1980s however, and they are continuing to increase. The later 1980s saw the rapid development of the category killer format as an international operation: Toys 'R' Us from the USA and IKEA from Sweden began to be very active.

By 1992, and the official completion of the European Single Market, cross-border moves were accelerating rapidly. There were probably more than twice as many moves in the 1990s as in the 1980s. Table 5.1 shows the most favoured locations for opening new operations. In the earlier years, the preferred destinations were Belgium, France and The Netherlands, reflecting a process of short distance border-hopping by retailers in the more mature markets of north-west Europe. The process continued through the 1980s, but Spain became a very important destination as foreign retailers saw opportunities to move into a fragmented but growing and maturing market. In the 1990s there was far greater activity overall than in earlier years, reflecting both the development of the 'Single Market' in the European Community, and the opening up of the countries of central and eastern Europe. The Czech Republic became the fifth most important destination, closely followed by Poland and Hungary.

By 1999 there were well over 3,000 international operations run by European retailers. The biggest 'exporter' was France (over 600), followed by Germany (over 400) and the UK (over 300). Two thirds of these operations were within Europe but the rest were in many parts of the world. Few individual retail companies, however, are themselves widely spread, even today, as Table 5.2 indicates.

Table 5.1 Top five destinations in Europe for cross-border moves

Pre 1980s	%	1980s	%	1990s	%
Belgium	15	Belgium	13	UK	9
France	12	Spain	10	Spain	8
Austria	11	Germany	9	Germany	8
The Netherlands	11	UK	9	France	7
Switzerland	8	The Netherlands	9	Czech Republic	6

Source: Jones Lang Wootton and OXIRM (1997)

Table 5.2 International sales of the largest retail companies

Size rank	Company	Country	MCap, 01/07/02 (US$ million)	International turnover as % of sales	Integrative measure of globalization
1	Wal-Mart Stores	US	241,973	16	1.2
2	Carrefour	FR	38,794	51	2.2
3	Tesco	UK	26,350	15	0.4
4	Ito Yokado	JP	20,614	34	0.7
5	Ahold	NL	19,281	92	5.2
6	Costco	US	17,177	18	0.2
7	Sears Roebuck	US	16,505	10	0.1
8	Hennes & Mauritz	SD	14,796	89	1.9
9	Pinault Printemps	FR	14,429	55	3.7
10	Safeway	US	14,016	8	0.1
11	Marks & Spencer	UK	13,727	15	0.7
12	Metro	BD	11,151	42	0.4
13	Sainsbury's	UK	10,815	21	0.2
14	TJX Companies	US	10,326	11	0.3
15	Castorama Dubois	FR	10,067	69	1.7
16	GUS	UK	9,380	26	1.3
17	Staples	US	8,939	7	0.1
18	Aeon Co.	JP	8,938	11	0.2
19	Boots	UK	8,838	9	0.2
20	Casino	FR	7,952	25	1.9
21	Kingfisher	UK	6,559	46	1.1
22	Dixons	UK	5,797	14	0.1
23	Office Depot	US	5,086	15	0.2
24	Tiffany & Co	US	4,961	51	0.0
25	Next	UK	4,702	3	0.1
26	Delhaize	BG	4,341	85	2.7
27	Karstadt Quelle	BD	3,000	10	0.2
28	Signet Group	UK	2,584	71	0.7
29	Michaels Stores	US	2,551	4	0.0
30	Esprit Holdings	HK	2,256	87	3.2

Source: Oxford Institute of Retail Management

There are no industry wide statistics on the international activities of American retailers, comparable with those given for European retailers. It is clear that fewer US retailers have international operations: naturally enough, as the domestic market is so many times greater than it is for a European firm. Very few large European retailers lack some international operations now. A recent survey showed however that there is widespread interest today among American retailers in becoming international (Vida, 2000).

Case Study: How to measure retail internationalization

The integrative measure of globalization (IMG)

Even today, the majority of retailers are entirely or largely domestic in their operations. Of the top 500 quoted retail companies in the world, only 120 have significant international operations. Table 5.2 shows the 30 biggest companies in the world. They have very variable amounts of international business. But even those with significant sales outside their home markets are not very 'global'. The challenge of how to become truly global still lies ahead of most retailers. To be considered truly global, a retailer must: operate mostly outside its home market; operate in a large number of countries; spread across several of the major regions of the world; and have developed the skills to enter a variety of different markets.

The IMG measures the first two of these. It is essentially a measure of concentration or dispersal. Even if a company has 51 per cent of its sales outside its home market, it cannot be regarded as global if its international activities are concentrated in just a few countries, or just one region or continent. IMG is a combination of three factors: percentage of international sales; number of regions in which a company is present (placed in a range 1–4) and the measure of regional concentration of international sales (ranges from 0.5–1.0). Arithmetically, IMG = international sales × geographic spread ÷ concentration of sales. IMG ranges between 0 and 8, the lower limit corresponding to purely domestic retailers, and the upper limit to entirely globalized retailers.

For example, Ahold: 91.7 per cent (percentage of international sales) × 4 (number of global regions present) ÷ 0.7 (the measure of regional concentration) gives an IMG of 5.2.

Strategic reasons for internationalization

What are the strategic reasons for venturing upon international operations, in the face of the conventional wisdom that retailing is a local business? Broadly, there are two sorts of motive: push and pull. Retailers need to consider their individual situations in making the decision as to where to seek growth – internationally or domestically, with the expansion of existing formats or through diversification into new products and formats.

Push

Some of the biggest early international players come from relatively small home markets. Growth has to be international for them. As the country markets have matured, with large company presence and similar stores throughout, growth opportunities for more of the same obviously diminish. The push is to find new markets for similar propositions and skills. It is not only small sized markets that have suffered from a degree of saturation, of course. France is full of hypermarkets and supermarkets; Japan has been saturated with department stores, and so on. Japanese department store retailers and French food retailers have long looked for opportunities in new countries. Saturation is a relative term: new ideas and new formats can be used to invade the most apparently saturated market. Regulation has tended to increase the difficulties however in many European countries – and Japan. New stores are difficult and costly to build, the process of obtaining permissions is time consuming and therefore costly. Foreign markets, especially in less developed countries, can seem far more attractive.

Pull

The opportunities in less mature markets or where there are market gaps are highly attractive. Economic growth, or more precisely growth in consumer spending, is the most fundamental pull factor retailers should consider. Population growth and the growth of middle classes with money to spend on consumer goods are clear attractions in some countries. Economic growth of 5 or 10 per cent per year in places like China encourages international retailers to enter.

The pull factors include less tangible but nonetheless important considerations about corporate philosophy and indeed management ambition.

Growth

All of these factors or motives of course should be seen in the context of the need for growth. For public corporations especially, growth is rewarded and lack of growth is punished, by market valuation and related financial assessments – leading to virtuous or vicious cycles in the ability to invest and grow further. It is no coincidence that the big European retailers who do not have international operations are voluntary groups or co-operatives of one form or another, who are not so much subject to this demand. But whatever the form of the organization, in broad terms there is a perception that opportunities for growth are no longer solely or most obviously in the local market.

Retailers themselves do not much emphasize the 'push' motives, as we can see from the interviews in Part III, but emphasize opportunities in certain countries and their abilities to exploit the strength of their brands or their expertise. Later in this chapter we look at the problems firms encounter in actually doing these things.

The decision to move internationally should not be made simply on the basis of the factors identified in Table 5.3. Many factors may trigger, facilitate or hinder international activity. We should not ignore the 'band wagon' effect: 'if they are doing it, we had better do so'. This effect has been in part increased by the influence of the stock markets: analysts have valued anticipated international growth quite

Table 5.3 Push and pull motives for international development

Push	Pull
Mature markets, few opportunities	Growing population in host country
Intense competitive pressure; declining market share	Economic growth; growth of consumer spending in key groups
Saturation or impending saturation in floorspace provision	Presence of niche market; desire to export a formula that works well in home market
Slow economic growth	Removal of barriers to entry
Low population growth, changes in demographics	Strong product brand
Regulation restricting store building, especially large store formats	Fragmented competition
Regulation restricting growth via corporate takeover	Company skills and strengths
High operating costs	Corporate philosophy to become international business
	Opportunity to learn about international retailing/establish base for further expansion

Source: Oxford Institute of Retail Management

highly, encouraging companies to seek and to declare such expectations. Chance plays a part: the financial crisis in south-east Asia 1997, for example, was largely unforeseen, but it gave a considerable impetus to the activities of international retailers there. They were able to acquire assets relatively cheaply, or indeed had to acquire the assets of local partners in difficulties, in order to ensure the continuation of their businesses.

Strategic choices

Retailers need to consider the push and pull factors that might lead them to international development. However, this is only the beginning. There are many strategic choices to be made in setting up international businesses. This section considers the main choices.

Types of retail business

First, it is worth noting some differences amongst types of trade. The first international retailers were very often manufacturers or suppliers of novel products – like Singer sewing machines, or van den Bergh margarine – looking to develop their own distribution networks. Some of the most successful international retailers since the 1960s have also been those with strongly branded products, often as part of a branded format. The most obvious are suppliers of luxury, niche products, such as Armani, Cartier, Hermes or Louis Vuitton, who have set up some stores, or concessions within department stores, to promote the brand within the country. Operating the store or concession offers the advantage of increased control over factors that affect the brand.

There is a bigger group of retailers who also have a relatively long track record of internationalization. These are more mass-market product brand formats, often in the clothing or fashion sector, and sometimes taking the franchise route to expansion. In Europe, companies in this category, such as Bally, Bata, Benetton, Stefane, Yves Rocher and Hennes and Mauritz have dominated 'border-hopping' international activities.

Retailers such as these have succeeded on the basis of brand management skills and the ability to exploit similar market niches in many countries. The risks and difficulties of internationalization have been relatively low: that is not to say that it has been risk free and easy. Local franchisees have often supplied much of the capital and the know-how about opening and operation in new locations.

Grocery chains

A recent interesting trend is the emergence of international strategies among the largest retailers, who are mostly grocery chains. Conventional wisdom was that food retailing was the most difficult business to transfer from one country to another. First, tastes are very local. Secondly, a food – or general merchandise – retailer apparently has no product advantage, as the necessary products are widely available. Thirdly, the business model of the efficient large grocers of today depends on close integration with a network of suppliers. Carrefour, with the longest history of expansion from one country to another, has based most of its strategy for organic expansion in new countries on the hypermarket format. This very large format is more 'stand-alone' than the smaller grocery store format. Individual stores tend to manage their own buying and supply to a greater extent. Companies with smaller grocery stores that depend on efficient networks, have possibly a more difficult requirement to develop many stores rapidly so that the network reaches economic size. Aldi entering the UK market for example, faced particular problems in obtaining enough sites and permits to build its network rapidly.

The most internationalized grocers, Ahold and Delhaize, have small home markets in The Netherlands and Belgium respectively. Their 'push' outside national boundaries was natural enough. However, over the last few years, the large European grocers have almost all taken international steps as well. Undoubtedly

Table 5.4 The largest retailers in central Europe

Rank	Company	Home country
1	Metro	Germany
2	Rewe	Germany
3	Tesco	UK
4	Tengelmann	Germany
5	Ahold	The Netherlands
6	Jeronimo Martins	Portugal
7	CBA	Hungary
8	Co-op H	Hungary
9	Carrefour	France
10	Casino	France

Source: Lupton (2002)

the 'push' is greater. Modern stores are almost everywhere; a few large companies with large market shares dominate most west European countries; there are relatively few places for them to go at home. Competition authorities within the EU limit the opportunities for many of them to take over rivals within the same country. That is not to say that innovative retailers cannot increase sales at home but foreign opportunities have come to be perceived as more inviting. The nearest opportunities in the 1980s were in southern Europe: Spain especially, but also Italy and Greece, where retailing was then much less consolidated. Rapid development through the 1990s means that now the largest retailers in Spain are French and the largest in Greece are French and Belgian. The opening of central and eastern Europe has brought further opportunities. German firms dominated the first moves in this direction, but others such as Tesco have become very significant players. Table 5.4 lists the largest retailers in central Europe in order of size of sales.

Choice of direction

The choice of destination or direction is a critical one. The last section discussed some European directions. More recently, attention has moved to Asia and South America. Carrefour found early opportunities in the growing and less consolidated markets of Latin America, entering Argentina in 1982, and later Chile, in 1998. Economic difficulties in Argentina in 2002 illustrate the risks of moving into less stable environments. The decision as to which new market to enter may be seen as one of weighing risk against opportunity. The most obvious risks are of political or economic instability. Balanced against these are the opportunities of undeveloped and/or growing markets. Consumer spending growth of 5 or 10 per cent per annum in tiger economies or elsewhere is far more attractive than a few per cent at home. Broadly static consumer spending has characterized Germany for instance, for some time. Timing – or chance – is often the key. B&Q took an opportunity to move

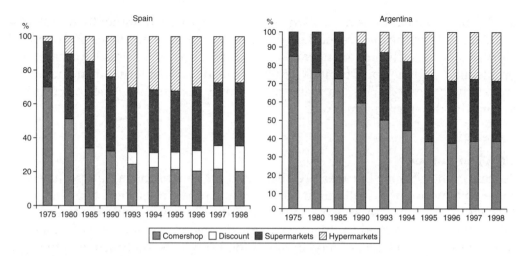

Figure 5.1 Channel evolution

into Turkey in 2000 when a suitable partner appeared. Turkey, with a fast growing, young, population, on the edge of the EU and seeking to join, is an attractive market. Hyper inflation has however made the business difficult: with greater stability in the future, there may be very large opportunities for international retailers in Turkey.

Riding the wave of modernization

When spending growth is combined with the opportunity to restructure the market, by developing a new format or taking substantial market share from fragmented domestic competitors, we have seen the most substantial moves by the grocers and general merchandisers. The strategy of 'riding the wave' has been particularly successful for hypermarket companies. The growth of the hypermarket and supermarket sectors in Spain, Argentina or Thailand has largely been because of the success of international retailers in those countries. Their success has been to offer a wide range of low priced merchandise, in a modern format with the virtues of consistent availability, range and quality, based on the systems and skills developed elsewhere, against relatively weak competitors. In each country, new retail channels have evolved as part of a process of modernization in retailing, and in each case the process has been led by international retailers (particularly Carrefour).

Market gaps

Market gaps, whether in mature or less developed countries, are attractive for retailers with a strong format proposition. Lidl's 2002 entry into Finland with its small scale, hard discount format is the most recent case of a company spotting and occupying such a gap. Just a few domestic retail groups dominate the Finnish market but none has done more than experiment with 'hard' rather than 'soft' discount formats. In the mature markets of Europe, especially northwest Europe, and North America, such gaps are now relatively rare. Ideas have spread, formats have proliferated, and the opportunities for retailers to develop international operations are relatively limited. This is a major reason for European and American retailers to consider the emerging markets.

USA and Europe

Success in the USA for European retailers, and for Americans in Europe, has been somewhat more elusive. Although Carrefour and others attempted to open hypermarkets in the USA, those experiments failed. The competitive landscape was difficult: well-entrenched companies had good consumer relations, and American consumers found the mix of food and non-food products unattractive in the light of existing competition. There were no doubt other factors involved, especially the difficulty of building supplier networks in a culturally different business environment. However, successful ventures include Tengelmann with Great Atlantic & Pacific, Ahold and Delhaize, and more recently Sainsbury's with Shaw's. These successful examples use various supermarket, food and drug focused formats, and it is clear that good local competitors existed. At least some of the success of these operations may be attributed to a careful process of acquiring and then extending chains that were already well established, with good store portfolios and a strong consumer bond.

American retailers venturing to Europe have very often taken their first steps in the UK, seeing the most culturally similar country as the most obvious starting point. Gap, Blockbuster, T K Maxx and Disney are good examples. Many, however, have progressed no further than the UK as dissimilarities have taken their toll. Higher land and property prices mean that different business models are required. Difficulties in building large-scale stores or out-of-centre stores have impeded the strategies of companies from Costco (warehouse club stores) to Toys 'R' Us.

Similarly, there have been several notable European failures in the USA. Dixons, the UK electrical retailer, made its first significant international move in the late 1980s. Deciding that its brands and formats were irrelevant to US consumers, it acquired the discount chain Silo. The acquisition proved ill judged, as operational weaknesses were exposed by recession. Large losses and perhaps most important, the consumption of disproportionate management time, led to the sale of the chain. Laura Ashley in contrast attempted organic expansion but was undermined by the costs of physical expansion, weak distribution and inventory control systems, and problems with extending the brand from fashion into furnishings.

It is important to recognize the problems that can be caused by unfamiliarity with the market. The unfamiliarity is natural but has been compounded in many cases by lack of research and planning. Choosing the wrong locations is a particular mistake. Probably more important is overestimating the strength of a brand or a concept and its potential in the new market. A different competitive landscape may mean in addition that a retail brand will be perceived differently from the way consumers see it in the domestic market, and indeed may mean that its owners must position it differently. At the least, it may mean that a different, more rapid campaign of brand development is needed in the new market, in contrast to the long process of growth in the domestic market. And retailers tend to be less experienced in the skills of brand development and brand management than other industries.

Asia

Asian markets have become very much more attractive for European and North American retailers, for various reasons. First is the diminution of opportunities elsewhere. It is instructive to compare French grocery retailer Casino, which came late to international activity, with its peers. It has 'leapfrogged' the border-hopping progression and learning process of European expansion of other companies. Casino was largely domestic until 1996, with a substantial market share in France. Narrowly escaping a takeover by Promodès, Casino was shaken into international investment. Casino's first opening was in Poland but then very soon it has moved into much more distant markets.

The second reason for growing interest in Asia is the process of learning. Unlike Casino, many firms tend to go through a process of experimenting with international operations, gradually gaining experience of the necessary skills, in markets regarded as close or relatively less risky than distant ones. Border-hopping comes first, followed by more distant expansion. As international strategies develop, they become more courageous, or well founded, and interest expands. This is not to say that there is a neat set of stages that retailers must or do go through: strategy often evolves in a messy way. Nor is it to say that we can see a neat process of outward expansion, as retailers have become larger and more international. Indeed leapfrog is a better metaphor for what many are doing, than a steady march forward.

Case Study: Casino: a later starter reaching the front ranks

Casino is a most interesting case. It remained largely domestic until recently, though it acquired 53 per cent of the Smart & Final cash and carry chain in 1984. In France, it runs 115 Geant hypermarkets, over 1,200 supermarkets and discount stores, and over 4,000 convenience and franchise stores. In the mid 1990s it had a large market share but rather poor performance and was showing little real growth. The punishment for lack of growth and lack of ambition was the threat of take-over. It narrowly escaped being consolidated into Promodès (itself now part of Carrefour) in 1996. Much later than most of its peers, the firm then embarked on serious international expansion. It also invested heavily in logistics and category management, and restructured its buying department. The bulk of Casino's sales growth recently has come from new international operations however.

Casino's first new opening was in Poland but then it moved into five countries of South America and into Taiwan. In 1999 Casino acquired 66 per cent of Big C in Thailand. Most recently, Casino moved into the Indian Ocean region. Casino's strategy has been to acquire good businesses on which to build, though in several cases it holds only minority shares. Casino has not spent time in trying to enter European markets long dealt with by its rivals but is trying to 'leap-frog' into places where it sees greater opportunities, principally for hypermarkets but also for its discount leader price format.

	France	International
Stores	6,385	1,155*
Sales growth	6.3%	18.1%**

* as at end September 2002
** 9 months to end September 2002, constant exchange rates

Opportunity is clearly a key driver as Part III illustrates. The opportunity presented by the opening of China to foreign investment, encouraged by the accession to the World Trade Organization, is one of the most important current challenges to international retailers.

Market selection and timing

The questions of destination and timing are closely connected. Timing is crucial – taking opportunities as they arise, particularly as markets open to foreign investment, and as consumer spending reaches absolute levels and levels of growth that are sufficient to support a new entrant. The UK was and remains an attractive destination for international retailers: consumer spending is high. Japan has possibly an even more attractive consumer spending profile: it has been difficult to enter because of regulation and also hidden or informal restrictions. The question for many is whether the time is now right to enter: recent times have seen considerably increased interest, including interest from Carrefour and Wal-Mart. Restrictions on imports have been eased; the Large Store Law which restricts much development has been reformed. Still few international retailers have gained significant market share there. HMV Media is an exception – in Part III (Chapter 15), the chief executive, Alan Giles, discusses their approach. Timing for the big grocery or general merchandise retailers is particularly significant. First-mover advantage operates in a particular way for them in relation to site acquisition. Those who identify and occupy key sites for hypermarkets or modern grocery stores can gain strong positions in new markets. Tesco's particular strength in site and location analysis is undoubtedly one of the foundations of its international success.

Waves of interest in different markets at different times have been seen and the earlier part of this chapter identified some of these. Keen interest must focus on where the next waves will be.

What growth strategies can international retailers employ?

Helfferich *et al.* (1997) brought together a wide variety of analyses of international retailing and suggested some terminology (Table 5.5) that can be used to distinguish types of international retailer. Different authors have used terms in various ways.

Of course, firms do not always fit neatly into the classification but the broad distinctions in Table 5.5 help to identify the strategic decisions that need to be made. Global strategies, focusing on exploiting similar market niches across the world and developing and benefiting from economies of scale, can be described as diametrically opposite to the multinational strategies of operating diverse, relatively independent units. Transnational strategies seek the advantages of both. Appropriate strategy for any particular retailer must involve processes of fitting both to markets and to organizational capabilities, and may well involve a mixture of the elements described in this table.

Table 5.5 Five parameters of international retailing and four kinds of international retailer

	International	Global	Transnational	Multinational
Geographic scope	I continent	2 or more continents	I or more continents	I or more continents
Cultural spread	I cultural zone	2 or more cultural zones	2 or more cultural zones	2 or more cultural zones
Cultural orientation	Ethnocentric	Mixed	Geocentric	Polycentric
Marketing	Expansion of home format or international alliances	Minimal adaptation, homogeneous markets	Medium adaptation, heterogeneous markets	Major adaptation or diverse formats, heterogeneous markets
Management	Domestic HQ	Centralized control	Integrated network	Independent units

Source: Helfferich *et al.* (1997)

Mode of entry

Retailers can choose various strategies for entering new countries. Broadly they can be seen as less to more risky:

- supply of goods
- concession in others' retail outlets
- franchising (from strong to weak control agreements)
- minor share acquisition of existing operation (and probably exchange of know-how)
- majority or full share acquisition of existing operation
- establishment of new venture/organic expansion (with a significant partner)
- establishment of new venture/organic expansion (without a significant partner).

Marks & Spencer, who became one of the most widely spread and widely known major retailers before retreating from many of its international operations in 2001/2 because of troubles in the domestic market, began international operations almost inadvertently, through supplying goods to retailers in other markets. Loose franchise agreements were followed by more formal ones, for instance in Korea. Existing well established retailers – Brooks Bros and a supermarket chain – were acquired in the USA. A joint venture with Cortefiel to establish new stores in Spain was followed by the company taking full control from its partner, and eventually full control or organic ventures were made to develop stores in France and Germany. Marks & Spencer's international operations are now re-focused on franchising.

The advantages and disadvantages of each form of expansion are partly dependent on the environment: markets that are more distant culturally and geographically are often seen as best served by local retail partners for example. However, difficulties with partners, and difficulties in adapting to new environments are general issues, and we will return to these below.

It is notable that franchising accounts for a high proportion of international stores generally, and particularly in the fashion and clothing trades where product and format are more likely to be branded (whether strongly or weakly) so that franchises can be built on supply of goods and use of brand logos, etc.

Boots from the UK has recently taken the reverse of Marks & Spencer's route, with high risk ventures gradually replaced by a lower risk form of expansion. Early acquisitions in Canada and France were eventually sold. A more recent phase of internationalization began in 1997 with operations in the neighbouring Netherlands. 'Leapfrog' took the company to Thailand in the same year, where they could see both a good market opportunity in a rapidly growing class of consumers with money and interest in strong brands, combined with few restrictions on foreign investment and store opening. In a fully Boots owned enterprise, they rapidly opened stores, at first very similar indeed to British stores, even to using store fittings shipped from the UK. Products of course had to be adapted and labelled to comply with local taste and local regulation. Many were Boots branded. The company opened stores very rapidly to reach a network of almost 100. The process of gaining approval for new products or imported products was not easy. Recognition of the Boots brand, though it grew rapidly, was of course nothing like as high as the almost universal recognition and trust in the home market. In the UK the Boots brand is mass market, not a luxury one. In Thailand, it was perceived as a luxury, expensive brand (even though strenuous efforts were made to reduce costs and prices). The interview in Part III (Chapter 16) comes from this phase of rapid expansion in 2000.

Boots has now retreated from this high cost, high risk strategy of trying to establish its brand in a new market and develop its own stores. It has sold its interests in The Netherlands, and is reducing the number of stores in Thailand and instead establishing concessions within grocery stores opened by Tops (Ahold). Boots entered Japan in a partnership with Mitsubishi, but managed to open only two stores. It is now entering other Asian markets through concessions in discount drug stores owned by Watsons (Hutchison). The investment of time, people and resources for sales achieved will be much less; the potential return in terms of size of the business in each market is also likely to be less than that of the earlier vision.

Partners

The textbooks tell us that partners are more or less necessary in entering more or less unfamiliar markets. Partners provide know-how about consumers or ways of doing business, and key assets, whether stores, people, brands or other things. In some cases, partners may be essential because of regulation of foreign ownership. In others – and some particularly uncomfortable situations – partnerships have resulted from the negotiation of a partial takeover. Retailers should take great care in selecting partners and obtaining agreements with them. There have been some very difficult experiences in the past. Negotiating and maintaining the relationships can be time consuming for senior managers. There are issues of control and of communication. Problems also relate to the key question of adaptation (see below).

Retailers tend to move to acquire control of joint ventures when they can, or as they grow in experience. Early international efforts with shared control are followed by those with greater or full control sought from the beginning. Generally speaking, these moves may be accounted for first by growing experience and confidence and secondly by the intrinsic difficulties of partnerships. Conflicts are generated by the partners having incompatible goals, different views of the decision-making process, and different perceptions of the local market. Problems may simply arise because of a slow or complex decision-making process, involving local and central organizations. Some of the difficulties experienced by US video rental chain Blockbuster in Japan for example, are attributable to its failure to obtain good sites, because site acquisition decisions were made, slowly, in Australia, not Japan. In addition, local management's perceptions of best product mix and of most appropriate locations were different from the headquarters' view. Eventually the US company withdrew from the venture.

Local partners can have very different views of what is appropriate in the market. Such views may be precisely what the market entrant wanted to acquire, but if they lead to modifications of key brand attributes, or to the firm's normal or expected ways of working, problems ensue. There are no prescriptions: successful firms are those who have the skills to adapt sufficiently, to learn constantly, and to balance the exploitation of what has made the firm successful at home, with what is required for success in a new environment. The balancing is particularly difficult for general merchandise retailers, without strong product brands of their own.

Acquisition

The acquisition route to expansion is becoming more common in grocery and general merchandise retailing especially. In mature, highly regulated markets, the new store building route to expansion is difficult. It also requires patience and deep pockets, as it may take a long time to build sufficient scale for economic operation. In northern and western Europe for example, acquisition is seen as virtually the only route for Wal-Mart to expand significantly, as indeed it is for electrical retailers such as Dixons or Mediamarkt, or a do-it-yourself retailer such as Home Depot. Acquisition of existing retailers provides a base for further expansion quickly in eastern Europe, as Tesco for example has shown in Poland. Acquisitions may be seen in strategic terms as providing a base of know-how and a foothold, or in terms of providing major assets in the form of stores, brands or networks.

For some retailers, acquisition is the preferred mode of expansion and is symptomatic of the 'multi-national' form of organization and approach to markets. Ahold notably has sought to acquire well-established and successful retailers, such as ICA in Sweden, Giant Food and Stop & Shop in America, and to operate them as largely separate enterprises. Networking behind the scenes means they seek to share best practice from one organization to another. Contrast this approach with that of say, Wal-Mart, re-branding stores and integrating the new organizations into centralized systems.

In Part III (Chapter 18), Roland Vaxelaire provides a view from a company acquired by Carrefour. Chapter 6 discusses the financial aspects with some salutary warnings about the difficulties of achieving real value from corporate acquisitions. Finding suitable, available targets is often difficult. The most obvious examples are recent takeovers in Germany. ITM, with a very large market share in its home France, and determined to enter Germany has bought Spar but faces considerable difficulties in raising performance levels in a very mixed portfolio of stores. Similarly Wal-Mart could find few opportunities to acquire large, well-positioned stores. Kingfisher, seeking to enter, has acquired part only of Hornbach. Consolidation in the USA has provided some better opportunities. Sainsbury's and Ahold, like the domestic grocers, have expanded by acquiring regional chains.

Despite the difficulties, companies continue to seek acquisitions. If this is the route to international growth that is available, they must take it, if growth is what they seek. There is an analysis that suggests that the end game of current developments among the big retailers is a situation with a handful of dominant players, and the rest swallowed, or disappeared or pushed into niche strategies in smaller markets. This analysis sees scale as the key to dominance. Strong domestic performance gives the ability to buy at low prices, attract the best staff and acquire the best sites. Increased cash flow enables acquisitions. The transfer of best practice across the extended organization strengthens it. Increased scale again gives greater bargaining strength, especially in product supply. Lower prices and improved performance in turn give greater cash flow and further increases in acquisition ability and so on. One particular feature of this strategy is the ability that increased international scale brings to reduce domestic prices, and further dominate local competitors. There is evidence that this cycle is working, but we must also bear in mind that no retailer is yet anything approaching 'global'. Countervailing problems of adaptation, control and communication also mean that it is not clear that such strategies will bring success in the short or even medium term.

Adaptation

Some of the debate about whether global strategies with minimal adaptation of formula are more successful than multinational ones with format and product adapted to new markets, is rather pointless. In fact every international retailer adapts to some degree – even McDonald's adapts its menus without adapting the essence of its brand (consistency, speed of service, appeal to young people, etc). In considering adaptation we must focus on what needs adapting, and what essential basis of success, including product, supply chain skill and store management skill, must be transferred or replicated. A store may have totally different products from those sold in the home market, yet the overall offer, the format including mix, price, store environment, may have similar brand qualities and similar appeal to the consumer, as in the home market. B&Q's international director, Steve Gilman, makes some interesting comments, as does Metro CEO, Dr Hans-Joachim Körber regarding this factor in Part III (Chapters 13 and 14).

Some adaptations are forced on international retailers. Building and planning regulations may mean particular restrictions on the locations where firms may operate and the size and style of store. Belgium's 'Padlock Law' is just an extreme example of restriction, meaning that stores over certain sizes cannot be built. Some retail trades, especially pharmacies and alcohol are licensed and restricted in some countries. In France for example, chain pharmacies are forbidden: it is therefore highly unattractive for Boots, with its format including pharmacies. Food and health regulations, tariffs and other import restraints affect the products retailers may stock. Restrictions on pricing and promotions may require adaptation of selling practices, rather than product itself.

Case Study: So you think selling is the same the world over?

Many retailers who were operating at national level are discovering the complexities of rolling out successful national strategies onto the European stage.

An example helps demonstrate the extent of the problem. In the field of commercial communications (advertising, sponsorship, direct marketing, sales promotions and PR services) whether it be in traditional retailing or in e-commerce, the importance of promotional offers, from discounts through to loyalty premiums is well recognized by commerce. Yet how many major UK or French retailers are aware that their loyalty card schemes would be considered illegal in Germany or that a 50 per cent offer would not be allowed in a number of European countries or that joint offers (i.e. premium offers) are also banned in a number of key European markets? . . . You may be interested to know that the right to make a discount (for certain products and services they are strictly regulated and sometimes banned), the manner a discount is displayed, the type of discount offered (e.g. 10 per cent off, or three for the price of two), the period of the year when it can be made and announced (in some countries you cannot announce discounts immediately prior to the seasonal sale periods) are all already regulated by national statute . . .

To keep within the law in each and every member state you decide to develop your business into will require a new marketing strategy. The associated adjustment costs can be enormous and moreover it is worth remembering that you will be testing out new strategies whereas the incumbents will have worked with their regulatory environment for many years making your successful entry into their market all the more difficult.

Extracted from an article by Bergevin (2000)

Store size, and consequently product offer, often requires adaptation. American category killer firms entering European or Japanese markets have certainly found this. Office Depot in Japan for instance, whose stores in the USA are typically 2,000 square metres, started developing stores of over 2,000 square metres in Japan but soon moved to experiment with stores of just 500 square metres. Another US category killer firm entering Japan in 1995 was Sports Authority, in partnership with Jusco. Sports Authority initially opened large stores of 4,000 or 5,000 square metres but high property and staff costs led to losses. The retailer reduced store sizes, while keeping the same number of products on offer. Sports Authority also clearly adapted its product mix for the Japanese market and introduced more seasonal change than at home.

Other adaptations are more matters of strategic choice, related to perceptions of opportunity, competition, and consumer taste and expectation. A dramatic adaptation is that of Tesco. At home, Tesco success was built on rapid growth of superstores, focused on grocery products, though with strong recent additions of categories such as health and beauty products. The company also built a capacity to segment its formats, opening much smaller Metro stores in high streets, Tesco Express convenience stores attached to petrol stations, and carefully tailoring larger and smaller superstore offers. Tesco had in the past developed non-food household goods and clothing departments but abandoned these many years ago. However, Tesco international ventures are focused on developing hypermarkets, with both non-food and grocery departments. It is highly unusual in this approach – and indeed even more notable for the success, which runs counter to the conventional textbook wisdom. Part III gives some views from Dr Hans-Joachim Körber, CEO of German retailer Metro. Perhaps the lesson is that what is being transferred and exploited internationally is know-how, skill and systems – not format.

Learning

Successful international businesses learn from the process of extending their operations. The process is not necessarily one-way, from home market to new markets. Ahold is a good example of a company that has developed the ability to share ideas and best practice internationally. Although its various chains are run separately and kept quite distinct, it organizes what it calls 'networking' to identify expertise and share knowledge via a series of mechanisms such as virtual knowledge centres, directories of people's experience and benchmarking databases. Tesco is another firm that has begun to import ideas and systems from new markets to the home market (see Table 5.6).

Table 5.6 Tesco: transfers of management know-how

	Source of transfer to other regions
Retail operations	
Basic operation systems	UK
Hypermarket operation	Central Europe, Thailand
Seasonal sales promotion	Central Europe
Fresh food operation	Korea
In-store bakery operation	Central Europe
Non-food operation	Thailand
Opening 24 hours	UK
Loyalty card operation	UK
E-commerce	UK
Buying	
Private brand strategy	UK
Development of simple private brand	Thailand
Retail supply chain	
Basic supply chain management	UK
Central replenishment system	UK
Composite distribution centre	UK

Source: Oxford Institute of Retail Management

Culture

Adaptation involves far more than appreciating different consumer tastes. Business practices and institutions vary across countries. The structure of supply and of supplier relationships can be very different from that in home markets. Perhaps the most extreme example is the difference between Japan and the UK. The multi-layered complexity of supply in Japan, the rigidities in the system and the difficulties of making changes, provide a different and unaccommodating environment for foreign retailers seeking to introduce working practices from elsewhere. Staff recruitment, training and management are further obvious issues. Retailers are no different from other firms in that they must learn or acquire the skills related to working across cultural boundaries in order to become international. What is different about today's retailers is their lack of experience. The cadre of managers in retailing who have significant experience of international development is currently small.

Conclusion and summary

Few retailers are yet truly international, but many see their future as lying beyond their domestic markets. Cautious and sometimes ill-judged experiments are being replaced with expansion strategies but few are finding easy returns. Niche retailers and luxury goods retailers are those who can be seen in many cities around the world. The really big firms however – those who have entered the Fortune 500 list over the last decade – are mass-market operators. Profit in mass-market retailing depends heavily on scale economies in stores or store networks, and sales growth on the steady expansion of physical space. These are the fundamentals that just a few retail companies are beginning to achieve in unfamiliar markets.

No easy recipes exist for international success. Part III gives some views and interesting food for thought from those responsible for strategy. This chapter has attempted to provide some context, rather than sets of checklists. What does sustained international success require?

First, we consider skill in location analysis and site acquisition. First movers do not always win but those early movers who focus on obtaining the right sites in the right place will build good positions in new markets. In order to establish a significant presence and a viable network rapidly, this skill is even more important in entering new markets than it is in building on mature positions at home.

Next, we consider the importance of skill in brand building. Establishing and building a brand is crucial in entering a new market where the retailer is probably unknown – even if selling recognizable products. The competitive landscape may be quite different from the domestic market and require new work on targeting and positioning. Retailers will have to develop explicit brand tactics for each market. There are additional public relations skills in dealing with possible xenophobic reactions to foreign firms. Beyond this, the PR and negotiation skills of building and keeping relationships with local and national governments must not be ignored. There are some distinct contrasts among big retailers in this area.

Skill in finding and managing the alliances or partnerships that ease the entry into remote markets is a further important factor. There are plenty of examples of unhappy relationships which have not delivered the hoped for success but as the opportunities for retailers become more remote from home, they become more necessary.

Success requires focus. Many international ventures are rather tangential to the main concerns of management teams. A franchising or international department exists, but it does not have high corporate visibility. This can be something of a chicken and egg situation, as the small size of many international operations deters the investment of management time. It is clear however that top management must drive the activities of firms that are seeing rapid international growth and success.

Review questions

1 What reasons might a European retailer have for seeking to develop international activities?
2 What growth strategies can international retailers use?
3 Who are the most international retailers?

Discussion questions

1 In what ways might retailers in different sectors have to adapt themselves to new international markets?
2 Should companies proceed internationally by first developing in new markets close to the home country?
3 How can retailers avoid repeating the international failures we have seen in the last two decades?

References

Alexander, N. (1997) *International Retailing*. Blackwell, Oxford.

Bergevin, J. (2000) 'Commercial Communications, eCommerce and the Single Market for Retailing'. *European Retail Digest*, **25**, March.

Burt, S. (2002) 'International Retailing'. Chapter 14 in P. McGoldrick (ed.), *Retail Marketing*. McGraw-Hill, Maidenhead.

Davies, R. and Yahagi, T. (2000) *Retail Investment in Asia/Pacific: Local Responses and Public Policy Issues*. Oxford Institute of Retail Management, Oxford.

Dawson, J. (1993) 'The internationalization of retailing'. In Bromley, R.D.F. and Thomas, C.J. (eds) *Retail Change: Contemporary Issues*. UCL Press, London.

Fernie, J. and Arnold, S.J. (2002) 'Wal-Mart in Europe: prospects for Germany, the UK and France'. *International Journal of Retail and Distribution Management*, **30**, pp. 92–102.

Helfferich E., Hinfelaar M. and Kasper H. (1997) 'Towards a clear terminology on international retailing'. *International Review of Retail, Distribution and Consumer Research*, **7**, pp. 287–307.

Jones Lang Wootton and OXIRM (1997) 'Shopping for new markets: retailers' expansion across Europe's borders'. JLW, London.

Lupton, R.A. (2002) 'Retailing in Post-socialist Central Europe'. *European Retail Digest*, **33**, March.

Retail Intelligence (1999) 'Retail sans frontieres: the internationalisation of European retailing'. Retail Intelligence, London.

Vida, I. (2000) 'Determinants of International Retail Involvement: The Case of Large U.S. Retail Chains'. *Journal of International Marketing*, **8**:4, p. 37.

Yahagi, T. (2003 forthcoming) 'The internationalisation process of Tesco in Asia'. *Proceedings of Asia Pacific Retail Conference*, Beijing, Nov. 2002.

Chapter 6

Prospects for e-commerce

Jonathan Reynolds

Whilst disillusionment with the so-called 'new economy' would appear to have reduced the attractiveness of business-to-consumer (B2C) e-commerce as a viable source of revenue growth for retailers, writing off electronic distribution channels may be premature. Retailing appears to be polarizing between those companies willing to embrace e-commerce for longer-term benefit and those for whom e-commerce is not seen as a desirable route to growth. Similar polarizing effects appear to characterize consumer behaviour. The indirect, informational effect of the Internet on the consumer buying process and the perception of retail brands are further unanticipated but significant considerations for those contemplating multi-channel futures. The practical logistical and fulfilment challenges of e-commerce provide further barriers. Nevertheless, this chapter seeks to show that the integrative challenges of multi-channel retailing are capable of being resolved in more than one way, through an examination of retail choices and constraints.

The rise and fall of the new economy

The student of retailing might well question the merits, if not the good intentions, of many of the early academic contributions to the debate on the transformative nature of e-commerce:

> There is a euphoria these days about the possibilities offered by eCommerce. Consumers see low prices and easy shopping; investors imagine cashing in on Internet IPOs; and start-ups hope that their business model will be the one that transforms their industry.
>
> Sinha, 2000

Two years ago, this author warned: 'Internet businesses remain at the whim of fashion, sentiment and confidence on the part of their investors.'

Substantial academic evidence of the ways in which business-to-consumer e-commerce operations might affect the established retail order started to emerge (Bakos, 2001; Brynjolfsson and Smith, 2000; Mayer *et al.*, 2001; Sinha, 2000). However, at the same time, the 'whim of fashion, sentiment and confidence' (and poor financial management) led to many of those same businesses, in which so much hope for the new economy had been invested, cutting back the scope of their operations and finally closing altogether. Indeed, the only profitable ventures for some former Internet high flyers proved to be publishing *post mortems* of their experience (Kaplan, 2002; Malmsten *et al.*, 2002).

One immediate consequence was that many retailers de-emphasized the perceived threat of e-commerce on their strategic agendas. Table 6.1 shows, for example, how home shopping fell to twelfth place in 2002 amongst European food retail CEOs from being amongst the top four agenda items in 2001 (and indeed ranked second in 2000). Business-to-business (B2B) exchanges – the next enthusiasm in the pipeline – fared little better. E-commerce divisions were disbanded, or given ambitious (and largely unachievable) breakeven targets, and pilots and experiments scaled down (IMRG, 2002a).

But have retailers been right to downplay the threat of e-commerce so significantly? Perhaps the pendulum has swung too far and too unreasonably against e-commerce? Certainly, in addition to the scaling down of online competition, alternative electronic channels to market – such as digital television and mobile commerce – have not been as successful as had been previously anticipated (Kehoe, 2000; Mayer *et al.*, 2001). In the UK, for example, the terrestrial digital television

Table 6.1 The strategic business concerns of food retail chief executives across Europe

Rank 2003	Issue	Rank 2002
I	Customer loyalty and retention	3
2	Food safety/security	2
3	Internationalization of food retailing	I
4	Global recession and consumer demand	4
5	Formats, services, assortment	5
6	Technical standards/supply chain efficiency	7
7	The retailer as a brand	6
8	Recruitment and retention	8
9	Environment/sustainable development	9
10	Accountability	n/a
11	Public image of retailing	n/a
12	B2C e-commerce	12

Source: CIES, 2003

platform ITV Digital went into administration in early 2002 and the two interactive cable television platforms, NTL and Telewest, have pulled back from an ambitious e-commerce strategy. Nevertheless, the online population and the value of online transactions has been increasing, even if more slowly than many had allowed for.

Further, we can argue that, whilst the direct impact of e-commerce has been relatively small in transactional terms, the informational leverage that Internet accessibility provides for increasingly large proportions of the population in most developed countries serves to offer a different kind of challenge: a more *informed* consumer, able and willing to challenge the *status quo* of retail brands. Finally, we can see that there are some significant choices and constraints facing existing retailers determined to pursue e-commerce goals: most particularly around resources and degree of integration.

The state of the art: US versus Europe

Electronic commerce is a difficult term to pin down. Statisticians have developed relatively narrow definitions of what such activity entails. In the US, the US Bureau of the Census, in thinking about ways in which the electronic economy can be measured, suggests that:

> 'Electronic commerce is the value of goods and services sold over computer-mediated networks', whilst electronic business is 'any process that a business organisation conducts over computer-mediated networks'.
>
> Mesenbourg, 2001

The UK Office of National Statistics preferred a more precise definition in its thinking on this subject:

> e-commerce occurs where the decision between seller and buyer to transfer ownership of goods or services has occurred over an electronic network. In other words, e-commerce occurred where the order was placed electronically and payment or delivery can be by other mechanisms.
>
> Williams, 2001

Focusing on transactions of priced goods has been the natural focus of most statistical agencies. However, these definitions naturally ignore the many indirect effects of the Internet on retail sales through pre-purchase marketing and brand-building and post-purchase customer service, potentially leading to increased customer satisfaction and patronage, which may be expressed through electronic or – more likely – conventional commerce.

Internet penetration is still very much a phenomenon of the developed economies. Even across Europe, a 'patchwork quilt' of connectivity reduces the

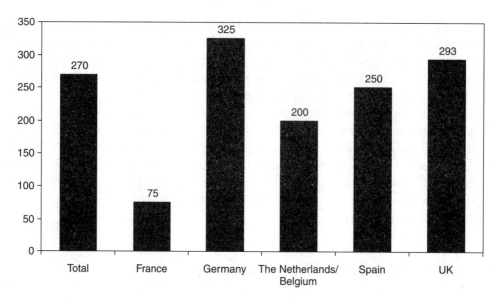

Figure 6.1 Growth in selected European country e-commerce market volumes, summer 2002

Note: Autumn 2001 = 100

Source: http://www.gfk-webgauge.com

economies of scale in markets potentially available to retailers. Further, European e-commerce appears to be taking a more varied technical journey from that in the US, with broadband, interactive TV and mobile platforms being much more evident in consumers' adoption patterns and some European consumers (notably from the UK) having a higher propensity to buy online than a simplistic innovation-adoption curve would suggest.

The media monitoring group GfK reported that whilst e-commerce sales volume was up overall by 170 per cent between autumn 2001 and spring 2002 across six European countries (rising from €4.2bn to €11.5bn), there were marked inter-country differences, with Germany and the UK experiencing a trebling of sales volumes, and France experiencing a decline (Figure 6.1).

UK sales have been particularly buoyant. The UK Interactive Media in Retail Group (IMRG) has been tracking UK online sales patterns for over three years (IMRG, 2002b), albeit based on returns from only 63 contributing businesses. In July 2002 they reported online sales growth at between four and five times 2001 levels, with sales volumes in November 2002 reaching nearly £1 billion: 'online retailing is still growing exponentially', they reported, in particular growing some 'nineteen times faster' than UK high street sales over the same period (Figure 6.2).

Figure 6.3 shows that according to the US Census Bureau, e-commerce sales in the US have grown from 0.7 to 1.3 per cent of all US retail sales between the fourth quarter of 1999 and the third quarter of 2002. Sales exceeded $11 billion for the first time in the fourth quarter of 2001 (US Census Bureau, 2002). More importantly, as in the UK and parts of Europe, online sales have been growing at

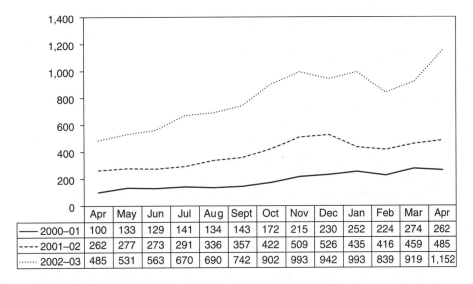

	Apr	May	Jun	Jul	Aug	Sept	Oct	Nov	Dec	Jan	Feb	Mar	Apr
—— 2000–01	100	133	129	141	134	143	172	215	230	252	224	274	262
---- 2001–02	262	277	273	291	336	357	422	509	526	435	416	459	485
······ 2002–03	485	531	563	670	690	742	902	993	942	993	839	919	1,152

Figure 6.2 Estimated UK online sales, April 2000–April 2003
Source: IMRG, 2002–3

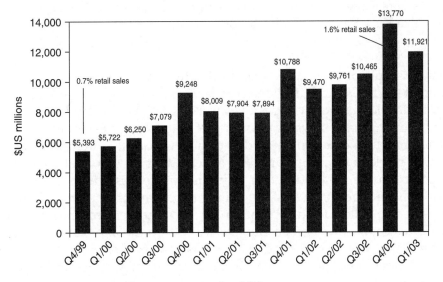

Figure 6.3 Estimated quarterly e-commerce sales, USA
Source: US Census Bureau, 2002

a significantly faster rate than retail sales as a whole. Between the second quarter of 2001 and the second quarter of 2002, online sales grew by 24.2 per cent compared to a 2.5 per cent growth in total retail sales. This progress in sales growth (which is of course from a low base) has served to confound many commentators who saw the complete demise of e-commerce in the downfall of many dot-com businesses. Furthermore, many retailers in the US reported that their e-commerce operations were 'already profitable by 2001' (shop.org, 2002). Whilst operating margins in the US online retail market averaged a net loss of 6 per cent in 2001, this was an improvement on an average net loss of 15 per cent in 2000, with fully 56 per cent of respondents reporting profitable online operations (shop.org, 2002).

How can this be reconciled with the anecdotal reports of retail businesses, especially in Europe, streamlining new channel operations or even withdrawing altogether from e-commerce? One explanation may be that it is not especially appropriate to learn from early US experience on this occasion:

> The very idea of following in the footsteps of the United States was probably inaccurate anyway: for a variety of reasons, e-commerce in Europe was always likely to follow a different course. For one thing, the technological and cultural infrastructures are much more heterogeneous in Europe than they are in the United States. Moreover, European players have had the benefit of hindsight from seeing what has succeeded and failed in the United States. The later entry of European companies into e-commerce also gives them the advantage of applying technology that has advanced considerably over the past two years.
>
> Cornet *et al.*, 2000

A classic example of this can be seen in the growth of mobile telephony and in the attempts of telecommunications companies and virtual network operators in Europe to develop interactive applications. Not all these attempts have been successful by any means, but in the examples of SMS (short messaging services) and music and mobile phone wallpaper downloads, we can see interesting and potentially large markets in Europe and to a lesser extent in Asia, that are simply not yet apparent in the US (Figure 6.4). What is not clear is whether such customers (typically younger segments) are willing to pay the price premiums that more sophisticated so-called 'third generation' transactional services may have to command for telecommunications companies to recoup the expenditure incurred in their acquisition of 3G licenses and of other businesses; nor is it clear to what extent traditional 'bricks and mortar' retail businesses will play a role in this particular electronic channel.

A further explanation of the differences between the US and Europe may lie in some of the clear strategic choices made especially by UK retailers. Recent research undertaken for KPMG shows that retail e-business in the UK is by no means uniform in its penetration and in fact has become quite polarized (KPMG Consulting, 2001). In what they call a 'quiet revolution', the researchers make a clear distinction between types of business that can be regarded as 'e-pioneers', 'e-followers' and 'e-laggards' based upon the extent to which they engage in different types of e-commerce activity and comment that, whilst e-pioneers are to be found in all industry sectors, it is retailing – remarkably, given the industry's historical

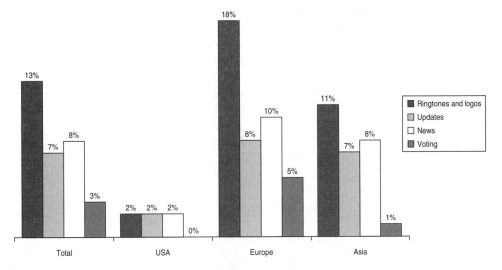

Figure 6.4 The extent of mobile phone transactions, 2002

Note: Base = Internet Phone Users. Data shows proportion of people in a panel-based survey saying that they have undertaken transactions

Source: AT Kearney, 2002/Mobinet #4

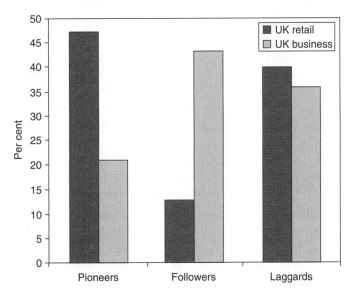

Figure 6.5 Business involvement in e-commerce: UK retail versus UK business as a whole
Source: KPMG Consulting, 2001

attitudes to the application of new information technology (CEC, 1991) – which is characterized by an 'all-or-nothing' approach to e-business (Figure 6.5).

The origins of this polarization become apparent when we examine some of the recent penetration and conversion data from UK online retailing. Table 6.2

Table 6.2 Numbers of users of UK retail sites, December 2002

Rank	Website	Number of users
1	Amazon	6,718,000
2	eBay	5,066,000
3	Argos	2,562,374
4	Tesco	2,186,779
5	Kelkoo	1,894,000
6	Comet	1,458,945
7	John Lewis	1,237,070
8	Currys	1,126,089
9	Dixons	904,907
10	Dealtime	847,648

Source: Nielsen NetRatings, 2003

provides data on the performance of UK retail websites during the critical Christmas 2002 period. More than 12 million people in the UK visited an Internet retailing site in December 2002 – 60 per cent of the country's online population and an increase of 3.8 million over December 2001. This information, from the data consultancy *Nielsen NetRatings* service, makes it clear that – apart from amazon.com and amazon.co.uk – the top 10 is made up almost exclusively of existing UK retail businesses. Apart from Amazon, the exceptions are new kinds of business model peculiar to the Internet: the eBay C2C auction site and two price comparison engines – the French-owned kelkoo.com and Dealtime. Further, when we examine the effectiveness of converting 'reach' into actual sales, Nielsen reports 'the UK's conversion rate from browsers to buyers is also the highest in Europe so it's a safe bet that actual online spend has risen over the year'. (In the US, 88 per cent of all Internet users who have ever shopped online did so again for gifts in the holiday 2002 period according to analysts retailforward.com. Three-quarters of this same group made a purchase.) One conclusion we might draw from the presence of so many established retailers is the effectiveness of brand recognition and established retail operational excellence working in combination. The small number of established retailers who have chosen to make the investment can indeed be successful pioneers in this marketspace.

Three key issues in electronic commerce

If growth in e-commerce sales and retailer involvement has so far been slower than many commentators expected, a question remains over the extent of its future growth. Many agree that a small number of key driving forces affect the pace

Table 6.3 Driving forces affecting the development of B2C e-commerce

Area	Selected factors	Elaboration
Consumer acceptance	Ease of access	Fall in price, extent of availability of technical means and reliability of access to electronic channels
	Time poverty	Extent of perceived time poverty amongst target consumer segments and consequent attractiveness of direct channels to market
	Fashionability	Extent to which electronic channels to market become a 'fashion accessory' amongst consumers
Technological progress	Convergence/ standardization	Speed of hardware and software standardization
	Interactivity	Extent to which software developments are able to increasingly mimic or enhance conventional retail experiences
	Capacity	Speed with which improvements in bandwidth and compression technology will enhance the speed and reliability of the online experience
Competition	Non-traditional competition	Ability of new entrants to stimulate consumer demand and prompt a competitive response by conventional retailers
	Global competition	Extent to which conventional retail internationalization will further complicate choices for conventional retailers seeking growth
	Internal competition	Extent to which e-commerce investment wins out internally in competition with other ways of allocating a company's resources to achieve growth
Legislative and institutional	Free trade	Extent to which harmonization between trade regions exists in respect of electronic commerce transactions
	Infrastructure	Speed of provision of competitive infrastructure, through telecoms deregulation, strategic alliances and partnerships, etc.
	Consumer protection	Existence of uncomplicated, but trusted and effective pan-regional consumer protection legislation.

Source: Reynolds, 1999

of change in the adoption of e-commerce. Table 6.3 provides one such summary. However, as increasing evidence emerges of actual company experience as well as of revealed consumer behaviour, new insights into some features affecting the scale and character of future adoption of e-commerce are emerging that have challenged the early rhetoric. We focus on three of these below.

Consumer acceptance: buying behaviour

One of the key reasons for the high degree of retailer polarization lies in the emerging characteristics of consumer behaviour online. Despite the apparently impressive scale of e-commerce sales online reported above, the most recent comprehensive US research shows that shopping online is simply one small part of Internet user behaviour. Even experienced users spend less than 5 per cent of their time online, on average, engaging in shopping activity (UCLA, 2001). That shopping is not the 'killer application' that many had anticipated must work to reduce the size of the strategic opportunity – or threat – once perceived by many retailers. It may simply be not that big a deal and, in terms of the factors in Table 6.3, greater business benefits may come from investment in other, more conventional growth opportunities.

Nevertheless, these same experienced users spend some 13 per cent of their online time just browsing – an activity second only to sending and reading incoming email (23 per cent). An element of this browsing behaviour may be linked to shopping. A US National Retail Federation study based on some 5,000 interviews in September 2000 found that 34 per cent of store shoppers surveyed looked for or purchased something in-store that they had seen on the retailer's website. Equally, some 27 per cent of store shoppers looked for or bought something online that they had seen in the store (Shop.org, 2000).

Importantly, therefore, there is a clear role in the consumer buying process for the electronic channel and, whilst this might not be strictly e-commerce according to the definitions of statisticians, the emerging evidence is that interaction between physical and electronic marketing channels is becoming a more significant issue for an increasingly large minority of the online population in making both store and product choices. This interaction can take two forms. The rhetoric of the early days of e-commerce proposed that the greatest threat to established businesses came from the so-called *showroom effect*. It was suggested that the bricks and mortar branches of conventional retailers would become merely showrooms in which consumers would browse, freeload on the service and advice offered by store staff, before returning to their computers and ordering the identical items more cheaply online. As a result, a web presence for the established retailer would be important in order to be in a position to capture some of these sales that would otherwise be lost to online competitors. Contemporary evidence from the US (Figure 6.6) in practice shows that this is still something of a minority pursuit for consumers.

In practice, the use of the Internet to browse at the 'pre-purchase' stage prior to making a physical purchase in store seems to be an increasingly common form of consumer behaviour, with nearly a quarter of US online consumers reporting that they would 'often' behave in this way. (We have no comparable evidence from non-US markets on this form of behaviour, however.) A further 42 per cent consulted web pages 'sometimes' before making a physical purchase (UCLA, 2001). Such 'pre-purchasing' behaviour allows consumers to establish product availability,

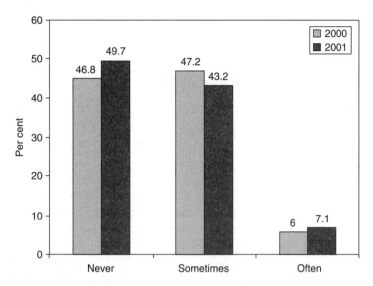

Figure 6.6 The 'showroom effect': percentage of US customers browsing in store before making a purchase online
Source: UCLA, 2001

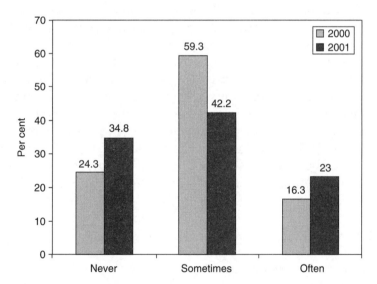

Figure 6.7 The informed consumer: percentage of US customers consulting websites before making a purchase in store
Source: UCLA, 2001

specifications and rudimentary price comparisons as well as equipping them for better-informed conversations in store (Figure 6.7). The Internet has, in practice, become just one more feature of the consumer's market research toolkit, and we might hypothesize that it will play a particularly important role in this regard in relation to products or categories of expenditure in which consumers are highly involved, or where price is important.

Consumer buying behaviour: the role of price

The apparent importance of price in the online consumer's mind-set was one of the foundation stones of early commentary on e-commerce and one that frightened many retailers. The threat was best summed up by *Business Week* columnist Robert Kuttner, writing in 1998:

> The Internet is a nearly perfect market because information is instantaneous and buyers can compare the offerings of sellers worldwide. The result is fierce price competition, dwindling product differentiation, and vanishing brand loyalty.
>
> Kuttner, 1998

Since Kuttner's observation, researchers have sought answers to many of the questions raised by his assertion (Table 6.4). In doing so, the rhetoric of the efficient market and rational economic models of price as the ultimate determinant of consumer choice online has been challenged, perhaps fatally so.

In part, this may be a consequence of crude and perhaps costly early technological interfaces and the very slow movement of some of the driving forces outlined in Table 6.3. In part, it may be a consequence of the different motivations of early adopters, which may be other than price (Degeratu *et al.*, 2000). But it may also be a consequence of consumer irrationality and uncertainty expressed in more general terms and which confound purely economic notions of consumer behaviour. In an environment of greater choice, it appears that in general terms, consumers plump for the brands they trust (Brynjolfsson and Smith, 2000), even if identical products cost less. The cheapest site does not always attract the most buyers. Evidence shows that, in certain online categories, consumers hold even smaller brand

Table 6.4 Prospective dimensions of internet market efficiency

Dimension	Research question
1. Price levels	Are the prices charged on the Internet lower?
2. Price elasticity	Are consumers more sensitive to small price changes on the Internet?
3. Menu costs	Do retailers adjust their prices more finely or more frequently on the Internet?
4. Price dispersion	Is there a smaller spread between the highest and lowest prices on the Internet?

Source: Smith *et al.*, 1999

portfolios in their heads than in conventional shopping activity (Degeratu *et al.*, 2000). The most trusted site will stand a better chance of attracting return visits and, ultimately, of becoming profitable, if it performs this role consistently and effectively.

Of course, the mechanics of and context for price-setting, as well as attitudes towards price amongst consumers, may not be inherently stable over the longer term (Bailey, 1998; Reynolds, 2001). Nevertheless, Bakos (2001) argues that whilst lower search and information costs should push markets towards a greater degree of price discrimination, the reality is that Internet technology provides a means for retailers to create differentiation for which price premiums can in practice be charged. As a result it may be that:

> The much heralded shift in market power from producer to the consumer that many associate with electronic commerce may be premature, overstated or incorrect.
>
> Bailey, 1998

Distribution and fulfilment issues

Of course, it may be easier for established brands to be trusted, but a transition for an established retail brand to an electronic channel is not always straightforward. It is no accident that many of the most profitable e-tailers have managed to avoid the pitfall of having to physically distribute goods:

> top e-tailers sell services that are almost entirely virtual – an e-ticket from Expedia, an auction platform from eBay. Once fixed costs are covered, they're cheap to run and a hefty share of incremental sales drops to the bottom line.
>
> Mullaney, 2002

We know that product-based fulfilment presents a significant obstacle to profitable business (Kämäräinen *et al.*, 2001; Department of Trade and Industry, 2001). Indeed, no other aspect of electronic commerce has been subject to more complaint by consumers than that of fulfilment. Early e-tailers neglected the distribution aspects of their businesses, to their cost. Contemporary debate centres on factors influencing consumers' attitudes to fulfilment, and the identification of an appropriate operational design to deliver sustainable competitive advantage whilst maintaining alignment with these attitudes (Table 6.5). In the grocery retailing arena for example, this has centred on the relative merits of store-based or warehouse-based picking systems alongside delivery modes ranging from timed or unattended home deliveries to collection points.

However, there is now a much better understanding of the implication of different business models for distribution costs: at least amongst retailers. Logistics and distribution costs clearly require careful evaluation and monitoring. Tollington

Table 6.5 Factors that affect home delivery options

<table>
<tr><td colspan="2" align="center">Factors related to customer behaviour</td></tr>
<tr><td>Whether customers order from many different firms or a few firms with larger product ranges</td><td>If customers order several goods at a time from a single firm with a large product range this will generate fewer trips and vehicle than ordering in individual items from nay different companies</td></tr>
<tr><td>Customer acceptance of in-full delivery</td><td>If customers are prepared to wait until their entire order is available this will reduce the number of deliveries and vehicle trips</td></tr>
<tr><td>Customer's order frequency</td><td>High order frequencies result in more trips and vehicle requirements</td></tr>
<tr><td>Whether customers only purchase part of their regular grocery needs by e-commerce and still visit a shop for the rest</td><td>Means that both car and goods vehicle trips take place</td></tr>
<tr><td>Whether customers need to view goods in person at a shop (especially true of large, expensive items)</td><td>Means that both car and goods vehicle trips take place</td></tr>
<tr><td>Whether customers use their time savings to make other trips</td><td>Net effect could be increase in van trips with no reduction in car trips</td></tr>
<tr><td colspan="2" align="center">Factors related to company strategy/operation and customer behaviour</td></tr>
<tr><td>Whether customers demand and companies offer rapid order fulfilment</td><td>The shorter the lead time between order and delivery, the greater the number of delivery trips</td></tr>
<tr><td>Whether goods are delivered to customers' homes or to local collection points which customers pick their goods up from</td><td>Local collection points would overcome problems posed by vans in residential streets, but may increase total number of vehicle trips needed to get goods to customers' homes if customers use cars to collect their goods</td></tr>
</table>

Source: Department of Trade and Industry, 2001

and Wachter (2001) observe that e-tailing is a niche market that works best when retail inventory 'throughput' is maximized, while, at the same time, favouring activity-based costing, because of the substantial fixed overhead costs incurred by retailers – by many of the major supermarket companies, for example.

But consumer perceptions of the perceived relative costs of different models of fulfilment remain remarkably stubborn. Punakivi and Saranen (2001) estimate that grocery goods e-commerce can be as much as 43 per cent cheaper than conventional store visits by consumers – if only they properly accounted for the costs of using their own car and for the value of their spare time.

Retail choices and constraints

We conclude this chapter with a discussion of the comparative experience of Screwfix.com and Tesco.com in the UK.

Case Study: The case of Screwfix Direct

Screwfix Direct was recognized as e-tailer of the year by the UK trade magazine *Retail Week* in 2002. Screwfix Direct is positioned towards the trade customer, or para-professional, segment of the home improvement market and offers 100 per cent stock availability, next day, evening and weekend delivery. Its experience, as a business acquired by retailer Kingfisher's B&Q home improvement division, demonstrates the subtle back office integration of an acquired company, building upon well-known consumer attitudes towards the category. Screwfix Direct manages over 6,000 product lines. In addition to producing four 280-page catalogues every year for a database of 2.5 million customers, the business functions increasingly online, with web-based sales accounting for 15 per cent of the £140 million total annual revenue in 2001/2, according to press reports. Sales through the web channel are growing faster than the business as a whole. It is a tightly-focused segment and the business has, according to its managing director, 'a cult following' (David, 2002). Although Screwfix Direct has just 0.5 per cent of the UK repair, maintenance and improvement market, it commands over 20 per cent of the RMI direct market, according to analysts. However, the Screwfix Direct business – ordering, fulfilment and branding – is kept separate from B&Q stores and, indeed, from the B&Q web presence, www.diy.com, although the companies share a buying office in the Far East. A full interview with John Allan, managing director of Screwfix Direct, can be found in Part III (Chapter 11) of this book.

Case Study: The case of Tesco.com

In contrast, the considerably better documented and much more broadly-based Tesco.com business (winner of the same award in 2001) infiltrates the existing store network, maximizing capacity utilization and benefiting from the sunk costs of an established infrastructure. The Tesco brand acts as the unifying feature of the Tesco service irrespective of channel and the Tesco Clubcard provides the seamless information flow from shoppers: assisting in the identification and development of detailed customer segments, which may well be multi-channel. By definition, common buying and merchandising functions service both physical and virtual channels. From this established base, the brand has been extended into a series of virtual warehouses for categories of product that are not available (and for which there is no space) in store. For the parent business, tesco.com contributes some 3 per cent of UK sales – £1 million per day – with turnover in 2001/2 at £356 million, that is some 77 per cent higher than the previous year. (For the record, this is approximately twice the penetration that e-commerce sales in the UK have at present.) Analysts estimate that the existing store network has the capacity to allow online sales to grow to between £1.4–1.5 billion before more radical solutions are required. Tesco.com has had a first-mover advantage within the grocery marketspace. It remains to be seen how its online market share (some 45 per cent of the UK online grocery market) will withstand the growth of competitive offers from Sainsbury's, Asda and Waitrose.

Summary

Whilst there may be many strides to be made in integrating the content, style and values of informational retail websites with their respective store brand images and to matching transactional services to the changing nature of consumer demand and expectations, the longer term challenge for the most dedicated retailer is to achieve some degree of overall marketing and distribution channel integration. If the lesson of this chapter is the not unreasonable assumption that e-commerce sales will be only a small proportion of the sales of most retail businesses that engage in the practice, and a higher proportion in only a few – at least in the medium term future – then *cost-effective* integration of distribution channels becomes even more important, even for those businesses with the deepest pockets. Of course, channel integration has been a major theme in e-commerce amongst retailers for some time:

> The notion that the Web is going to replace bricks and mortar
> belongs in a fantasy novel. What the Web may bring to retail is a
> more effective way to integrate distribution and marketing.
> Underhill, 2000

Whilst significant obstacles still exist to the multi-channel aspirations of store-based retailers, it would appear that selected established retailing interests both in the UK and US are winning the battle for integrated distribution channels: either through selective acquisition (as in the case of Kingfisher/Screwfix or John Lewis/Waitrose) or through the extension of their existing operational excellence (as in the case of Tesco/Tesco.com). In both countries, the recognition that retail brands already command has enabled those 'e-pioneering' established retail businesses to capture the high ground within the online consumer's 'consideration set' (Degeratu *et al.*, 2000).

Review questions

1 What are the key driving forces determining the speed of adoption of B2C electronic commerce?
2 Why might the indirect effects of electronic commerce be more significant to retailing than the direct effects?
3 What are the comparative merits of different forms of fulfilment systems?

> ## Discussion questions
>
> 1 'Price is now overtaking convenience as the key factor for consumers in deciding to shop online'. Do you agree?
> 2 How might online business build customer loyalty?
> 3 Have retailers been right to downplay the importance of electronic commerce in the long term?

References

Atkinson, R.D. (2001) *Revenge of the Disintermediated: How the Middleman is Fighting E-Commerce and Hurting Consumers*, PPI Policy Report, http://www.ppionline.org/ppi_ci.cfm?contentid=2941&knlgAreaID=140&subsecid=292

Bailey, J.P. (1998) 'Electronic commerce: prices and consumer issues for three products: Books, compact discs and software'. Internal Working Paper, OECD/GD(98)4.

Bakos, Y. (2001) 'The Emerging Landscape for Retail E-Commerce'. *Journal of Economic Perspectives*, **15**:1, Winter, p. 69.

BBC News Online (2002) 'WorldCom admits massive fraud'. http://news.bbc.co.uk/hi/english/business/newsid_2066000/2066731.stm

Brynjolfsson, E. and Smith, M.D. (2000) 'Frictionless commerce? A comparison of Internet and Conventional Retailers'. *Management Science*, April, http://ebusiness.mit.edu/papers/friction

CEC (Commission of the European Communities) (1991) 'The impact of new technology and new payment systems on commercial distribution in the European Community'. Directorate General XXIII.

CIES (2003) 'Special Report: CIES Top of Mind Survey'. *Food Business News*, January.

Cornet, P., Milcent, P. and Roussel, P.-Y. (2000) 'From e-commerce to Euro-commerce'. *The McKinsey Quarterly*, **2** Europe, pp. 30–8.

David, R. (2002) 'Company profile – Screwfix Direct – Screwfix builds sales from strong foundations'. *Retail Week*, 10th May.

Degeratu, A.M., Rangaswamy, A. and Wu, J. (2000) 'Consumer choice behaviour in online and traditional supermarkets: the effects of brand name, price and other search attributes'. *International Journal of Research in Marketing*, **17**:1, pp. 55–78.

Department of Trade and Industry (2001) @ *Your Home; New Markets for Customer Service and Delivery*, Retail Logistics Task Force. http://www.foresight.gov.uk/servlet/DocViewer/docnoredirect=2857/Retail@YourHome.pdf

IMRG (Interactive Media in Retail Group) (2002a) 'Argos and Woolworths Abandon iTV'. Press Release, 23rd January, IMRG, London.

IMRG (Interactive Media in Retail Group) (2002b) *IMRG e-Retail Sales Index Report July 2002*. IMRG, London, http://www.imrg.org/IMRGindexJuly2002.pdf

Kämäräinen, V. *et al.* (2001) 'Cost-effectiveness in the e-grocery business'. *International Journal of Retail and Distribution Management*, **29**:1, pp. 41–8.

Kaplan, P.J. (2002) *F'd Companies: Spectacular Dot.Com Flameouts*. Simon & Schuster.

Kehoe, C. (2000) 'M-commerce: Advantage Europe'. *The McKinsey Quarterly*, **2**, pp. 43–5.

KPMG Consulting (2001) 'The Quiet Revolution. A report on the state of e-business in the UK'. CBI/KPMG, London.

Kuttner, R. (1998) 'The Net: a Market Too Perfect for Profits'. *Business Week*, 11th May, No. 3577.

Malmsten, E. *et al.* (2002) *Boo Hoo: A Dot Com Story*. Arrow.

Mayer, M.D. *et al.* (2001) 'PCs vs TVs'. *The McKinsey Quarterly*, **3**.

Mesenbourg, T.L. (2001) *Measuring the Digital Economy*, US Bureau of the Census Working Paper, http://www.census.gov/eos/www/papers/umdigital.pdf

Mullaney, T.J. (2002) 'What's glowing online now'. *Business Week*, 2 September, No. 3797.

Punakivi, M. and Saranen, J. (2001) 'Identifying the success factors in e-grocery home delivery'. *International Journal of Retail and Distribution Management*, **28**:4, pp. 156–63.

Reynolds, J. (1999) 'Electronic Commerce: A discussion paper'. Prepared for *Commerce 99: Seminar on Distributive Trades in Europe*, Eurostat and Enterprise DG, Brussels 22–23 November 1999.

Reynolds, J. (2001) 'eCommerce: a critical review'. *International Journal of Retail & Distribution Management*, **28**:10, pp. 415–44.

Reynolds, J. (2002) 'E-tail marketing'. In McGoldrick, P.J. (ed.), *Retail Marketing*. McGraw-Hill, Maidenhead.

Shop.org (2000) 'The State of Retailing Online 3.0'. Boston Consulting Group for shop.org.

Shop.org (2002) 'The State of Retailing Online 5.0'. Boston Consulting Group for shop.org, www.shop.org/press/061202.html

Sinha, I. (2000) 'The Net's Real Threat to Prices and Brands'. *Harvard Business Review*, 78 (March–April), pp. 43–8.

Smith, M.D., Bailey, J. and Brynjolfsson, E. (1999) 'Understanding digital markets'. In Brynjolfsson, E. and Kahin, B. (eds), *Understanding the Digital Economy*. MIT Press, Boston, MA, USA.

Tollington, T. and Wachter, P. (2001) 'ABC/TA for Internet retail shopping'. *International Journal of Retail & Distribution Management*, **29**:4, pp. 149–55.

UCLA (2001) *Surveying the Digital Future. Year Two*. The UCLA Internet Report 2001, http://ccp.ucla.edu/pdf/UCLA-Internet-Report-2001.pdf

Underhill, P. (2000) *Why we buy: the science of shopping* (2nd edition). Texere, London/New York.

US Census Bureau (2002), *US Department of Commerce News*. CB02–74, 30th May, http://www.census.gov/eos/www/ebusiness614.htm

Williams, M. (2001) 'Measuring E-commerce – the ONS Approach'. *Economic Trends*, **568**, pp. 33–5, or http://www.statistics.gov.uk/articles/economic_trends/Measuring_E-Commerce.pdf

Chapter 7

The financial implications of retail strategy

Dmitry Dragun

In an internationalizing world, there is a growing pressure on retailers to perform. They now have direct access to the world's financial stock markets to replenish the capital necessary for continuous expansion of business. Yet they are also subject to the discipline of those same stock markets, with the relentless emphasis put on the next quarter's earnings and sales projections. Although not all retailers are as yet included in the cycle of analytical assessment, pressure to become more accountable begins to be felt by even the smallest unquoted companies. Financial performance has become the pinnacle of competitive success, a tool that can either enhance the competitive standing of a company or lead it to destruction. This more extensive chapter, the final functional chapter in Part II, reflects in its breadth and depth the contemporary emphasis placed upon effective financial management. It starts with financial model of the retail business. It then provides an illustration of retail financial statements, in order to highlight the particular financial performance characteristics of retail businesses. The next step focuses on financial performance evaluation and indicators (financial ratios). Building on ratio analysis, ways are discussed in which ratios can be built into a model suitable for assessing the company's performance in a strategic context. The balance of the chapter examines the interaction between financial performance and stock market returns. Specifically, the chapter focuses on the performance parameters that the stock market believes are important for valuing the retail sector, including sales growth, profitability and market share.

Introduction

In the US, Wal-Mart's excellent financial performance over the last 20 years has become a major competitive weapon and the company's springboard to global expansion. Conversely, Marks & Spencer's patchy financial performance, with significant deterioration of sales and profitability in 1997–2001, remains a burden even after positive changes effected in later years. Another pressure for improvement comes from a combination of the financial reporting authorities and the analysts' community. Until very recently, retailers have been content to report annual accounts in formats prescribed by national accounting standard-setting authorities. However, in the late 1990s and early 2000s more and more companies, including the medium-sized retailers with no prior record of international reporting, have sought to present their accounts in a format suitable for comparisons across national borders. In a climate of improving financial and operating transparency, financial performance serves as a crucial tool for diagnosing and improving the fundamentals of retail business.

As Chapter 5 noted, internationalization is a multi-faceted phenomenon. Strategic reasons for internationalization, changing patterns of international growth, factors of success and failure are issues requiring continual attention and awareness on the part of retail practitioners and analysts. This chapter examines financial performance – the pinnacle and ultimate goal of a successful retailer. Businesses are ultimately judged on their ability to perform financially. Domestic growth, international expansion, strategic repositioning – each and every strategic decision is punctuated by the need to generate corresponding financial returns. Understanding the drivers of financial performance, their roots and causes is a must for sound retail management.

Financial model of retail business

Figure 7.1 presents the basic financial model of retail business: a generic view on how financial performance fits the general operating processes in retailing. In reality, the picture is complicated by the presence of other groups such as credit card companies, banks and property operators and the leasing companies.

The financial cycle starts with suppliers providing merchandise at the retailers' request (Step 1 in Figure 7.1). Often, this is supplemented by goods manufactured under the retailers' own brand names. After the merchandise is received, the retailer prepares the goods for sale (Step 2), which includes assortment and format assembly, spatial arrangement of the stores, shelf space allotment by categories, and various other steps intended to ensure that merchandise is accepted by customers as goods available for sale. It is on this stage that the value in the retail business is created, and it lays the foundations of sound financial performance in retail business.

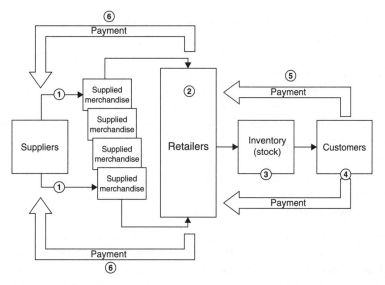

Figure 7.1 Financial model of the retail business
Source: Oxford Institute of Retail Management

Having passed the merchandise formation stage, goods now become inventory, or the products available for sale (Step 3). The impact of this stage on financial performance is 'passive' in a sense that the customer-facing trading process has not yet begun. However, this impact is nevertheless significant because essential parameters such as pricing schemes and cost formation are determined here. The next stage (Step 4) puts retailers in a direct contact with customers, both operationally and from a financial perspective. Operationally, retailers are now selling goods to consumers and collecting proceeds at the end of the process (Step 5). Financially, this generates cash proceeds and provides a basis for payment by retailers back to the suppliers (Step 6).

Although there is an appearance in Figure 7.1 that the cycle starts with suppliers and continues with retailers to reach customers in the end, it must be borne in mind that retail is a business entirely driven by customers. However successful the retailer might be from a viewpoint of supply chain management or development of pricing policies, unless customers subscribe to the company's strategy by generating enough sales (and corresponding profits), financial performance is bound to flounder. Therefore, it is also appropriate to see Figure 7.1 from a different, customer-driven angle. Specifically, starting from Step 4 and moving backwards gives a clear indication of how reliant financial performance of the retail business is on the customer base. For example, the inventory stock-outs – common in UK retailing practice – usually occur not because insufficient inventory was ordered in Step 1 but because the customer demand in Step 4 had not been assessed with sufficient precision. Resultant loss of sales and profits is a direct consequence of ineffective decisions related to customer-facing functions.

Importantly, financial performance under such conditions becomes customer-driven too. If customer tastes are not met or the target audience is misjudged, financial performance is immediately affected. For example, after acquiring Kwik Save in March 1998 Somerfield attempted to reposition a significant number of Kwik Save stores by re-branding them for up-market consumers. The efforts failed, with significant repercussions for Somerfield's operating and financial performance: Kwik Save's divisional sales plunged by 16 per cent on average, and Somerfield lost market share in 2000–01.

As retailing is an intensely cash-generative business, an important characteristic of any retail operation is ability to 'recycle' cash received from sales. This capacity is often described as the *cash conversion cycle*.

The cash conversion cycle is a result of interaction among three components:

1 **Cash tied up in inventory.** This component influences the cycle negatively, since the longer it takes the retailer to convert inventory into sales, the farther away will be the period in which cash is actually received.
2 **Cash in receivables.** This component also has a negative impact, since the proceeds not yet received from suppliers increase the overall length of collection period, thereby reducing the cash conversion cycle.
3 **Payables.** This component can have a positive influence on the cash cycle, since it represents payments that are not yet made by the company. Put differently, payables represent an offset against the earlier two components. That is why the cash conversion cycle is sometimes called the working capital cycle, or the time in days it takes the company to turn its working capital into cash.

Based on three components, Figure 7.2 develops the concept using two practical examples as illustration, one for Home Depot and the other for Carrefour. Home Depot has a significant amount of capital tied in inventory (this is dictated by nature of the business, home improvement), hence a significant number of inventory days (70) in the cash conversion cycle. The next component, cash in receivables,

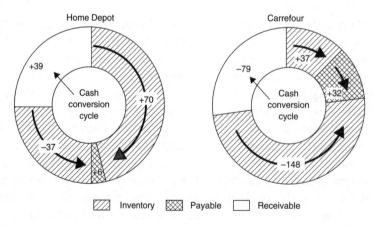

Figure 7.2 Cash conversion cycles for two retailers
Source: Oxford Institute of Retail Management, Templeton Research, Datastream

is insignificant (6 days), and reflects the fact that most of the company sales are in cash. Finally, the third component, cash in payables, to some extent offsets the combined impact of two earlier components, producing the final number for the cash conversion cycle of 39 days. Interpretation of this number is straightforward: Home Depot turns over its working capital more than nine times (365/39) during the course of a calendar year. Whether such working capital 'speed' is competitively sufficient can only be established in relation to sector peers. Lowe's, the closest such comparator, has a cash cycle of 4 days (working capital speed 91 times a year), and Courts in the UK, 73 days (five times a year).

Carrefour is the more interesting case in that its cash conversion cycle is negative (−79) implying that the cash tied up in inventory and receivables is more than offset by the payables owed by Carrefour to suppliers. Some comparators (e.g. Tesco and Ahold) also have a negative cash conversion cycle, whereas some (e.g. Kroger and Walgreen) have positive cash cycles of 7 and 26 days correspondingly.

Retail financial statements

Three financial statements form a base from which the financial performance of the retailers can be examined: the balance sheet, the profit and loss account (P&L or income statement), and the statement of cash flow. We will consider each of these statements in turn, with the financial statements of Wal-Mart being used as an example throughout the discussion.

Balance sheet

The balance sheet is a point-in-time representation of a retailer's assets (economic resources) and liabilities (claims to these resources) at some specified date, usually the end of the financial year. Table 7.1 presents a balance sheet for Wal-Mart.

Although Wal-Mart is the world's largest retailer, its balance sheet is fairly similar in structure to that of other retailers.[1] A major component of the retail balance sheet is *inventory* (stock). For Wal-Mart, it constitutes 27 per cent of the total assets, average for the sector. Another large component on the asset side is *property, plant and equipment* (PPE), which accounts for over 50 per cent of the asset base. Among

---

[1] A common problem while comparing a company's performance over time is constantly changing firm size. The companies merge, divest of assets, acquire new units and start new lines of business. All these changes affect the firm's scale of operations and, by extension, size. In order to standardize the financial statement components and hence be able to compare across companies and sectors, *common-size statements* are used. These express the components of the financial statements as percentages of total assets and sales for balance sheet and P&L account, correspondingly. They also provide useful information with regard to causality of factors affecting financial performance. For example, substantial changes in income over time may reflect the variation in costs of good sold. Common-size statements are therefore the first line of attack while considering the historical progression of retailing business. Financial statements produced in this chapter provide both the common-size and reported formats alongside.

Table 7.1 Wal-Mart, consolidated balance sheet (amounts in millions US$)

Fiscal years ended January 31	2002	2002 (common-size)	2001
Assets			
Current assets			
Cash and cash equivalents	2,161	3%	2,054
Receivables	2,000	2%	1,768
Inventories at LIFO cost	22,614	27%	21,442
Prepaid expenses and other	1,471	2%	1,291
Total current assets	28,246	34%	26, 555
Property, plant and equipment, at cost			
Land	10,241	12%	9,433
Building and improvements	28,527	34%	24,537
Fixtures and equipment	14,135	17%	12,964
Transportation equipment	1,089	1%	879
Subtotal	53,992	65%	47,813
Less accumulated depreciation	11,436		10,196
Net property, plant and equipment	42,556	51%	37,617
Property under capital lease			
Property under capital lease	4,626	6%	4,620
Less accumulated amortization	1,432		1,303
Net property under capital leases	3,194	4%	3,317
Other assets and deferred charges			
Net goodwill and other acquired intangible assets	8,595	10%	9,059
Other assets and deferred charges	860	1%	1,582
Total assets	83,451	100%	78,130
Liabilities and shareholders' equity			
Current liabilities			
Commercial paper	743	1%	2,286
Accounts payable	15,617	19%	15,092
Accrued liabilities	7,174	9%	6,355
Accrued income taxes	1,343	1%	841
Long-term debt due within one year	2,257	3%	4,234
Obligations under capital leases due within one year	148		141
Total current liabilities	27,282	33%	28,949
Long-term debt	15,687	19%	12,501
Long-term obligations under capital leases	3,045	4%	3,154
Deferred income taxes and other	1,128	1%	1,043
Minority interest	1,207	1%	1,140
Shareholders' equity			
Common stock	445	1%	447
Capital in excess of par value	1,484	2%	1,411
Retained earnings	34,441	41%	30,169
Other accumulated comprehensive income	(1,268)		(684)
Total shareholders' equity	35,102	42%	31,343
Total liabilities and shareholders' equity	83,451	100%	78,130

Source: Wal-Mart Annual Report 2001–02

other significant components *intangible assets* is perhaps the most noteworthy. In the course of international expansion, Wal-Mart has acquired a number of companies for which consideration paid had been in excess of the net asset values of the companies acquired. Such excess is recorded in balance sheet as 'Net goodwill and other acquired intangible assets', a category amounting to 10 per cent of Wal-Mart's asset base. Although such proportion is unusually high for the average retailer, intangible assets are often present on the balance sheets of many retail companies.

On the *liability* side, the balance sheet is often divided into *current liabilities* (due within a year) and *long-term liabilities,* with expiry periods extending beyond one year. The biggest current liability for Wal-Mart – as indeed for many retailers – is *accounts payable,* a component representing approximately 19 per cent of total assets. Other current liabilities include *accrued expenses* such as deferred revenue, unpaid interest and income taxes. These collectively account for 10 per cent of the assets. Among the long-term liabilities, *bank debt* and *capital lease obligations* (23 per cent jointly) are the largest categories. One of the most important liabilities on the balance sheet is *shareholder equity,* or the capital contributed by owners of the business. Usually, it consists of three components: common stock at the nominal (at par) cost (US$445 million or 1 per cent of the total assets for Wal-Mart); capital in excess of par value at a time of issuance (US$1,484 million or 2 per cent of the assets); and retained earnings (US$34,441 million or 41 per cent of assets). *Retained earnings* are undistributed profits generated and retained in business during the prior years of operation. Commonly, retained earnings are the single most important source of internal funding for retail companies. They also serve as the major indicator of the financial health of a company. Large and consistently growing retained earnings are a sign of financial health, since they provide a clear indication of the financial cushion available to a company.

Income statement (P&L) and Cash flow statement

Table 7.2 presents the income statement for Wal-Mart in both the conventional as well as common-size formats. The structure is fairly typical for a retail company. A major expense category, in proportional terms, is *cost of sales* (79%) followed by the *selling, general and administrative* (SG&A) expenses, 16 per cent. Although the exact constituents for each expense category differ among retailers, they generally include all expenses necessary for delivering merchandise to the stores, preparing it for sale and closing the transactions by collecting cash from customers. In case of Wal-Mart, SG&A expenses are comparatively low as percentage of sales, although the proportion of cost of sales is higher than the industry averages. In some measure, this is a reflection of the 'lowest possible price' strategy Wal-Mart has been pursuing: the lower retail prices generally mean the higher percentage of costs of goods sold. *Net income* represents 3 per cent of sales, a comparatively low number in relation to the retail industry as a whole.

One of the interesting features of the income statement is a number reported close to its bottom, *net income per common share* (earnings per share, or EPS). This

Table 7.2 Wal-Mart, consolidated statement of income (amounts in millions US$ except per share data)

Fiscal years ended January 31	2002	2002 (common-size)	2001
Revenues			
Net sales	**217,799**	99%	191,329
Other income-net	**2,013**	1%	1,966
	219,812	100%	193,295
Costs and expenses			
Cost of sales	**171,562**	79%	150,255
Operating, selling and general and administrative expenses	**36,173**	16%	31,550
Interest costs			
Debt	**1,052**		1,095
Capital leases	**274**		279
	209,061	95%	183,179
Income before income taxes, minority interest and cumulative effect of accounting change	**10,751**	5%	10,116
Provision for income taxes			
Current	**3,712**		3,350
Deferred	**185**		342
	3,897	2%	3,692
Income before minority interest and cumulative effect of accounting change	**6,854**	3%	6,424
Minority interest	**(183)**		(129)
Income before cumulative effect of accounting change	**6,671**		6,295
Cumulative effect of accounting change	**–**		–
Net income	**6,671**	3%	6,295
Net income per common share:			
Basic net income per common share:			
Income before cumulative effect of accounting change	**1.49**		1.41
Cumulative effect of accounting change, net of tax	**–**		–
Net income per common share	**1.49**		1.41
Average number of common shares	**4,465**		4,465

Source: Wal-Mart Annual Report 2001–02

indicator provides a link between financial performance and the stock market. Traditionally, prediction of EPS has preoccupied analysts and the investor community, and companies are often judged on their ability to 'deliver' the expected, or 'consensus' quarterly earnings. Although often criticized for their inadequacies, such as exclusion of risk and short-termism, EPS do provide a good indication of the corporate financial success or failure. For example, ability to grow EPS in line, or in excess of, sales growth is often perceived in retailing as a sign of robust financial performance and of a sound operating strategy. The reverse is equally true. For example, several quarters of the lower-than-expected earnings growth by Ahold in late 2001–early 2002 led to a US$10 billion loss of stock market value during this short time. Conversely, eBay's rapidly progressing earnings caused the stock market capitalization to increase by roughly the same amount.

The last financial statement to consider is the cash flow statement. This complements the balance sheet and profit and loss account, although its importance as a standalone analytical tool cannot be overestimated. The cash flow statement reports cash receipts and payments in the period of their occurrence, classified as operating, investing and financing activities. (In the UK, as in a number of other countries, prescribed formats of cash flow statements may differ from the one presented here.) *Operating activities* are the actions of the company in pursuit of its line of business. In retailing, this would include anything that leads to selling merchandise to customers, e.g. sourcing, format arrangement, assortment and collection of receipts. Operating activities result in cash being collected. Under normal circumstances, such 'operationally-produced' cash represents an overwhelming part of the total cash proceeds generated by the business. For Wal-Mart, the operating cash flows amount to US$10,260 million (see the cash flow statement in Table 7.3). It is quite clear that operating activities provided the bulk of overall cash generated by Wal-Mart. Any indication that the operating cash flows are proportionately insignificant should generally be taken as a sign of underlying financial weakness.

Investing activities in the cash flow statement are defined as those that result from acquisition of sales of property, plant and equipment (PPE); acquisition or sale of a subsidiary or segment; purchase or sale of investments in other firms. For Wal-Mart the largest element of investing cash flow is acquisition of PPE (US$8,383 million). The number reflects asset consequences of the relentless programme of international expansion the company has been pursuing for a number of years. The other significant component is the costs of termination of investment hedges (US$1,134 million), the appearance of which on the cash flow statement is mainly due to the recent introduction of US accounting standards with regard to financial derivatives.

Cash flows from financing activities include cash flows related to the firm's capital structure (debt and equity), including the proceeds from issuance and repurchases of equity and debt, dividends paid to shareholders in cash, principal repayments of debt and lease obligations. The main cash source of Wal-Mart's financing activities is proceeds from issuance of the long-term debt in the order of US$4,591 million.

Table 7.3 Wal-Mart, statement of cash flow (amounts in millions US$)

Fiscal years ended January 31	2002	2001
Cash flows from operating activities		
Net income	**6,671**	6,295
Adjustments to reconcile net income to net cash provided by operating activities:		
Depreciation and amortization	**3,290**	2,868
Cumulative effect of accounting change, net of tax	**–**	–
Increase in accounts receivable	**(210)**	(422)
Increase in inventories	**(1,235)**	(1,795)
Increase in accounts payable	**368**	2,061
Increase in accrued liabilities	**1,125**	11
Deferred income taxes	**185**	342
Other	**66**	244
Net cash provided by operating activities	**10,260**	9,604
Cash flows from investing activities		
Payments for property, plant and equipment	**(8,383)**	(8,042)
Investment in international operations (net of cash acquired, $195m in fiscal 2000)	**–**	(627)
Proceeds from termination of net investment hedges	**1,134**	–
Other investing activities	**103**	(45)
Net cash used in investing activities	**(7,146)**	(8,714)
Cash flows from financing activities		
Increase/(decrease) in commercial paper	**(1,533)**	(2,022)
Proceeds from issuance of long-term debt	**4,591**	3,778
Purchase of company stock	**(1,214)**	(193)
Dividends paid	**(1,249)**	(1,070)
Payment of long-term debt	**(3,519)**	(1,519)
Payment of capital lease obligations	**(167)**	(173)
Proceeds from issuance of company stock	**–**	581
Other financing activities	**113**	176
Net cash provided by (used in) financing activities	**(2,978)**	(442)
Effect of exchange rate changes on cash	**(29)**	(250)
Net increase/(decrease) in cash and cash equivalents	**107**	198
Cash and cash equivalents at beginning of year	**2,054**	1,856
Cash and cash equivalents at end of year	**2,161**	2,054

Source: Wal-Mart Annual Report 2001–02

The rest of the components are cash uses; they have negative impact on the cash flows from financing activities. Chief among them is repayment of the long-term debt (US$3,519 million) followed by the repayment of principal on the short-term commercial paper (US$1,533 million).

The resultant cash position of Wal-Mart is a combination of the initial cash position and changes in components of the cash flow during a year:

Cash and cash equivalents at beginning of year	2,054m
+ Net cash provided by operating activities	10,260m
− Net cash used in investing activities	7,146m
− Net cash provided by (used in) financing activities	2,978m
− Effect of exchange rate changes on cash	29m
= Cash and cash equivalents at end of year	2,161m

Compared to the previous financial year (31 January 2001), Wal-Mart's cash position appears to have strengthened. Cash flows from operating activities increased from US$9,604 million to US$10,260 million (+7%). The main positive features were increased accrued liabilities (cash flow impact of $1,114 = 1,125 − 11$), decreased inventories ($560 = 1,795 − 1,235$), and reduction in accounts receivable ($212 = 422 − 210$). Cash flow from investing activities has changed significantly; however this was mainly related to termination of the net investment hedges mentioned earlier; investment in PPE has in fact increased. Cash flows from financing activities were characterized by a significantly increased level of debt repayment, which was likely to be caused by the changing environment in which the falling interest rates made higher-interest debt an unnecessary burden. As a result of counterbalancing influences, the end-of-year cash position changed little, from US$2,054 million to US$2,161 million.

Analysis of cash flows, whether performed from the timeline perspective for a sample company, or on a comparative basis, is a very helpful diagnostic tool. K-Mart, in bankruptcy since January 2002, developed signs of cash flow weakness well before that date. In the financial year 1999, the company reported operating cash of US$1,084 million of which net income contribution was US$633 million. A year later the operating cash flows, although seemingly healthy at US$1,114 million had nevertheless indicated significant profitability problems: negative net profit of US$244 million and restructuring charges of US$728 million were reported. Also in that year, capital expenditures remained broadly the same, even though it was becoming clear that deteriorating profitability might not support the usual pace of business expansion. In the latest financial year 2001–02 (in which the company was *de facto* bankrupt although not formally so), the cash flow statement registered continuing profit erosion (net loss of US$2,587), increasing reliance on debt funding (proceeds from issuance of debt increased from US$400 million to US$1,824 million), and growing restructuring and impairment charges (US$1,262 million). Taken together, the early warning signs alerted the analyst community to the possibility of bankruptcy in 2001–02 and reduced K-Mart's stock market value by US$6 billion in the short period from September 2001 to September 2002.

Whether such deterioration could be interpreted as leading towards financial distress or bankruptcy is a topic covered in the next section, which deals with financial performance evaluation.

,formance evaluation

, f financial performance usually starts with analysis of financial ratios. /stem' of financial performance comprises metrics designed to convey ehensive picture of financial performance. (Analysts use financial ratios .inancial numbers in isolation are not especially informative.) This ratio syste. is often referred to as the *DuPont model*, after the company that pioneered the concept. In focusing upon those ratios of most use to retailers, we first describe the main groups of financial ratios, which then leads us to consider the basic and extended DuPont systems. (Throughout, the annual report of Tesco for the financial year 2001–02 is used to illustrate calculations; excerpts are provided in Table 7.4.)

In retail practice, four groups of financial ratios are utilized:

- Internal liquidity ratios
- Profitability ratios

Table 7.4 Tesco, excerpts from financial statements (amounts in £ millions)

Fiscal years ended February 24	2002	2001	Source
1. Sales	23,653	20,988	P&L
2. Cost of sales (cost of goods sold)	21,866	19,400	P&L
3. Administrative expenses	465	422	P&L
4. Operating profit (1-2-3)	1,322	1,166	P&L
5. Total tax charge	371	288	P&L
6. Tax rate (5/4 × 100)	28.1%	24.7%	P&L
7. Earned for ordinary (net profit)	830	767	P&L
8. Interest expense	202	168	P&L
9. Earnings before interest and taxes (EBIT)	1,403	1,222	P&L
10. Cash and equivalents	670	534	Balance sheet
11. Total equity (shareholder capital and reserves)	5,530	5,014*	Balance sheet
12. Current assets	2,053	1,694	Balance sheet
13. Total assets	13,556	11,732	Balance sheet
14. Current liabilities	4,809	4,389	Balance sheet
15. Accounts receivable (trade)	1,830	1,538	Balance sheet
16. Long-term debt (>1year)	2,741	1,925	Balance sheet
17. Total interest-bearing debt	4,230	3,338	Balance sheet
18. Total long-term capital (11 + 16)	8,271	6,939	Balance sheet
19. Cash flow from operations	2,053	1,937	Cash flow statement
20. Capital expenditures	1,835	1,910	Cash flow statement
21. Principal repayments	24	46	Cash flow statement
22. Dividends paid	297	254	Cash flow statement

* restated
Source: Tesco Annual Report 2001–02

- Financial leverage ratios
- Earnings coverage ratios.

Internal liquidity ratios

The ratios from this group measure the ability of the firm to sustain current and meet future obligations. Internal liquidity ratios usually compare the short-term assets such as cash and marketable securities with the near-term financial obligations such as accounts payable.

(a) Current ratio. One of the best-known metrics of liquidity, the current ratio addresses the question of whether short-term company resources (assets) are sufficient enough to meet corresponding liabilities.

$$\text{Current ratio} = \frac{\text{Current assets}}{\text{Current liabilites}}$$

For Tesco, the current ratio for 2002 is 0.43 (2,053m/4,809m).

(b) Quick ratio. Some analysts believe that total current assets should not be considered when gauging the ability of a firm to meet its near-term financial obligations, because inventories and some other assets included in current assets (e.g. accounts receivable and prepaid expenses) are not liquid enough to fit the definition. The measure reflecting such considerations is called the quick ratio.

$$\text{Quick ratio} = \frac{\text{Cash and equivalents} + \text{Accounts receivable}}{\text{Current liabilites}}$$

For Tesco, the quick ratio is 0.52 (670m + 1,830m)/4,809m.

(c) Cash ratio. This is the most conservative ratio, in that it only treats cash and equivalents as suitably liquid assets.

$$\text{Cash ratio} = \frac{\text{Cash and equivalents}}{\text{Current liabilites}}$$

Tesco's cash ratio is 0.14, calculated as 670m/4,809m.

(d) Cash flow from operations ratio. Sometimes, in order to overcome limitations of the previous three ratios, liquidity is assessed by comparing the actual cash flows from operations to current liabilities. The resultant ratio is called the cash flow from operations ratio.

$$\text{Cash flow from operations ratio} = \frac{\text{Cash flow from operations}}{\text{Current liabilites}}$$

For Tesco, this ratio is equal to 0.43 (2,053m/4,809m).

(e) Defensive interval. This measure compares the most liquid sources of liquidity (cash and equivalents and accounts receivable) with projected operating expenditures.

Although definitions of projected expenditures vary, these usually include cost of goods sold and administrative (or other) expenses necessary for continuation of the business.

$$\text{Defensive interval} = 365 \times \frac{\text{Cash and equivalents} + \text{Accounts receivable}}{\text{Projected expenditures}}$$

The defensive interval is usually interpreted as a 'worst-case' scenario indicating the number of days that the firm could sustain the current level of operations with the present cash resources *assuming* that there are no additional revenues. For Tesco, it is assumed that projected expenditures include cost of sales and administrative expenses. The defensive ratio is then equal to $365 \times (670m + 1,830m)/(21,866m + 465m)$ or 24 days.

Profitability ratios

Metrics from this group are designed to gauge the ability of the firm to achieve, sustain and increase profits. Profitability can be measured along a number of dimensions. First, there is a relationship between profits and sales (margin ratios). Secondly, profits are related to capital, or investment necessary to generate them (so-called return ratios). The ratios below reflect each dimension in turn.

Margin ratios
(a) Gross margin. This ratio is a 'top-level' indicator of margin sufficiency.

$$\text{Gross margin} = \frac{\text{Gross profit}}{\text{Sales}}$$

For Tesco, gross margin as a percentage of sales is 7.5 per cent, calculated as: $((23,653 - 21,866)/23,653)$.
(b) Operating profit margin. This ratio reveals the profitability of the retailer's 'core' business, excluding the combined effect of investments (income from affiliates), financing costs (interest rate expense) and tax position.

$$\text{Operating profit margin} = \frac{\text{Operating profit}}{\text{Sales}}$$

Tesco's operating profit margin is 5.6 per cent $(1,322m/23,653m)$.
(c) Net profit margin. Useful for comparisons across a broad range of companies, this ratio relates net profit to sales. As such, it represents the 'bottom-line' profitability of the retail business.

$$\text{Net profit margin} = \frac{\text{Net profit}}{\text{Sales}}$$

For Tesco, net profit margin is 3.5 per cent $(830m/23,653m)$.

Return ratios

(a) Return on assets (ROA). As a broad measure of profitability, return on assets measures the management's efficiency in utilizing assets for profit generation. Usually, ROA is computed on a pre-tax basis using earnings before interest and taxes (EBIT). The resultant return measure is unaffected by different capital structures (debt-equity) and tax positions across firms.

$$\text{ROA} = \frac{\text{EBIT}}{\text{Average total assets}}$$

Tesco's ROA is equal to 11.1 per cent, calculated as: $1,403\text{m}/(13,556\text{m} + 11,732\text{m})/2$.

(b) Return on invested capital (ROIC). This metric provides a return characteristic similar to ROA, but on the basis of invested capital, which is different from the total assets used in ROA calculations.

$$\text{Return on invested capital} = \frac{\text{EBIT} (1 - \text{Tax rate})}{\text{Interest-bearing debt} + \text{Equity}}$$

The numerator of this ratio is after-tax earnings the company would report if there were no debt in its capital structure. The denominator represents the sources of capital on which return must be earned. Therefore, ROIC is the rate of return earned on the total capital invested in the business regardless of whether this capital was represented by debt or equity.

Tesco's ROIC, on the basis of information provided in Table 7.1, equals 4 per cent.

(c) Return on equity (ROE). This measures returns accruing to the residual claimants – common shareholders. If equity capital contains preferred shares, the preferred dividends are excluded from the net income in the numerator.

$$\text{ROE} = \frac{\text{Net profit} - \text{Preferred dividends}}{\text{Average shareholders equity}}$$

Tesco does not have preferred shares in its capital structure; its ROE is 7.6 per cent.

Financial leverage ratios

From the shareholder viewpoint, leverage represents a trade-off between risk and return. The greater the leverage (proportion of debt in the capital structure), the larger are the potential returns accruing to stockholders. This occurs because debt is a fixed obligation; for as long as the company honours its debt, all remaining extra profits accrue to the shareholders. However, such profit enhancement potential of leverage comes with higher risk attached. In an unfavourable business climate where the company's ability to sustain the level of profits is curtailed, increased leverage implies greater risk because debt obligations are fixed irrespective of operating environment. Leverage ratios serve to capture the extent to which a company is exposed to fixed funding costs. Table 7.5 provides a brief description of the most common leverage ratios, with the appropriate values for Tesco computed as an illustration.

Table 7.5 Financial leverage ratios

Ratio	Description	Formula	Value for Tesco 2002
Gross leverage	Indicates size of the asset cover from which accumulated debt is serviced	$\dfrac{\text{Total assets}}{\text{Total debt}}$	3.20
Debt-equity	Provides a gauge of size of equity cover in relation to accumulated debt	$\dfrac{\text{Long-term debt}}{\text{Total equity}}$	0.49
Long-term debt-total capital	Specifies the size of long-term debt versus the size of total long-term capital, including equity	$\dfrac{\text{Long-term debt}}{\text{Total long-term capital}}$	0.33

Source: Oxford Institute of Retail Management, Templeton Research, Tesco Annual Report, 2001–02

Earnings coverage ratios

In addition to the measures described earlier, investors and analysts often use metrics called 'earnings coverage' ratios. In essence, earnings coverage ratios evaluate the *flow* of earnings available to service the debt and lease obligations. In contrast to the 'point-in-time' ratios such as quick or gross leverage, earnings coverage ratios assess financial performance on a continuous basis as the financial reporting frequency allows. Table 7.6 describes three most common indicators.

Limitations of ratio analysis

Despite having an important role to play in strategic performance management, ratio analysis has certain limitations. First, the ratios described earlier are only suitable as a top-level analytical tool of financial management. Deeper understanding of the underlying business must rely on thorough appreciation of retail fundamentals and realities, supplemented by analysis of competitive environment and interaction of the interested parties ('stakeholders'). Further, ratio analysis is meaningful only if applied in time-series or cross-company contexts. For example, a value of the interest coverage ratio for Tesco (6.94) computed in Table 7.6 using the figures provided in Table 7.3, is not by itself informative or particularly useful unless put in a comparative context in relation to other retailers, or compared across time. Finally, ratio analysis ignores the different levels of operating and financial risk among the companies. If retailer 'A' has higher ratios, but also has a higher aggregate risk profile than retailer 'B' (e.g. more highly leveraged, has

Table 7.6 Earnings coverage ratios

Ratio	Description	Formula	Value for Tesco
Interest coverage	Indicates if the earnings are sufficient to cover the interest expense outlays	EBIT ÷ Interest expense	6.94
Times debt burden covered	Estimates the burden the company carries in *both* servicing and repaying debt	EBIT ÷ (Interest expense + Principal repayments*)	5.96
Times common covered	Determines if the earnings are adequate to cover the costs of all external sources of funding, including both debt and equity	EBIT ÷ (Interest expense + Principal repayments* + Common dividends*)	2.16

* Principal repayments and common dividends on a before-tax basis. Calculation: Principal repayments on the before-tax basis = Principal repayments on an after-tax basis/(1 − Tax rate). Common dividends on a before-tax basis = Common dividends on an after-tax basis/(1 − Tax rate)
Source: Oxford Institute of Retail Management, Templeton Research, Tesco Annual Report, 2001–02

greater exposure internationally, or pursues uncertain diversification strategies), these comparatively higher ratios will be misleading. On the contrary, retailer 'B' may have a relatively low risk profile even though its ratios are lower. The balance between the operating characteristics of a company and its risk profile is one of the most important considerations in the analysis of interaction between financial performance of retailers and their stock market valuation.

An integrated analysis using ratios

In order to overcome some of the limitations of ratio analysis, the DuPont model of financial performance is used. The DuPont model decomposes financial performance into easily accessible and highly informative performance factors. There are two variants of the model. The first ('basic') presents return on equity, ROE, as the product of three components: profit margin, asset turnover and gross leverage. The second, 'extended' model is a more detailed five-factor framework that provides additional insights into effects of financial leverage and tax position on the firm's financial performance. Both models are presented in Table 7.7.

Table 7.7 DuPont model

Model	Descriptive formula
DuPont basic	$\text{ROE} = \underbrace{\dfrac{\text{Net Profit}}{\text{Sales}}}_{\text{NET PROFIT MARGIN}} \times \underbrace{\dfrac{\text{Sales}}{\text{Total Assets}}}_{\text{TOTAL ASSET TURNOVER}} \times \underbrace{\dfrac{\text{Total Assets}}{\text{Equity}}}_{\text{GROSS LEVERAGE}}$
DuPont extended	$\text{ROE} = \left(\underbrace{\dfrac{\text{EBIT}}{\text{Sales}}}_{\text{OPERATING PROFIT MARGIN}} \times \underbrace{\dfrac{\text{Sales}}{\text{Total Assets}}}_{\text{TOTAL ASSET TURNOVER}} - \underbrace{\dfrac{\text{InterestPaid}}{\text{Total Assets}}}_{\text{INTEREST EXPENSE RATE}} \right)$
	$\times \underbrace{\dfrac{\text{Total Assets}}{\text{Equity}}}_{\text{GROSS LEVERAGE}} \times \underbrace{\left(1 - \dfrac{\text{Tax Paid}}{\text{EBT}} \right)}_{\text{TAX RETENTION RATE}}$

Table 7.8 Components of the extended DuPont Model for Carrefour, 1992–2001

Component	1992	1993	1994	1995	1996	1997	1998	1999	2000	2001
Operating profit margin	0.87%	1.19%	1.58%	1.84%	2.34%	2.92%	3.19%	3.45%	3.70%	3.54%
Total asset turnover	2.26	2.32	2.32	2.26	2.05	1.97	1.59	1.12	1.50	1.63
Interest expense rate	1.11%	0.97%	0.72%	0.50%	0.50%	0.48%	0.86%	1.39%	2.01%	1.54%
Gross leverage	5.50	4.45	4.54	4.14	3.97	4.17	4.40	5.28	5.67	6.09
Tax retention rate	71.0%	78.7%	71.0%	73.0%	68.0%	65.3%	65.4%	61.7%	61.6%	67.7%
ROE	3.3%	6.3%	9.5%	11.1%	11.6%	14.3%	12.1%	8.0%	12.4%	17.5%

Source: Oxford Institute of Retail Management, Templeton Research, Carrefour Annual Reports, 1992–2001

To illustrate how DuPont model is used for evaluating financial performance strategically, Table 7.8 provides components of the extended DuPont model for Carrefour during a ten-year period 1992–2001.

Figure 7.3 illustrates some of the implications of the data in Table 7.8. Figure 7.3(a) shows the progression of ROE during the study period. This is accompanied by the corresponding time series in Figure 7.3(b) showing the changes in two of the explanatory components, *gross leverage* and *total asset turnover*. During the ten-year period, Carrefour's ROE increased significantly, from 3.3 per cent in 1991 to 17.5 per cent in 2001. This increase, however, was not uniform: ROE suffered substantial decline during 1998–99 (from 12.1 to 8 per cent), followed by recovery in the subsequent years. As operating profit margins kept rising at a steady pace (Figure 7.3(a)), what other factors could explain the ROE fluctuations experienced by Carrefour in 1998–99?

Figure 7.3(b) provides the answer. During the short interval of 1998–99, Carrefour commenced a wide-ranging expansion programme, which culminated in acquisitions of Comptoirs Modernes in October 1998 and Promodès, in August 1999. The company also scaled up its presence in a number of strategically important

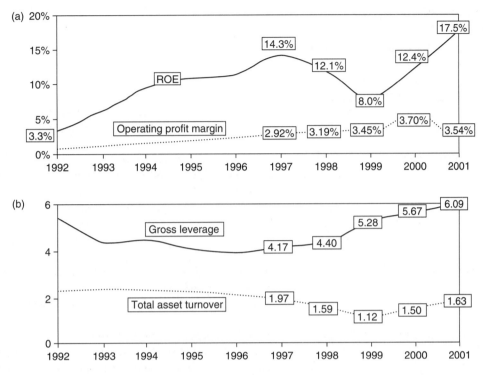

Figure 7.3 Components of the extended DuPont model for Carrefour, 1992–2001

emerging markets of Central Europe and Latin America. To finance the growth effort, Carrefour had to borrow massively, thereby increasing financial leverage. An immediate impact on ROE was positive, according to the formula for the DuPont extended model. (Growing debt causes the proportion of equity in the total amount of debt and equity to decline, hence the enlarged proportion of company's profits accrue to a smaller equity base, boosting ROE.) However, this positive impact was more than offset by negative effect inflicted by declining asset turnover. This happened because the consolidated company, although having increased the asset base, had not yet realized commensurate returns. Post-merger integration usually requires some time to execute; Carrefour's acquisitions were no exception. An auxiliary sensitivity analysis shows that if Carrefour's leverage remained the same in 1999 as it was in 1998 (4.4), ROE would have declined further to 6.7 per cent. As the other factors in the model (operating profit margin, interest expense rate and tax retention rate) did not change significantly during 1998–99, the interaction between total asset turnover and gross leverage determined the overall dynamic of ROE.

As Carrefour's example demonstrates, both the basic and extended DuPont models allow for meaningful analysis of various factors underpinning financial performance. From the managerial perspective, these models could be used to pinpoint the exact causes of changes in return on equity. Table 7.9 summarizes

Table 7.9 DuPont model actions

Components of the DuPont model	Expression	Actions
Operating profit margin	$\dfrac{\text{EBIT}}{\text{Sales}}$	Augment operating profit as percentage of sales by leveraging the store portfolio, sustaining and enhancing format profitability, and streamlining supply chains and store delivery systems
Total asset turnover	$\dfrac{\text{Sales}}{\text{Total assets}}$	Increase asset productivity by reducing fixed asset base (land, buildings, equipment and fixtures) and optimizing the working capital requirements (inventory, receivables, prepaid expenses and payables)
Interest expense rate	$\dfrac{\text{Interest paid}}{\text{Total assets}}$	Minimize the interest paid in relation to asset base by borrowing at appropriate times and by leasing instead of borrowing
Leverage	$\dfrac{\text{Total assets}}{\text{Equity}}$	Achieve a level of debt in the capital structure which would allow efficient use of interest tax shields without causing financial distress or excessive servicing requirements
Tax retention rate	$\dfrac{\text{Tax paid}}{\text{EBT}}$	Minimize corporate taxes in relation to operating income by utilizing the permitted tax allowances and using tax offsets among national jurisdictions if allowed

the actions that might be required to enhance each of the components of financial performance, according to the DuPont model.

Notice that the managerial actions described in Table 7.9 are forward-looking in nature even though the ratio analysis itself is based on historical data. This illustrates the dilemma that retail practitioners face. On the one hand, all the financial information is historical, and hence is not particularly relevant for a fast-changing, constantly evolving business environment. The only constant present in formulation and implementation of retail strategies is uncertainty. It is uncertainty that eventually leads to acceptance of the strategy as a distinctive competitive advantage and a driver of financial performance in retailing. On the other hand, historical financial performance conveys useful information and forms a basis for sustainable business development. Also, it is often argued that historical results are the best predictor of the future, since they constitute the only reliable dataset readily available for decision-making.

The job of reconciling the rear-mirror view – as portrayed by historical data – with the forward-looking picture – as represented by the changing business environment – is often left to the stock market. In the context of efficiently functioning stock markets, the financial performance of each quoted company is continuously scrutinized, benchmarked and valued. The resultant stock market valuations combine historical data with the expectations of future returns. The modes and outcomes of interaction between retailers and financial markets are often complex, uncertain and multi-directional. In the next section, we consider some of the elements of such interaction.

Financial performance and the stockmarket

Valuation factors

The assessment of an individual retail company by the stock market is a multi-stage continuous process (Figure 7.4). As the starting point, the *retail business environment* is assessed. This includes an evaluation of the macroeconomic climate (current and projected growth in GDP, consumer and manufacturing confidence, expected inflation and industry fundamentals). At the next stage, the *strategy* pursued by a retailer is evaluated. Various parameters of the strategy, such as brand positioning, store portfolio development and intended versus actual growth are assessed.

The subsequent stage, *sales growth*, is particularly significant in retailing. Given the relative scarcity of other sources to enhance financial returns, expanding sales is the singular most important driver of financial performance in retailing. A manufacturing company, for example, may use its product research and development (R&D) base to augment sales and profits via a range of new products. There is

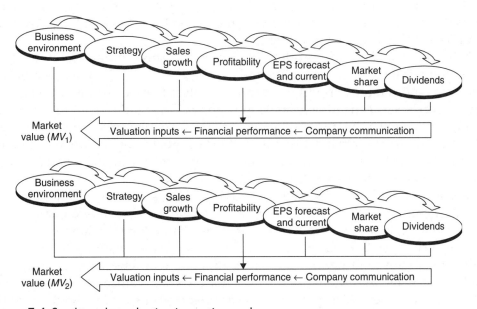

Figure 7.4 Stock market valuation in continuous loop

no product *per se* to develop in retailing, and gains to be potentially reaped from innovation come mainly via more skilful (and thus more incremental) changes in the composition of stores, formats and merchandise. As a result, analysts tend to pay more attention to sales growth in the retail sector.

Profitability follows sales growth as a factor of importance. Operating and net profit margins complement the sales figures analytically, by giving additional insights into the nature of sales growth. In the financial community, there is a firm belief that successful retail businesses grow both 'top line' (sales) and 'bottom line' (profits).

As we have suggested, both *forecast and current earnings per share* (EPS) provide the first visible link between financial returns achieved by the company and the stock market valuation of these returns. Commonly, EPS is interpreted as a simple measure of the company's 'fundamental' earning power. EPS is perceived as 'fundamental' because its shows the ultimate ability of the management to deliver returns per unit of shareholder stock, irrespective of other factors such as size, strategy, and business models. Thus, EPS may serve as a uniform gauge of financial performance across companies and sectors. Growing EPS is interpreted as a sign of sound financial performance. Conversely, slowing or declining EPS is often seen as a warning signal.

Market share, although not an immediate concern addressed in course of a stock market assessment, could nevertheless have significant repercussions on valuations. In the UK, the declining market share of Sainsbury's during 1997–2000 led to a profound *de-rating* (lowering of the stock market valuation) of the company. Generally, market share trends are essential in assessing financial performance of smaller-size or niche retailers. This is so because for such retail operators each basis point of market share lost to the larger rivals is much more intimately linked to the survival of the business. For the bigger retailers, on the other hand, market share gain is proportionately less important.

The final factor, *dividends*, is often considered a permanent feature of retail financial performance. Being in an intensely cash-generative business, retailers are usually in a position to support dividend payouts ratios exceeding those of some other sectors such as manufacturing and services. Dividend payout ratios are not uniform across the industry however; they vary by country and format affiliation. In the US and the UK, retail dividends tend to be higher than in Europe and Japan. Discount operators such as Wal-Mart and K-Mart have traditionally had dividend payouts lower than those for department store retailers.

After factors in Figure 7.4 have been assessed ('discounted', in the language of analyst community), the evaluation process culminates in market value MV_1. This is depicted in the figure by a straight arrow. Valuation is an iterative process, and the cycle repeats itself to arrive at MV_2, the market value of the company in the next assessment period. Such a continuous loop ensures that all quoted retailers are subjected to on-going evaluation. Market values estimated at each cycle of the loop represent point-in-time approximations that integrate both the historical information and forward-looking assessment of business potential. The system is never stationary: continuous input, combined with diversity of analysts' opinions, ensures that the stock market attitude towards the company is always in flux. Hence, as noted above, the interaction between financial performance and the stock market valuation is essentially dynamic, non-linear and uncertain.

Stock market metrics

We noted that ratio analysis, although a useful tool of financial assessment, has a number of limitations such as the exclusion of risk from consideration and an essentially historical orientation. In trying to overcome the limitations of ratio analysis, the stock market uses a number of other metrics described below.

(a) *Price-earnings (pe) ratio.* One of the most widely used indicators of relative valuation, the *pe* ratio is a simple quotient of current share price over current earnings per share. Figure 7.5 provides an illustration of the *pe* ratios for the leading European retailers. As can be seen from the chart, the ratios vary widely. Carrefour commanded a ratio of nearly 50 in December 1999 whereas Ahold has recently posted a value of only 9.3.

Although the *pe* ratio is a simple and convenient tool of comparative valuation, it also has significant limitations. One such limitation concerns risk. Specifically, by its very composition, the ratio does not provide 'risk equalization' across the companies compared. In other words, the higher ratio for Carrefour in comparison with Ahold may be interpreted as a higher stock market award for better financial performance on part of Carrefour. However, the higher *pe* value for Carrefour may also reflect a lower risk attached to the company shares by comparison with Ahold's. The composition of the *pe* ratio (in part attributed to financial performance and in part to different levels of risk) can never be established with precision. This seriously limits applicability of

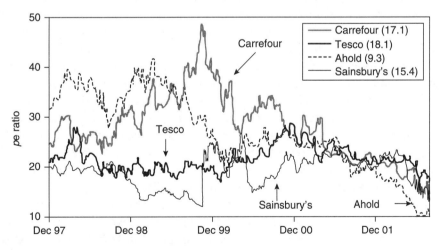

Figure 7.5 *pe* ratios of the leading European retailers
Note: The ending values as at 8 September 2002.
Source: Bloomberg, Datastream

pe ratio as a valuation tool beyond quick, rule-of-a-thumb applications. Another, often overlooked, limitation of the *pe* ratio lies in its definition. The ratio can be computed using either the past period earnings in denominator or the earnings projected for the next period. The method preferred by the analyst community is to use the latter as it is believed that the next period earnings are forward-looking and thus have better informational content. However, this opens the door for subjectivity, dubious inter-pretations and inflated valuations, especially since the next period earnings tend to be 'revised' by the analysts on a regular basis. Under such conditions, no amount of analyt-ical effort will ever be enough to establish the true, or 'intrinsic' value of the company because it will always remain a product of revised estimates, not factual data.

(b) The *price-to-book* (PB) ratio is also a tool of relative valuation, computed by dividing the current share price by the book (balance sheet) value of the common equity. The ratio has received considerable attention since Fama and French (1992) found it to be a good predictor of future returns. In a practical context, the measure is usually used to estimate how valuable the intangible element of company value is. A PB value close to 1 is regarded as a sign of weak valuation and low productivity of intangible assets such as brand, market position, and innovation. A PB value well in excess of 1 is usually considered a positive signal implying profitable utilization of the company's intangibles. There is no consensus, however, as to the optimal range of PB values. Is a PB value of 3 too low in light of the company's dominant position in a particular market? For another company, is PB value of 12 too high considering the declining sales momentum, hence implying over-valuation of the company shares? The definitive answer has yet to emerge, hence the price-to-book ratio should be used cautiously as a supplement to other valuation metrics.

(c) *Dividend yield*. We suggested that the dividend payout is one of several factors con-sidered by the stock market in assigning values to companies. We also noted that regular dividend payouts are long accepted by investors as a permanent feature of retail business. Dividend yield, on the other hand, is a variable metric expressing the dividends paid per share as proportion of share price. Wide variation in dividend yield is a common feature, and short-term fluctuations are usually not considered particularly meaningful. However, under some conditions, such as in a period of falling valuations and with the uncertain earnings projections of the general stock market observed in 2000–02, dividend yield does become important. This happens because as share price appreciation is limited or non-existent, dividend payouts provide the lion's share of total income from the stocks (share price appreciation + dividends). Table 7.10 reports the current dividend yields for a number of retailers.

As the dividend payouts remain very stable in absolute terms, it is useful to remem-ber that the dividend yields are often a mirror reflection of the share price. They also reflect the stock market valuation of a particular retailer relative to its peers. For example, dividend yields for Wal-Mart and H&M are the lowest (see Table 7.10). How-ever, this is not because these companies do not pay sufficient dividends. Instead, the explanation lies in relative valuation: Wal-Mart's and H&M's *pe* ratios are the highest in the group. Dividends paid per share are compared against relatively higher share prices; hence the lower dividend yields for Wal-Mart and H&M.

Table 7.10 Retail dividend yields

Company	Country	Dividend yield, %	pe ratio
Ahold	The Netherlands	4.5	9.3
Carrefour	France	2.0	17.1
Delhaize	Belgium	5.1	18.8
Hennes and Mauritz	Sweden	1.0	37.0
Metro	Germany	4.4	10.0
Tesco	UK	2.9	18.1
Wal-Mart	US	0.6	32.0

Note: Values as at 8 September 2002
Source: Datastream

Value metrics

Dissatisfaction with the limitations of ratio analysis and stock market metrics has led to the emergence of a relatively new class of measures called *value metrics*. The idea behind a value metric is simple and powerful: value is only created if the company generates return on capital exceeding the cost of that capital. A publicly quoted retailer usually has two sources of capital in its disposal: debt and equity. Each of the sources has its cost. For debt, the cost is interest expense required to serve the debt. For equity, the cost is the rate of return on common stock expected by the shareholders. Cost of debt is easier to deal with, since the cost of the debt capital is simply the interest rate fixed in the indenture (debt finance agreement). The cost of equity capital is harder to establish because it depends on the uncertain factors such as overall stock market risk, return expectations and the risk-free rate of return available to investors. The model most widely used to assess the equity cost of capital for an individual company is capital asset pricing model or CAPM in short (see Brealy and Myers, 2002 for details). CAPM defines the cost of equity capital as

$$r_e = r_f + \beta \times (r_m - r_f)$$

where r_e is a cost of equity capital (expected return on the common equity), r_f is the risk-free interest rate, β is the sensitivity (covariance) of the company's stock price to movements of the general stock market, r_m is the observed stock market return. In essence, the cost of equity capital is a sum of two components: risk-free interest rate (r_f) and premium for holding the risky stock $\beta \times (r_m - r_f)$. In this later expression, ($r_m - r_f$) represents the equity risk premium (ERP), or extra return on equity investors demand comparatively to safer instruments such as government bonds.

After having established the cost of debt and equity capital for a company, the weighted average cost of capital (WACC) is computed as the weighted average of the two, with the proportions of the debt-equity capital used as weights. For example, if a company's cost of debt and equity capital is 5 per cent and 8 per cent respectively and the capital structure is 40 per cent debt financed, WACC will be calculated as follows:

$$0.4 \times 5\% + (1 - 0.4) \times 8\% = 6.8\%$$

In contrast to standard indicators of returns such as ROA or ROE, value metrics explicitly recognize the cost of equity capital by adding a charge on the capital employed to the total cost of running business. Traditionally, such adjustment is never reflected in the financial statements, as accounting rules prevent putting on balance sheet the assets and liabilities whose values cannot be measured precisely. Such calculations nevertheless could lead to a concept of *economic profit*, or all-inclusive costs of running a business.

The most widely used measure of economic value is *economic value added* (EVA), patented and propagated by Stern & Stewart Co. EVA is calculated according to the following formula:

$$\text{EVA} = \text{Net operating profit after taxes} - \text{WACC} \times \text{Capital}$$

The equation presents EVA as a difference between net operating profit after taxes (NOPAT) and the capital charge as described earlier. In practice, there are also a number of accounting adjustments made to convert the numbers as reported in financial statements to their 'economic' equivalents. For illustration purposes, Table 7.11 presents simplified EVA calculations for Home Depot in the financial year ended on 3 February 2002 (for more detailed explanations see Ehrbar, 1998).

EVA as computed in Table 7.11 is significantly lower than the net income reported by Home Depot in the financial year 2001–02 (US$3,044 million). The comparison illustrates that economic profit measures such as EVA are unforgiving performance indicators. By explicitly incorporating the cost of equity capital into a cost base via accretion of capital charge, EVA sets a high performance hurdle for any company. Taking a step further with the Home Depot example, we may also calculate an economic profit return, by relating the economic profit, or EVA, to the capital base that generated this profit: 961m/19,337m = 5 per cent. Comparing this number with the average cost of capital of 10.4 per cent makes it immediately clear that the company destroyed value, *even though* it reported significant accounting profit. The example demonstrates a general principle used in construction of the value metrics: if the economic profit return is lower than the cost of capital, value is destroyed; if the opposite happens, value is added.

The *market value added* (MVA) metric is also a measure of value creation. However, in contrast to EVA, MVA is a purely stock market-based measure. MVA is calculated as a difference between the market capitalization of the equity and the capital employed in business. For Home Depot, MVA was US$96.1 billion as at 3 February 2002 (market capitalization of $115,437 million minus $19,337 million of capital employed). Rather than looking at the absolute value of MVA (which is highly positive in case of Home Depot), *changes* in MVA are usually measured to see if stock

Table 7.11 Calculation of EVA for Home Depot

Component	Amount	Calculation/source of information
1. Operating profit before taxes	4,901	Income statement
2. Income tax expense	1,913	Income statement
3. Decrease in deferred taxes	6	Balance sheet
4. Tax benefit from interest expense	10	Interest expense (US$28m) × Marginal tax rate (35%). Income statement
5. NOPAT	2,972	Item 1 − Item2 − Item 3 − Item 4
6. Capital	19,337	Total capital invested in business (interest-bearing debt 1,255m + equity 18,082m). Balance sheet
7. Debt-to-equity ratio	6.9%	Interest-bearing debt/Equity (1,255m/18,082m). Balance sheet
8. Cost of debt	5.9%	Footnote information
9. Cost of equity	10.7%	CAPM was used; equity risk premium assumed 5%. $r_e = r_f + \beta \times \text{ERP} = 4.9\% + 1.15 \times 5\% = 10.7\%$
10. WACC	10.4%	Weighted cost of debt and equity capital: $5.9\% \times 0.069 + 10.7\% \times (1 - 0.069) = 10.4\%$
11. Capital charge	2,011	Item 6 × Item 10
12. EVA	961	Item 5−Item 11

Note: Amounts in millions US$. Fiscal year ended 3 February 2002
Source: Oxford Institute of Retail Management, Templeton Research, Home Depot Annual Report 2001–02

market value is being added. Continuing with the Home Depot example, MVA on 3 August 2002 or six months after the reporting date stood at US$47.6 billion (market capitalization of $66,949 million minus $19,337 million of capital employed). Loss of value during the six-month period from February to August 2002 was therefore US$48.5 billion (calculated as difference between MVA in February and August: 96.1 − 47.6).

Table 7.11 for the EVA calculations and the MVA example presented above demonstrate some of the weaknesses of value metrics. For EVA, one of the major practical shortcomings is the complexity of calculations. Adjustments necessary to transform the reported accounting items into their economic equivalents are often non-intuitive, cumbersome and time-consuming. In their proprietary versions of EVA, Stern & Stewart Co. utilize up to 160 such adjustments. Although perhaps useful as the 'ultimate' measure of value, an EVA constructed in such a manner is most likely to be incomprehensible to anyone without accounting certification. For MVA, the main criticism hones on perceived inadequacy of the measure as a tool of practical management. Main ingredient of MVA, share price, reacts to a plethora of factors among which the management's actions are only a subset. Thus, day-to-day operating activities cannot be guided by MVA as there is little or no relationship between changes in MVA and managerial actions. It is perhaps because of these limitations that companies in the retail sector do not make extensive use of value metrics, although some of them – Ahold, Escada, JC Penney – are starting to use the logic of added value to reduce operating costs, improve the margin performance and develop incentive schemes.

Does corporate consolidation in retailing destroy value?

The financial performance consequences of corporate consolidation are a topic of active debate among academics and practitioners alike. Academic researchers emphasize the important role corporate consolidation plays in disciplining under-performing managers and imposing operating efficiencies (Healy, 1992; Jarrell *et al.*, 1988); practitioners view it as a forthright tool of market share expansion and an effective response to a plethora of competitive challenges (Howell, 2002; Read, 1999).

Retail consolidations, although a small proportion of the total consolidating activity, remain the pinnacle of attention because of their huge impact on pub-lic welfare, environment and businesses involved in supply and transportation of merchandise. As the world's largest retailer, Wal-Mart has become a sizeable player in a number of the key European markets via acquisitions in the UK and Germany. The French national champion Carrefour responded by first acquiring Comptoirs Modernes in 1998 and merging with Promodès in 1999. Although a flurry of consolidation activity had been anticipated ever since, the actual con-solidation trends were more subdued. With the exception of Casino-Monoprix merger in October 2000, the leading European retailers preferred to pause for a while, in the meantime expanding into the emerging markets of Latin America and Europe.

A significant body of evidence has been accumulated regarding the value effects of mergers and acquisitions (M&A), the most visible form of consolidating activity. From the stock market perspective, this evidence (called 'stylized facts') suggests that M&A activity generates positive gains for the shareholders of the target com-panies, but brings no benefits to shareholders of the acquiring companies, and leads to a systematic reduction of the post-merger share price in the year following the event (Dodd, 1980; Eckbo, 1983; Jensen and Ruback, 1983). From the financial per-formance perspective, the results of various studies are more contradictory. Healy (1992) discovered that mergers did improve asset productivity and operating cash flow for 50 companies studied, but Loughran and Vijh (1997) concluded that the long-term investors in 947 acquisitions did not experience any post-merger gain arising from operating improvements.

Retail-specific consolidation studies are sparse. Hazel (1997) reviewed the US retail scene and the regulatory and legal implications of the continuing consolidation drive of American retailers. Read (1999) undertook to analyse the direction and impact of consolidation on the global retail landscape and leading retailers. Both authors did not arrive at any testable conclusions. One of the most recent studies (Dragun, 2002a) attempted to establish the value effects of corporate consolidation in the context of European retailing (26 M&A transactions were studied). The study findings were broadly consistent with the stylized facts. M&A transactions generated stock gains for the shareholders of the targeted retail companies, although this added value was transient and reverted to losses within a year after the transaction took place. Also, M&A deals destroyed value for the shareholders of the acquiring retail companies. Taken together, these results suggest that corporate consolidation in European retailing is not an area where value is created.

The global picture is not as clear-cut, mainly due to the lack of relevant studies. The most recent large cross-border acquisition, of Asda by Wal-Mart in the UK, appears to have changed little, apart from an immediate increase in sales for the parent. Under the Wal-Mart umbrella, Asda centralized its customer service response system, streamlined the supply chain, and generally aligned the business processes with those of the parent. However, the changes have not yet fully found their reflection in Asda's operating performance or market share comparative to other UK retailers.

Summary

The implementation of strategy requires retail managers to be aware of the financial implications of their decisions. In such an intensely customer-oriented and detail-driven business as retail, there is always a temptation to see financial performance as something for senior executives to worry about. This view is mistaken. Unless the financial factors of success are clearly understood by everyone in the company and applied for improvements in financial performance, no operating strategy has a chance of succeeding.

This chapter introduced a financial model of the retail business. Major components of the model are customers, suppliers, and the retailers themselves. Building upon the model, we then reviewed real-world retail financial statements. The purpose was to understand the structure, linkages and interaction among various parts of the statements, as well as to form a fundamental understanding of the financial side of retailing. A review of financial ratio analysis followed, supplemented by discussion of how disparate ratios could be integrated into a model suitable for evaluation of the company's financial performance from the strategic perspective. A framework used for such evaluation (commonly referred to as the DuPont model) reflects various factors of financial return, and also provides the operating guide for improving financial performance.

Useful for analytic purposes, DuPont models have limitations, of which one in particular relates to the fact that the managerial actions required to improve performance are forward-looking in nature whereas the data used in calculations are historical. Thus the model alone may not be sufficient to provide adequate support for a rapidly evolving retail environment. Counterbalancing such a view is the realization that historical financial performance does convey valuable information by providing a basis for understanding of where the business currently stands. Also, it is argued that historical results may be the best available predictors of the future, since they constitute the only reliable dataset readily available to retail decision makers. The chapter addresses these issues by describing the interaction between financial performance and stock market returns. The market's agents such as stockbrokers, asset managers and research analysts are the forces that drive the expression of the company's financial performance in the stock market domain.

This expression is the market value, or the total worth of the company's common stock. It is determined by a number of factors, such as business environment, sales growth, profitability and market share, to name but a few. Stock market assessment is a continuous process (valuation cycle), and it results in a value being assigned to the company's shares. In order to sustain the positive interaction with and flow of communication to the stock market, the retailers are required to demonstrate the sustainable financial performance and ability to generate ('add') economic value. Measures of the economic value (EVA and MVA) are presented in the chapter, with the concluding remarks devoted to discussion of advantages and deficiencies of such metrics.

Review questions

1 Describe a financial model of the retail business (it does not necessarily have to replicate the one presented in the chapter!). Include the major players (components) and the interactions among them. On the basis of your description, make the case for or against the following statement.

2 Financial performance in retail is a fluke because it never depends on retailer. The only players determining financial performance are the customers and suppliers. The best way to improve financial returns is therefore to cater most effectively to the needs of these two groups, by giving the best prices to both.

3 Explain the concept of cash conversion cycle. Why is it important in retailing?

4 Describe (and provide formulae for) the most common ratios used to assess financial performance in retailing. As a retail manager, how would you go about improving each of the ratios you described? What might be the impact of improvement in each ratio on the overall financial performance?

Discussion questions

1 Discuss what is meant by 'financial model of retail business'. Does every retailer have a unique financial model? To what extent do you think the financial models differ among retailers? What are the factors that account for such differences, if any? Could a single, uniform financial model suit every retailer?

2 An excerpt from the interview with Michael Mirrors, CFO of Ahold, is given below (*source:* Fair Disclosure Financial Network, transcript of June 6, 2002).

> We don't manage credit rating and obviously we give full disclosure to the rating agencies. But when we look at our numbers and our indebtedness we look at two ratios; one, is interest coverage ratio, and the other is net debt over EBITDA [earnings before interest taxes depreciation and amortisation]. We do not expect our net debt to go up until we expect a rolling EBITDA to improve over the year as a result of the impact of the acquisitions.

(a) Explain why the interest coverage ratio is important in sustaining creditworthiness.

(b) Discuss possible reasons for Ahold's preference to use EBITDA instead of EBIT. (Consider Ahold's growth strategy and impact of acquisitions on profitability.)

(c) What does the last sentence in the quote tell us about Ahold's current and future debt policy?

3 Assessment of financial performance by the retail analysts often produces contradictory conclusions. Below are the statements made by two analysts describing the financial results of Sainsbury's for the first quarter of the financial year 2002–03 (*source:* InvesText)

> Sainsbury fails to maintain momentum. Sainsbury needed to show in this quarter [April–June 2002] that it could sustain the outperformance and recovery of last year, in order to achieve a better rating versus industry leader Tesco. But the outcome announced today was disappointing, with 3.1% LFL [like-for-like] growth in the UK barely better than that for the struggling Safeway. The slowdown to only 0.5% LFL sales growth in the US for Shaws [Sainsbury's US subsidiary] is also disappointing.

Nick Bubb, SG Securities, 25 July 2002

> [Sainsbury's] Q1 sales were a shade drab reflecting aggressive promotions by competitors. But momentum has improved significantly and the margin/cost interplay

> looks more attractive than the peer group. The company has
> begun to win back the customers lost to Tesco. Customer
> numbers increased by 2–3% we estimate in Q1 and the
> momentum has picked up further in Q2 we believe.
> Sainsbury's profit recovery remains on track due to a
> combination of sales growth, margin stability and cost
> efficiencies.
>
> Simon Dunn, Dresdner Kleinwort Wasserstein, 24 July 2002
>
> 4 Discuss why the analysts' views might differ so substantially. From the stock-
>   market interaction perspective, what is more beneficial for a retail company
>   to attract – diversity of opinions or their uniformity?

References

Black, B. (2001) 'Employment relations and national culture: continuity and change in the age of globalisation'. *Industrial Relations Journal*, **32**:2 (June), p. 177.

Brealy, R. and Myers, S. (2002) *Principles of Corporate Finance* (7th edition). Higher Education US Editions.

Dodd, P. (1980) 'Merger proposals, management discretion, and stockholder wealth'. *Journal of Financial Economics*, **8**, pp. 105–38.

Dragun, D. (2002a) 'Q&As for M&As: value implications of corporate consolidations in European retailing'. *The European Retail Digest*, **34**, pp. 51–9.

Dragun, D. (2002b) 'The "ideal" financial performance retailer: Is globalisation worth it?' *Working Paper*. Templeton College, Oxford.

Eckbo, E. (1983) 'Horizontal mergers, collusion, and stockholder wealth'. *Journal of Financial Economics*, **11**, pp. 241–73.

Ehrbar, A. (1998) *EVA: The Real Key to Creating Wealth*. New York, John Wiley & Sons.

Fama, E. and French, K. (1992) 'The cross-section of expected stock returns'. *Journal of Finance*, **47**:2, pp. 427–65.

Hazel, D. (1997) 'What's next for retail mergers?' *Chain Store Age*, **8**, pp. 35–7.

Healy, P. (1992) 'Does corporate performance improve after mergers?' *Journal of Financial Economics*, **31**, pp. 135–75.

Hedemann-Robinson, M. (2000) 'Defending the consumer's right to a clean environment in the face of globalisation. The case of extraterritorial environmental protection under European community'. *Journal of Consumer Policy*, **23**:1 (March), p. 25.

Hobson, J. (2002) 'Globalisation makes of states what states make of it: Between agency and structure in the state/globalisation debate'. *New Political Economy*, **7**:1 (March), p. 5.

Howell, D. (2002) 'Bankruptcies, closings and M&As'. *The DSN Retailing Today*, **7**, pp. 25–36.

Jarrell, G., Brickley, J. and Netter, J. (1988) 'The market for corporate control: the empirical evidence since 1980'. *The Journal of Economic Perspectives*, **2**:1, pp. 49–68.

Jensen, M. and Ruback, R. (1983) 'The market for corporate control: the scientific evidence'. *Journal of Financial Economics*, **11**, pp. 5–50.

Loughran, T. and Vijh, M. (1997) 'Do long-term shareholders benefit from corporate acquisitions?' *Journal of Finance*, **52**:5, pp. 1765–90.

Perraton, J. (2001) 'The global economy – myths and realities'. *Cambridge Journal of Economics*, **25**:5 (September), p. 669.

Read, N. (1999) 'UK: Emerging mergers'. *Retail Week*, December 3, pp. 12–15.

Reilly, F. and Brown, K. (2000) *Investment Analysis and Portfolio Management* (6th edition). Fort Worth, The Dryden Press.

Walters, D. and Hanrahan, J. (2000) *Retail Strategy. Planning and Control*. Houndmills and London, Macmillan Press.

White, G., Sondhi, A. and Fried, D. (1998) *The Analysis and Use of Financial Statements* (2nd edition). New York, John Wiley & Sons.

Part III

The view from the bridge

Chapter 8

Supply chain: a core competency for retailers

Interview with Armin Meier, IT and logistics director of Migros

Migros-Genossenschafts Bund, Limmatstraße 152, Zürich 8005, Switzerland
Tel.: +41(0)1/27 72 11 11; +41(0)1/2 77 25 25

Richard Cuthbertson

Switzerland is a federation of 26 independent states or cantons in the geographic heart of Europe. The country borders France, Germany, Austria and Italy, and German, French and Italian are all official languages. Switzerland recently once again decided it did not want to join the European Union, although dialogue continues.

Despite being a small country with a population of only just over 7 million, Switzerland is one of the wealthiest nations in the world and has a highly competitive economy. Retail concentration in Switzerland is high, and dominated by a small number of domestic players, particularly in the food sector.

With gross retail sales in 2002 of around €14 billion, employing over 80,000 personnel (Migros is Switzerland's largest employer) and nearly 2 million co-operative members, the Migros Group is the largest retailer in Switzerland.

The Migros community comprises ten regional co-operatives with a high degree of regional autonomy. Sales in the Group are roughly equally split between food and non-food. Outlets include bookstores, department stores, DIY stores, hypermarkets, office equipment, sports and leisure, furniture stores and others. Migros are to be found on garage forecourts, in out-of-town centres and high street locations throughout Switzerland. The Migros online shop is a small part of the business as a whole. Migros is also involved in activities such as financial services, publishing and printing.

Migros has a small presence in neighbouring France and Germany, with no immediate plans for further expansion beyond the domestic borders.

In this chapter, Armin Meier, IT and logistics director, discusses the chains that supply Migros supermarkets and restaurants in Switzerland.

Migros supply chains

There are three main supply chains in Migros: non-food, dry products and fresh products. Migros has 530 supermarkets and over 200 restaurants. The regional supply chain of fresh goods and fresh products and the fastest moving dry goods assortment are delivered out of ten distribution centres throughout Switzerland with about 7,000 SKUs and over 20,000 pallets per day. However, with 40 specialist markets such as do-it-yourself and garden outlets, the national supply of non-food products has over 200,000 SKUs and about 6,000 pallets per day. The dry product supply chain of slower-moving food and beverages has about 4,000 SKUs and roughly 5,500 pallets per day.

In addition to those three main supply chains, we have specialist supply chains for frozen goods, e-business and home delivery. Currently, the e-business and home delivery supply chain is centrally organized. However, we have observed the Tesco model and we might consider commissioning the goods in one or more stores. Tesco have in any case hinted that they may go to a centralized system and so the debate continues. The question is how the market develops in terms of volume and acceptance of e-business throughout Switzerland.

It has become more and more obvious that specialization of the supply chains makes a lot of sense. As already mentioned, we have frozen goods home delivery and small shop delivery, and we have now acquired a company whose core business is to deliver to restaurants, hospitals and other institutions. It may be that in the future we concentrate the whole supply chain for restaurants on this company, because, as discussed, our core supply chains are based on pallets, but pallets are not necessarily very practical in a kitchen.

Balance between centralization and regionalization

Supply chain systems for non-food and dry foods are centralized because the assortment is highly standardized throughout Switzerland and there are no huge regional adaptations. They can be managed much more effectively centrally, supported by a SAP system. Centralization brings considerable advantages such as professionalism of the assortments, centralized delivery and centralized replenishment.

In the dry goods area, about 90 per cent of our goods are private label. Many of those brands are produced and delivered through our own industry. The producers are supplying our chain directly and we believe that we can get many synergies out of centralization, for example in the way we deal with each other, the way we keep the stocks, and the way we deliver, thus providing efficient processes that we can exploit. However, the fresh products are regionalized: currently in 10 regional centres. They are the fast movers and they have to be on the shelves quickly to be seen as a really fresh product. We believe that the regional distribution centres make a lot of sense in the case of fresh products in terms of delivery time, transportation, distance, and so on. In fact, many fresh products are sourced regionally. They are regional products that have been produced regionally and consumed regionally – our customers like that very much. That is part of the reason why we believe that regionalization also makes sense, even in such a small country as Switzerland.

Supply chain is a core competency of a retailer

It is our belief that we should control the logistics, and that logistics and the supply chain is a core competency of Migros as a retailer. Therefore, it is quite natural that we outsource very little of the management control of the supply chain. Of course, we control the supply chain centrally in the case of the centralized supply chains and regionally in the case of the regional supply chains for the fresh products but we do not transport it ourselves. Here at the Federation of Migros Co-operatives we do not own trucks but sub-contract to either Migros regional trucks or to external companies. We make extensive use of the rail system in Switzerland because roads are heavily loaded already. For example, a standard waiting time for a truck at a mountain pass is four hours, making delivery of fresh goods impossible. Also, we are not allowed to move trucks during the night. Rail is slower, but rail is much more predictable, which is an important part of our promise to the stores. In general we keep control over our supply chains as much as necessary but the transportation is heavily outsourced. With very small exceptions, all the distribution centres are Migros-owned and run by Migros employees.

We have established comprehensive control of our logistics and the task is to ensure that we do not lose time, money or people over the whole supply chain. Rene Meyer and his group offer consulting services to the individual activities in the supply chain, bringing know-how to improve those activities. The group also has the task to control the whole supply chain in terms of, for example, knowing the money we spend on logistics, the time we lose, the problems we have, the warehouse space we need and the head count. He reports twice a year to the board. We have certainly improved over time but we need to do still more. We are in the middle of a reorganization of the whole logistics landscape and the whole supply chain. We have not completed the implementation but the results so far are promising.

Careful decision-making for speedy implementation

We are a co-operative of co-operatives, the headquarters is a co-operative that is owned by co-operatives. There is a contract in place between those co-operatives so we know each role. We have quite a strong influence on the regional co-operatives. They are allowed to take their own decisions but we are all so dependent on the whole network.

Typically, it takes a long time to get a clear decision in such a network but when you have a decision it is quick to implement because by that time everybody has 'bought in'. In other companies the decision-making may be easy but implementation is made much more difficult as people are not convinced about the change. Here it takes a long time to discuss, sit together, influence, convince and make the arguments but when you have the decision it is easy to implement.

However, we believe that a regional anchor is very important for us because people for example in the western, French speaking, part of Switzerland are different from people in the German speaking eastern part of Switzerland and again compared to the southern part of Switzerland where people are more influenced by an Italian culture. They see the world differently and we have to adapt to those different needs. That is why the regional presence with a limited amount of regional decision taking also makes a lot of sense.

Responsive and flexible

The reorganization of the logistics function means we are on the right track for the future, prepared for a world that will be much more competitive. We came from an organization where the whole supply chain was carried out regionally in 20 or more centres and we are transforming that to a more responsive structure.

Centralized product assortments are replenished automatically, typically within 24 hours. Twenty-four hours is our standard order delivery time for dry goods as well as for non-food. However, in non-food it does depend on whether the product needs to be replenished within 24 hours. It may be that 48 hours is appropriate and seasonal products may be longer if warranted.

Each shop has the opportunity to influence the number of goods replenished, so if a shop manager thinks of a special situation he has in his surroundings, for example a celebration or festival, he might increase the number or type of goods delivered the next day. Therefore, he has a window every day where he can influence the number of goods replenished. Our expectation was that about 2 per cent of the goods would be influenced manually every day. In reality, some shops are much higher and others are lower.

In fresh goods, where the supply chain is distributed, things run a little bit differently. There, the manager of the shop orders what he needs and he gets it within 24 hours, and it is possible to make a delivery within a couple of hours if necessary.

Planning is the key

Obviously, when you are replenishing an item that has a fairly standard, predicable demand (no item seems to have constant demand) when it is well managed with good information systems it works well. However, promotions are a very important part of our business as well, requiring a more intelligent response. Planning is the key.

It is possible for a regional centre to run a promotion on fresh products but the standard promotion is a centralized, countrywide promotion. This requires a promotion to be organized, involving several departments as well as logistics. With the changes we have made to the supply chain, people have had to re-think and re-learn their role because they have new responsibilities. Previously, someone responsible for buying goods would pass them to the shop and the shop did the rest but now the whole process has to be considered. So the volumes are planned and each and every shop receives an initial delivery either directly from the supplier or delivered through our supply chain but without waiting at a distribution centre. Subsequent re-ordering during the promotion time is done in the standard way. So the initial planning is essential, and the closer you get the better it is.

Following the promotion, we have a de-briefing. We want to know whether we can learn anything, and the learning cannot be achieved through the systems but through people. People need to understand what can be done better next time. Undertaking a good assessment of the situation, trying to understand what went wrong, leads to better results next time.

Seasonal periods such as Christmas or Easter have the same dimensions as big promotions. For example, at Easter, all stores are filled with Easter bunnies – thousands of pallets. Normally, there is the initial stock order and then replenishment through the normal process. Except this year. At Easter 2002 we had a problem because a distribution centre burnt down with all the Easter products. Forty per cent of the Easter chocolate was lost in one night! Four million Easter bunnies! So we had to re-produce it. Part of the reason we were able to manage that is because the supply chain is very integrated. The producers of chocolate for Migros, rather than take their usual break after the seasonal production, continued to produce.

In addition, there was no space available in the burnt-out distribution centre. It was necessary to create a new system of delivery for one week while all the products were distributed; using services we had in hand for other operations. That is a demonstration of the strength of our supply chain and this kind of distribution.

Products were moved to another distribution centre and after one week it worked again, with the information system installed.

Integrating people and processes

Something that struck me on arriving at Migros is the very high professionalism of the people. There are many people who have been working for Migros for many years – 20 years and more – and they really think in an integrated way. We have been growing and building different channels but Migros people still think as part of a whole – and that was very important in the Easter bunny crisis. People sat together and developed solutions, and the next day it worked. They are flexible and pragmatic.

To support integration, we have to a great extent standardized the IT landscape. The whole supply chain is SAP, including the suppliers and stores. Every supplier is able to see and understand the stock behaviour. They are also ready and able to adapt their production plans according to the needs of the stores. Numbers are updated overnight. So for today, the suppliers have figures available from yesterday. Naturally, we also do some forecasting automatically, taking into account the day of the week, the season and so on.

With the external suppliers, it depends if they are linked to the system as an efficient customer response supplier, linked using EDI or not linked at all. Therefore, we have different levels of linking suppliers to our supply chain. The level of linking largely depends on how important the supplier is to Migros.

Performance measurement across supply chains

When it comes to measuring supply chain performance, it is again the area where Rene Meyer and his team excel. They do the planning mainly for the core supply chains but also for the specialized supply chains. For example, they are currently conducting research to understand whether it makes sense to concentrate the restaurant supply chain into one channel, and another to consider frozen goods. Where volumes are small, frozen foods for a petrol station for example, a pallet or a trailer unit is very big.

When we remodelled our supply chains, we defined targets for dry food, non-food and fresh goods. Different formats need different supply chains and this is where Rene Meyer and his team are working on different models. They undertake a variety of studies aimed at really understanding the market, and according to what they discover we start to adapt. For example, should the distribution be more regionalized via trucks or centralized via rail? We consider the combination of factors, such as space utilization and head count that allow us to reach our own targets and compare ourselves to the European standard. For example, we can benchmark the fresh food distribution across the distribution centres each month.

They can compare their key performance indicators such as cost per employer or per case as required.

Global and local suppliers

We have a number of global suppliers in non-food and some even in food. We have an importation centre and naturally there are some differences in the way we operate outside the region but the methods of collaboration remain very similar. Pet food, for example. Our own label pet foods are made by the two or three global manufacturers but in the same way as for any Swiss-made products, we decide on the promotions and we work together with the manufacturer. Buying is a part of the marketing function, which is normal and reasonable.

Reverse logistics

Switzerland is top of the world league in recycling packaging materials and this is an important aspect of supply chain management. In fresh goods, the backstream is around 80 per cent of the forward stream at Migros, since we take re-usable crates, pallets and packaging material. There is a substantial area in each fresh distribution centre for all the reusable and recyclable materials, and we have recycling centres there. We also bring back out-of-date or unsold goods and seasonal returns. In time, consumers will be forced by law to return products such as batteries and electrical devices, and we already take back bottles.

Retailing is all about distribution

The Migros logistics function is essential to what Migros is doing as an organization. The contribution to the commercial value of Migros as whole is tremendous. Logistics and the handling of goods in an efficient way is a core competency of Migros and it is also a huge portion of the total costs. About one third of the total operational costs of Migros might be termed 'logistics' so it is both essential and a considerable cost to the whole operation.

There is a threshold that logistics has to provide in terms of the service that reinforces the marketing of Migros as a fresh food retailer. If shelves are empty, then the logistics may be at fault, but if it works, you don't see it. That is real success.

One of the main added values that a retailer provides to the consumer is logistics because we collect together all the items the consumer wants at a location that is convenient. Without the retailer, the consumer would be forced to go to the farm for eggs. Sometimes, when we think of retailing we see the stores and the products but really retailing is all about distribution. We bring the goods to the consumer. Nothing more, nothing less.

Outlook for Migros

The big issue is optimization of the whole logistics network throughout Europe – constant optimization of time versus cost. Ideally we would like to deliver the products to the shop five seconds before the customer enters the shop and takes the products away. If that were possible, the costs would be very high. On the other hand, if you try to be on the safe side and keep stocks on multiple levels then you also run into cost problems. So the question is how to optimize the whole logistics network.

The stock should be on the move. For example, in dry goods: before we started the logistics re-organization, we had an average stock time of 32 days from when it arrived into the Migros system until it reached the shelf. That is a very long time and now we are aiming at ten days or even lower. It is different for different products of course but we are approaching a more just-in-time behaviour. On the other hand, we see that transportation is getting a really big issue, and that will be a challenge for the future.

The second challenge we see is that there is increasing regionalization. Even in a small country like Switzerland, people want to see a regional product in their regional shop. Many consumers value their regional products as highly as, for example, branded products or organic products. They want to see products from local farmers on the shelves. This is a logistical problem, timing versus money.

An additional challenge for us in Switzerland is expansion. We would like to expand our network and grow the service but we have very limited opportunities remaining within the Swiss border. For example, it is very difficult to get permission to build a new shop. We see continuing consolidation of small chains here in Switzerland as in other parts of Europe. The small chains are either very much focused on a niche where they are strong but limited in size or they are getting sucked in by other chains. It is tempting to expand that way but it is always a question of price. It is a strong competition and the tendency is that you pay too much for such an acquisition. It is necessary to maintain a balance and be reasonable in decision taking. We have an expansion plan set up and agreed, and we are starting to implement it. The advantage of being regionalized is that we can use a variety of methods to expand.

Chapter 9

Bridging the gap between IT and the business

Interview with Dick Dijkstra, chief information officer and Eric Polman, director, IT strategy and architecture, Ahold

Royal Ahold, Albert Heijnweg, 1, 1507 EH Zaandam, The Netherlands
Tel.: +31 75 659 9111; Fax: +31 75 659 8350

Christine Cuthbertson

Ahold is a multi-channel food retailer and food service operator with 35 companies trading under their local brand name, in 28 countries across four continents. The Ahold company network generates considerable synergies in facilities, knowledge exchange, and innovation. In this way, they can operate locally in many countries while leveraging the advantages of scale, co-operation and network. Ahold outlets in Europe range from large full-service supermarkets, hypermarkets, compact hypermarkets and speciality stores, to neighbourhood convenience stores in 13 countries, with sales in 2001 of €21.8 billion.

Dick Dijkstra is chief information officer at Ahold's European Competence Center in Zaandam. The European Competence Center was established in 1999 to share know-how and maximize synergies across different businesses. With a background in consultancy and eleven years with Ahold in various positions, including four years in a non-IT capacity, Dick Dijkstra considers himself a retailer.

Eric Polman is director of IT strategy and architecture. Eric joined Albert Heijn, the flagship supermarket company of Ahold in The Netherlands, in 1994 after nine years

> with consultants Accenture and Deloitte & Touche. Eric's background is very much in supply chain and IT. Like Dick, he would not call himself a technician but a generalist working with business processes using information to realize the business strategy.

IT-oriented business people and business-oriented IT people

In both our backgrounds there has always been an element of IT but not 'hard' IT for its own sake. It has always been from a business perspective. Of course, there is an important role for the IT specialist. However, the real challenge lies in ensuring that IT is linked to business. Increasingly, people in the rest of the business are likely to know about IT, but there is always a struggle when linking IT to business imperatives.

We did some research to explore the options for leveraging IT at a global level. One of the topics in that research was the position and background of the CIO. One began with IT specialists and increasingly IT-oriented people became business-orientated people because everyone experienced the gap between what business people wanted and what IT people provided. However, we see some organizations going back to recruit more IT-orientated people to senior positions. I think it has to do with attitude in senior management. Management itself feels somewhat more comfortable and no longer see IT as something they should not touch but similar to finance or human resources or logistics. Senior management increasingly realizes that an IT specialist is not somebody with a screwdriver in hand but is a professional. When business managers have a greater understanding and awareness of IT and its potential, communication becomes easier, IT is not such a risk and you can forge the link with the business.

At Ahold, business management feels responsible for IT. The present generation is knowledgeable about IT and it is so important for the present operation. This is particularly true in the retail industry, where IT has been used to gain and sustain competitive advantage, in logistics, consumer marketing and so on.

More than a collection of companies

Ahold has several operating companies, or 'OpCos', in Europe. By the end of 2001, Ahold operated over 6500 stores in 13 countries. In The Netherlands, Ahold operates five store chains: supermarket company Albert Heijn, speciality stores Gall & Gall (wine and spirits), Etos (health and beauty), De Tuinen (natural products) and

Deli XL (food service provider). At www.albert.com, Ahold's joint Internet-based home delivery service in The Netherlands, customers can access all five Dutch subsidiaries in completing one order. We have a joint venture with the ICA Group, with stores in Sweden, Norway, Denmark, Latvia, Lithuania and Estonia. In Southern and Central Europe, Ahold operates stores in Spain, Portugal, Poland, the Czech Republic and the Slovak Republic.

All these companies have their unique propositions in their own markets because they are very different in terms of buying power, culture, maturity, etc. This approach is also partly because of acquisitions, since it makes no sense when you join forces with a popular Swedish brand like ICA, to change that brand. So all the companies are focused on their local customers. Company CEOs have a strong bottom line responsibility, all directly reporting to the Ahold executive board.

It is natural to query whether Ahold is more than simply a collection of world-class companies. The answer lies not so much in trying to find synergies in the front office but in working backstage. So, as far as strategy is concerned we have made that distinction between the front office and the back office: buying, real estate, finance, HR, logistics, retail development and IT. Our approach is to do only those things that make sense in terms of delivering synergy benefits. Each function is treated differently. For example in buying, we have centralized some of the sourcing responsibilities so we have a central buying department where applicable.

We have been actively looking for synergies since the late 1990s. Before then there was some synergy within Ahold companies but that was incidental. There was no structure in place to initiate, control and co-ordinate. The structure is now provided by the European Competence Center, which we have had in place for about three years and now we have a vision to increase and create synergy in the back office. For buying, much of the sourcing process can be centralized but for logistics it is more limited because logistics are, by definition, very regional.

The synergy effect is growing and we are learning to distinguish between processes that are suitable and those that are not. However, we do not have the luxury of unlimited time. There is a need, an urgency to work together because our competitors are doing so too. So this is really a thing we have to do, rather than a matter of choice. However, a big European headquarters with responsibility for Europe is not the answer. We have tried to do it the smart way.

It is really finding a balance between local autonomy, speed and commitment but at the same time sharing business opportunities, creating economies of scale, cost savings and so on. Different retailers tackle it in different ways. It might be called 'the race to the middle', with Wal-Mart and Tesco coming from one angle and Ahold from another. Wal-Mart and Tesco are rather more centralized. They take one format and try to adapt it to the local markets. We come from another angle where we have a strong position, and strong brands but autonomous operations and we have encouraged co-operation in order to be as efficient as our competitors on a multi-local scale.

Role of the European Competence Center

Of course, it is impossible to draw a line to say where the front office ends and the back office begins. There is tension in this model but the tension is necessary to keep everyone sharp. There are no absolutes. The European Competence Center is correctly named because it is not a central functional department, not a European 'Polit Bureau', but it is about competence. We are delivering competence and that should be our commitment to all Ahold companies.

Each company has a CEO and of course ultimately, they 'call the shots'. We are part of the meeting but they define the problem. Of course, we give direction where possible in our functional area. We present proposals that ensure we gain optimum benefit from our scale, and determine the direction in terms of architecture but ultimately it is the business that decides what is to be done. For example, at ICA we are dealing with an operating company with a long history of autonomy and of being very successful in the local market and we can still learn from each other. In our vision, we all want to compete in an international market with the big operators around who are able to leverage their scale. We have only been working together for a short time and we are getting into shape, becoming more and more of a team. Although we are all different, you will see Ahold vision emerging out there, and it is the European Competence Center that is helping to make the change.

Competence Center organization

The real estate organization based here in Zaandam has satellites in each of the markets responsible for the really big projects. In Poland, for example, we have developed complete shopping centres including entertainment and that is specialist work. The CFOs in the operating companies report to finance in the Center. Human resources is responsible for direction-setting in the different countries but it also has to be part of the execution. For example, management development should always be in one place.

For logistics, it does not make any sense to operate a distribution centre in Poland from Zaandam but it makes sense if one of the expertises in Holland is in how to set up a distribution centre or how to organize your supply chain between suppliers and retail. The role of the European Competence Center is very much in this area of knowledge exchange, dissemination of best practice and help in setting direction. We really want to leave it as mean and lean as possible.

Shaping the organization

What we are really doing is shaping the organization, and a year from now you will see a completely different picture. The Center has to be very sharp in determining where we place the responsibility, on a European or on local level. And the other important question is whether it is a task, a responsibility, a process that we should do ourselves or should we look to outsource. The answers to those two questions will determine the future shape of the organization.

We want to implement systems cheaper and faster to support the business. An important way of achieving those kinds of efficiencies is in a convergence of our application portfolio. Although it is in no way our intention to standardize overnight, we believe that greater efficiencies lie in having the same systems in our application portfolio. For example, two or three years ago, many of the ICA Group's core applications were reaching the end of their useful life. At around the same time, we were establishing a European vision and so it was decided that the ICA solution would be a common initiative. This means that the core applications being developed now have been selected as part of a common application portfolio. The migration is not forced but the opportunity came in response to the business need to innovate. So, the main drive is not towards standardization but is in supporting a business strategy and doing that in the cheapest and fastest way.

A pre-requisite for achieving that is sufficient overlap in synergy in the business strategy and business process. This is also the role of the Competence Center and the vision of the board. We believe that despite the differences in culture and market position, there is a lot of agreement on how to compete for the future. Ahold wants to compete by bringing very consumer-specific added value in retail and broadening the retail scale. We can see this happening. In every operating company and joint venture partner you will see it differently but there is a lot of overlap in what every company is doing in its local market and the processes that are needed to operate on an efficient scale. That also requires the development of specific IT solutions. We are confident that all European companies will eventually benefit from those solutions, and ICA and Albert Heijn are very much leading that process.

So when we say we are converging we need to have a focal point where we will converge and the Center is here to define the path and the tools required to get there. The business strategy is not developed centrally but the business strategy is very much centred on providing a customer-specific offering, entering a world where Ahold will have a network of contact points with our customers. It is a challenge and to win we have to do it in an efficient way without losing differentiation. Lots of added value that goes beyond being the cheapest but having the right product, at the right time, with added value, lots of choice, rather than becoming cheaper and cheaper.

That vision has been translated into timescales and methods to meet that challenge in a cost effective way. Our most important role is to try and link business process, the applications architecture and the technical architecture within Europe. In this way we are developing back-office synergy to support front-office diversification. So the business strategy is the main input and there is very close communication with operating companies because it is there that the process modelling takes place. We give direction from the Center, the implementers are working in the operating companies and they have to bring those ideas to life.

Communication and innovation

The Center provides the structure by networking, communicating and working together. We have described functions but this is not a hierarchical relationship. The Center has a few technical architects who define technology and standards. There is a lot of knowledge in people in the business as well. There is a formal decision process that sets the direction and we will advise. Communication ensures we share knowledge and achieve commitment.

The way we organize our business is innovative in itself. We are innovating from the heart of our business. The tools required are completely new tools. For example, typical enterprise resource planning solutions are not suitable so we cannot simply select an ERP package and roll it out throughout the organization. We select a combination of packages for the less core or competitive processes but undertake custom development in the areas where that is appropriate.

For example, merchandising or replenishment, both of which are very much at the heart of a retail business. We have typically seen that the standard tools on the market are not really appropriate. They either come from a non-food or manufacturing standpoint, and so our core processes are not supported. This has led us towards developing some of our own systems and integrating them with the existing environment. Integration is a big issue because you are not building one system, you are building various components and not at the same time and so integration in all these steps is naturally a big issue for us.

At the moment, we are working mainly with ICA and Albert Heijn. Our vision gives us a step-by-step approach to identifying and incorporating those parts which it makes sense to include in a consolidation of the operating companies, and to really share operational service centres for some of the major operation areas, such as running a European network and running a Unix service centre. We are at the beginning of that change. If we see that any software facility service provider can do it cheaper, then we consider outsourcing.

We have progressed in aligning ideas at a global level because the structure here is more or less mirrored in the US and the communication between Europe and the States is strong. We have centralized IT procurement and can approach the big suppliers on a European or even a global scale. We approach IT suppliers more and more often as one customer whenever possible.

Two important balances, then, are between in-house or outsourced and centralized or decentralized. We strongly believe that our core competence is in finding the balance that is right for the business. And not just *the* business but *our* business, and even more specifically, the Albert Heijn business, the ICA business or whatever. If our intention is to produce the best solution for the operating company, then it does not make sense to have all the IT people in a big building in the centre of Europe, well away from the business. They should know their business.

It is very clear, from the CEO level down, who is the owner of all the IT developments. There is always someone clearly accountable and the Center retains a functional line into the operating companies. So the operating company IT groups do all the day-to-day applications support, and they run the applications development projects but their remit is always one operating company and usually one competence such as merchandising or supply chain. So, for example, when we undertake the development of the next generation of merchandising systems, we will bring those specialists together in a joint or common project. The project members, then, are not resourced from a centre pool but are resourced from the operating companies' pools to participate in common projects. For example, the merchandise project is hosted by ICA and therefore they may bring a little more business commitment but the co-operation and benefits are wider, especially in the first stages of the project where we have the definition phase and some of the design takes place. There you can really see that there is very much in common and it does not make sense for the two big operating companies to separately design screens or whatever. So we have this concept of the lead operating company, where one operating company takes the development deliverables and develops something that can be rolled out later throughout Europe.

Project and programme management

The interesting question comes when we consider how IT developments that span operating companies and have the direction set centrally are justified, appraised, funded and evaluated. It is essential to have highly structured and well-formulated project governance around this kind of project. In Ahold, there is always a steering committee. The chair is the business representative of the lead operating company and there are representatives from the other operating companies. For example, in a merchandising project, the merchandising VP from ICA will be chair, the VP merchandising from Albert Heijn is a member, as are IT directors from both operating companies, and myself as CIO.

For programme management, we have an IT policy board in each operating company. As members, we have the CEO, the CFO, the IT director and myself to ensure that the operating companies go in the required direction and that we are not going to re-invent the wheel. There is also the European IT policy board, comprising the CEOs and IT directors of the main operating companies as well as myself, all working together, to get the right alignment and an escalation level throughout Europe.

As for funding, we have recently agreed funding principles, and although they may be reconsidered, they are working at the moment. During the definition phase of each project, we establish a role for each operating company: lead operating company, development partner or implementer or external consultant. Once the roles are identified, it is how the project is to be funded. There is no central budget and so the Center does not fund any part of the project. It is not an easy thing to achieve, but the good thing about this whole scheme is that the project has commitment from the start. Nothing is developed unless there is a business need to drive the change. It is their project and they do it together, they run it together, they own the budget and they own the benefits so if an operating company has a share of the benefits, they also have a share of the costs.

At the European Competence Center, we determine the rules of engagement, ensure the deals get done and support the project along the way but it is not our project, it is their project and that is the way it should work. Implementing a new system is not the main objective. We are chiefly interested in getting real business value out of such a system, and that only can be done in the operating companies. This is more or less a federated model.

The operating companies really do have to justify when they are going to make a major investment in a system that is not aligned with the plans and the business strategy. This has the effect that over the last eighteen months or so, over 80 per cent of major developments within Albert Heijn and ICA have been within the context of this programme. Whether you call it decentralization or democratization, when you really look to the deliverables, it is very much centralized.

Our core competence is really using IT, understanding the business, and understanding how we can benefit from our scale. We will increasingly use third parties for development, and also perhaps make them responsible for maintaining some applications. For example, in Poland, we could start from scratch, and we have learned from experience so we do not have developers there. Albert Heijn and ICA have a history, but they have also moved in that direction. The policy has an effect on the way we hire people and how their career is developed. It should be natural that people spend some time in IT but then work in other areas of the business. Our own careers are an example and although it is not general now, it will be in the future because it is really necessary.

There is a place for the specialist, of course. We need technical expertise to, for example, evaluate new technologies but they should be real experts and in there is a dearth of real experts.

Ahold has traditionally been excellent in operational activities, and also excellent at a conceptual level. With our mission to bridge the gap between IT and the business, what we are developing is the ability to translate the conceptual into the operational. We need people, middle managers, who can understand and explain the concepts so that the concepts are implemented in a timely and practical way. Without those people bridging the gap, there is the danger of spending too long in the exploratory stage, and a chance of losing a potential source of competitive advantage.

This is perhaps particularly important in retail, where vast numbers of people are on the shopfloor. They are selling – that is what retail is all about. Even the store managers are very operational of course. Many members of our middle management are operators and it is a challenge to develop or attract middle managers with the capability to conceptualize to take on this essential bridging role.

E-business initiatives

We take e-business very seriously so we have www.Albert.com. Although Albert is more associated with Albert Heijn, it is conceived as a brand in its own right, bringing together Albert Heijn and the speciality stores in The Netherlands.

The website has been launched to some acclaim and from a functionality point of view, it is regarded as a top site. It does not bring in big money yet but it is perhaps a pre-requisite to be successful in the future. It is still very much a strategic issue, initiated because of a strong belief that it will continue and will grow.

If you talk about B2B in the sense of co-operating with suppliers, I think you can say that Ahold has always been very advanced. We are a very enthusiastic supporter of ECR (efficient customer response) and I think Ahold has always tried to co-operate well with suppliers because it benefits us and will benefit them. So we were, at least in The Netherlands, the trendsetters for EDI standards.

We have been implementing EDI traditional technology very intensively and of course the new technologies are a natural progression. For example, Albert Heijn has a very advanced supply chain system giving regular updates to our main suppliers on stock positions in the warehouse to really make the supply chain very responsive. We use B2B websites and Ahold is a founder member and strong supporter of WWRE (WorldWide Retail Exchange). WWRE plays an important role in establishing the infrastructure and the architecture and CPFR (Collaborative Planning, Forecasting and Replenishment) too will help implement new concepts. We will support developments of that kind. It is not going as fast as we sometimes hoped but I think as far as that is concerned, it has been important and it will continue to be important.

Standards are a requirement to make progress in this field. We have an internal department representing WWRE in Ahold, working on a global level. They are translating the business needs of Ahold into WWRE and the other way around. One project, for example, is to develop a 'buying catalogue' and associated buying systems to support all the buying departments of Ahold in Europe. The team are using tools and concepts that are co-developed with the WWRE.

Technology is not unimportant. The B2B market places do struggle with some of the technology issues. However, we see the WWRE and B2B very much as business-driven and of course the technology helps but in the end it is about business processes and co-operation in businesses, which we have been doing for several years and will continue to do. There is nothing new there!

Chapter 10

Leisure and retailing: LEGOLAND parks

Interview with Mads Ryder, head of LEGOLAND parks and director of LEGOLAND, Billund, Denmark

LEGOLAND A/S, Nordmarksvej 9, DK-7190 Billund, Denmark
Tel.: +45 7533 1333; Fax: +45 7535 3179

Jonathan Reynolds

There is much talk across Europe amongst retailers of the future importance of leisure services, entertainment and of theatre in retailing. Consumers, goes the argument, are tired of the sameness of retail formats and are eager for different experiences. It also appears that consumers are willing to pay more for services than for products and that leisure services therefore provide an attractive and potentially profitable route to brand differentiation for retailers. One strong brand to have sought differentiation through leisure is LEGO, with four LEGOLAND theme parks.

First produced in 1932, the distinctive LEGO brick was named Toy of the Century in 2000 by the British Association of Toy Retailers and in 1999 by Fortune Magazine. Over the past 60 years global sales of LEGO bricks have exceeded 320 billion – the equivalent of 52 LEGO bricks for each of the world's 6 billion inhabitants. LEGO is a privately-owned business, seeking to offer children and young people 'creative, developmental and amusing products and experiences'. In addition to the basic play materials, this has included software (including PC-programmable bricks), lifestyle products (such as clothes and watches), retail stores and leisure parks. A number of joint licensing deals, with companies as diverse as Warner Brothers, Disney,

Nike and HIT Entertainment (producers of *Bob the Builder*), have allowed new and contemporary themes to be developed.

Financial performance at LEGO has recovered somewhat following extensive I billion Danish kroner losses in 2000 and subsequent restructuring. Lego Systems posted a net profit of 530 million Danish kroner for 2001. LEGO forecasts a 4.0 per cent year-on-year increase in turnover for 2002, although the important fourth quarter was disappointing because of poor US and European Christmas sales.

Here we interview the head of LEGOLAND, Mads Ryder, to determine how straight-forward brand extension into leisure services can be and what lessons can be learned by retailers.

Origins and growth

Mads Ryder hands me two business cards. 'I have two cards but only one salary', he observes sadly. Ryder is both director of the first LEGOLAND at Billund in central Denmark (which attracts over 1.5 million guests every year) and head of the parks business unit, incorporating parks in Windsor, UK, California and the new development in Germany that opened in 2002. He certainly seems to have enough energy for two jobs, as he leaps across the office to show me a neat, customizable LEGO pen set. He offers me a boiled sweet. First name terms are the rule in LEGO and this is indicative of an informal business culture so common amongst Scandinavian organizations, in this case derived from the continuing family interest in the company (now in its third generation). The values associated with this culture have strongly determined the way LEGO's leisure services have developed.

The Billund LEGOLAND opened some 33 years ago, largely as a result of the number of requests the company had to 'see behind the scenes'; tour the factory (adjacent to the park) and meet the designers. Almost certainly, says Ryder, LEGO had not intended to enter the theme park business but got there by accident. Some 250,000 visitors in the first year and 600,000 in the second meant that the company had to get serious about managing this new venture. In the early 1990s, with visitor numbers running at 1 million per year (half of these from outside Denmark), it was agreed to examine the potential for international growth. An early joint venture in Germany had not been successful and in examining the reasons behind this, it became clear that the significant challenge was ensuring that the company's values were translated into an effective theme park experience.

Brand values and positioning

Ryder has just two objectives in running the parks: they must make a profit (in other words the parks are not a marketing cost to the business but standalone business units); and they must act as a 'brand house' for LEGO, providing a means of exhibiting the product and the values attached to that product. LEGO's value set is unusually clearly articulated. It centres on relatively innocuous themes of fun, coolness and interactivity; but there is also a set of strong moral messages. LEGO is about family togetherness; it focuses upon achievement through construction, backed up by a systematic approach to the task in hand. He gives an example: the pen-cum-construction set he showed me earlier epitomizes the creativity and interactivity of the brand, based upon the building block system. The owner has a choice about how the pen looks and feels and it's fun to put together (it is, too). Another example – a LEGO-branded product sample plastic mug – is less clearly linked to the value set. It's less distinctive and could be advertising anything.

The LEGOLAND theme parks seek to differentiate themselves from the competition through this focus on creativity, on the product, and through the target demographic – 2–12 year-olds (2–10 in California). Ryder suggests that there is actually relatively little for this age group in LEGOLAND's host countries, with most theme parks aiming at teenagers. Perhaps, I suggest, this is because many kids – particularly towards the end of his target age spectrum – no longer find leisure offers ostensibly aimed at them fun – they are continually aspiring to teenage activities. Ryder agrees; he believes kids are getting older younger. The combined effects of television, of the Internet and of computer gaming also create expectations that can be difficult to deliver against in the 'real' world.

Financial challenges

The LEGO Group has expanded rapidly over the last five years. The new product development cycle has been especially quick. Extraordinarily creative mainstream products such as Mindstorms and Bionicle have sought to address children's more sophisticated expectations; product tie-ins such as Star Wars and Harry Potter exploit cross-selling opportunities, whilst staying true to LEGO brand values. The brand has also been extended into software and clothing. This expansion, in the context of a fall in sales worldwide during 2000, caused the company some financial problems. Non-core activities were closed down and costs reduced; some production facilities were closed.

What has been the impact of this on the theme parks? The parks themselves are distinctly core, Ryder emphasizes, a natural and logical extension of the company's core business of toy production. Whilst there is unlikely to be short-term growth in park numbers following the opening of the German park in 2002, he believes that 2003–04 will see new developments being commissioned. Not least, this will avoid splitting up the talented team that Ryder and his colleagues have put together to create the parks. Three designers are at the heart of this team, responsible for translating product into attractions on the ground.

The diversification of the product range brings with it new opportunities and challenges for the parks. Whilst there is never a shortage of new product ideas, the life cycle of theme park attractions needs to be considerably longer to justify the initial investment of resources. For example, the UK TV character Bob the Builder may have a two or three year spell at the front of children's consciousness – a ride or other attraction may have to last ten. Managing the mix between short-term fashion and longer-term attraction is a difficult balancing act. LEGOLAND manage this by using 'soft' investment in events and theatre to complement the strategic investments in such attractions as Pirateland and Adventureland. The Billund site has an Imagination Theater presently featuring the Bionicle product. They also seek to identify 'generic' themes that can be promoted in the longer term. For example, racing is a theme that will be actively supported through the development of Technics ranges and matching attractions in the years ahead.

Marketing and local differentiation

Each of the park sites has its own set of issues. In Windsor, for example, the historic nature of the site and the UK development control process means that planning any new investment can be a protracted and prolonged affair. Its closeness to Windsor Castle and the Great Park carries additional sensitivities. Yet the UK park is only the size of Billund (itself on a restricted site) and the scope for expansion is considerable. Billund, on the other hand, faces an over-trading problem; with very high peaks in demand during the Danish and German school holiday periods.

Marketing the non-Danish parks is a continuing task. In Denmark, only some 5 million people live within 2 hours of Billund. In the case of Windsor, the figure is nearer 15 million. Yet the visitor numbers are similar – between 1.4 and 1.6 million per annum. The new German park attracted 1.2 million visitors in its first season. Whilst in Billund's case, half these visitors are foreigners, increasing visitor numbers and loyalty is still a challenge for the parks business. Season ticketing has worked well in improving customer loyalty and increasing the number of return visits. In Billund, off-peak season ticketing (April–June and August–October) has proved popular, with some 60,000 Danes visiting up to four times a year. Shifting 100,000 visits from peak to off-peak days has a significant effect on reducing overcrowding.

Focus groups in Denmark and California explored the sensitivity of guests to discounting as part of season ticketing and found, surprisingly, that price was not necessarily an issue for the most loyal guests. What they wanted was exclusivity and the ability to get closer to the company – especially access to the factories and designers. Breakfasts with model builders have proved very successful in California, for example. The team of 60 or so model builders are the creative heart of the business and have a wacky sense of humour. In the UK and Denmark, going 'behind the scenes' and invitations to preview launches of new attractions, has allowed the company better to cultivate enthusiasts for the brand.

The website lego.com is also seen as a legitimate marketing tool by LEGOLAND, although it is a self-contained business unit. The site is very successful for the company in terms of numbers of hits and LEGOLAND itself has ambitions to sell and allow guests to print out park entry tickets from their PCs.

Retail opportunities

I was surprised to see so many shops on the Billund site, compared to Windsor. There are 12, some by the exit, but other themed units are sprinkled around the park, designed to allow guests to buy products related to the attraction they have just visited. This is a difficult area for LEGO, admits Mads Ryder. The opportunity to cross-sell is clearly an important one – there are visible synergies between the leisure and retailing functions – but at the same time, the commercial aspects of the operation must not be allowed to eclipse the entertainment value of the parks and the philosophy of the brand. 'So many parks', says Ryder, 'force you to go through the gift shop on the way to the exit. We must be careful about balancing commercial pressure and brand values.' So although the Windsor park saw more shops being introduced during 2002, including a childrenswear outlet, this will always be a measured introduction. What we have also seen is the marketing of the park as a retail destination in its own right. Since Christmas 2001, UK visitors have been able to shop without necessarily entering the park. LEGO has also experimented with a standalone shop in the Bluewater development in Kent and in Milton Keynes. The company has been approached on numerous occasions by shopping centre developers wanting a mini-LEGOLAND in their developments. Only the Mall of America has one at present – an indication of LEGO's desire to keep the brand exclusive.

Nevertheless, Ryder is quick to say that as retailers, LEGO still have much to learn in terms of store design and operations. Has LEGOLAND then thought of outsourcing the retail aspects of their parks business? Ryder observes that, whilst there are a number of product partners in the parks (for example, Nestlé, Coca-Cola, Carlsberg and Fujifilm, and Audi in Germany) these are more in the way of vendor relationships than true partnerships. LEGOLAND, he feels, would not be averse to identifying what he calls a 'megapartner' with whom to work – but the degree of brand alignment between LEGO and any prospective partner would be critical, as would the logic of the brand association. It would be ineffective to have – say – a carpet company sponsoring an attraction, if there was no apparent relevance to the attraction. It is interesting to note that in November 2002 LEGO announced a global strategic alliance with Nike, centred around the Bionicle product range.

The future of brand extension

Despite its present financial difficulties, LEGOLAND is always looking for ways to extend its brand directly to support its core activities. I had just been ejected from my room at the Hotel Legoland – adjacent to the Billund park – because the hotel would be full on the following night. Ryder was sympathetic but not surprised. The Danish hotel runs at 83 per cent capacity year-round (catering for business guests and conferences outside peak holiday periods). This is a figure many in the hotel industry would love to achieve. If he had planning permission, Ryder says he would build a Hotel Legoland in Windsor 'tomorrow'. But these developments would be to support the parks – LEGOLAND is not in the hotel business. In the same way, the German LEGOLAND has a LEGO campground adjacent to the development, for those guests not wanting or able to afford hotel accommodation.

What lessons can LEGO offer retailers seeking to use leisure services as a way of extending their brands? Brand extension works, concludes Mads Ryder, when it is a relevant, natural and logical extension of the core brand. It was a short leap for a family-centric toy manufacturer to move into family theme parks – for a retailer it might be a very different proposition. Further, LEGO's core values and the product itself provides for exclusive and differentiating features in the LEGOLAND offer that are significantly distinctive from the competition. Mads shows me out into the park. 'Have a fun time and come back soon,' he says, looking at the blue sky 'it shouldn't be too crowded – it's going to be a 3–4,000 guest day.' Leaving Mads smiling at the door, I am startled by a loud snore from the life-size LEGO statue of an old man sitting on a park bench. Clearly, the model-builders have struck again.

Chapter 11

Everything for the trade – next day: Screwfix Direct

Interview with John Allan, managing director of Screwfix Direct

Screwfix Direct, FREEPOST, Yeovil BA22 8BF, UK
0500 41 41 41

Jonathan Reynolds

Screwfix Direct was founded in 1970 as the Woodscrew Supply Company. Now owned by the Kingfisher Group, the company is estimated to have turnover of some £200 million. The company is active in the repair, maintenance and home improvement market in the UK, of which it has a 0.5 per cent market share. However, it commands over 3.5 per cent of the UK trade market, and is the dominant player in the RMI direct market. Screwfix Direct operates one of the largest DIY websites on the Internet. It seeks to offer the lowest prices, with next day delivery and superior service.

Presently headquartered in Yeovil, Screwfix Direct also operates from a warehouse facility in Leicester and is constructing a new headquarters in the Potteries, in the North Midlands.

In this chapter, John Allen, managing director of Screwfix Direct, discusses some of the distinctive characteristics of the business and the reasons for the company's success in managing hybrid channels to the consumer.

Older than you think

The reception area, the corridor to the managing director's office, and the office itself, are full of awards. UK company Screwfix Direct has just picked up the *Investors in People Award*, as well as *E-tailer of the Year 2002* and *West of England Business of the Year*. No wonder John Allan, Managing Director since 2001, is looking pleased. He leans across the table: 'I love this job.' Many people would be forgiven for thinking that Screwfix Direct was one of the few companies to emerge with flying colours from the dot.com debacle in 2001. In fact, the business has substantially deeper roots. Founded in the late 1970s as the Woodscrew Supply Company, it relied on mail order and advertising in *Exchange and Mart* for its business. The company had no way of recording the names and addresses of its customers and dealt with one-off orders from tradesmen. But it prided itself, as it does now, on product quality, depth of offer and customer service. The business was purchased by Kingfisher in 1999 as it sought to develop a portfolio of new ventures that might enhance the future strategic development of the group and which might harness the electronic sales channel. It has proved a canny acquisition.

Growth and transition

The transition from an essentially entrepreneurial small business turning over £100,000 in the early 1990s to over £1 million by 1995 and to a concept worth, according to analysts' estimates, some £200 million in sales today, created many of the challenges typical of a fast growing firm. Great commercial success led in particular to significant infrastructural challenges. At the end of the 1990s, the business was trading out of just 80,000 sq ft of warehousing. Allan's appointment in 2001 was prompted by the need to put into place the systems, processes and resources required to manage a nine-figure turnover business and an exponential growth curve. Screwfix now trades from 580,000 sq ft from a range of buildings in Yeovil, has a sister unit of 500,000 sq ft in Leicester and an extendable facility of 317,000 sq ft opening in 2003 in Trentham in Staffordshire. 'On the growth curve we are on, the business planning process must be different. It takes four years to put in place what we know now will be needed by 2005.' Screwfix sources over 6,000 product lines. In addition to producing four 280-page catalogues every year, the business functions increasingly online, with web-based sales accounting for an estimated 15 per cent of the £140 million total annual revenue in 2001/2.

But there are dangers in becoming too efficient from the supply side perspective, stresses Allan. Whilst a supply chain discipline is critical, mechanization and ultimate supply side efficiency can work against the customer's interest. With a fulfilment system that is especially designed to handle small orders, too much automation in any case is difficult and expensive (as companies like Webvan discovered). John Allan's more flexible focus on the customer creates a virtuous circle in which the business can be seen to respond to not just exceptional circumstances, but evolving customer needs.

The cult of Screwfix

And these customers are very particular animals. 'Screwfix Direct does what it says on the tin', says Allan. 'It's as simple as that.' And that is 'Everything for the trade, next day and at trade prices'. The business is fortunate enough to have a highly defensible and arguably low risk niche market. The key target is the 'light trade' buyer. Although Screwfix has just 0.5 per cent of the UK repair, maintenance and home improvement market, it commands over 3.5 per cent of the UK trade market and is the dominant player in the RMI direct market. Screwfix is driving the direct market – and there's plenty of headroom. The light trade and so-called 'paraprofessional' market (the grey market of individuals who slip in and out of self employment alongside professional DIYers) has been on a long term growth trend in the UK. Typical is the customer who has learned a trade at some point in their life and who undertakes a big project in their own house – and who then may go on to help out a neighbour – and is paid in cash. And for these customers, Screwfix has become something of a cult. Screwfix is not for the Changing Rooms generation. Allan thinks that the Changing Rooms bubble has burst. By far the more reliable market is the 'bread and butter' collection of serial house renovators and the growing number of self-build home-makers. There is also a growing interest in the business from facilities managers. Indeed, as Figure 11.1 shows, the business's market segmentation provides a number of complementary avenues for growth.

How resilient is this market to the prospective slowdown in the housing market and to the economic rumblings of UK plc? Allan regards the business as being well

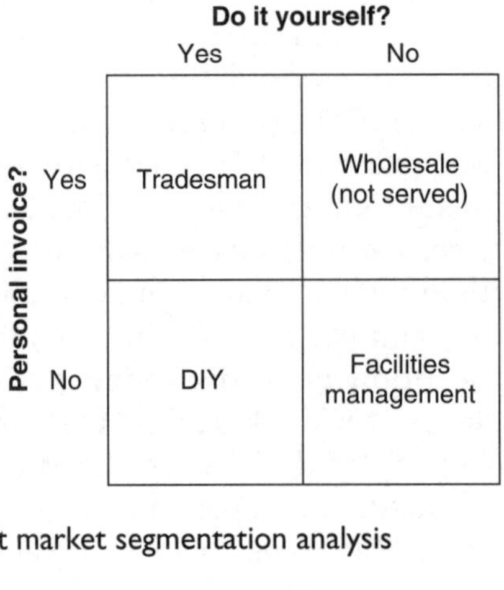

Figure 11.1 Screwfix Direct market segmentation analysis

protected from the economic cycle. If the market turns down, people stay with their existing homes and invest more in them. In any case, Screwfix does not sell, by and large, to those individuals; it sells to the largely self-employed who work on properties. Nor is the market especially seasonal: the month-on-month sales range from slow growth to accelerated growth. There is a modest January–March peak, and Christmas is usually quieter, but the even nature of demand compared to other retailers means that staffing levels can be kept constant.

Culture club

Allan's commitment to customer focus and requisite flexibility, and his rejection of efficiency and mechanization for the sake of it, is most clear in terms of the Screwfix Direct culture. 'Culture is a fascinating thing', he comments. 'It comes from the workforce – it's not something that can be hammered in.' Allan sees the profit-and-loss as the scorecard, not the game. The game is meeting customers' needs.

For example, the contact centre staff has no targets on call duration, as is common with other call centres and this leads to a much more positive atmosphere. They make sure that the customer gets what the customer wants, no matter how long it takes. Both they, and the distribution centre staff, are 'tuned into success' and are flexible. Whilst I was waiting in the reception area, the receptionist shifted smoothly and professionally from handling visitors to handling a customer query that had come through to the head office number by mistake. Rather than forward it to the call centre and putting the caller on hold, she dealt with the request then and there.

Of course, the historical origins of the business and its primary location in the small town of Yeovil has made it one of the biggest employers in the area and makes a 'local', more intimate culture easier to maintain. But the huge change of moving from 24 people in 1995 to 1800 today has provided considerable challenges; and these are not likely to be reduced as the company now operates from a second facility in Leicester and will shortly be commissioning its Staffordshire distribution centre. How does Screwfix Direct manage to maintain its flexible performance culture in the context of exponential growth? Allan claims that this is because although they recruit frequently and often, the business brings people in in small numbers, allowing them to become 'infected' by the existing workforce. Opening the Leicester warehouse as a new build operation with large cohorts of new recruits was a significant challenge in cultural terms: how to recreate and sustain the achievements and values fostered in Yeovil? 'We took a few disease carriers along,' chuckles Allan, 'and they did the job for us.' The business is not unionized, although USDAW has been making strident efforts to force recognition on the retailer. Richard Butler, Screwfix Direct's HR director comments that whilst 'we respect USDAW's right to canvass our staff, we don't want formal presentations. We think we have a dynamic, fair and supportive business.'

Where's the web?

It seems curious that a case selected to address e-commerce issues is only now turning to the company's objectives and achievements in relation to its website. This is not accidental. The fundamentals of a rapidly-growing established business must be well understood and sound irrespective of the superficial merits of its online platform. John Allan's view was that many potentially successful dot-com businesses got to a scale where they were comfortable managing themselves entrepreneurially in terms of turnover – say between £30 and £50 million – driven by the capabilities and constraints of their web presence, but could not get beyond that point.

But a further important consideration is that Screwfix Direct – despite being recognized as 2002's e-tailer of the year by UK trade magazine *Retail Week* – is not dependent upon the web for sales. It is a truly integrated business in terms of marketing channels. The business deals with all direct channels: web, phone, fax and even a few orders received by post. Allan says that he has sought to turn on its head the usual rhetoric about 'a single view of the customer'; he wants the customer to have 'a single view of the organization'. This requires a meticulous consistency of approach in relation to sales channels. So there is no deliberate incentive for customers to order online (unlike other businesses such as easyJet, who provide discounts to online customers as a way of reducing the costs attached to other marketing channels). Indeed, until the end of 2001, the web channel performed a complementary role to the catalogue as an alternative ordering channel. Only recently has it started performing as a sales generator in its own right. Allan wants the web channel to 'reach its natural level'. Its success to date, he believes, also comes from its being very basic and very simple.

This simplicity has meant, so far, that it has not been possible to offer the degree of personalization and flexibility in the web channel that has been available, for example, over the phone. This is soon to change. A beta site is undergoing user acceptability testing and will better harness the Internet's capabilities to personalize the customer's online experience. The site, developed with the support of Javelin Group (whose clients include Marks & Spencer, John Lewis as well as other present and former operating companies of Kingfisher) will include order history and tracking and targeted promotional merchandising and is due for release next year. The redesign will also better integrate the website with the contact centre and fulfilment operations.

Conclusion

What comes out of a discussion with John Allan is that, not surprisingly, it is the viability of the business concept, the durability of the market positioning, the capabilities of the people and the culture within the firm that must be right before issues to do with the practical mix of marketing channels used to deliver sales can be addressed. Effective channel integration is a consequence of the clarity of this vision and attention to detail in the quality of execution. What also becomes clear is that a business concept does not have to have been invented yesterday in order to be relevant to or successful in an electronic marketing environment. The Woodscrew Supply Company found its niche well before most of the Internet generation were born.

As we leave the building, John Allan shows me the first flyer produced by the company in the early 1970s, framed alongside some thirty other flyers and catalogue covers. Although the xeroxed sheet of paper has not weathered well over the years, it is possible to make out a preoccupation with product quality, knowledge and customer service that still prevails today.

Chapter 12

Uniquely Auchan: retailing as invention

Interview with André Tordjman, marketing director of Auchan

Auchan, Rue de la Recherche, 200, 59650 Villeneuve d'Ascq Cedex, France
Tel.: +33 3 28 37 67 00; Fax: +33 3 20 67 55 20

Richard Bell

In France, Auchan has over 100 hypermarkets and over 260 supermarkets with a combined staff of over 60,000 making net sales of over €27 billion in 2001. Auchan now has a presence in 14 countries, including 160 outlets in Spain and others in Portugal, Italy, Morocco, Asia, and central and eastern Europe. With a reputation for surprising the customer, Auchan makes an interesting marketing case study.

Auchan perspective

Retailers sell goods and the goods that one retailer, for example Carrefour, sells are often the same as the goods that another retailer, perhaps Auchan, sells. The question is how to create a unique positioning, a difference between us and the competition. In the past, the key to retailing was to buy at the lowest price in order to sell to the consumer at the lowest price. Although this has led to success for retailers in the past, it will not be enough to be the best in the market of the future. Today, we are moving from a distributor focus to a brand focus. However, there is still a lot of work to do. First of all it is necessary to change the way of doing business. In the past, retailers sold what they bought. Today, we have to first define what we want to sell. If we want to become the best and to achieve uniqueness, it means that we have to have a brand mission. When we sell 450 different categories, from fruit and vegetables to computers, to clothing, to pet food – what could be the common element that makes us different from the competition?

Creator of better solutions

At Auchan, we want to move away from being a distributor of products to being a creator of solutions that improve the standard of living for the majority of people. However, there remains the question of how to organize to make sure that this positioning brings uniqueness to the market. First, becoming a brand means providing proof every day of the meaning and value of the brand. Creating and delivering solutions means thinking about products, packaging, services and the store, in a way that improves shopping and living. We have done this with Auchan products on a day-to-day basis.

A simple example of an innovative Auchan product is found in our plastic food storage boxes. The main difficulty when opening a cupboard to retrieve a storage box is to find the lid that fits the box. The colour on an Auchan box matches the colour of the lid. So if you see a red box and a red lid, it means that they fit together. It is a small thing but we have perfected it. For a further example, a child at a swimming pool or the sea might have an inflatable ring. The main difficulty for a small baby using a ring is that he cannot move his arms. We have developed an inflatable that is not round but is in a figure-of-eight so that the baby has freedom of movement.

For an example of uniqueness in services, if a customer buys a washing machine in Auchan and the washing machine is out of order for more than 48 hours, we have to find a solution. When a family of four has no washing machine, it is a disaster. Our commitment is to provide a washing machine during the time that we fix the machine. For another example, if a customer wants to have dinner tonight but is unsure what to cook, she can telephone Auchan and ask a chef for recipe ideas. If the customer is trying to lose weight, on the same telephone number Auchan can provide advisers.

A further example of uniqueness is provided by our new store concept, organizing a store not as a manufacturer might, by product category, but in the way that people consume the product. The Auchan store in Valle D'Europe is organized this way.

These small examples demonstrate Auchan's unique approach to the product lines, stores and services – improving life on a day-to-day basis. But why have we become inventors? The answer is that our role is no longer to copy but to solve a problem from a consumer point of view, in using, eating or handling the products, whatever the problem. This creates the Auchan uniqueness.

L'Institut Auchan

To further Auchan's mission, we have created L'Institut Auchan as the guardian of customer values throughout the company. The institute is responsible for monitoring the evolution of some aspects of French society, and undertakes research on the way that people – seniors, the young, people on holiday – live, move and communicate. Reports are produced that offer insight into French society. All of the Auchan management receive the report summarized and in full. Each report considers an aspect of the evolution of society and the implications for Auchan.

It is important not to have the research divorced from the operations. So although the researchers are from my market research department, the people who decide which studies should be undertaken and the implications of the results of the studies are the operational people – store managers, market managers and category managers. This way, we make sure that we are people-oriented. With a prime task not to write the report or to research, but to make sure the research we have done answers the questions that the operational people have asked.

There is an operational committee, which is different depending on the topic. For example, we have an operational committee at the moment working on young people because we know that young people do not often go to hypermarkets. The committee is composed of people at the store, the market people at marketing level.

To summarize, the operations group identify the subjects for research, the institute undertakes the research, and then the operations side have to respond to the research with solutions to the problems that they had identified. In this way, they are their solutions, and so the solutions will be properly implemented.

Private-label products

In the Auchan view, private-label products are not essential to achieving uniqueness. First of all because the brand mission statement is to provide better solutions, a better life, and the better solutions cannot only be found with Auchan products. The Auchan product may be part of the solution but it is not always essential to the solution. Auchan should always provide the choice to its consumers. If we reduce the choice, we reduce the solutions.

We must keep the big and high quality brands and add our own products to these brands. The market share of the Auchan product will be what the consumer decides, not what we decide for the consumer. We will never, never, never reduce the choice to the consumers and we will never decide that the Auchan product must be in a better position than the other brands.

Even with no Auchan products, we should be able to achieve uniqueness because the world of market management today is not simply to have an assortment based on what I have bought but to have an assortment of what we decide to sell. I ask each market manager for a marketing plan for his or her category. In this way, the manager demonstrates his or her understanding of the market and predictions for the future of the market but they also include what they want to be on the market. We cannot be everything to everyone. For example, we cannot sell every type of clothing to every type of person in France. We have to decide which clothing is for whom. This is why, even if we did not have any Auchan products, we could achieve uniqueness by managers deciding where they want to be in their market.

Consistent proposition

However, it is important to ensure that what one manager wants for his or her category is consistent with the overall proposition of the Auchan brand. This is part of the role of the marketing director. Each completed document comes to me and I make sure that it provides a clear analysis of the market, because if the analysis is clear, the position is good. For example, if I decide that Auchan will be the most environmentally friendly hypermarket in the world and I will sell only organic food, this is my position. I must make sure that in all the categories, the emphasis is on organic food – whether it is for pets or for humans. That would be my position, and I have to make sure that all the market categories are consistent with this position.

Brand equity

Once you begin to build a brand based on providing solutions, it raises the issue of brand equity. One classic measure of brand strength is that price elasticity is low. However, there should not be a conflict between branding and price position. The difference between branding in retailing and branding in manufacturing is that, for manufacturers, a good brand has 'good will' in the price. You are willing to pay more for a Mars Bar, for example. However, from a retailing point of view, it is very difficult to make a consumer understand that, because there is a better choice, a service is provided. For the consumer, if you take a bottle of Evian or Badoit, it is difficult to explain that there are two different prices. However, becoming a brand does not mean that prices should increase. We have to throw away the idea that marketing always brings higher prices. Marketing should bring value and value does not mean increased prices.

To be able to afford to invest in our research and development, to innovate, to invest in new concept stores, to improve stores, to invest in service; we should try to lower our costs. The best method of lowering our costs is not in buying but in better economy of costs in the stores. Today, many members of our sales force are responsible for replenishment. However, we should be devoted to consumers, and so we have to find a way to be more competitive in the methods of replenishment. This is why, while we are creating the brand, we have to find economy of scale by better information systems, which provide free time for employees to devote to consumers. For the first time since the creation of the hypermarket, we are fashioning a new organization for the hypermarket. We will still have a store manager but below him or her there are two important roles, a marketing director and a logistics director. The marketing director is responsible for defining the marketing plan for the store.

The brand gives power to the promotion. The brand campaign gives my promotion more importance because the brand campaign is unique. Anyone can reduce the price of a bottle of Badoit, but the brand campaign makes the promotion unique. Part of each advertising budget should be invested on pure branding. Now, the question is, can you communicate both on values and on promotion? This is how Auchan communicates in advertising, consumer material and promotional activities. Sometimes principally communicating the brand and sometimes chiefly the promotion but always the same great product.

For the future, Auchan can do more in terms of the upstream functions of the business. However, our main focus is to be very good at the basics. Basics means that the store is clean, the products are on the shelves, the tag is well done, and so on. These are the basics. You cannot become a good brand if the basics are not right. It is a little like an iceberg. The tip of the iceberg is what we see in terms of consumer loyalty but below this level there are a lot of activities going on to ensure delivery at store level.

Marketing directors at store level

The retail brand exists only at the store level. If we are not able to have 52,000 ambassadors of the brand (that is to say, the employees of Auchan) we are not able to become a brand. To be able to achieve both global and local strength, the role of marketing is not to decide on the store identity. The role is to give the framework within which each store acts. A marketing director at the store level cannot try to be marketing director for all of Auchan because we cannot afford to have 120 marketing directors. The brand is unique, so we cannot have 120 brand mission statements and 120 different ways of communicating. We have one brand mission statement.

However, each store is different: different in size, competition and consumers. Therefore, the store is left to define the store position, and to identify the most important markets. For example, in an area where there are a lot of young, working people, I may not carry bicycles for children. I will have bicycles for young managers wanting to de-stress at the weekends. However, where there are a lot of children, Auchan should carry bicycles for children. I, as marketing director for Auchan, should not decide what each store should carry but I should decide what position Auchan wants to have on bicycles, provide a number of different models and let the store chose. However, they must select a consistent position. A store cannot be a little bit of this and a little bit of that. This approach would not produce a clear image. The brand provides the framework and the store nourishes the framework. To make that possible, it is necessary to elevate the competences in marketing at the store level. It is why, today, we have a marketing director at the store level. The decision must be taken at the place closest to the consumer.

The role of the marketing manager

There is a lot of talk about category management. I never use the term category management in my work at Auchan because what has been done well in category management has been done principally by manufacturers and does not adapt well to retailers. I do not ask people to manage a category, but rather to understand the market, identify a place in the market and only then decide on the category. Today, we need to build a marketing plan rather than undertake complex data analysis. That is not to say that I do not need to know the size and other properties of the category. We do analyse all these characteristics, but it is most important to define your position in the market if you want to be ahead of the market. In the past, stores were always the same because they were created around the categories. Now the question is one of market position, and this makes for a very different strategy.

This is a world that is going to be dominated by the marketing manager. For example in meal solutions, perhaps Auchan want to be good and cheap. Well, that is good news; it is better to be good and cheap than bad and expensive. However, that is not enough. Meal solutions may be ready to eat, ready to cook, use organic products, gourmand meals, exotic, traditional, speciality or every day. It is not easy to identify a market position, but when the marketing manager is able to define a position, only then it is possible to perform an analysis.

So, the term marketing manager, rather than category manager, focuses on the market and focuses on the consumer. We have separated the buyers from the marketing managers. The marketing managers define what we want to sell and the give the buyers the responsibility of negotiating the buying. This means that the buyers are no longer deciding what we are going to sell. The marketing manager decides what we are going to sell and the buyer executes the buying. We have separated the functions and the marketing manager must make sure that what we want to do is consistent with the marketing strategy.

Suppliers have marketing people that understand the consumer potential and they have sales people who negotiate with buyers. Our marketing people talk to the marketing people of our suppliers. This is an enriching and constructive dialogue, and will become more so in the future. We have to change. We have hired people from outside and they have to learn what we are doing in the market. We have people from Auchan, and they have to learn what marketing involves. The combination of the two types of people is very powerful, now they start to talk to suppliers. My role as marketing director is to elaborate some dialogues at the strategic level. The problem I face today is that suppliers have been used to defining the strategy they think we want Auchan to have. Now, they might provide input to the strategy and we might share ideas but they no longer formulate the strategy. I am not going to delegate that role.

Summary

In less than two years we have built the brand mission statement, we have reorganized, we have created the new advertising campaign, we have a new concept for the stores, and the new product Auchan design. Now this is all very new. In the future we will be able to tell manufacturers what we want to be about. For example, we might want to provide solutions for pets, food, health and so on. We might ask a manufacturer to help. However, they would have to understand that we are not willing to carry all the product categories but we are going to take products that support our position. It is why my store will be different from Carrefour because Carrefour may have a similar approach but will not be doing the same thing.

Chapter 13

Straightforward British approach works in China

Interview with Steve Gilman, international director of B&Q

B&Q plc, Portswood House, 1 Hampshire Corporate Park, Chandlers Ford, Eastliegh, Hampshire SO53 3YX
Tel.: +44 (0) 23 8025 6256; Fax: +44 (0) 23 8025 7480

Elizabeth Howard

B&Q was founded in the UK in the late 1960s and is now the UK's leading DIY and garden centre retailer. The format has proved popular in other regions of the world, and B&Q now has over 20 stores in Asia and further outlets in Poland and Turkey. B&Q had a turnover in 2002/3 of £3.7 billion, with a profit of £360 million and over 30,000 employees.

Steve Gilman is the international director of B&Q and sits on the B&Q main board reporting directly to Bill Whiting, the CEO. B&Q is part of CDI, a joint venture between Kingfisher and Castorama. Steve has been with the business for 22 years in total, joining as an assistant store manager. Today he spends about two weeks out of six in Asia, as well as time in Turkey and Poland.

B&Q's international focus

Most of the focus over the last three and half years has been on China and Taiwan. B&Q is part of CDI with Castorama of France, and Castorama have an international division just as B&Q do. We have an informal agreement about where we focus our time, so the Castorama international team is focused on European development and South America. I focus my time and energies on Turkey and the East. Kingfisher own about 34 stores in Poland under the NOMI brand, and I run those as well.

B&Q have five stores in Turkey. That was a relatively recent entry, where we bought a 50 per cent stake in Koçtas, a subsidiary of the Koç Group. The Koç Group is a big conglomerate, very much like Samsung in Korea or Mitsubishi in Japan. Because of the volatility of the Turkish economy, many western partners get concerned. The indigenous companies feel more comfortable with hyperinflation, hyper interest rates, cash management and all things that we have had to learn in a new way in Turkey.

However, we inherited a number of stores, we closed one small store, we built a brand new warehouse and we did all that during the course of 2001, which has been one of the worst years economically for Turkey. We are still there and we are doing OK. We will continue to work out how we are going to build a business in Turkey.

Excitement and potential in China

If the market in China keeps on growing at 7–8 per cent, they will catch up with America over the next 25–30 years or so, which in China, they consider a blink of an eye. For the last two years we have been talking about our pan-Asian vision. We entered Taiwan initially on a fact-finding mission in 1995. Our partner in Taiwan was Tony Ho – the CEO for Test-Rite. Test-Rite have been a major supplier for B&Q for about 20 years. Tony had a vision that Taiwan was ready for a home improvements store. We opened in a low cost way, realized that there was a market and we have been building that business for the last five years. B&Q now have 13 stores, we are profitable and we are opening another three stores this year. It has been a great test bed. Taiwan is a good place to start for western companies that have never worked in an Asian context before. Arguably, Hong Kong is better but more expensive.

Taiwan is a good starting place partly because of the American influence over the last 50 years. The facilities, such as schools for westerners, are good. There is empathy for working with westerners. Shanghai has a similar sort of appeal when you enter mainland China and it is likely that most B&Q employees who have worked out there would say they would rather live in Shanghai than Taipei. And I think I would as well if I was to go back there.

Learning as a team and as an individual

We are fairly confident that we know what makes a good person for us. One of the necessary skills is the desire to learn. When you first go out there, you do not know the language, you do not know the culture, you do not know the customers' behaviour at home, you do not know what is important and not important to them and you do not know how to motivate people. You realize you have to start again. Now that is part of the fun because you start to learn that it is about relationships. The Chinese will say that a contract is just an intention to do something, and a handshake means it really will happen. That is not the way we do business in the UK. So a lot of the time you are conducting business the reverse way you do things in the UK. Good communication skills, even if you are unable to speak Chinese, are crucial.

We are having Chinese lessons, and there is a couple in my team who can speak passable Chinese. Personally I am careful about my tone of voice. I deliberately slow down and am much more measured. I am quite excitable but until my relationship with somebody is very good I am much quieter in the way I speak. You have to learn so much. I think I have still got an awful lot to learn and the same goes for anybody in the team.

Approaching the Chinese market

Obviously, what B&Q 'brings to the party' is all our experience. Our approach to any country is enter in a low cost way, delivering what we believe the customers want and having done the market research. Once we establish that the customer is there and that we can find an economic format that will work, then Kingfisher, our parent company, is very supportive.

For example, in information systems. Our initial system in mainland China came from a Chinese domestic software company, who were a derivative of the Chinese missile programme. They had developed a retail software package for a couple of local retailers. Working in collaboration, we reached the stage where it was good enough to do what we needed to do, and at relatively low cost. The system was not going to be the solution for the future but now we have replaced all our local systems with SAP, again in a low cost way. It may have been more expensive than the original, but low cost from a European perspective.

B&Q's principle is not to go in with big investment until we know that we can make money. Being low cost is a real quality. If you look at our businesses you see that we try to get as much of an international standard as we can but with the lowest possible cost. Boots and Marks & Spencer – and I would not necessarily want to criticize them – have always gone in with a much bigger budget. They have put in state-of-the-art stores, which means the economic model is built on a difficult cost base. Obi, a German competitor of ours in China, is trying something similar currently.

B&Q image in China

We have only five UK expatriates in mainland China. Of the top four management positions, one is English and three are Chinese. Our president is Chinese. Certain jobs in Carrefour, in contrast, are nearly always expatriate jobs, so it produces a glass ceiling with the locals.

You can find very, very well educated young people in China, who are very ambitious, and want to learn. In China, if I said 'tomorrow morning at 3 a.m. we are going to run a course on . . . whatever' we would probably have 100 people attending voluntarily! When we are recruiting, obviously salary is important but it is not as important as the learning opportunity. People have a tremendous desire to learn.

The next challenge is how to get people to think 'outside the nine dots', that is, to think more widely. To do that we must provide an environment where they start to believe that this is not a traditional Chinese environment, this is a Chinese/British environment. That takes a while, and comes back to personality and attitude and learning. If they want to take an initiative, even if you are pretty sure it's wrong, it is good to let them have a go. Then don't shoot them when they make the mistake. The Chinese are very self-critical anyhow, that is part of their education system. So my inclination if someone comes and makes a suggestion is to consider how can I make that happen for them and what is the risk? If the risk is small, then I encourage it. That is the behaviour that you really want people to learn. In the beginning, most of the initiatives in store were British and now it is probably 50/50. In a few years time, it will be 80/20 Chinese, which is probably where it should be.

Customers and lifestyles

Chinese customers, Turkish customers and Polish customers all want to live in a better way than they did before. In China, previously state-owned housing is now being sold off very cheaply to people who have lived there a long time, and virtually all new housing is private. So there is massive social change in China. And everyone wants to improve his or her home. Chinese employees want to live in a better home and their customers want to live in a better home, but none of them has had the 30–40 years experience of home improvement that we have. Initially it is about bringing in the plumber or the decorator, but then more and more customers choose their own things and learn how to do-it-yourself. We promote it as being something that is fun and enjoyable. We encourage with 'how to' displays in our stores, with our learning centres, and with our demonstrations.

Another important aspect is that in China (and in most countries) people believe that workmanship standards are quite poor and shoddy. So if they bring in someone to do something, they are probably not going to do a very good job. The risk of them using fake or poor quality products is also high. If they come into a store like ours, they know that if it says ICI on the can, it is ICI inside. Our own brand paint is also particularly successful. It will cover all surfaces. Now that is quite attractive to the UK customer, but to an Asian customer who is worried about how to do things, it is brilliant. So the B&Q brand means an awful lot more to consumers in Asia than it does in the UK.

Differences from the UK business

We include more furniture in China than in the UK. It is a different product range to the UK: more tailored to the customers. We also set up our own home decoration service, first in Shanghai and later in all the businesses in China. About 20 per cent of our turnover is driven through the decoration service. We will go into the typical, completely bare, new flat, and we will design it with the consumer. We will understand their budget, their lifestyle, whether they want modern or ultra Chinese. Then we will give them a quote that shows the cost of all materials bought from a B&Q store, the cost of labour, and a management fee. If they say yes, then over two to three months we will completely do out their whole apartment for them.

Customers perceive us as very experienced and knowledgeable, with high quality, and reasonable value for money. They do not see us as the cheapest, even though most of the time we are actually leading edge on price. Even people who have never even been to a B&Q store have enormous trust and confidence in us. When they actually go to a store then they also say that our prices are OK.

Trust in the brand

Let me tell you a story about trust. About a week after we had set up the decoration service, a guy came into our first store, and said: 'I'm a local from Shanghai but I live most of my time in the UK now and I know B&Q. Here's 100,000 renminbi (RMB). I have just bought an apartment and I like a fairly modern style, please get on and decorate it for me.' He gave us the keys to his apartment and gave us the cash. A week later we faxed him a copy of a design for the apartment, he said it looks good, just get on with it! The next he knew was when he came back three months later and it was finished. That says something about B&Q branding in the UK but it also says an awful lot about the brand in China.

Private-label strategy

Private-label will probably be greater elsewhere than in the UK for B&Q. In all the countries we are in, the vast majority of products that we want to sell are manufactured in those countries. We import to add innovative and different products. In China, one of the reasons for going for private label is that many of the big brands are already available in the marketplace, but they still account for a small proportion of total turnover. For example, we own-brand a large proportion of our lighting – now that is not the case in the UK. That reinforces confidence in our brand but it also helps us to differentiate ourselves in the market place. Chinese consumers are very, very price conscious. If we can put a product out that is ours, which we believe offers very good value for money and is guaranteed in the consumer's mind by B&Q, then the price comparison is less in the customer's mind.

For example, the B&Q brand of paint has been developed in the UK with the UK in mind. The tub is clear plastic so you can see the colour of the paint. The presentation is innovative and the quality of the paint is very good. We were shipping some of this paint from Germany, where it was manufactured, directly to Shanghai or to Taiwan. I was paying shipping costs and import costs and did not have the language right. So own-brand paint became a very expensive and not necessarily very innovative product in the range. We will launch paint manufacture in China in March. The tub is still being made in Europe but it is now completely Chinese labelling, in fact we have distinguished between the simplified Chinese for mainland and the complex Chinese (Mandarin) for Taiwan.

We still make the tub in Europe, but this is Asia so you know it will get copied fairly quickly. Soon we will be able to do this in China as well. The development cycles are much quicker in China, and it is not simply copying. Think about money for instance: the UK went from cash to cheque, and then to credit card. China has just moved straight from cash to credit card. They do not simply go through some of the cycles more quickly – quite often they leapfrog. That is one of the interesting things about China: some things are 20 years behind Europe and some things are 10 years in front.

The Castorama connection

The main thing that Castorama have learnt from us about internationalizing is probably our approach to property. If we want a piece of land then my team will negotiate and get a price. Then I will introduce an international property company and they will give their opinion on the value of the land. That then gives my Chinese team and me a new target. It is Castorama's view to go in and buy land more quickly. I think ours is the best way on that, but there are aspects of their business that we learn from.

B&Q and Castorama have very different approaches. For example, B&Q have as few expatriates as possible and a mostly local management team. Then we have an experienced central team who support all the functions in each of the businesses. Castorama's way is to build a slightly bigger expatriate team who are able to do most things in their local country, with a slightly smaller central team. But Castorama has of course been a decentralized company at home in France. They have been becoming a more centralized company over the last 12–18 months.

Triggers for entry into new markets

It is only four years ago that the Chinese government made retail an 'experimental industry'. It is still experimental although I think it will be completely de-regulated within three years. So it is really only in the last four or five years that the opportunity has existed. The next thing is that you have to have the guts to go and do it. Because we said we were prepared to enter in a low cost way and learn, we were able to go in when other people did not. Obi had an office in China for nearly two years before we did, but they opened their first store six months after us. I think that says something about us and about what our values are.

'Can do' has always been a B&Q value. Basically we have said: biggest market, biggest opportunity – we will make it happen. There is a bit of bloody-mindedness about B&Q, about me and about the people in our team. It has given us the first mover advantage.

Meeting Hansen Tian, now our president in China, was also important. About six years ago, the first home improvement store in China was opened, an indigenous one called the Homeway in Tianjin. Bill Whiting asked me if I would go over with three other guys to have a look at this business. They were looking for an investor. In the end our recommendation was that we should not invest but while we were there we met Hansen, their finance and systems VP. We do unearth some excellent people and when people spend a little bit of time with us they love the culture.

When they compare us against, for example, the French or the Germans or other Asians, they think that we British are unique. Government officials seem to like working with the British, certainly since Hong Kong went back to China. They perceive us as being straight: if we say we are going to do something, we actually do it. They see the French as being nimbler than the British but perhaps feel that they cannot trust them as much. The Germans are seen as too pedantic. The Americans love the investment but do not like the need to rely on trust. We fit in pretty well there at the moment. Being British is quite helpful in a lot of ways with our negotiations.

Possibilities in Japan and Korea

We had an office in Japan for nearly a year that we closed down last year. Japan is the second biggest market in the world after the United States but it does have 3000 home centres already, that is ten companies with more than a US$1 billion turnover. The opportunity is there and there are ways of entry but all require a very deep pocket. The supply chain is just bizarre and needs to be taken apart. For example, a one-ring gas burner: a couple of years ago we were selling them in the UK for £10, in Taiwan we were selling for £5 and in Japan they were £25. A basic 16oz steel claw hammer we were selling for £2.99 in the UK. It retails for about £2.00 in Taiwan. The cheapest one in Japan is about

£14.00. The examples are endless. The opportunity is there but property is enormously expensive, people are relatively expensive, and the supply chain needs re-structuring but no domestic retailer wants to start that process and it would be a long fight.

We have an office open in Korea and we are still investigating the Korean market. I believe the Korean market is a good one. We still have not found the right way of entering that market but we are working on that.

Partners and relationships

The situation with partners is different in every country. In Poland we now own 100 per cent. Our other three businesses are all partnerships, and in Korea we have being looking at partnerships but also considering the possibility of working without a partner. Our preference is to have a partner. Obviously in mainland China a partner is essential because the maximum we are allowed to own under current law is 65 per cent.

With all our partners we are very clear about what we have to offer and about what we want the partner to provide in the relationship. Absolute clarity is essential from the outset. We provide investment and 30 or more years experience of retailing. We can adapt and adopt our format based on market research to satisfy customer needs. We know we are not going to get it right with the first store and that is good: we always make mistakes but we know how to learn from them, and get it right before we start to move out. We have got an approach that works for us. We want the partner to be very flexible and prepared to be a partner. It is also important to us to have the possibility of an opt-out some time in the future.

There are two things we really want partners to bring: political relationships and property. We want them to bring us political relationships, they need to help us with that, though we are not completely reliant on them because our management team are very able at building these relationships too. In China you have to hit all levels at the same time. People that can help with that and even low level things like getting your gas supply turned on a bit quicker than normally is very helpful. The other side is property: having people who can help you find the right sites at the right price. For instance in mainland China, as a foreigner you have to pay taxes when you buy land use rights, there is no such thing as total freehold. We do 40-year deals, however – almost freehold. You can hire lawyers and property consultants but having people who actually know the way things work means that you can buy property at the lowest possible price for a foreigner. It will always be more expensive than for the locals but you can shrink the gap quite considerably. Advice about strategic direction and cultural advice is important, but the two key things are political relationship and property.

B&Q's future in China

Geoff Mulcahy, Kingfisher's chief executive, announced some six months ago that we would open 58 stores by the end of the year 2005. That is the target we are working towards. It is mostly on the eastern seaboard but we are looking at Wuhan, which is considered western and we are already trading in Kunming, which is near the Vietnam border. Whether we achieve 58 in 2005 or not is dependent on lots of circumstances: it is a very ambitious pace. We have five stores trading now, we will open another six this year with plans to open seven or eight next year. Therefore, 20 stores by the end of 2003 is the interim target.

I want to make sure we open all our stores well and not just quickly. Some of that is about making sure infrastructure is in place and a lot is about people. We continue to recruit excellent people, but quite often with relatively little experience in what we want them to do. Training is necessary but training is also time-consuming and costly.

Another fundamental building block is the SAP system, which we launched very successfully in December 2001. The next is logistics. China is a very big place, so we have entered into an agreement with Maersk Logistics and they are providing the logistics to our two stores outside Shanghai. Kunming is 1,958 km from Shanghai: 50 per cent of the stock will come from the central distribution centre in Shanghai and 50 per cent will be Kunming sourced. You cannot start moving plasterboard from one end of China to the other – it does not make sense. Together we are learning how to make the logistics work. We have only been out there three years and we are already accelerating away. I must stress the importance of the balance between being quick and doing it well. I am not by nature 100 per cent – getting 80 per cent result through 20 per cent effort does me fine.

Most of the countries in Europe are mature home improvement markets, and there are big decisions to be made if you want to enter. My decisions at the moment are smaller decisions, involving smaller amounts of money. I will worry about how I can justify relatively small investments in these countries that do not drain resource from the main business but a few years out when the company is looking for real growth streams of profitability, then I will be ready. My vision is that in ten years time the international businesses will be a very significant part of B&Q's total profitability. It is not just about opening new stores. We probably have 2,500 or 3,000 new manufacturers supplying us in China that have no relationship with the UK or France. Obviously we're starting to build those bridges. New manufacturers will bring new products to Europe, which will also help the profitability of the business.

. . . and finally

If I could be granted one wish, it would be for access to more and better people. That does not mean to say that the people I have got are not great, but I would like even more of them and even better. This business is all about people, the people who are making things happen.

Chapter 14

Metro in China or a Chinese Metro?

Interview with Dr Hans-Joachim Körber, chairman and CEO of Metro AG

METRO AG, Metro-Straße 1, 40235 Düsseldorf, Germany
Tel.: +49 211 6886 0; Fax: +49 211 6886 2178

Richard Bell

Metro AG was created in 1996 as a result of the merger of Metro Cash and Carry, Kaufhof Holding AG and Asko Deutsche Kaufhaus AG. In 2002, the group generated net sales of €51.5 billion and today has over 2,200 outlets in 26 countries. The six sales divisions of the Metro Group are Metro Cash and Carry GmbH, Real SB-Warenhaus GmbH, Ezxtra Verbrauchermärkte GmbH, Media-Saturn-Holding GmbH, Praktiker-Bau und Heimwerkermärkte AG and Kaufhof Warenhaus AG. In addition to the sales divisions, the Metro Group has several cross-divisional service companies to perform such tasks as purchasing, logistics and IT.

Dr Hans-Joachim Körber has been CEO of Metro AG since January 1999. In this chapter, Dr Körber discusses some of the issues facing a truly international retailer.

Global retailing?

Food retailing is still far from being a global business. The top ten food retailers have a worldwide market share of approximately 11 per cent. No retailer has a comprehensive presence in all regions of the 'triad' – North America, Western Europe and Japan – and the triad regions account for more than 65 per cent of world retail sales. For example, Wal-Mart is only in ten countries and 90–95 per cent of Wal-Mart's business is the United States.

Nevertheless, given more or less stagnating home markets and the growth opportunities abroad, internationalization is a major part of the strategy of many of the big players in retailing. With a sales share of more than 42 per cent outside our home market, Metro is one of the most international retail companies.

We saw a lot of merger and acquisition activities in European retailing in 1999, including Wal-Mart/Asda and Carrefour/Promodès. The year 2000 was rather quiet in this respect. We have seen no bigger national consolidations and no significant cross-border alliances. One reason is a higher valuation of possible take-over targets. Such prices can only be financed by synergies and synergies are still very hard to realize across borders. It is still very difficult to create synergies across the whole of Europe. Additionally, integrating acquired companies can be a difficult task, as we can see from Wal-Mart's last acquisitions in Germany.

For the future, I expect consolidation to gain momentum again. In the long run, global retailing will be characterized, but not dominated, by global players. At the end of this decade I estimate that the top ten retailers will have a market share of around 20 per cent. There will always remain sufficient potential for successful national niche competitors. In other words, the mix of retail players is likely to be similar in the future to the mix we see today; some international, some cross-border, some national, some regional and some local.

Strategy for growth

One major value driver of Metro AG's strategy is sales growth, especially through international expansion where we achieve above-average growth rates. We are taking four of our six operating concepts abroad. Over the last few years, we have consequently increased the foreign sales proportions of operating divisions and of the group.

Metro AG is targeting store openings primarily in those divisions where the concept is most advanced and therefore the value creation is highest, namely cash-and-carry and consumer electronics. With our ambitious store-opening programme, we will generate approximately 50 per cent of Group sales abroad in the medium term via organic growth.

It is worth commenting that internationalization is not a one-way street. For example, Metro Cash and Carry, France, has very extensive know-how in fresh food. This helped us to improve our fresh food offering at Metro Cash and Carry, Germany. For formalized knowledge transfer, we founded the Metro Fresh Academy affiliated to Metro France.

Concept adaptation

Among the most difficult tasks of internationalization is surely the adaptation of the concept to the specific market conditions. Retail relies more than other sectors on interaction with people. In contrast to the production industry, retail never functions as an enclave, for example like a factory does in another country. In order to be successful, a retailer must integrate with the community and the society of a country. So the concepts, and especially the assortments, must be adapted to the different languages and customs of the consumers.

Different attitudes and shopping behaviours arising from different customs, religions, climatic conditions, etc. require that the assortments be individually adapted to each country. For example, we have learned that 'fresh' in China, with regard to fish, means nothing less than 'alive'. Although consumer habits are converging in certain product groups, there are still significant regional differences in consumption and taste. The varying purchasing power of the customers and widely differing income distribution require individual adaptation of the assortment structure, particularly in the non-food segment. The only answer is local and national management. We could have a Metro in China, or a Chinese Metro. It is always more successful to develop a Metro in China.

It is important to have a supporting structure, a super-national organization on top of a national organization. Most of the assortment is sourced in the country. With retailing you are doing business in a country, with a country, with the people in the country. In this respect, retailing is much more complex than, for example, manufacturing. Some retail concepts have relevance in certain countries but do not necessarily have a universal relevance. For example, Carrefour demonstrated the applicability of the hypermarket concept to Latin America, southern Europe and Asia-Pacific but have never been successful in Germany.

To be a successful international retailer, you need a success story in your own country. You should never go abroad if you do not have a successful formula. The question is then concerning the extent of adaptation necessary. There may be one format for Europe or many adaptations by country or region. The extent of adaptation is not easily determined.

Human resource issues

In order to ensure an intelligent adaptation, Metro generally employs country managers who are from the respective country and are therefore very familiar with the local market conditions. Before beginning their jobs, these managers go through a comprehensive training programme in our company in various countries and divisions.

We have a strong human resource development programme that has evolved over many years. Whatever you have in mind, you need the people who know the concept and you need people who know the country. So normally at the top levels of country management we have a mixture of people from the country and people from Germany. It is attractive for young employees to work in a company that has international opportunities.

International, national and group culture

When you judge the success of any kind of merger or internationalization, the really crucial issue is culture. When you see the failure of acquisitions, the difficulties are also cultural. Despite a need to adapt, it is necessary to create an international culture. For example, in our cash-and-carry business, from the secretaries to the top management the language of business is English. A member of a local cash-and-carry is also part of the bigger group. However, creating an international culture takes more than thought. Retailers really need to invest in human resources.

A corporate culture is also very important. What makes a Chinese manager proud to do his job for a German company? Is it the way we think, the way he is treated, the opportunities he is offered? It is not easy to determine the answer. The big food retailers like Metro and Carrefour have a long-term development programme of internationalization. When a retailer has been internationally active for more than thirty years, it is easier to speed up. To start from scratch, as Wal-Mart did, is not so easy.

Identifying new markets

When Metro AG are seeking opportunities in new countries, we always start with a comprehensive feasibility study. We send a very capable and knowledgeable management team. They analyse the whole infrastructure, the environment, distribution and customer structures, the legal and tax frameworks, and so on to find out whether cash-and-carry is possible.

Then we have some discussion about the opportunities offered. We start with the big international suppliers and explore the nature of the consumers. You have to procure for the local demands of the customers and then the adaptation is about knowing the assortment, layout, and so on. It is not prescriptive.

The cost of land is an important issue. In some countries land is extremely expensive. For example, in high inflation countries, like Turkey, it is extremely expensive. It is then a question of construction, labour costs and margins – so we have a ten-year business case.

Usually Metro Cash and Carry reaches break-even in a country within two to three years. After an initial investment of €15–20 million per store, a country will autonomously finance further expansion with three stores. This strong self-financing capability due to high stock rotation and a high negative net working capital is a major asset of cash-and-carry. Of course, profitability always depends on the speed of expansion. For us it is most important that we see that our concepts work in the country.

We may sometimes use partners. We started our European operation with partners. At that time, in the late 1960s, early 1970s, we believed that it was necessary to have somebody for issues such as tax and licensing. However, our experience with partners has not been good in the long term. In a lot of countries, for example in China, we are forced to have a partner. In other countries, when we fear that countries are fairly difficult, perhaps because of the legal framework, then we look for a partner. This is the case in Japan. So it depends on the country.

The efforts to enter a country are always the same. You have to put in a management team, and you have to conduct the feasibility study. Once an opportunity is identified, the rest is almost mechanical. So our focus is on the most appropriate areas and cultures for our successful formats.

Benchmarking

We see benchmarking as a key measure of success in each of our formats. We started a benchmarking programme in the mid-1990s. Every one of our distribution divisions has a national, and an international benchmark, not in the sense of copying but in identifying and exploring the differences so that we can have a much more informed discussion on strategy. We go much deeper than simply turnover per square metre. Productivity is an issue but I am more interested in a discussion about concepts. We look at how our competitors structure their shops, how they present themselves, what kind of lighting they use. In this way we can follow developments across the world.

Our benchmarking may be based on our observations or on open discussions with our competitors. We try for some kind of cooperation. Sometimes that is not possible but our intention is to have open discussions and most retailers are open-minded. It has helped us to have an informed discussion about our opportunities. In retailing it is very simple: you should know your competitor locally, regionally, nationally and internationally.

Multiple format strategy

Cash-and-carry is a core business for Metro, a great strength, and it is a system that supplies professional customers like independent retailers, businesses and institutions. All over the world there are professional customer groups. Their formats and businesses may differ and the products that they sell may differ but fundamentally the price of products is reduced for them. That is truly a global concept. It is the reason we are in 22 countries today, and have decided to have a stronger focus on Asia. There is always an opportunity for a cash-and-carry business, adapted to the local needs.

Cash-and-carry is our most international format. We achieve 75 per cent of sales outside Germany. Major expansion regions for cash-and-carry are eastern Europe and Asia. Asia will account for 15 per cent of sales in the medium term.

In many countries of Europe we see the decline of department store retailing but Germany has been much more successful. There are only two significant players in German department store retailing, Kaufhof and Karstadt. Kaufhof with its

Geleria concept is the quality leader in this segment. It is important for the quality of the distribution infrastructure of the country to provide attractive retailing propositions out-of-town as well as on the high street. Innovative department store retailing will always have potential. Our success is the result of investment. We have invested a lot in the stores. We have moved away from the original strategy of the department stores to have 'everything under one roof' and towards creating a life-style approach for customers. We have a much stronger focus on fashion. We are very much in the lead in this segment.

Autonomous management teams run each of the six operating divisions. In regular meetings we discuss strategy, targets and business development. Our central management tool is EVA – economic value added. In this respect we at Metro AG level act as portfolio managers. Service companies that take care of cross-divisional synergies in purchasing, IT, advertising and logistics support Metro AG's infrastructure. Analysts are always fast to determine sum-of-the-parts values without taking into account group structures and benefits. Metro AG's portfolio still bears enormous potential for value creation. From an economic point of view there are no right or wrong portfolios but only successful and not successful ones.

The responsibility for the assortment is in the divisions. Although the decision on assortment is made in the divisions, synergies are found across formats on the import side. We have a structure where sales is separated from buying but there is a strategic unit bundling the volume. Nothing interferes with the local assortment but there should be some benefit to being an international retailer. It is necessary to manage the complexities and gain advantage from the structure.

The benefits of internationalization are not obvious in all retailers. At Metro AG, the clear answer is to have businesses that are close together so that synergies can be realized and the formats can support each other in entering a country.

Retail branding

Retailers can only be successful if they succeed at building a brand. Of course, when you take over a company there is always a discussion whether you convert the original brand name, as we did in Germany with Allkauf and Kriegbaum, or do what Carrefour is now doing with Promodès. Long-term, the only solution is one brand. But when you change a brand name, you have to change something and normally the customer reacts. It is not always easy to see what makes a brand attractive to the customer. We have not yet made the decision as to whether we change Makro to Metro or the other way around but I believe it will be more successful as one brand.

Brands provide differentiation. For example, Lidl and Aldi. Aldi has only private-label products. Lidl has brand products and so there is the differentiation. The highest brand of all brands in Germany is Aldi. Nobody can copy Aldi. Our own brand strategy is that we have two kinds of product, the first one is a low cost, low price product, and then we have the higher quality own brand. This provides an additional way for the customer to get lower prices.

Branding is principally an emotional relationship with our customers because you can copy a store and you can copy the product range but you cannot copy the emotional relationship with the customer. The customer relationship is built on system delivery and the build up of trust over time. And the relationship depends on qualified staff.

The Wal-Mart factor in German retailing

Wal-Mart are, as we all know, the biggest retailer in the world, mainly on the basis of their US business. There have been all sorts of comments written about their approach in Germany. In the longer term, Wal-Mart is an international competitor but they are not better retailers than we are. Germany is a difficult market and, as said, adaptation is a crucial success factor.

The essence of Wal-Mart's success in the United States has been based on a very efficient logistics system, which enables them to take cost out of shelf replenishment, range rationalization and bring the price down for the consumer while still making money. So they have made money through efficiency. If they apply that concept in Europe, one of the consequences may be that they would induce the same levels of efficiency in European replenishment as we see say in Wal-Mart in the United States.

However, Wal-Mart has not yet reached European standards. For example, they presented 'every day low price' in Germany as something new. They still have to adapt to Germany. For Wal-Mart there is a long way to go.

Chapter 15

Music, movies, more: the specialist retailer

Interview with Alan Giles, chief executive of HMV Media

HMV Group plc, Shelley House, 2–4 York Road, Maidenhead, Berkshire SL6 1SR
Tel.: +44 (0) 1628 818300; Fax: +44 (0) 1628 818301

Christine Cuthbertson

The HMV Media group was formed in March 1998, and includes HMV music stores and Waterstone's bookstores. The principal markets for HMV are the UK, Canada and Japan. HMV is also market leader in Hong Kong and Singapore, number two in Australia and has a smaller presence in the US and Germany. Waterstone's, the leading UK bookseller, is principally a UK brand. In May 2002, HMV Group plc was listed on the London Stock Exchange.

Alan Giles was educated at Blandford School, Dorset, Merton College, Oxford and Stanford University. He was appointed chief executive of HMV Media in 1998, after positions with Boots and WHSmith. Alan Giles is also a non-executive director of Somerfield. In this wide-ranging interview, Alan Giles explains the management challenges facing a specialist retailer in today's marketspace.

The HMV and Waterstone's brands

Both HMV and Waterstone's are great brands because there is an immediate and very strong association on the part of a group of valuable customers. The primary appeal of both brands is to the most committed, knowledgeable and frequent consumers of music and books. Consumers of music and books might appear quite fanatical in their interests. This commitment gives the brands some protection from the economic cycle because people who are passionate about books and music don't stop buying books and music, they give up something else. What makes the brands great is much less a consequence of imagery developed through advertising and much more about the consumer experience. The format of the stores, the layout of the stores and the commitment to width and relevance of range are all-important elements of the proposition.

We do actively promote, edit, select and recommend, and there is a plethora of choice available to the consumer with both books and music. All our experience is that even very knowledgeable, very committed consumers want some advice in making those choices. The help comes partly through the format and management of the stores but also through the expertise and enthusiasm of the employees.

Branding and the employees

The brands are inextricably linked with the culture of the organizations, including the attitude and nature of the employees. The great strength of both brands is that the employees are also consumers because the people who work in Waterstone's and HMV are incredibly passionate about books and music. Our employees have a tremendous shared interest with the customers, and one of the most important and powerful things we do is to present our customers with store-based personnel who are as knowledgeable and enthusiastic as they are themselves.

Similarities in the brands

There are many similar characteristics in the HMV brand and the Waterstone's brand. Both have incredibly wide ranges. An average supermarket rarely has more than 30,000 SKUs. The largest Waterstone's and HMV stores have 250,000 SKUs. Within that, 20 per cent will change during the course of the year, so managing a product lifecycle is incredibly important. Even very professional retailers like food retailers tend to be found wanting in these markets because they are not used to having to manage products with a very short life expectancy. Clearly, a lot of grocery goods are perishable but out-of-date bananas are replaced by more bananas. In music and books the replacement is a completely different title.

There is a strong element of needing to respond to, and perhaps lead, fashions in consumer taste. Books in particular are an indicator of broader interests and trends in society. People read about what they are interested in. So what the brands also have in common is the appeal to the high-end, committed, most frequent purchasers.

The brands also share the consumer perception that shopping for books and music is not really shopping. It is a pleasurable experience. It is a recreational activity, more akin to going to a gallery or a restaurant rather than shopping. This has implications for the type of environment that we try to create in the stores.

Brand evolution

It is true that the brands are constantly changing but there are many core attributes, giving continuity. An area in which the brands do have to adapt and develop is in the channels to consumer. For example, with both brands we have developed an on-line presence. There is clear evidence that when consumers shop on-line they feel comforted by the reassurance and security of known brands, brands that they recognize, brands that have a certain stature and physical presence, and brands that they trust. In both the markets, and perhaps in society, there is a trend towards the mainstream – the obvious becoming more important. So, if you look at music over the last two or three years there has been a pronounced resurgence in mainstream pop and more demanding types of music have proved more difficult to market and sell. In books, there is a clear move to a concentration of demand on a narrower range of more popular titles. Again, more demanding literature is proving more difficult to sell.

The change is consumer-led. A difficult judgement for us is the extent to which we will follow those trends. Strategically, those trends could be viewed as not particularly helpful for specialist brands. Both brands have been given a broader appeal, so that the less confident, less familiar consumer can feel comfortable in going into the stores and not feel threatened by lack of knowledge. At the same time, we have to be careful not to reduce the quality of the experience for the very committed customer – and that is a difficult trick to pull off.

Employees have an effect on the titles we stock. Whilst in order to secure economies of scale because we have 200 bookshops, we have had to move some of the decision making away from the stores, there is still not a single book that appears on the shelf in a Waterstone's store without it being a proactive decision on the part of someone based in the store.

In most stores, the majority of people who work in the store have a specific area of buying responsibility. There are over a million titles in print and the task of optimizing the selection of which 150,000 you put into the store in Oxford is impossible to do from the head office, no matter how sophisticated your information systems. Much the most effective way is to put the decision making into the hands of people working on the shop floor in Oxford, and make sure that they have the skills and the expertise to know.

A happy consequence of that is that it is a more fulfilling job. It gives a sense of focus, so it allows us to recruit and maintain a higher calibre of personnel than would otherwise be the case. And the customer gets access to somebody of higher calibre than would otherwise be the case. So despite pay rates typical of retailing,

80 per cent plus of the Waterstone's store-based personnel are university graduates. That is quite a telling statistic.

Many people who are very interested in books will also be very interested in film and music, so there is a significant cross over. We know and can measure that because our gift vouchers are redeemable in both brands and there is a lot of cross purchasing.

The specialist market

Strategically, a weakness for both businesses is that we are somewhat exposed to the creative cycle. So you have years where there are a lot of great albums and you have years where there are not. The same is true to a lesser degree with books. That lies beyond our control. We are not publishers, so we do not go and find artists and authors. A fashion chain can 'make luck' by sourcing and developing merchandise but we are exposed to what other people are able to bring to market.

The creative cycle has hit us quite hard in a place like Hong Kong, where the record labels, because of the economic difficulties, have significantly reduced their investment and artist development. There is therefore a dip of new artists now coming to the market and other than lobbying the record companies, as we do, there is nothing that we can directly do about it.

Competitors

The supermarkets now offer both books and music but the supermarket share is static. In both books and music, the sector that is gaining share is the specialist. There are significant limitations on what you can achieve in the supermarket in terms of width of range, staff expertise and knowledge and relevance of store environment. A supermarket feels like shopping, so it is a very different psychological experience. Supermarkets do have a valuable opportunity for impulse purchases, and books and music can be used to reinforce price credentials. Ultimately, however, supermarkets find it difficult to justify investment of space in books and music.

From the point of view of HMV Media, the supermarket offer is good news, particularly on something like books where the specialists can be intimidating. It is great if there is a way of putting books in front of potential consumers. In the longer term there is benefit for us in that. Additionally, if an eight year old is in an environment where she can persuade her parent to put a CD in the trolley and that creates an interest in music, then we will reap the benefit in subsequent years.

Segmentation

There is always going to be scope for some segmentation because the nature of the market means that it is difficult to create a store proposition that effectively meets the needs of all purchasers of that category. We have had to broaden the offer at Waterstone's but there are limits as to how much you can do before the quality of the experience for the heavier, more committed, purchasers becomes diminished.

There are quite a few differences, some contradictory, between different types of consumer. It would be impossible to develop a model that satisfied them all. There are consumers whose requirement is to get in and out of the store very quickly, to select something that someone else has effectively chosen for them at a low price, very quickly. There are other people who greatly resent any efforts from the retailer to help them with their purchase, who just want to get lost in an oasis of books. It is quite difficult to develop a format that caters for both needs.

Technology in book and music retailing

Technology is fundamentally important in any retail business. The vast majority of the technology we have is store-based because that is where most of the decision making takes place. Most of the investment we make is in inventory management systems. One of the benefits of bringing the businesses together is a world-wide, common systems infrastructure, with software which has been extensively adapted. It is backward integrated with the accounting function, so the whole back-office is integrated with the front-end and in HMV the off-line presence is also integrated with the same back-office on a common systems platform. So, for a group that prides itself on decentralization, systems *have* allowed some consistency world-wide and that has been very helpful. Like most retailers, over the last ten years, we have come up from no technology at all to it being one of our most important areas of expenditure.

It is interesting from a broader technological standpoint, to see the pressures created by the greatly enhanced expectations of our customers. The investment required to fulfil those expectations is very significant indeed. The investment of demonstration facilities is very high. For example, in our new HMV store in Oxford Street we have put in a DVD cinema. It is an expensive investment but it really brings home the power of the sound and visual experience that the digital technology permits.

The number one issue on the minds of all executives in the music industry world-wide is how to plot a transition from the old model towards a future in which digital signals can be delivered to the consumers. And there is a vast amount of experimentation going on with a whole array of different pricing models, some of them being more akin to a rental model as opposed to an outright purchase model. New models challenge the traditional creative concept of the 40–70 minute album. That may not be what the customer wants and maybe the customers want to choose the order and content. However, there are a significant number of barriers to further progress.

Barriers to progress

The technology is a barrier in some cases. Clearly the potential is there but the bandwidth is very limited. A consideration of WAP technology shows that it is very easy to fall into the trap of promising more than can be delivered.

The second barrier is the original creators of music. Artists have quite legitimate views on how their work should be presented to the consumer. However, the technology offers the consumer the opportunity to alter the product and the original intention is lost. Artists may have contracts that prevent alteration to the product downstream in the supply chain.

The third barrier is clearly around fears of piracy, and music communities like Napster are creating a huge impediment to unlock what the technology can do because the creators, promoters and distributors of music will not get the rewards of their investment if it is pirated.

The fourth impediment is the attitude that consumers have towards the Internet. There is a perception that somehow the Internet is not about commerce but about free and cheap products. Therefore there is a big question over whether customers are prepared to pay the premium for home selection and delivery.

Both online and in our stores we are doing a vast amount of experimentation with all of these models. It is easy to think that tomorrow everybody is going to stop buying CDs or books but I do not believe that is the case.

The pressures in book retailing are in fact not as acute in music. Imagine that the only way in which you were being able to experience the creativity of an author was in what could be displayed on a screen. If I suddenly produced out of my briefcase an aesthetically pleasing paper-based format with portability, resilience, convenience, the ability to dip in and out – you would think it a great technological breakthrough. So, having been in book selling for about 15 years, I am a great believer of the enduring characteristics of the book as a form of communication.

There are going to be some areas in which technology can provide greater functionality – reference works and some learning material – but that it is the exception rather than the rule. What authors such as Stephen King have done is interesting and there is a lot of experimentation going on. Reactionary as it might sound, I would be surprised if that becomes a very significant channel to market for that type of author.

The technological advance makes disintermediation a very real possibility, in both markets. However, whilst there will be an inevitable period of challenge and uncertainty, ultimately in the new channels to market it will all settle down with a kind of grudging recognition of the role of the other protagonists in the supply chain.

Supply chain management

The underlying IT systems play a huge part in modern retailing. However, human expertise is an important factor. Anyone who is experienced in running a record store will know that there are certain bands with a very strong, committed following that will have huge week one sales and then sales will collapse to virtually nothing. There will be other, more mainstream bands that appeal to less committed music enthusiasts, where the shape of the demand curve is much broader and lasts for much longer. Although it is not done quite as scientifically as selecting from a range of mathematical models, intuitively that is how decisions in the stores are made. When you then build more sophisticated central inventory management systems, that is the type of methodology that has to apply. But there is huge complexity, and books are more complex than music. Astonishingly, last year Waterstone's dealt with over 7,500 different publishers.

I read with amusement about food retailers wanting to reduce their number of suppliers from 600 to 400. For book publishers, barriers to entry are very low and the way in which print technology has evolved means that there is nothing to stop anyone publishing a book in a back bedroom. That is valuable for society but it does mean that there is complexity, cost and difficulty in automating the accounting procedures. One of the opportunities is that the much lower cost and widespread distribution possibilities of the Internet mean that we should be able to develop much lower cost electronic invoicing systems, which in EDI were only realistic for the large, more sophisticated suppliers.

New business models

What Amazon has done, has been done with enormous skill but also with an extraordinary sense of timing. There was a brief period in which dot.com entrepreneurs were actively encouraged to develop any business at virtually any cost. That has proved to be very short lived but there were a few businesses who secured their capital while that window was open and who now have significant cash resources to continue to develop the business.

For most of the others, the business model that has been used is just not sustainable. Indeed, I don't think any of us can know for sure that it is possible to develop a valid, sustainable business model for the sale of books and music online.

My guess is that it can be done but there will be prerequisites. One requirement is for prices to the consumer to increase because there has been a rather reckless quest for customer acquisition without any thought of profitability. Even now, some on-line retailers are selling things below cost and, at the end of the day, retailing is simple – you buy something at one price and you attempt to charge a higher price when you sell it on to the next guy. So prices will have to go up and consumers must lose the perception that the Internet is about getting products for nothing or very cheap.

The second thing I would say is that you need to give the customer the assurance of brand attributes. There are one or two people, including Amazon, who have created a fantastic brand with fantastic attributes. However, in the vast majority of cases the brand is going to be about leveraging off another brand, like our own.

And it is not only the brand that we can leverage. We have got a lot of buying power, staff expertise and promotional power.

Our online presence is still relatively small. In books, Amazon is very large and very powerful and it is a question of leveraging our assets to get ourselves properly into that game. In terms of music, we are either the leader or close to being the leader online, in most of the markets that we offer in – particularly in Japan where we are the number 3 offline music retailer, we are the number 1 online player.

Property

The property plays a very important part in the proposition, in that ideally you want the building itself to contribute something to the recreational experience. If you have a restaurant, you want a building of character that makes a positive contribution to the customer's experience. That is most certainly true with bookshops and to a lesser degree with music.

In the Waterstone's portfolio there are buildings that were previously churches, music halls or cinemas. A building that others would see as difficult and lacking in clean regular spaces is actually an attraction for a bookshop. Both books and music, however, also benefit from a large degree of impulse purchases. To benefit from impulse sales, it is a good idea to be in a relatively high traffic location, so we do tend to pick prime sites. Compared to other product categories however, multiple retailing is easier for us because the goods are physically small and easily carried up and downstairs. In addition, because customers are immersing themselves in a browsing experience, they are less resistant to being led up or downstairs than more purpose-driven types of retailing.

The flagship stores play a significant role. Customers would recognize that Waterstone's might have a flagship on Piccadilly but they don't expect you to have a flagship in Camden. People are rational about their expectations of the scale of the offering that you make. It could be that the future entry model for new territories is a flagship store in the major city centres and then an online presence to service the rest of the country. For example, if we looked at Taiwan, we would probably have a flagship in Taipei, plus a website.

In each business there is a centralized property division that identifies new sites but not for the group as a whole, though they do talk to each other. We are just changing a Waterstone's in the city to create adjoining HMV and Waterstone's stores, so there is co-operation. However, there are no plans to bring books and music under one roof. Consumer feedback suggests that if there is more space in Waterstone's customers would rather have more books, or something to add to the experience, like a coffee shop.

Environmentally, the intention is to create a very different atmosphere for each brand. Now, in some locations we have put them next door to each other but with a physical dividing wall – and that works well. And because these two brands have not been in the same ownership for very long it may be that we have not done as much as we could in terms of shared back-of-house facilities. However, the consumer environment we want to create is sufficiently distinct between the two that separate stores work well.

Recruitment and training

For HMV Media, being a good employer is about giving people early responsibility and trusting them. Traditionally, retailing in the UK has been seen as a low paid, low skills environment. However, retailing can appeal to high quality young people who want a career and more work needs to be done to change perceptions. We are trying to give people good opportunities for advancement. Employees need the opportunity to make decisions and to be held accountable. People like to perform and for that performance to be measured. The collegiate atmosphere of the stores helps, and that the employee base in both brands is usually young and like-minded. Several people have commented that Waterstone's is almost like an extension of university life. If I go to somewhere like Waterstone's in Durham, I would imagine that 60–70 per cent of the employees in that store are recent Durham graduates who didn't want to leave the city.

Some go on to build a career in Waterstone's and others move on. There is a perfectly valid, unwritten agreement in Waterstone's, that very few of those people come in thinking that they want to retail books. In many cases, they leave us after 12, 18, 24 months and in a way that is fine. That has worked for us as well as for them. There are a significant proportion who like Waterstone's, and whilst the entry level rewards are not good, able and committed employees reach store manager quickly, and go on to have good, fulfilling careers.

One of the things we have found has grown over the last four or five years, is that new employees look for training, as a close second to money. There is an appetite for developing and broadening their skills. The training we can provide is not about the products. Through self-selection, people who come to us are already well-read or have listened to a lot of music. Being in the business enhances knowledge but we do very little to promote product knowledge. However, what we can do is to help develop their interpersonal and decision-making skills.

During the last five or six years, personal development has become increasingly sophisticated. There is a growing demand for it and there is a real appetite for the use of high quality, accredited, outside third parties, such as Templeton College, to help deliver the programmes. Employees obviously feel the benefit of it enormously. It provides a rare opportunity to escape the workplace and to build stronger relationships with contemporaries and other business functions. It also provides the stimulus of more theoretical, broader outlook and frameworks that help them create more of a sense of meaning about what they have been doing.

Perhaps we should be doing more to hang onto the really good people we have. We delegate a very high degree of decision making to the stores. If you were to draw a graph of the acquisition of expertise, some through formal training but a lot of it through doing the job, there is a fantastically steep learning curve. Someone who has been a bookseller for 18 months is of infinitely greater value than somebody who has been a bookseller for only 6 months. Something we have not done is considered the true cost to the organization of losing people after 18 months. We need to develop more appropriate policies to retain and motivate good people.

Globalization

We have to ensure that what happens globally is catering to local needs. There is an underlying belief of delegating decision making to the lowest level. Decisions are made in the local country, local region. The interesting thing about somewhere like Canada, perhaps unsurprising given the geographic extent of the country, is that there are probably more acute differences in culture and consumer taste between the various provinces of Canada than there are between many of the countries in which we operate. A highly decentralized model is needed to make that work.

Another thing that we regard as very important is employing a huge proportion of locally based management. For example in Japan, where we employ over 1,000 people, only three of them are not Japanese. The effect of that is that over 40 per cent of what we sell in Japan is Japanese music. The vast majority of Japanese customers view HMV as being a Japanese business and that is the best possible result. They are not buying into some notion that this is an outpost of western culture.

What we strive to do is to have the relevance and energy of the really good independent bookstore or record store but to have the quality assurance and buying power of a chain. I would hate it if our employees and customers consciously thought 'this is a store in a chain'. Most people who are really passionate about books or music would choose an independent as their favourite store.

Brand positioning is certainly not as uniform as a retailer like Gap. Some of the overseas territories are less effective at having broadened the base beyond music. In the UK, HMV is very accomplished at selling DVDs, videos and games. Sometimes for good reasons but sometimes for bad reasons we are less effective overseas. The good reasons are because other types of retailer often use games as a loss leader and therefore it is an unattractive market in overseas territories. But it is sometimes because the management that we have are there because they love music and are not very good at embracing new product categories.

Interestingly, the dog and trumpet logo is not an HMV trade mark in overseas territories. In Japan it is used by JVC and in America it is used by RCA. Therefore we cannot even use the same trademark world-wide, though the product is broadly similar, the range authority position is broadly similar, as is the decentralization, and the appeal to the more frequent customers.

So it is a brand that we have optimized by allowing it to adapt to the local environment, the local competitive situation and the local culture. Somewhere there is a balance between uniformity and customization. The question is, where does that optimal trade-off lie?

We obviously have planning and performance monitoring processes and that is inevitably about financial performance. However, there is also a battery of softer characteristics that we consider. There have been territories where we have concluded that, to achieve financial success, we would have to significantly change the position of the brand and we have chosen not to go into those territories. We are prepared to adapt our brand but only so far.

Chapter 16

Consumer wellbeing: wellbeing.com

Interview with John Hornby, managing director of Digital Wellbeing

Digital Wellbeing Ltd, 1 Thane Road West, Nottingham, Nottinghamshire NG2 3AA

Richard Cuthbertson

The Wellbeing Network was jointly established by Boots and UK media company Granada in October 2000, and sought to give customers access to a wide range of Boots products, information and advice, as well as providing a digital TV channel. In December 2001 the wellbeing TV channel, partly as a result of a decline in the advertising market, together with a delay in the rollout of broadband infrastructure, was closed. Digital Wellbeing, now solely comprising the e-commerce website, made losses last year of £16.9 million. In 2002, Boots agreed to acquire Granada's 40 per cent stake in the business for £1. Nevertheless, 'customer satisfaction ratings of wellbeing.com, are very high: 95 per cent say they will use the service again and 85 per cent rate the fulfilment process as above-average', according to the company. It expects average order values to rise as it introduces a growing number of premium fragrance and cosmetics brands. It is presently the only UK website authorized to sell Chanel products, and one of only two approved to sell Estée Lauder and Clinique.

In this chapter, we interview John Hornby who became commercial director of Digital Wellbeing Ltd when it was first created and took over from Richard Holmes as managing director in February 2002.

Unique positioning

We do not consider ourselves as simply participating in the health and beauty market. Wellbeing is where health, beauty and fitness converge and that is very much reflected in the contribution that products make to the site. We are 'Boots online' as far as consumers are concerned and at its simplest, it is a place where people can come and buy Boots products. However, in the UK, the e-commerce channel in the health and beauty market has been one of the slower markets to take off, lagging behind markets such as books, music and electricals. The underdevelopment is positive for wellbeing.com because there is plenty of potential. Wellbeing.com is firmly positioned as the only significant player with a dedicated offer online. There are a number of other players who participate in elements of the product set within wellbeing.com but we are the only website of significant size that has a health and beauty focus. The unique positioning of wellbeing.com reflects the unique positioning of Boots offline. A consistent theme when considering various issues relating to the business is that many of the issues that apply to Boots offline apply equally to wellbeing.com.

Online and offline strategies

Wellbeing.com has sought to recruit existing Boots customers and so we would not expect to have huge numbers of customers that are new to Boots. Our customers tend to come from the most valuable segments of the Boots customer base. By definition the only people with whom we are interacting are those with Internet access and there is a demographic skew, which is becoming less marked over time. Women are rapidly matching men in terms of Internet access and online shopping, thus developing an online environment that better reflects the offline situation. This is positive for wellbeing.com and Boots because 90 per cent of our customers are women.

Obviously there are very close links between the store-based business and wellbeing.com, and in particular a two-way relationship between our customer offer teams. However, there may be physical constraints that suggest that elements of our product set will never work in stores. Wellbeing.com has fewer constraints on space. Where consumers are buying relatively bulky items or 'high' ticket items, the convenience of delivery to the door is very attractive. We may see some 'showcasing' of higher ticket items in stores with wellbeing.com operating as a fulfilment service. The consumer gets the best of both worlds by being able to physically see and test the merchandise but not having to take away a heavy or bulky item. It would be delivered at a time and place that is convenient for the customer. That is a good example of where wellbeing.com can interact positively with stores, not just to drive incremental sales but also to provide a much more rounded experience for the consumer. As we develop there is likely to be more examples where we are taking the Boots offer and extending for consumers online. However, that will be very much driven by consumer needs rather than for the sake of creating a larger range online.

There are a number of other ways that wellbeing.com supports the Boots strategy. Customer communication is an important element of Boots strategy and wellbeing.com provides some interesting new ways for Boots to communicate with its customers. For example, wellbeing.com has a number of sub sites or micro sites promoting various elements of the Boots product or service offer, and that provides a more rounded means of communicating with Boots customers out of store.

Trust in the brand leads to success online

There may be the potential for foreign operators to enter the UK health and beauty online market but the more we operate within this territory, the more we believe that ultimately, it is the trusted, well-established brands that will be successful online. That is not to say that to be successful online you have to be an incumbent retailer. Amazon, for example, has done a fantastic job of building a great brand online with no physical presence. However, that is expensive and takes time, and in areas where the consumer really needs to trust the retailer it is going to be difficult for an unknown brand to make an impact in the UK. There are some interesting parallel operations in the States, for example drugstore.com, which encompasses beauty.com. We are not complacent about a threat from the US but my judgement is that it would be difficult for someone like drugstore.com to transpose their US operations to the UK.

Boots is such a great retail brand that it may seem odd that we chose not to use the Boots brand online but developed a new brand in wellbeing. There are some very practical reasons and the most significant is that when we launched a year ago we were launching both an Internet site and a TV channel. The TV channel had an entertainment license and the regulations do not allow it to be called 'Boots TV'. Given a strategy of greater convergence of the two platforms, we were very keen to co-brand the TV channel and the Internet site. As TV and Internet technologies converge, it is naturally important to be able to offer an integrated proposition. The TV channel has since closed, largely due to the speed of convergence (it seems to be some way off). Additionally, the advertising/sponsorship market was, and remains to some extent, problematic. There was no real willingness to shoulder the losses and to wait patiently for convergence. We are certainly not ruling out TV participation in some form in the future but we will choose the point at which it is appropriate commercially. Wellbeing.com has offered an interesting opportunity to build a brand and we have a significant number of people accessing the site. It is open to us at some point in the future to re-brand as Boots.co.uk or Boots.com but for the moment we have elected to stay with wellbeing.com.

We are very passionate about research and one of the things about being online is that you do not see your customers, day-in and day-out. We know about customers purchasing behaviour but we are not meeting them and getting that intimate feedback so we are very keen on getting feedback in other ways, either through the contact centre who are talking to customers on a day-to-day basis or through customer research. We have developed the site significantly since launch based on customer feedback. For example, over time we have introduced a much closer association with the Boots brand. The development of the wellbeing.com brand is driven by what consumers say they want us to be in relation to Boots. There is real merit in not introducing additional customer confusion by having a pricing strategy or a promotional strategy different to Boots. We take Boots prices, so that there is no confusion as to whether people have to price compare with Boots offline in terms of our online prices.

Promotional activity

We have done a lot of work over the last year to expand the number of Boots promotions online and we can now run almost all Boots offline promotions in an online context. That is an amazing challenge from a technical perspective because Boots has probably the most extensive promotional programme of any UK retailer. Providing such a programme online has posed the technical team some incredible challenges in terms of understanding how some of these promotions work online and identifying how consumers will understand the promotions in an online context.

Wellbeing.com also runs exclusive online promotions quite regularly. They tend to be about the free delivery threshold. We sometimes expand some Boots promotions. For example, when Boots runs a double Advantage points weekend we often extend the promotional period because many online consumers are shopping from work and may not be able to take advantage of a weekend promotion. We are also running an increasing number of specific product promotions. However, in terms of the week-to-week promotional programme, there is real merit in avoiding customer confusion by broadly mirroring the offline programme, online.

Card Advantage

We use the Advantage card in a number of ways. First, from a customer acquisition point of view, there are various points of interaction that Boots has with its Advantage cardholders, in particular a certain number of those Advantage cardholders receive regular magazines. Wellbeing.com takes space in those magazines for customer recruitment purposes and to encourage people to shop online for the first time with Boots. Boots have 14 million Advantage cardholders, offering wellbeing.com great opportunities in terms of customer acquisition.

The research we did before launch said that it was absolutely essential that we offered Advantage card points online. Once again, it is not an insignificant technical challenge but from the wellbeing.com launch, customers could earn Advantage card points online, credited automatically to their card. If they shop online, the next time they go into a store and put their card into a kiosk or a till point, the points they earned online will be credited to their account.

At the moment we are not offering redemption online. It poses some very interesting technical challenges, not least because the Advantage card is a 'smart' card and therefore points are accumulated on the card itself. Clearly it is a real challenge to offer online point redemption when a customer does not have a card-reader to hand. It is something that we will continue to develop and collaborate with our colleagues at Boots to understand the real benefit to the consumer of online point redemption.

Halo effect

From the beginning, Boots decided not to worry about taking customers away from the store and putting them online – so-called 'cannibalization'. At its very starkest, without wellbeing.com it would be open to someone else to 'cannibalize' Boots sales. The issue simply does not arise because one of the advantages of the card is that we can do some very extensive and quite sophisticated mining of data, and in particular look at the behaviour of the people who surf or shop online against their behaviour in store. Wellbeing.com was launched over a year ago and we understand how wellbeing.com customers change their behaviour in stores. The results are very positive and constitute exactly the opposite of cannibalization. We know that people who shop with us online shop more often in store than those who do not shop at wellbeing.com. Even more importantly, we know that people who use the site to browse but do not go on to make online purchases also spend more in store. Our findings agree with much of the research, particularly from the US, suggesting that offering multi-channels allows customers to shop more across all channels rather than cannibalizing offline sales.

There is a 'halo' effect in store both for our shoppers but also for people who browse online. Browsing certainly makes sense because wellbeing.com, although it is a shop with transactional capability, provides an excellent way for someone to have a look at the breadth of Boots products in the comfort of their own home. In that sense, we are providing a service to the Boots group as well as converting a significant number of browsers to online purchasers. A further issue is that not everyone has the same Boots store on their high street. Wellbeing.com offers considerable advantages to people who regularly access small Boots stores and want access to a much broader range of merchandise, particularly at Christmas. Boots has a fantastic Christmas offer and small stores can only carry a small element of that offer. We provide a way for those consumers to access a broad offer, perhaps at Christmas but all the year round as well.

Sales and information

We see content as working on two levels. Direct content is that which drives consumers ultimately directly into buying something. Since launch we have taken account of customer research and customer feedback and increased the proportion of direct content. Much is magazine-type content that is relevant at a particular point in the year. We now spend much more time producing magazine-type content than we did at launch.

However, we still believe there is a place for more static content, particularly in the health arena because people wanting to interact with Boots online expect information on health issues. We are absolutely happy to provide that information and we have teamed up with two of the most trusted partners, the British Medical Association and Dorling Kindersley. Together, we provide some absolutely fantastic health content online that does not have a direct link to product sales. We see the advantage in the extent to which people do come back and buy something. Indirect content users are often wellbeing.com customers as well. However, people looking for indirect content arrive at wellbeing.com in a very different state of mind. If they want to do some research on a particular medical condition they are most unlikely to want to go and shop for shampoo, fitness equipment or gifts. We acknowledge the difference and it is reflected in the way we structure the site. We have a small proportion of customers who use us for information only, and that is fine. What is more important to me is that we have a lot of customers who may sometimes want information and sometimes want to shop, or perhaps read the magazine content before shopping. We are comfortable operating with customers in different modes.

Operational certainty

We see the customer experience as being from the point at which they enter the site to the point at which the driver hands over the merchandise. We know, because we have asked them, that people want an experience that is relatively clean, simple and easy to use. Usability is something we take very seriously, and we do a lot of work to make sure that our site is easy to understand and easy to manoeuvre around. The site needs to be sufficiently fast and it is necessary to limit the type and number of images carried. Much has been learnt over the year since launch and, in particular, we are able to offer fantastic imagery without weighing the pages down.

Once people get into shopping mode, we give them certainty. Right from the beginning we aimed for transparency, so that if a product appears in stock on the web front then we are in stock. Delivering that level of certainty sets some significant challenges. However, we made the investment because we felt that it was absolutely crucial to the customer experience. We provide a straightforward, robust and secure shopping process. There is seamless fulfilment at the back-end so the consumer can always see the stages of their order. We have an efficient warehouse that gets the right product out, picked in good condition and into the carrier network so that we can fulfil our delivery promise. This is something we have spent a lot of time on and we believe that we have significant advantage over some other e-commerce players in the UK.

Fulfilment

We have our own dedicated warehouse north of Nottingham, run by Boots logistics using a collaborative approach. The warehouse is effectively a pick and pack warehouse, developed from the warehouse previously used for catalogue operations at Boots. There was a limited amount of re-purposing to make sure that the warehouse was appropriate for an Internet offer. We have a dedicated team who pick and pack, and prepare the product for despatch.

We use four different carriers. We have a very intelligent system that works out the optimal carrier to use in a particular circumstance. At its simplest, the carrier depends on weight or product but our system is more sophisticated, for example placing an individual package with an individual carrier based on their performance in a particular part of the country.

About 85 per cent of the stock we take into the warehouse is through the Boots supply chain, and that offers us enormous advantages. Wellbeing.com has all the handling and buying efficiencies from Boots, and we also have the advantage of daily replenishment so we can hold stock levels on the basis that we can pull stock into our warehouse overnight or in extreme circumstances within a day. Again, the close proximity of our warehouse to the main Boots warehouses in Nottingham really helps.

Once the stock is taken into our warehouse (either from Boots stock or directly from a third party) that stock is dedicated to wellbeing.com. This is because a 'pick and pack' for a consumer operation is very different from an operation where stock is being provided in larger quantities direct to store. They are radically different operations requiring different physical configurations, systems and techniques.

Patterns of demand

As you would expect, our March 2001 launch means that we have a limited track record, although we always knew that we would have a very heavy skew towards

Christmas because gifts are such an important part of our offer. In broad terms we would expect around 50 per cent of our sales to be in the last quarter of the calendar year. Christmas starts relatively early for us online because a significant number of our shoppers are very organized and find the opportunity to do their holiday season shopping, even as early as October, very attractive. For Christmas 2002 we also offered the ability to shop early on site and to name the day of delivery up to eight weeks later. We guaranteed that the items would be delivered on that date.

For consumers, to shop at wellbeing.com for a gift is attractive because the full inventory is available. They can shop from home or work at times when it is impossible or difficult to visit the high street. We can gift wrap items and have presents delivered direct to the recipient. For any number of reasons we are incredibly attractive to many customers at that point in the year. The most important categories to us at the moment, without the pharmacy element to sustain wellbeing.com throughout the year, are beauty and mother and baby.

Managing the peaks is not as difficult as it might be because the seasonal peak was taken into account in the design of the operational configuration. In the warehouse and the contact centre we are able to add variable resource at any time in the year but particularly at Christmas. We do not have a very significant chunk of fixed cost to carry throughout the year. Obviously, part of our challenge is to increase the level of business throughout the year and we are having some success.

It is slower than the gift offer but each month our re-purchase rates for consumers increase in terms of all year round business. Developments such as online prescription and over-the-counter medicines will also help in driving business throughout the year.

Support from IT

To a large extent the IT architecture for wellbeing.com stands alone, as do the IT team. However, we are constantly talking to our colleagues in Boots to identify areas where they can support us and vice versa. Many elements of the architecture are specific to running an Internet channel and so we have to be self-supportive in a number of areas. We run different core systems to Boots. For example, we use SAP and at present Boots are not operating on a SAP platform. That presents us with some challenges in terms of operating and supporting a core system that is not supported in Boots but we have the ability. We have arrangements either in-house or with third parties to provide effective support for those operations where appropriate, 24 hours a day, 7 days a week.

Private-label and branded products

Boots has a large amount of private-label products and wellbeing.com can take advantage of Boots integration. As far as Boots inventory is concerned, whether private label or a proprietary brand, we simply place orders against the Boots supply chains. However, we have to carefully consider ranging issues, and make the decision based on what the consumers want online. Most of the ranges that Boots carries we also carry and there are many examples of where Boots gives us the advantage against any competition. For example, we are the only authorized stockists on the Internet of Channel products in the UK and soon we will be the only authorized stockists of Lancôme. With Estée Lauder and Clinique we are one of only two authorized online stockists in the UK. Once again we provide security for consumers who want to be sure they are not buying counterfeit products.

In terms of sales of the private-label versus proprietary brands, the overall profile is a little skewed by the proportion of Boots sales that fall into the health category, since overall sales at wellbeing.com in health are fewer than in store. However, in individual categories such as beauty, the profile is very similar to Boots. In mother and baby, we have a bit more of a skew towards proprietary merchandise, because we do extend the range of mother and baby to certain third party brands such as 'Mommas and Papas', as demanded by the consumers.

Commercial implications

The decision was made for investment up front to provide the infrastructure and all the systems and processes to support the website. It was intended to deliver a platform that is robust, scaleable and flexible. Flexibility is very important because we have learnt much over the last year or so about how consumers want to interact with us. Flexibility of platform and infrastructure is crucial to be able to respond quickly and also cost effectively. Having made that level of investment, we are trying to move towards breakeven – in line with the original indications that were given at launch. Success is ultimately about increasing top line sales and being more efficient. That is not about making compromises in terms of our customer promise but it is about running our contact centre and warehouse more efficiently, and it is about running our systems more efficiently with less costly support. We are working very hard and we are starting to make significant progress. A demonstration of that progress is that the breakeven point that we need to achieve in terms of e-commerce sales is coming down literally by the month. We will move aggressively on the top line, bringing in new customers and looking after our current customers. Our financial year ends on 31 March 2003 and we are anticipating reaching breakeven, based purely on direct revenues, in the following financial year. Of course, as already discussed, we have probably also increased sales in stores and overall basket size. In addition, there is a more modest revenue stream around advertising sponsorship online. We are increasingly working in some quite novel ways with our suppliers to produce interesting sponsorship and advertising packages for them, where they can learn more about consumer behaviour online, and ultimately sell more products. Our breakeven calculations take that into account but do not include any halo effect for Boots, be it directly, in terms of product sales or more indirectly in terms of marketing benefit.

We look at customer behaviour, in particular through the Advantage card database. Because around 90 per cent of wellbeing.com visitors are buying online and over 80 per cent of the people who are registered with us have an Advantage card, we have the ability to compare their behaviour online with their behaviour offline. There are some restrictions as to what we can and cannot do but we can identify online buyers and surfers and watch their behaviour in store. This ability to monitor customer behaviour illustrates the tremendous power of the Advantage card in understanding both the economics of our business but also the consequences of wellbeing.com in our business on the high street with Boots.

Outlook

Primarily we will consider wellbeing.com as a revenue stream. We will see consumers with more means of accessing and transacting with us. At the moment we are a PC/browser-driven business. I discussed iDTV earlier and there will be a point at which purchasing using the TV will be a significant part of our business. I am not quite sure how significant and when but we are monitoring the situation closely to make sure that we are making investments in that area at an appropriate point in time. I am less persuaded by the mobile technologies in the context of our business, although the use of mobile telecommunications together with other technologies may offer some interesting developments.

The advantage we have got, coming back to my earlier comments on scalability and flexibility, is that we have an IT architecture that is platform neutral. This means that for modest further investment it is possible to accommodate different modes of access for consumers, and the flexibility makes the incremental investments to allow for different consumer behaviour more palatable for our shareholders.

We have existing competitors, the supermarkets for example, and we would expect some of those competitors to extend what they are doing. It is unlikely in the short- to medium-term that we will have a 'pure play' start-up without an established brand trying to replicate wellbeing.com. The main barrier to a new entrant must be the breadth of merchandise, and in particular the premium fragrance and cosmetics brands. However, we cannot be complacent because there is very credible competition cutting across certain elements of our product set already. The supermarkets, for example, offer consumers a convenient way to add our product areas to an online grocery shop. We see those players increasing their participation potential, and maybe extending to other areas in which we are operating. For that reason, the advantages of the Boots brand and the trust that consumers place in the brand are very important. Equally we must look for relevant extensions to broaden our base beyond product or service areas within which Boots either participate now or will participate in the future.

If you asked ten people about the future of e-commerce you would probably get ten different answers. I believe that e-tail through the various access points will, over the medium- to long-term, represent in excess of 4–5 per cent of all retail sales in many product areas. Trusted brands will dominate e-tail, whether it is an existing retailer or pure play e-tailer.

From an industry perspective we will see an increased focus on operational efficiency. Just as we are striving hard to drive down our breakeven point, so most of the other players are doing the same to begin to realize the benefits of online retailing.

The other significant areas where we will see most e-tailers devoting a lot of time will be in customer relationship management (CRM). There are a number of players who have achieved a reasonable level of sophistication but many are really only 'scratching the service' of the potential of a very data rich environment. Certainly, wellbeing.com is committed to CRM and we will become increasingly sophisticated over the next few months and years in terms of the way we use data to understand our consumers in order to offer them absolute relevance. We are in some ways in a better position than many but I expect much attention to be devoted by the whole industry, and further investment made, to really enable e-tailers to grab the benefit from CRM.

Chapter 17

Freshen up: differentiation through fresh foods

Interview with Antoni Gari, deputy general manager of Supermercats Pujol SA

Supermercats Pujol SA, 307 Ind El Segre Cl Victoricano Munoz Parcela, 25191 Lleida, Spain
Tel.: +34 973 351818; Fax: +34 973 205262

Christine Cuthbertson

This small chain of Spanish supermarkets numbers some 59 outlets, half company-owned and half as franchises. All of them are located in the provinces of Lleida, Barcelona and Tarragona in northeast Spain. Pujol supermarkets have more than 50 years of experience in the distribution sector. At the moment the company employs nearly 550 and in 2001 it had revenues of 11,330 million pesetas (€68.1 million), a 9.4 per cent increase on the previous year.

Spain is the second in Europe only to France in territory size and, in Madrid, has the third largest urban population in Europe after London and Paris. Although international retailers such as Ahold and Carrefour increasingly dominate Spain, as in the rest of Europe, there is a dense network of local grocery stores and fresh markets that continue to play an important role. Spanish food shoppers still prefer to make frequent trips to local stores, with trips to the hypermarket for non-perishable goods restricted to once or twice a month. The Spanish consumer is becoming more health conscious and is seeking more information, improved customer service and high quality produce.

In this interview with Antoni Gari, deputy general manager of Supermercats Pujol SA, we explore the concerns of family-owned, national operators, and find some surprising ways of growing.

In this environment, Supermercats Pujol presents itself as a Catalan, family-owned business that includes the Plus Fresc chain of 59 neighbourhood shops. The chain started more than 50 years ago, with a wholesale and retail outlet in Catalonian Lleida. Innovation began in the 1960s with the introduction of self-service in three new stores. It was the second generation of Pujol's that reigned over a big expansion in the 1970s. At that time, Plus Fresc were known as discounters. The end of the 1980s saw a change of direction when Plus Fresc began to offer instead a value proposition that increased the range and quality of the products on sale, and emphasized fresh foods. The stores in the chain range from 200 m^2 to 1,000 m^2. The stores are located in small communities with a population typically of between 1,500 and 2,000 – and there are plans to introduce new shops into areas with even smaller populations. Around half of the stores are under franchise. With sales in 2001 reaching just over 111.3 million pesetas (€68.1 million) and a workforce of 550, Supermercats Pujol is a small fish in a large sea, and swimming against the swelling tide of global retailers.

Focus on fresh

Supermercats Pujol is too small to compete on volume and so we compete on fresh products. The emphasis on high quality fresh foods – raw, ready-to-cook and ready-to-eat products – brings Plus Fresc more customers, more frequently. One of our extra guarantees to the customer is that if they find a product that is out-of-date, we will give them a fresh item for no charge. This, together with a 'no quibble' returns policy, improves the confidence that customers have in the freshness of our goods and our honest, open approach to retailing.

Food safety

Of course, we need to ensure food safety and this is a very big issue in Spain today. Spanish consumers have always wanted quality, convenience, availability and price and in the past this has been enough but now consumers also want a full guarantee on safety. Interestingly, although consumers do associate organic foods with greater safety, they are not willing to pay extra. The challenge is to provide conventional, safety-assured products at no extra cost.

Our safety objectives are reached in a number of ways. There are as yet no standard forms of certification and regulations are different in each of the 16 regions of Spain. However, all our fresh food is bought from suppliers that are certified in some way, perhaps by larger retailers or trade associations. Although the medium-term goal of Plus Fresc is to sell only products grown under the label 'integrated production', that is, grown using the minimum of chemicals and ensuring full traceability, the concept is not as yet well understood by Spanish consumers. There are moves to provide a European framework for food safety, and we welcome such initiatives, as they may give greater confidence to consumers.

All-important partnership with producers

We have established and maintain a close partnership with the smaller producers so that the needs of our customers are properly communicated and satisfied. For example, for bread, we have an exclusive agreement with two traditional bakers. Another example is in our fish, which arrives fresh daily from the Mediterranean and we never sell thawed fish. Currently, there is no traceability on fish raised in fish farms but there is a need to ensure traceability for the future. All our veal comes from a single producer. When a close relationship develops, the supplier better understands and is better able to provide for the Plus Fresc customer. We take as much of the processing as possible in-house. We therefore have a butcher in each store and prepare some pre-cooked meals in our own kitchens. As this facility grows, so we must find more, equally reliable suppliers, and the relationship with the supplier becomes a critical success factor.

Responding to health scares

Health scares can easily cause a crisis for retailers. For example, veal has been a popular meat in Spain but the recent problems, while not apparently affecting the health of Spanish citizens, have caused a huge drop in sales. Large retailers have the power to make demands on suppliers. They have their own veterinary staff, for example, and can have highly integrated production. However, measures are still open to smaller retailers to ensure the quality of fresh foods. We now buy from one local supplier and have full traceability so we are able to give the customer full information about the rearing of the calf such as when the animal was born, what it was fed on and when it was killed. This is such an important issue that, even as quite a small retailer, we have our own meat processing plant conforming to ISO9002, giving us better control 'from farm to fork'.

Euromadi Iberica

For dry goods, Plus Fresc uses a buying group and selects high brand products that complement our range of fresh goods. In fact, our customers tend to reject value goods. Supermercats Pujol belongs to Spain's first purchasing group, Euromadi Iberica, part of the European Marketing Group (EMD). Euromadi Iberica has over 200 members and volume of sales of over €9,000 m, representing nearly a quarter of the food retail market in the Spain. Belonging to the buying group gives tremendous buying power and access to many suppliers throughout Europe. The group makes a tremendous effort to continually grow, and all the partners benefit from this continual expansion with a greater range of suppliers and products and greater technological innovation to gain the advantages of business-to-business operations.

Plus Fresc customer profile

Nearly 50 per cent of the population of Spain is under 45 and the number of young, working women is growing. Consequently, 30 per cent of Plus Fresc customers are busy working women and they account for 60 per cent of sales. Our commitment to very fresh produce is in response to the type of customer that wants value, quality and convenience from a retailer that they can trust. In adapting to the needs of this busy, demanding group, we have made many changes. For example, Catalonian law allows retailers to stay open no more 72 hours a week but to satisfy the needs of our customers, in some shops we have abandoned traditional hours in favour of a split day with a closing time of midnight, Monday to Saturday. This has proved very popular. Further examples include the installation of automatic packing machines at the checkout and a home delivery service where the customer shops and the goods are delivered within a chosen two-hour time frame up until 23:00. Delivery is free to customers who spend over 8,000 pesetas (€48).

We seek feedback from customers both informally and formally. We encourage customers to first contact staff in the store. At the store, the customer can make a suggestion or a complaint and have a problem solved immediately. They can leave a message for head office and even send an e-mail to the chairman, all from their usual store. We seek more formal feedback through a council of customers. The chairman attends meetings of the council. He is very often able to answer queries immediately or might set in motion some change on the basis of council discussion. In this way we have been able to gradually draw closer to our customers so that now we are better able to predict their requirements.

Customers have shown an interest in both the environment and the local community, and many, for example, donate their 1 per cent discount cheques to a charity of their choice, through our own payment systems. As a local chain, we think it important to do what we can for the community and environment. For example, we use photodegradable bags and recycled paper. Our signage and advertising is in Catalan as well as Spanish. The changing requirements of our customers have also initiated a recruitment policy change. Now our ideal employee is not necessarily the one most concerned with high productivity but with more of a focus on interaction and empathy with our customers.

Enabling technology

Information technology has been very important in providing speed, efficiency and innovation. For example, our ability to trace a calf from beginning to end is achieved with low-cost IT solutions, and we also use IT for customer profiling and to customize our response to the customer at the point-of-sale with special promotions and information.

From July 2001, at www.plusfresh.com we have been running a pilot scheme for Internet ordering by picking from three of our larger stores and delivering to the area covered by all our stores. Now, Spain in general might be seen as behind the rest of Europe in terms of e-commerce and the e-commerce activity is usually associated with only the largest players or specialist retailers but we have found that innovation is one of the keys to our success and information technology has enabled Plus Fresc, as quite a small operation, to constantly improve our offering to the customer.

Our loyalty card, the Plusi card, is based on cards from the larger food retailers with a 1 per cent discount given to the customer for previous purchases in a cheque every four months, together with coupons for promoted items. However, costs of mailing are prohibitive and so we have had to be inventive. Every point of sale has a mailbox. When the cardholder's card is swiped, the customer receives her or his quarterly cheque, and may have other messages highlighting new products, special promotions or giving extra discounts on featured products. The customer may also ask questions and receive answers via the in-store kiosk.

The loyalty programme was initially developed entirely in-house with the help of the Department of Computer Science at ESADE. It is unique in Spain, and won us the 1998 Global Electronic Marketing Award for the best electronic marketing programme from a non-US company (an award previously won by SuperQuinn in Ireland). We have been running our loyalty scheme for four years and so now perhaps the initial impact is spent. Some changes may be in order and we are considering, for example, a catalogue of rewards rather than simply a discount.

The future for Plus Fresc

In Catalonia, Plus Fresc has been the leader in food sales for many years. We are known as the 'local chain' but being local is not enough. We are opening new stores with a new format – a supermarket focused on pre-packaged foods and pre-cooked products. Our current store design is eight years old and so a fresh approach is needed. The new design is focused on convenience and will be refined as new stores open and old stores are refitted. We will continue to look around the world to bring best practice to Spain and not be afraid to innovate. Our customers want and expect it.

Chapter 18

Integration, challenge and change

Interview with Roland Vaxelaire, president and CEO of Carrefour Belgium

Carrefour Belgium, Avenue des Olympiades 20, 1140 Evere, Belgium
Tel.: +32 2 745 03 11; Fax: +32 2 729 29 87

Richard Bell

Belgian grocer GB has until recently held GIB Group's interests in subsidiaries operating in the supermarkets and hypermarkets in Belgium. The French retailer Carrefour, who already had a 27.5 per cent stake in GB as a result of the Promodès acquisition, acquired the other 72.5 per cent from GIB Group in July 2000. GB currently consists of 57 hypermarkets and 347 supermarkets and affiliates and 94 convenience stores, with 16,000 employees and 2 million customers in Belgium. The company generated over €5 billion in sales in 2001.

Roland Vaxelaire was appointed managing director of GB in January 1988, and continued as managing director following the Carrefour acquisition. He has worked within the food sector throughout his career. After a period with Nestlé Group (in the USA and France), he moved to Danone where he occupied management positions with Kronenbourg and then Evian before being appointed managing director of Alken-Maes breweries in 1993. Roland Vaxelaire is vice-president of FEDIS (Fédération des Entreprises de Distributeurs Belges) and ERRT (European Retail Round Table) and he is an administrator of Eurocommerce.

> In this frank interview, Vaxelaire provides a unique insight into the challenges facing all major retailers in western Europe today, including issues of supply chain integration, franchisees, private label, labour relations and e-commerce. Since this interview, M. Vaxelaire has been appointed president and CEO of Carrefour Belgium.

Supply chain integration

We believe that the supply chain is not only the concern of the logistics department but is all the way from the supplier to the store. The first step is from the supplier to the buyer. In retailing you are transporting information before you are transporting goods. Very often, the problems the store has in terms of replenishment or out-of-stock items are not because of problems with goods transportation. It is much more likely, perhaps 80 per cent of the time, that the problem is with the timeliness, accuracy or relevance of the information.

To overcome the problem of poor information, we have combined the buying, logistics and IT departments under one manager. That gives us the full line of responsibility from the buyer to the stores, and questions of supplier relations, transportation, warehousing and so on are the responsibility of one key person in my organization, the supply chain manager. The supply chain manager's responsibility extends to delivery into the stores. Once it is in the stores it is the responsibility of the store manager. If a product is in store but not available for the consumer to purchase, that is the responsibility of the store manager.

I cannot say that we will have the integrated function in the future. Carrefour has another vision of the business, another vision of the supply chain. At Carrefour, currently the buying department is really another business from the logistics, although logistics and IT are together. However, at GB we had some problems with the supply chain and it was very important for me during my two years with the company to bring the people together and to stop departments playing ping-pong with a problem. The problem could be passed from buyer to transportation to warehouse, without being solved. Now we have one person accountable who can quickly identify and solve the problem.

I put the integration of the buying, logistics and IT departments in place in April 1999. It is important to be able to measure the benefits of the new organization. The first thing we did was to determine the service level. We considerably increased the service level to the store. We had to. When you have an integrated organization and there are out-of-stock problems, even though this is a problem for the business, the store managers will simply stop complaining if nothing changes. However, if the franchisees or affiliates find that their business is at stake, then that becomes a big problem for them and us. The fact that we have a lot of franchisees in GB and the fact that there were problems in the supply chain really forced us to change things.

What drives the system depends on the department in the stores. Some of the departments work on orders from the stores, for example clothing. The manager in the store sees the collection and decides how much to take. Other departments work on paper, for example the grocery department. We do not yet have an automatic delivery programme but we are moving towards an automatic ordering system.

Of course, extending the supply chain to point-of-sale data may undermine the authority of the store operations. That is a big question at the moment but I think that the important thing is to give the opportunity for the store manager to work on exceptions – to have a double check on what is automatically delivered. Most of the product lines will be automatically replenished but sometimes the store manager can make a better decision. I think it is a good thing for both the store and for the store manager. In food, most of the stock is held in the store and so the people responsible for the inventory levels are the store managers. We try, especially in groceries, to have a flow from the supplier to the store. For the non-food it is sometimes best to have a buffer.

Affiliates

Management information

The same supply chain that supplies the affiliates, supplies our own stores. The affiliates are responsible for their own store stock levels. We do not measure them on that. That is their responsibility. The information system for the running of the stores includes a certain amount of management information. The store manager automatically receives data relating to the manager's own store but if the store needs a benchmark, someone from head office will do the comparison. We have the information store by store but the decision-maker is the store manager. The supplier does not have the right to send the affiliate anything that he did not request. In the integrated system, we can do that but it is important to know the store very well.

Rebranding of Nopri and Unic

The process of rebranding Nopri and Unic to Super GB was completed in 2001. It was a really tough operation. You had 10 days to transform each store. All the goods were removed from the store, the store is transformed and the new goods brought in. It was really a very heavy process. Since Carrefour's acquisition, the company has decided to keep the GB name on its supermarkets, because of strong brand recognition in Belgium.

For the stores, it is really a change of attitude. In an integrated system it is possible to some extent to impose changes but when you work with affiliates you can only suggest and advise. This is really a change of mentality and change of culture.

Much more service-wise, much more looking at the client. The stores that have been rebranded have had an average increase in turnover of 25 per cent. Some have had a 60 per cent increase in sales. The affiliates are small family businesses and a 25 per cent increase in sales is really another business for the affiliate. This causes a lot of difficulties with the rebranding.

The major reason for bringing the affiliates under the GB banner was the increased competition in Belgium. There is an increasing specialization in supermarkets and hypermarkets. We wanted to do that, and separate brands and goods for Nopri, Unic and GB would be much more expensive than one brand, GB, for all three. The market in Belgium is very competitive with Spar, Delhaize, Intermarché and Colruyt. We need to concentrate our efforts on one brand. Unic was 150 stores, Nopri was 200/250 stores but really decreasing very quickly. Without coming under one brand we would have 100 stores with the brand Nopri, 100 with Unic and 100 with GB. Better to have a very large brand. It also provides the opportunity to have a national campaign and to have local stores. Nopri and Unic were in very small towns in local areas where GB had no presence.

We lost some stores. We lost in two ways. Some affiliates did not want to make the investment and to continue to run the business. It provided an opportunity for them to reconsider. We were asking the affiliates to change their brand and change their way of doing business. For someone towards the end of his working life, and perhaps without a successor or the financial basis to continue, it may not be an attractive proposition. So we closed a lot of stores. In Belgium that is not a big problem for the business because the density of stores is really too high compared to other countries.

Second, we were giving the opportunity to the competitors to move in. The affiliate is in a position of having to undergo a change and so it offers the opportunity to look at alternatives. We lost around 20 per cent of stores. A lot were the poorer performing stores but we also lost some good stores. It offered a real opportunity to change affiliation, and we had experienced a lot of problems with the supply chain.

The reaction of the affiliates to the acquisition of GB by Carrefour was a little bit like the reaction of the union. Carrefour is the second largest group in the world and the largest in Europe, so affiliates are keen to have the know-how and conditions that go along with that. Obviously, they may also be concerned at being very small compared to Carrefour but first reactions are positive. From 2001, 45 supermarkets were further remodelled in line with group concepts (an emphasis on fresh products and low price products, and a growth in promotional campaigns).

The Carrefour acquisition

One of the advantages for GB of the Carrefour acquisition is size but size is not everything because the retailing business is very local. There is the know-how, the competencies, the training from them, and the possibility that Carrefour gives to GB in the supermarkets and hypermarkets. Carrefour has branded the hypermarket Carrefour here and retained the GB brand for the supermarket. It is easier when you exploit the synergies of the two métiers. We can immediately go for the hypermarket with Carrefour and have the synergy with Carrefour in France and elsewhere. The same is true for the supermarkets. With information systems, we can immediately change the system and that is very important.

Though there are synergies in bringing Unic and Nopri under the GB brand, there are also advantages in having the two separate marketing strategies, GB and Carrefour, in Belgium. I brought the Nopri and Unic under the GB brand because GB is a supermarket brand. Hypermarkets and supermarkets are really two different métiers. The supermarket is 90 per cent food and 10 per cent or less in non-food business. The hypermarket is 70/30 or 40/60, mostly non-food. It's really another business. You only have to look at electrical goods, computers, clothing, sport and leisure to see it really is a different kind of business and for that you have to have two different brands.

The question of whether to have one or two supply chains in Belgium is difficult to answer. The question is whether to work by the type of business or by region. My feeling is that we will have two types of operation. One will exploit the size, and there will be limited handling costs. The other supply chain will have large handling costs because it is small packages, small units for the store and so forth. I think that the likely outcome of the discussion is two separate supply chains but it is undecided.

Consumer research

We will undertake very little consumer research to judge the Belgium consumers' reaction to a Maxi becoming a Carrefour. We have to take a long-term view. It is very difficult to make a decision based on consumer reaction to something that they cannot really appreciate. I really think that the location is very important. When you have a good location and you give a good service to the consumer, they don't really care what name is on the store. It may be that the offer of the GB Maxi to the consumer will change when it is rebranded as Carrefour and that is an opportunity to reposition them to make them more contemporary, more relevant and to provide services that we do not provide today. Carrefour can offer more services than we currently offer at GB. The 2001 year-end results from the modernized supermarkets show a significant rise in the number of customers and a 5 per cent increase in sales.

Private label

Private label is very big in continental Europe, and GB has been one of the major drivers of private label. Recent analysis from ACNielsen showed that the disparity between the value and volume share of private label was much greater in Belgium than in other countries, which implies a discounting of private label in terms of price. The strategy, certainly as far as GB is concerned, is really to have a very low price in each of the categories of value, market leader and high image. Colruyt work on a strategy of price and Delhaize on a strategy of quality. I have to work on a strategy of choice. I have to have products in each category and each category is very important.

The lowest price that we have in our stores is against the competition of the discounter but we have to be very careful what we compare. When you look at the German market, Aldi or Lidl, they have very high quality products that are also a very low price. Choice does give us our strategy but it's more difficult than competing on price. You have to consider the image you give to the client.

The marketing strategy is to gradually uptrade customers from the low price private label to the premium price private label. Obviously the rebranding with Carrefour offers more opportunity, and also provides the opportunity to give more choice because a larger choice is possible when you are Carrefour.

Labour relations and the power of the syndicates in Belgium

I think that the big challenge for us in the following two or three years is to mange the labour force. I would say it is the reason for GB's lack of success in the past. We were in a permanent conflict situation with the union. Much of the management effort in the past has been concentrated on social issues rather than business issues. Competitors, such as Delhaize, have similar issues with the syndicates. Delhaize was perhaps more consistent in terms of social politics and, also, they were smaller and because we were the leader and the workforce was large the workforce has potentially more power to disrupt. More recently we have tried to speak more with the union and to understand their complaints. We have tried to be more open. I'm not saying we have solved the problem but that we are on the right track.

The strike that we experienced in May was, I think, very important because it demonstrated to the labour force that you have to give something to get something and if there is no benefit to the company you can't have profit-sharing. There is a greater mutual understanding. That's very important.

E-commerce

We are exploring the implications of e-commerce with great interest. We can imagine that some consumers will see great benefits from this channel of distribution, which is why we launched www.Ready.be before the acquisition by Carrefour. The big challenge with e-commerce is the development of the interactive software and the logistics associated with home delivery, such as the speed of response and whether customer orders should be picked at the store or in a specialized facility. Carrefour are addressing the same issues in France and did not wish to be involved in a parallel experiment in Belgium. They therefore saw no merit in acquiring the Ready store operation. GIB are continuing with this in Belgium and we are assisting them by continuing to acquire and supply the grocery items. This is, however, very much an arms' length relationship.

Chapter 19

A passionate journey: creating the right culture in a food retail organization

Fiona Bailey, director for culture, Safeway Stores, Hayes, UK

Safeway Stores plc, 6 Millington Road, Hayes, Middlesex UB3 4AY
Tel.: +44 (0)1622 712987

This case study and the following one are unusual in that they are written by senior managers within the organizations concerned, rather than by an 'outsider'. It is no coincidence that both these cases address issues of culture. Readers are invited to reflect not only upon the content of the cases that follow, but also upon the style of presentation. In early 2003, Safeway plc was the fourth largest grocery retailer in the UK, with annual sales of £8.7 billion, over 92,000 employees and nearly 480 stores nationwide. As this book went to press, the company had become the target for a bidding war from five interested parties, including Tesco, Sainsbury's and Asda/Wal-Mart, following an initial recommended bid from Wm Morrison, the sixth largest UK chain. Fiona Bailey has been with the Safeway group since 1997. Before becoming director for culture she joined the operations board as trading director fresh foods, having previously held the position of business unit director non-foods. Fiona is also responsible for internal communications.

If you're not passionate about it, don't even bother. . .

Changing the culture of any organization is a long and difficult journey. It involves unearthing deep-seated values, changing attitudes and behaviours, 'changing hearts and minds', which all depends on the working climate that people experience every day. You therefore need to believe passionately in the worth of what you are doing, if you are to survive the journey of (typically) several years . . .

Why is a culture in which people enjoy work so important?

In food retailing there is an important and very visible link between the motivation and satisfaction of our people – and the satisfaction of our customers. Our customers shop very frequently with us, and have a great many opportunities to judge their shopping experiences and tell others about them.

'What it's like around here'

The culture within any retail outlet is heavily driven by leadership behaviours. It drives employee attitude, which in turn drives retention, behaviours and advocacy. This then drives the experience of our customers, which very directly drives their future shopping behaviours and advocacy.

It is therefore important to know exactly what drives employee attitude in your own company, so that you can address what's important. For Safeway, confidence in our strategy was important – over 70 per cent of our people believe we have chosen the right strategy to succeed – this boosts both trust and commitment. Other important drivers are trust and loyalty to management, and job satisfaction.

The start of the journey – ambition

What drives the ambition to change culture? In Safeway it was the catalyst of a new chief executive with a turnaround strategy for the company, which required us to work together in a new way. We moved from short-term survival to a desire for long-term excellence.

We developed a vision for how we wanted to work together, which was driven by the behaviours that had successfully driven our turnaround, our competitive position (weak) and our future (ambitious) aspirations. It was important for the operations team to own the vision, and gain ownership and commitment from our senior managers. They then had the difficult task of adapting the vision to their own working environments – stores, depots and support divisions.

We didn't start with the launch of any 'Big Initiative' but used symbols, rituals and stories to highlight required new behaviours – and, hard as it was for some, we had to start 'walking the talk'.

The first few months of my own appointment were spent talking to people in every division at every level about what it was really like working for Safeway. This enabled me to assess the gaps between where we were and where we wanted to be, analyse the resistance to change and understand the different sub-cultures that existed – for example every store had its own sub-culture, largely influenced by the store manager's personal management style.

Managing the perceived conflict between 'hard' and 'soft' objectives

The link between 'people drivers' and 'business drivers' can be a constant source of conflict *unless* both are aligned. This is where belief in the service-profit chain is tested. If both are intrinsically linked to business objectives and strategy, then that tension remains healthy – the 'what' and 'how' are balanced, and you can both deliver business results and make the company a better place to work in.

The 'mess' – achieving commitment in the middle phase

Changing the culture of an organization has been described as 'messy' – it is! As the end of the old culture merges with the green shoots of the new, it can feel uncertain and confusing. In any change process you have typically a small number of champions, and then a larger group of people inclined to believe the change is the right thing to do.

At the other extreme, this is repeated for the 'negative opinion formers', cynics or culture terrorists. The higher up in the organization they are, the more they can encourage resistance to change. But at least they have passion – I have seen some cynics converted to the change and they immediately become champions. The trick is to get that passion working for you and not against you!

But the easiest prize is the undecided majority – the 68 per cent – and that is the biggest prize too. . . . These 'spectators' will respond to being challenged and inspired by the change vision, and should be encouraged and supported.

Inspiring and effective leadership

In this middle phase those responsible for how to engage people, inspire them with a cause, and work through them, need to be coached and trained in new behaviours, so that they, in turn, can develop and motivate others. This facilitates the greater involvement of colleagues, as attitudes change, communication improves and colleagues and managers meet to discuss performance and issues facing the teams. This promotes accountability and ownership for the business. The importance of enjoying work shouldn't be overlooked – in our stores the 'retailtainment' we provide is for the benefit of Safeway colleagues as well as customers.

Time to review, learn and measure

An essential part of the change journey is reviewing policies, procedures and processes, to check that they are fully aligned to the new way of working. Best practice also needs to be supported and promulgated – where is the new culture working, and why?

Safeway took the step of measuring how we were doing on the journey of cultural change by carrying out an employee survey – a very public way of demonstrating commitment to change and willingness to listen and improve things. This is now a regular event in which every colleague is consulted and results for every store/depot/division are published and acted upon. The survey is also used to measure where we are against our corporate strategic milestones for our new culture.

Reward, promote, encourage openness

Rewarding and recognizing exemplars of new behaviour is a powerful message to others. We try and ensure that this is part of normal good management practice, and that it is thoughtful, timely and appropriate.

The types of people who you promote will also give a powerful message to others – are they just high performers whose management style may leave a trail of high labour turnover and absence in their wake, or are they exemplars of the management style you wish to create?

It is easy to talk about openness and accessibility but harder to live up to the words. Here we found that symbolism and ritual (in the form of a bi-monthly video conference involving up to 1,000 colleagues in a two-way business meeting with the board) helped to model the change.

New beginnings – the latter phase

The speed of any change is heavily dependent on the commitment to change of the leader in any team. Nevertheless, the speed of corporate change does at some stage start to gather more momentum, when a critical mass of managers and leaders commit to transforming culture. We saw the power base for change expand as personal and emotional commitment spread, and as those who were more cautious saw the personal and business success of those who bought into the change at an earlier period. In this phase we have also raised our expectations of our managers, embedding 'people drivers' into objectives and targets.

The expectations for change are high, and we therefore continue to focus on communication, measurement and feedback, and the development and training of our leaders. We are also seeing the hard benefits of change, such as lower labour turnover and reduced sickness and absence. The biggest reward is to see the teamwork in our stores; the commitment, the spirit and the pride in what they do.

The final furlong

Our final furlong will take a further two and half years. Our ambition to become first choice food retailer will only happen if we achieve it through our people – the only long-term differentiation for any company. This is why cultural change will remain high on the agenda of all our managers and leaders. I shall continue to act as champion, catalyst and critic, uniting the company behind a common vision of how we want to work together in order to drive our business success.

If I were asked to sum up what has really made a difference on the Safeway journey, what has created the right conditions for the engagement of our people, I would cite six key learnings:

- Gain the emotional commitment of your people.
- Develop inspiring and effective leaders to achieve commitment.
- Release the potential of your people by getting them involved in and committed to delivering business success – every role is important.
- Show you value your people's contribution and commitment.
- Make work enjoyable.
- Do it all . . . with passion.

It makes cultural change sound easy – it's not – but it's a tremendously exciting and unforgettable journey to share with others.

Chapter 20

Wal-Mart's entry into the German market: an intercultural perspective

Reinhart Berggoetz, HR, recruiting and developing, and Martin Laue, senior HR manager for operations personnel, Wal-Mart, Germany

Wal-Mart (Germany) GmbH & Co KG, Friedrich-Engels-Allee, 28, D-42103, Wuppertal, Germany
Tel.: +49 (0) 202 2829 1238; Fax: +49 (0) 202 2829 1421

This US retailer, which is based in Bentonville, Arkansas, is the largest retailer and the largest business in the world. It operates 3,244 cash and carry (C&C) stores (SAM's Clubs) and retail stores (Wal-Mart stores, Supercenters and Neighborhood Markets). Outside the US, Wal-Mart operates 1,170 stores in nine countries. The company employs over 1,300,000 associates worldwide, more than 300,000 of these outside the US. Sales volume for Wal-Mart Inc. at the end of January 2002 amounted to US$217.8 billion (over €240 billion), up 13.8 per cent. This case study deals with the cultural issues involved in Wal-Mart's entry into the German market and, unusually for this book, is written by two senior managers from the business.

German market entry: understanding different cultures

The financial significance of Wal-Mart's entry into the German market at the end of 1997 was based not only on Germany's status as the third largest national economy but also on Germany's importance as a basis for expansion into Europe. In December 1997, Wal-Mart entered the German market by acquiring *Wertkauf* GmbH with its 21 hypermarkets. Only one year later, the 74 *Interspar* stores of *Spar AG* followed.

In 1962 Sam Walton founded Wal-Mart and with it the Wal-Mart culture. It has been the company's 'heart and soul' for decades of continuous organic growth and has allowed Wal-Mart's tremendous economic success. With the takeover of *Wertkauf* and *Interspar*, Wal-Mart met with two strongly established and very different corporate cultures.

On the one hand, Hugo Mann, a charismatic entrepreneurial personality, had exerted a strong influence on the formation of *Wertkauf* since its foundation in the 1950s. The culture is best described as autocratic and conservative, leaving little room for innovation. The company was known among its competitors for its unbeatable proportion of non-food items in the assortment, its focus on internal growth instead of uncontrolled expansion, and concentration on profit and profitability expressed as a high productivity ratio. The workflow was structured by standard operating procedures. This system very much limited the store managers' room for manoeuvre. The company's below-average turnover stemmed from *Wertkauf's* ability to retain its employees by offering a clear, systematic and transparent corporate culture despite its strict cost reduction policy.

On the other hand, the 74 *Interspar* stores did not share a common corporate history and were a true conglomerate of different corporate cultures. Despite working at the same store, some associates had been employed by as many as six different companies – a change every 2–3 years on average. Cultural influences ranged from the union-affiliated *Co-op* to *Plaza* stores to the *Pfannkuch* group and its *Kolossa* stores (which in turn had been acquired by *Interspar* only one year prior to the Wal-Mart takeover). French influence over a period of approximately two years resulted in a 'cameo appearance' from *Continent*, which withdrew from the German market due to lack of success.

Thus, Wal-Mart had to cope with the heterogeneity of both companies' corporate cultures when it first entered the German market.

Wal-Mart culture

The entrepreneurial personality of Sam Walton shaped the Wal-Mart culture, and continues to thrive beyond his death in 1992. The Wal-Mart culture is founded on the Three Basic Beliefs: (1) Respect for the Individual, (2) Service to Our Customers and (3) Strive for Excellence. Sam Walton's anecdotes and adages quicken this vibrant culture. Sam Walton worked closely with the associates in the stores – the essence of his success. It is the associates who have the best ideas and closest contact to the customers, and are the key to the company's success. With this conviction, Sam Walton regularly held 'grass roots' meetings with the associates in the stores where he personally asked them for their ideas for improvements. These meetings often resulted in successful implementation of the associates' ideas.

The 'grass roots' tradition is continued in annual associate surveys at all Wal-Mart locations. Managers and associates discuss the results in order to jointly work on improvements. This leads to the requirements of an 'ideal' store manager. He or she is not an hierarchic and inaccessible leader but supports his or her associates through 'servant leadership', acknowledges every associate's efforts and their contribution to the team's success, coaches by walking around (CBWA) and fosters entrepreneurial thinking ('be a merchant'). This form of management requires strong communication skills and openness towards the associates. Managers cannot fall back on their position and status but must demonstrate and prove their quality as leaders.

For outsiders, the Wal-Mart culture is frequently identified by artefacts such as the 'Wal-Mart cheer' rather than by the clear entrepreneurial focus. Ultimately, the Wal-Mart culture focuses on the customer, whose shopping habits determine the company's economic success. Any action or programme, be it the every day low price (EDLP) policy, warranties, or the assortment, advertising support and so on, has the objective of communicating to the customer Wal-Mart's 'best value' policy.

Walton's 'commitments' and their influence on current corporate culture support customer orientation both directly in the form of customer service, and indirectly in associate appreciation. For example, Wal-Mart celebrates success with its associates, and encourages everybody to find some humour in failure, too. The company does not succeed by imitating the competition; its success is based on a unique combination of services and products, which can only be achieved by 'swimming upstream'.

In summary, Wal-Mart's culture is simple and relevant. It is transparent. It concentrates on the essential and is utterly pragmatic. The customer is number one and each individual associate's contribution to the company's success is valued.

Intercultural encounters

The Wal-Mart culture is often thought synonymous with the American culture, but in fact it is a set of globally applicable standards. The international implementation of the Wal-Mart culture needs to take regional differences into consideration. The results of intercultural studies provide a better understanding of experiences gained by US associates in the transfer of the Wal-Mart culture.

Compared internationally, in Germany relations focus on the task, in the US relations focus on people. The Wal-Mart culture, too, is composed of associate and customer relations, whereas the *Wertkauf* and *Interspar* culture focused on getting the job done. This form of communication was supported by slogans such as: 'The store has to be set', 'We need more hands', 'Associates are here to stock the shelves, not to think'.

Germans' tolerance of uncertainty is rather low, whereas US-Americans are prepared to take risks. Wal-Mart's motto is 'Let's do it'. Implementation issues will not throw them off the track for long. They often seem to accomplish the impossible. The German tendency towards problem-oriented thinking hinders swift action. For example, with instructions from an American advisor, an entire department was reorganized without lengthy planning.

The German system is characterized by punctuality, linear performance, sticking to the initial solution, and a long-term focus. At Wal-Mart, several different projects are being worked on at the same time. Decisions are easily abandoned for new ideas and the focus is on short-term objectives. After the acquisition of the *Interspar* group in 1999, for instance, the head office was moved to Wuppertal, the American merchandise information system was implemented in all stores, and the assortment structure and logistics were reorganized at the same time. A German planning process would have taken much longer.

An important difference is the German tendency towards consensus, whereas Wal-Mart fosters an entrepreneurial attitude among its associates ('swim upstream'). In critical situations, for example in the case of an angry customer, it is much better to apologize and contain any possible damage proactively than to remain passive. In daily business, the tendency towards collectivist behaviour in Germany manifests itself through employee co-determination (works agreements), employee protection and labour safety laws as well as wage scales. These facts stand in the way of an action-oriented and frequently spontaneous attitude. Therefore, it is difficult, for example, to explain to Americans the reasons why associate uniforms are subject to co-determination.

The biggest differences, however, are revealed in everyday communication. While German associates prefer direct communication and frankness as well as precise instructions, US-Americans appreciate indirect communication and implicit explanations as well as face-saving criticism. Frequent and individual praise is the most common instrument of motivation at Wal-Mart; however, effusiveness may cause scepticism among Germans. People can differentiate between an American or German manager when something is referred to as 'outstanding'.

Wal-Mart corporate culture, intercultural differences and implications for human resources

This discussion leads to the following thoughts on global human resources. Corporate culture and country culture are not the same (Wal-Mart culture is not US culture). However, the influence of the country culture on corporate culture must always be taken into account. Universal corporate beliefs have to be adapted to country-specific cultural aspects without losing their corporate identity.

Corporate culture not only requires supportive action (intercultural training, coaching) but also time and patience in order to grow within an acquired company with a cultural history of its own. There is no such thing as a pill for cultural transformation.

Corporate culture depends on cultural carriers. Particularly during the first phase after an acquisition, cultural promoters among the senior management are very important (top-down process). The acquiring company should demonstrate its sincerity and live up to its guidelines and culture.

With respect to the recruiting of external resources, the focus should be on qualifications and adaptability to the corporate culture ('Get the right people on the bus').

Cultural standards should be integrated into all personnel development measures (e.g. management/leadership training). The approach should focus on performance instead of education. With respect to internal succession planning, cultural skills take a significant part in building cross-positional culture promoters.

Development of active 'coaching for improvement' processes is supported by performance appraisals (also 360° feedback) and associate surveys on a regular basis. The appraisal criteria are based on company principles.

Managers acting deliberately and persistently against corporate culture should leave the company ('Get the wrong people off the bus') since they hinder consistent culture transfer.

In view of the high number of contact points with different national cultures within the Wal-Mart corporate culture transfer, the core competence of the human resources department is to support adaptability of its staff to the corporate culture and at the same time develop tolerance for the different national cultures within a global company.

Chapter 21

Ready to scale up: India's Shoppers' Stop

Interview with B.S. Nagesh, customer care associate, managing director and CEO, Shoppers' Stop

Shoppers' Stop, Eureka Towers, 9th Floor, B Wing 504, Link Road, Malad (West), Mumbai 400 064 India
Tel.: +91 (0) 22 880 0808; Fax: +91 (0) 22 880 8877

Elizabeth Howard

Shoppers' Stop is a pioneering chain of department stores in India. Thirteen stores of around 5,000 square metres each focus on garments and accessories, plus home furnishings, books and music, offering international domestic and own brands. Revenue in 2001/2 was 2,486 million rupees (about €50 million). 2002/3 saw same-store growth of 9% and company growth of 23%, moving from breakeven to around €2m.

When I first met BSN he gave me his business card. Customer care associate? I thought he was CEO? He is of course, and explained the card as follows. He said that everyone in his business is now called a customer care associate. 'This is about employee self esteem.' Retail salespeople should not be looked down upon. The idea started when he heard a story about someone who disapproved of his daughter marrying one of his 'salesmen'. Does this remind you of Asda's 'colleagues'? This was just the first of several times when I was struck by Nagesh's determination to apply the best ideas he can find to a new, growing business – and of the difficulties of persuading people that retailing can be a large scale, professional business in India. I met him again later, and he talked about the challenges in setting up and developing one of the very first modern retail chains in India.

Beginnings

I had been a postgraduate management student, then worked for three big companies: in luggage, electronics and footwear. In the last one I was running 128 small shops in the south of India – average size about 50 square metres. I was fed up with these small shops and dreamed that someone could open larger stores. It was chance more than anything that I met our parent company, the K. Rajeha Group, which is one of the largest real estate corporations in the country. They had a four cinema multiplex which had been closed since 1988 and were looking for something to do with it. I had never been in a store abroad at this point; I'd never travelled abroad. But I was ready to do something big and I joined them. I was the first employee of the new company, before even its brand name was selected. Most of the retail initiatives in India were taken in 1995/96, but this was back in 1991. Before we started there were some larger stores but these were highly specialized family businesses selling saris or jewellery. Outside these two categories there were no large stores. So when we started, nobody believed it would work: the biggest store they had seen was 5,000 square foot (500 square metres) and we were talking about 50,000 square foot. And retailing had never been professional.

So we started with an experiment and by June 1993 had completed occupation of that first property. We ran one store for two years then opened the second. It was only when we opened the second store, in Bangalore, that people suddenly looked at what we were doing. We were profitable in one store, and we were a profitable two-store chain.

From 1991 to 1996 it was a struggle. It was a struggle to get anyone to look at retail. I went to universities and took classes, I talked to people. I believe in openness and sharing information, anyway, though we are a private company. Then in 1996 Littlewoods of the UK came into India and opened their first store in Bangalore. After two years because of reorganization in the UK, and because they found it difficult here – they had 10 expatriate managers and you can't pay in pounds and earn in rupees – they sold out to Lakme. The stores are now called Westside, owned by Trent. So that was the second large corporate to get into retailing. The next was RPG going into food retailing in association with Dairy Farm of Hong Kong.

At that point we took stock, and took a very long-term view. We decided that there was something much larger to go for, and we developed three things: our vision, our mission statement and gradually, our value statement. Our vision is to be 'India's Number One Global Retailer'. That does not mean that we will open stores in the rest of the world! There's enough to do here. But we will bring the best of global practices to this country. The mission statement is 'nothing but the best'. We will not compromise on anything. We have also developed 10 values, which help and guide us. In 1996 I applied to IGDS (the International Group of Department Stores) and they accepted us as a member alongside companies like Selfridges.

During 1998–2000 we had the mission and vision and fire in the belly. With KSA's help we evaluated 10 software companies around the world, and shortlisted four. They refused to come to India! I begged them – have you ever heard such a thing, there's a customer and they won't talk to you. They said we were too small. Finally we selected JDA and we implemented their software. We implemented the full JDA software in 12 months when they wanted us to take two years. We were a two-store company and we opened three more stores in one year. I moved to a central distribution system. We took too many initiatives at once, so we had major problems, and losses for two years.

We've been lucky in the way our promoters have looked at us and in the confidence they have in us. After buying JDA we realized we had the track but we didn't know how to drive. We hired Keith Dunn (ex Littlewoods) to help us for two years. It was tough to be the flagbearer for the industry. When we did well everyone praised us, when we did not, people said it was the end of scale retailing in this country. I have a wonderful team and within one year of making losses we recovered fully. This year we are expecting fabulous results.

Now we have the software working: NMS for the backend and WMS for the frontend. There's automatic stock matching at the end of every day right across the chain. We have a totally automated warehouse – not escalators and cranes, but a total auto-replenishment system. Every night at 10.30 p.m. the signal is given and replenishment begins. We don't have even 100 square metres of backroom in any store. We do not stock *anything* in the store. Last year we turned stock round 5.2 times and hope for the same this year.

We are the only retail company in the country with B2B working: 85 of our suppliers are connected online. By next year I want all our 300 suppliers to be connected online. I don't think that retailers should try to exert power through holding back information. We should share it with suppliers; we should all look at the same screen. Last month we opened a totally wireless store. So the business is fully integrated. The last piece that is left is the planning software. We were using indigenously developed software, but intend to implement Arthur. My team is in Australia at the moment to complete that.

Although we are not a public company we follow every corporate governance rule. I am the only executive director on the board; there are three directors from the promoters, three from other major Indian businesses, Nitin Sanghavi of Manchester Business School, and also Vittorio Radice from Selfridges. We have an audit committee, a compensation committee and so on. We have introduced an employee stock option plan for the top 16 people, and this March it will be extended to the next level.

Our vision is always to be the global best. Every time we wanted to do something we went outside the country and benchmarked. We bought the best technology. We run customer and employee satisfaction surveys every six months. We are getting to the stage when we can link them: if employee satisfaction goes down, so do the customer scores. Store managers' bonuses depend on store EBITDA (earnings before interest, taxes, depreciation and amortization) but subject to achieving rising customer and employee satisfaction scores. At the department level, the manager's job is to ensure that feedback occurs, and so on.

We are introducing a balanced score card system now to make sure that mangers do not just look at the financials. Ideally I want the balanced scorecard to be the way we measure the business.

We have the biggest loyalty scheme in the country, based on a Citibank credit card. That gives us a huge amount of information about our customers. Three cards, gold, silver and classic, provide reward points at various levels, which can be used in gift vouchers.

No experience please

At sales level we take fresh undergraduates. We don't take anyone with experience. At managerial level we did not, until recently, take anyone from retail or textile backgrounds. I did not want anyone who came with the belief that we could not do it. Once we had five stores we started to look at how to improve merchandising and then we started getting buyers from fashion and so on. But we still employ very young people. The average age of the company is 28, and it is 23 at the front end.

I am proud of our 'kangaroo' programme. These are training programmes based on the idea that first people need to be in the pocket, and then they can leap forward. Through these programmes customer care associates can become supervisors, then there is another programme to help them become department managers and so on. I am very pleased that our latest store managers are both 'kangaroos'.

We have very good people here at headquarters too, but there is a very big gap to fill as we grow. How will we do it? Look, we will double in size soon, and that puts us in a good position to recruit the best. People will see us correctly as a US$100 million company.

Ready to scale

We are ready to scale. We have 11 stores today, and are opening two more in the next few weeks. We are already national, with stores in the eight major cities. In our catchments, we calculate we have 8–12 per cent market shares. Within five years we will have 35 stores.

Constraints

The biggest constraint on our development is suppliers' ability to fulfil. The whole supply chain is very weak. Secondly, the cost and time taken for distribution is very large. Thirdly, stock is not floor ready when it arrives. We have to do a lot to it. Next there is the fact that India operates a maximum retail price system. So the price we get for a shirt in my store is equal to the price you see everywhere. The result is that our margin is 28 or 29 per cent, when international companies might have 35 per cent. The necessary real estate development has not happened yet. We are just beginning to see malls of international standard. And finally: people. Getting enough people of the right kind is a challenge.

Opportunities

The biggest retail opportunities in India are for food hypermarkets. But in our sector there are also great opportunities. We could grow to be a €300 or €500 million company before thinking about doing anything else. Our aim is to capture the national urban market. Although 60 per cent of India is rural, it is the cities we will focus on. We have three formats for different catchments but they do not differ greatly.

My own role changes year after year. At first it was to build a business in an unknown industry. For the last three years it was converting the business into an organization. This year it is concentrating on growth. The next challenge is to triple the size of the business.

Nagesh is a pioneer in India. Before I left I asked whether there were lessons for retailers in other countries from his experience. He was clear there were. A weakness of European retailers is that they are often stuck with old technology and systems. They are often too inward looking. And finally, he says, don't spend too much time worrying about the detail of what the competition is doing: look at the consumer instead.

Chapter 22

Creating a global retail brand

Interview with Sir Geoffrey Mulcahy, former group chief executive, Kingfisher plc

Kingfisher plc, 3 Sheldon Square, Paddington, London, W2 6PX
Tel.: +44 (0) 20 7372 8008; Fax: +44 (0) 20 7644 1001

Richard Bell

With some 2,500 stores spanning 13 countries by the end of the 1990s, Kingfisher was being recognized – albeit not necessarily by consumers – as one of the world's leading retail brands. With proforma sales of £8.2 billion (€11.97 billion) in 1997/8, it ranked as the world's 36th largest retailer. In 2000, it became the leading European DIY operator, following a complex alliance between B&Q and Castorama. It also captured a larger share of the European electricals market with the acquisition of But, France's fourth largest electricals retailer, and a 60 per cent stake in German retailer Wegert, which operates the Promarkt chain. The prime mover behind the company's composition, strategy and success was Sir Geoff Mulcahy. This interview, conducted at a point at which the company reached the peak of its international breadth and reach, across a broad range of home-focused categories, provides us with a unique insight into its strategy for developing global retail brands. A postscript provides an update on subsequent events.

Group brand strategy

We view Kingfisher as a family of retail brands concentrating on the home and family at various stages of the lifecycle.

Table 22.1 Kingfisher plc five year history

Year ended	1998	1999	2000	2001	2002
Turnover	6,409.4	7,457.8	10,885.0	12,134.2	11,238.1
Home improvement	1,753.7	2,055.4	4,528.3	5,093.5	5,833.9
Electrical/furniture	1,937.9	2,458.1	3,188.0	3,564.9	3,784.8
General merchandise	2,618.0	2,840.9	3,065.5	3,358.4	1,498.6
Property	51.2	41.1	32.5	59.2	65.7
Financial services	48.6	62.3	70.7	58.2	55.1
Pre-tax profit	521.6	626.4	712.8	691.2	28.0

Source: Kingfisher plc

The three sectors on which we are now clearly focused are DIY, electricals and general merchandise. We believe that DIY and electricals offer excellent international growth potential, particularly in Europe which, in the context of these businesses, we view as a single market. Our decision to expand on an international basis was taken not just for the sake of creating a bigger business, but because we knew that in order to maintain unbeatable choice, price and service we have to have the benefit of scale. In order to pursue this strategy on an international front, we have to have a very strong home base. This is where our general merchandise sector fits in, and we are committed to growing that as well.

Our philosophy for both our UK and overseas brands is that they focus on the mass market; they offer the best price, the best choice, and the best service; and that they occupy the leading, or a good number two, position in their respective markets. Markets are usually chosen because they offer relatively strong growth potential.

Woolworths, for example, has prospered over the years because we have concentrated on developing good market positions – it is the leading brand in entertainment, confectionery and toys, and occupies a strong position in home and childrenswear. Our aim to be the leading market brand in growth markets is applied not only within the brand, but across the brand overall.

In terms of the group as a whole, Darty is the number one electricals retailer in France, whilst Comet is the number two in the UK. In DIY retailing, Castorama leads the French market, whilst B&Q is the leading UK operator. Woolworths holds premier position in several of its sectors, and Superdrug is number two in health and beauty.

Continuing to grow the brand

I do not believe that brands ever really run out of growth. The key to growing them indefinitely is innovation. At Kingfisher, we are continually looking at new ways to develop our businesses, moving in and out of markets and product areas where appropriate, and developing new formats to take the brand forward. Provided you look creatively at the business, you can continue to grow and develop the brand far further and longer than most people would have thought possible. Our brands strategy has always been to create market leading propositions which have clearly defined roles in the customers' mind about what they stand for. B&Q, Woolworths and Superdrug provide good examples of the effectiveness of this strategy.

Initially, B&Q was a smaller player than Woolworths in the DIY market. Even in terms of its superstores, it was number two or three. We realized that by taking DIY products out of Woolworths and channelling them through larger, dedicated super-stores we would create a more efficient, customer friendly vehicle for growth, with the potential for being the market leader. We wanted to create a brand with absolute authority, which would become the consumers' first choice for DIY products.

At the time, this caused us some problems at Woolworths, as we had to look at new ways of growing that business. Nevertheless, the results show that it was the right strategy. B&Q offered a greater opportunity for us to grow and gain leadership in the DIY sector, giving customers a wider choice, lower prices (through economies of scale) and, by specializing in that sector, better service. Taking this strategy one step further we developed B&Q Warehouse, massive stores of 150,000 sq ft, selling some 40,000 product lines. They offer a greater range, price and service than our smaller outlets, therefore satisfying customers' needs more completely. B&Q Warehouse not only reinforced our leadership, but enabled us to expand the DIY market at the same time.

In the case of Woolworths, some 20 years ago it had lost its way and become a 'jack of all trades'. Consumers were shopping there as a last resort, rather than as their store of choice. We had to recreate the brand, making it the first choice for customers and a destination store. We decided to concentrate on product areas where we could develop a market leading position – toys, entertainment, childrenswear and household products. As a result, adultswear and food were dropped from the range, as these were areas where we felt that as a general merchandise operator, we would never have been able to establish a market leading position. Although this meant eliminating £250 million (€350 million) worth of business, by reallocating space taken up by food and clothing, we were able to trade a lot more effectively in our chosen markets.

Another integral part of our strategy to grow our brands is innovation in mer-chandise. At Woolworths this has involved developing leading private-label toy and childrenswear labels – Chad Valley and Ladybird – as well as having exclusives in confectionery. Furthermore, Woolworths was the first retailer to sell prerecorded, low price videos creating a new market of which we still have a leading share.

Since acquiring Superdrug in 1986, we have repositioned the brand away from its traditional position as a discount drugstore to a value health and beauty store in the personal care sector. It now has a really competitive offer to challenge Boots. The recent addition of pharmacies to 200 Superdrug stores has been an important part of that process.

Maintaining the brand essence

Knowing and defining what the store brand means to the customer is one of the most important things to consider when making changes to the product range or store format. If you have retained the brand's essence and attributes, customers will continue to come back to the store after changes have been made. The essence is much more than the particular products sold within the store.

Woolworths is a particularly interesting example. It is one of the few stores that you can sell virtually anything in and the customer would not be surprised, it has a sort of universal branding. The essence of the Woolworths' brand is a warm, friendly environment, family products, good value and hassle free shopping. These values can be applied across a variety of product categories provided that you set out and establish authority in these categories over a period of time. Woolworths has some very strong brand attributes, not only in the UK, but also in the other countries in which it operates, such as the US and Germany. People's understanding of the store brand is exactly the same across all of these countries.

Failure to understand these brand values was one of the reasons why Woolworths floundered during the 1970s, leading to the change of ownership in 1982 and the creation of what is now known as Kingfisher. As is often the case in retail brands, the brand image is created by the inventor of the brand – a person who has an intrinsic understanding of what he is trying to offer the customer. When creator Frank Winfield Woolworth died, the chain lost customers as the business did not have any intrinsic understanding of what the brand values were and was therefore unable to evolve and meet new customer demands. It got stuck in history, as it was unable to adapt those intrinsic brand values to the new customer environment.

The B&Q brand conveys many of the same values as Woolworths, but it is regarded as the place to go for home improvement. This gives you a broad canvas on which to hang your merchandise selection.

Overseas expansion

In order to continue to grow our business, we must now think about the market in terms of Europe, and indeed the world. Going back 10–15 years, retailers really only competed within their home markets. This has now all changed and the industry can no longer afford to think in these narrow terms.

Europe needs to be looked at as one market. As trade barriers come down, there are some huge economies to be gained by organizing oneself on a European basis. However, we cannot restrict ourselves to Europe, what we are seeing is the emergence of global retailing.

By expanding into Europe, and indeed across the world, we will be able to significantly enhance our buying power and therefore economies of scale. This will place us on a more even playing field to our American counterparts, many of whom have reaped the benefits of a huge domestic market to fund overseas development.

Not only does it make financial sense to operate on a European basis, but also it is important from our customers' perspective. They are seeing and experiencing products from further afield by travelling, watching television and using the Internet. Consequently, they demand the best that is available internationally. Add suppliers to the equation, and we are all having to think globally.

Once you have to think about your market in these terms, you then have to ask yourself how you are going to operate across Europe and the world. In the process of internationalizing our business and acquiring new companies, we are trying to create a company that has a common sense of customer values and management attitudes. It is essential that we understand and are at ease with our partner's brand and business.

In the case of Castorama and Darty, we spent a lot of time trying to understand the underlying business and management ethos of both companies. It is important that we all have a similar perspective with regards to the customer, investment in infrastructure and the supply chain, etc.

Local marketing and global supply

I think the key to being successful abroad is to understand how the local markets operate and how you can get efficiencies out of the back of the shop – the supply chain, infrastructure and relationships with suppliers, etc.

At the front end, the marketing end of the business, whilst it is true that you require some different product specifications, you can still apply best practice methods. Despite all the talk about globalization and Europeanization, you have to recognize that customers are different in different countries.

Nevertheless, regardless of the type of washing machine a customer prefers (top-loading in France; front-loading in the UK), the retailing principles are very much the same. The customer wants to be satisfied that they are buying it at the best price, that they have the best range of products to choose from, that they are getting the best advice in terms of what machine will meet their requirements, and that they are getting the best after sales service.

Furthermore, if you can offer a supplier the advantage of scale, then he can generate efficiencies that are passed on to the retailer, and ultimately the customer. The trick is local marketing and global supply.

Developing common brand values

Kingfisher is currently going through an evolution, a transition process. Our markets are rapidly moving from local markets to European and global markets. Each country has different, well known brand names that are trusted by the customer.

The first stage to harmonizing these brands is to ensure that they are managed in the same way, so that they truly mean the same thing to customers in different countries. We aim to manage the brands so that they develop a common set of values.

In 1993 (when Darty became part of the group) we established KERL (Kingfisher Electrical Retailing Ltd) in order to maximize the benefits from having a European network of electrical retail outlets. One of the objects of KERL is to make sure that the brand harmonization process happens across these outlets. This process may be at different speeds in different countries, reflecting the varying positions of each country's electrical brands.

Furthermore, KERL tries to ensure that we get some efficiencies out of the back end of the business – supplier relationships, distribution infrastructure, systems, etc. I think it is unlikely in the foreseeable future that we will move to a common electrical brand name across Europe, but I would not rule it out totally, depending on how fast the industry evolves.

New technologies such as the Internet and satellite television, as well as consumers travelling abroad more, are prompting us to continually review our branding strategy. If a customer visits the web sites or retail stores of Comet, Darty, Promarkt (Germany), BCC (the Netherlands) and New Vanden Borre (Belgium), he may question why each one has a different offer, in terms of range, price and service, when it is owned by the same company.

Private label

Developing a private label offer is a conscious part of our strategy, which is applied in different ways in different markets. In electricals for example, the customer is actually looking for branded products such as Sony, Philips, Toshiba and Whirlpool. They want these brand names and therefore we market them. As a result, the position of our private label in electricals is set in relation to those branded products. In other markets, private label could be a higher proportion of the mix.

In terms of developing a common private-label name across the various markets in which we operate, we are already marketing the same name across several countries in Europe. Obviously, the price levels in the various European markets differ, not because the retailers impose different prices in different markets, but because over the years suppliers have priced differently into each country.

The interesting thing about private label is that we are in control of the total supply chain, product specifications and the cost of the product. Therefore, when pricing the product we are not carrying the baggage of different price levels in different markets, enabling us to price at a level that is in tune with the local market. This could possibly lead to the development of a Europe-wide price.

Price differentials

The most well known example of different prices is the price of electricals in the US and Europe. The differential is not retailer driven, but manufacturer driven. Consumers are becoming more aware of these differentials as they see the price of products on the Internet, etc. However, it is not simply a question of retailers pricing products differently, it goes right down the supply chain. This may reflect product specification – Europeans tend to demand a higher quality and are more concerned about the environmental impact of particular designs. Furthermore, the costs of supplying individual European countries are higher than the US, as the market size is much smaller and less homogeneous.

Nevertheless, as Europe becomes a more truly single market, we are likely to see greater economies operating. With 350 million people, a larger population than the US, there is no reason why we cannot enjoy the same economies of scale provided that manufacturers organize themselves properly. We should therefore be in a position to be able to see why these price differences are really there. If price differences are not driven by product specification, then there is likely to be more pressure from consumers to equalize them.

Private label may be the route for us to develop price harmonization. Once we start to expand this area of our business, we could generate enormous purchasing power that could be levered across all of our European businesses and passed on to the consumer.

Currently, we are not that big on a global scale, we rank 36th in the world. However, we are aiming to compete with retailers such as Wal-Mart, Home Depot and Metro, in order to gain greater buying power and scale economies. Last year, we saw how Carrefour used its global scale to run an excellent promotion celebrating its 30th anniversary. It was run across a number of different products across its worldwide business. They were promoting it to their customers as the benefits of Carrefour's global scale.

However, buying power is not the only issue. If internationalization is going to work well, you have to have an integrated supply chain. To get the benefits of scale through to the customer, it is necessary to develop new ways of working so that factories can be made more efficient and we can move to just-in-time manufacturing practices. By doing so, we can give manufacturers the scale of orders on which to get true economies of scale and to run their factories in a highly efficient way. Therefore, it is not just a question of buying muscle but using that scale to improve the efficiency of the total process. You have to be big to do this, as a manufacturer cannot change his production methods for a lot of individual retailers, but he can for a small number of large ones.

To a certain extent manufacturers face the same issues as retailers. One manufacturer recently told me that he was operating 25 different brands across Europe, with 25 different sales forces often selling to the same retailers. This situation would then put competing demands back on the same factories. The question is, do you really need that number of brands? You might have one brand that works better in France than the UK for example, but there is no reason why the underlying product needs to be different. If you can achieve that, you can enjoy the efficiencies of scale.

Developing a multi-cultural organization

In the transition that we are making towards becoming an international company, we have to assimilate not only different languages, but also cultures and working practices. In order to achieve this there are three steps that we take.

The first thing that we do, is to spend quite a lot of time in preparation prior to acquisition, or indeed setting up an operation in another country. We try to understand the culture of the country that we are moving into, or the management style of the company that we are acquiring. Although nationalities may be different, we really try to understand the management of a company, so that we can satisfy ourselves that we have a common set of cultural and ethical values.

The second step is to make sure that people understand that different nationalities have different cultures, it is not a fact that one is better than the other, just different. A common mistake is to think that because we speak the same language we share a common culture; for example, the Americans and the British.

Thirdly, we concentrate on bringing together the management team so that they share a common vision and idea of the way forward. Once a clear vision is established, we can concentrate on the business issues and then work through to a common solution.

In terms of the organization structure, for certain functions I can see that in time as we become more international we are likely to move towards a more decentralized, multi-cultural team. This is particularly the case for front-end roles such as labour relations and marketing, where it is very important to understand the local market that you are operating in, rather than for distribution, logistics and sourcing for example. In distribution it is possible to envisage Frenchmen working in Germany; Germans in the UK and Britons in France. This will be much more difficult to achieve in the front end roles. To a certain extent, I think that this is a generation game, with younger people far more used to travelling and open to new cultures than the older generation.

Postscript

Sir Geoff Mulcahy retired from the Kingfisher board in 2002. Having initiated and led the expansion of the business, he spent 2000–02 rationalizing the business to reflect the higher growth potential of the home improvement category. Kingfisher sold its chain of about 700 Superdrug stores (even though it was the UK's second largest cosmetics/health and beauty chain, behind Boots) in early 2001, and it disposed of its Woolworth and other general merchandise stores in a public offering in August 2001.

The separation of Kingfisher's electricals businesses in the form of a management buy-out was due to be completed during the second quarter of 2003. The company confirmed in February 2003 that, outside the UK and France, it would now focus its international resources solely on growing market-leading businesses in Poland, Italy and the Far East where it is already successfully established. On a smaller scale, development work would continue in Spain, South Korea and Turkey. As a result, it planned to withdraw from Castorama's German business and exit from its Canadian, Belgian and Brazilian operations together with its NOMI subsidiary in Poland.

The new CEO, Gerry Murphy, commented in February 2003:

> In home improvement – soon to be our sole focus – Kingfisher is now well positioned, has clear momentum and strong operational management teams throughout the business. Looking ahead, we can concentrate on growing our business and delivering real value for our shareholders. Our top priorities are to keep improving our customer offer, grow our market share, continue to drive profitability and improve shareholder returns. The current environment is uncertain but we remain cautiously optimistic for the year ahead.

Chapter 23

Consolidation in the European mail order market

Interview with Kurt Ebert, former marketing director, Quelle Schickedanz AG & Co

KarstadtQuelle AG, Theodor-Althoff-Straße 2, D-45133 Essen, Germany
Tel.: +49 (0)2 01 7 27 9633; Fax: +49 (0)2 01 7 27 9853

Richard Bell

In October 1999, Germany's second largest home shopping operator Quelle, merged with Karstadt, owner of the country's third largest mail order retailer and largest department store chain. The enlarged company is now the biggest home shopping operation in Germany, with total group sales in 2001 of €16.1 billion (of which mail order contributed €7.81 billion (48.6 per cent)), €333 million pre-tax profit and 112,000 employees. Shortly after the merger, Dick Bell discussed the background to it and the future plans of the company with Kurt Ebert, marketing director of Quelle.

Since this interview took place, Herr Ebert has left the combined KarstadtQuelle business to become Associate Director (Germany) of Javelin Group, a multi-channel retail consultancy. The remarks attributed to him at the time of the interview may or may not now correspond to the present strategy of the combined KarstadtQuelle business. Some financial performance data has been separately updated and a short postscript to the interview is designed to bring the reader up-to-date with KarstadtQuelle's strategy in relation to its mail order activities.

Merger with Karstadt

In the early 1990s, Quelle's owners, the Schickedanz family, decided to refocus their business interests. They concentrated on retail and financial services, and sold their industrial shareholdings. As part of this strategy, the family acquired a 48 per cent stake in Karstadt. However, it was soon realized that in order to benefit from all of the possible synergies between the two companies, a full merger was necessary. In April 1999, this merger was announced.

One of the main opportunities presented by the merger was the ability to achieve cost savings in back office functions, such as buying, logistics and IT. One of our first priorities was to combine our buying offices around the world. Not only would this make it easier to work in the Far Eastern markets, but it would also improve our buying power with suppliers across the world. However, from the customers' perspective it will be important that they continue to view us as two separate companies, with individual identities and brands.

Karstadt, for example, is the outright owner of Neckermann, the third largest mail order company in Germany. From the customers' point of view, it would be completely wrong to merge Neckermann with Quelle, as we would lose our profile and sales. From the front end, the two must be seen to be independent. Therefore, we will maintain our separate brands, deriving synergistic benefits in terms of operational efficiency.

In order to manage this structure, we will be setting up a holding company with three or four branches each with their own director – mail order, retail, travel and perhaps services. Below this holding structure there will be four companies – Quelle AG, Neckermann AG, Karstadt AG, and CNN AG (services). Services include for example ServiceLogiQ, carrying out fulfilment for other companies (for example, fan club articles for football teams). The services company would serve the house brands as well as external brands.

Business strategy

Quelle's long-term goals are twofold – to expand the Quelle brand internationally and to develop in speciality markets. Over the next ten years, the split in terms of growth is likely to be 50/50. With regards to our international growth strategy, we plan to expand in those countries in which we already operate and move into new ones. Currently, we are highly concentrated in Germany, although we do have a presence across most of the countries in middle and middle eastern Europe.

Our largest foreign market is Austria where we have operated since 1958. Quelle is the country's leading mail order retailer. In France, we are also a fairly strong player. We pulled out of Italy in 1993. Because of its fairly old fashioned retail structure and inefficient postal service, Italy is the most difficult mail order market in Europe.

Table 23.1 Internationalization of Quelle

Country	Year of entry
Austria	1958
France	1966
Switzerland	1972
Belgium	1985
Croatia	1988
Spain	1989
Czech Republic	1993
Slovakia	1993
Hungary	1993
Poland	1993
Slovenia	1993
Portugal	1996
China	1997

Source: Quelle Schickedanz AG & Co

With regards to central Europe, we are currently active in Poland, the Czech Republic, Slovakia, Hungary, Slovenia and Croatia. With the exception of Poland, we are by far the biggest mail order company in each of these markets, with a very well known brand name. We use the national postal services in each country, which although expensive, is efficient. Similarly in Germany, we use the German post which handles the total volume for the group, enabling us to obtain very competitive rates. In each country we assess the competitiveness and efficiency of the national postal service, and if we are unhappy with it then we use private companies. We are not tied to any particular method.

Other interesting markets for further development are the UK and the US. The UK represents one of the largest mail order markets in Europe, and with a stable economy is attractive to overseas retailers. Similarly the US offers excellent potential for growth with a very large customer base and a tremendous economy. However, both of them are difficult to enter. In the UK, we are currently testing the market for organic growth via our French subsidiary La Source.

Management

With regards to the management of our subsidiaries, our aim is to make them as independent as possible. However, the degree of responsibility depends on the size of the company and its experience in the market. Our Austrian and French subsidiaries for example, have full responsibility for their business, from choosing the range through to logistics and delivery options. This contrasts with the situation in smaller, developing countries like Slovakia. We entered the market in 1993 and have found that it is more effective to manage the assortment, catalogue printing and delivery from Germany, with only customer service, order taking and some marketing taking place in the actual country.

Therefore, the range of responsibility varies from quite independent companies with goals set centrally to a very rigidly managed company in new or smaller countries. As each company grows and gains experience, it will be given more independence. Mail order retailing is very much a local business and it is very difficult to run it in another country. In the long term, if it is possible and profitable, we like the subsidiaries to run independently.

Specialization

In addition to the Quelle 'big book' we also operate a series of specialogues marketed as Madeleine, Elégance, Peter Hahn, Mercatura and AGS (recently acquired). These niche catalogues are fairly independent, with most consumers not even realizing that they are part of the Quelle organization. Indeed, they virtually operate as separate companies. Each of them develops products and new catalogues to suit their local market as well as undertaking international expansion. Madeleine

Table 23.2 Quelle specialogues: international coverage

Specialogue Gross Sales DMbn 1997/98	Country
Peter Hahn DM397bn	Germany France Switzerland Austria
Madeleine DM207bn	Germany Switzerland Austria France
Elégance DM162bn	Germany France Austria Switzerland UK
Mercatura DM178bn	Germany France

Source: Quelle Schickedanz AG & Co, 1999

for example recently expanded into France. Furthermore, an Alpine clothing catalogue was developed in Austria and then launched in Germany, and we have
introduced an underwear catalogue in France. They are specialogues marketed
under the Quelle brand.

Not only are we looking to expand the number of specialogues, but we would
also like to create new ones, as part of the trend towards consumer fragmentation.
However, although specialogues are becoming increasingly popular, we do not
believe that they spell the end for the 'big book', with both types of publication
having a role to play within the market.

All of the information on consumer lifestyle trends points towards the growing
need for retailers to cater for smaller, more discrete groups of consumers. Quelle
has recognized this need for specialization, and we believe that this gives us a
competitive advantage over generalists such as Marks & Spencer and C&A.

Ladies fashion is currently the most successful product for the specialogues.
However, in the long term, we are looking to develop a wider variety of merchandise such as bicycles, shoes and home textiles, etc. This will be facilitated by
the introduction of the euro.

Competition

In terms of the European and international market, we face two main
competitors – Otto Versand and La Redoute. British companies tend to be more
concentrated on the British market, although GUS, for example, is the second
largest mail order retailer in Austria and therefore competes directly with us.

Impact of new technology

Although there is certainly a lot of potential in new modes of shopping such as
the Internet and interactive television, I am not convinced that in 3–5 years time it
will represent our total business. We have a 10 per cent stake in HoT (Home Order
Television), the biggest television selling channel in Germany (renamed Home
Shopping Europe). We are also active in Internet retailing, and last year we had the
highest sales of any Internet company. Although this has rapidly grown, it is still
a relatively low level of sales.

We have to be involved in these new forms of retailing, as it represents the future.
But, it is still difficult for most of our customers to use the Internet alone, so at the
moment it complements our book based business. However, in 10–20 years the
situation may have changed, with the next generation likely to use it far more.
I think the Internet will become as commonplace as the telephone with no bias
towards sex or age. At the moment, it is still a young media, but it is becoming
older and more normal in terms of demographics.

One of the interesting issues that has arisen with regards to the Internet is whether it will enable suppliers to go direct to the customer. In my experience, most of the suppliers who talk about serving the customer directly have not fully thought through the issues involved in terms of fulfilment, accounting, customer services, payment terms, etc.

Synergies between mail order and retailing

I do not believe that many synergies exist between 'big book' mail order shopping and retailing. If you look at the US for example, both Sears and Montgomery Ward have abandoned their 'big book' business. Furthermore, Quelle used to have a department store chain and closed it. However, in terms of specialogues it does make more commercial sense. Elégance, for example, has a chain of shops across the world which co-exist alongside its mail order business.

Own-brand development

In the 1960s, we launched our own range of electrical appliances in Germany, marketed under the Privileg name. At this time, there were few well known brand names and we were able to establish a position of superiority. Privileg is now the German market leader in sewing machines, microwaves, fridges, dishwashers, washing machines and freezers. However, extending the brand outside Germany is very difficult. In new markets, where we are relatively unknown, it is very difficult for us to communicate our brand values against major international names. We have been relatively successful in Austria, but have had more problems elsewhere in Europe.

Postscript

Since this interview took place, there has continued to be integrative development in the mail order business. With its Quelle and Neckermann brands, KarstadtQuelle is market leader in Germany (market share 30 per cent). It retains strong positioning in 17 European countries through more than 120 subsidiaries. Mail order operations are categorized as 'universal' or 'special'. Universal mail order brands (the 'big book' business) include Quelle and Neckermann – with a familiarity rating of over 90 per cent and sales of €6.5 billion. The universal business distributes 38 million catalogues and 68 million parcels per year. The specialogue business includes brands such as Madeleine, Elégance, Mercatura, Mode & Preis and Baby Walz – over 178 catalogues. Seventeen countries receive KarstadtQuelle specialogues. Sales exceed €1.5 billion. 'Strategic measures' proposed by the company in a presentation to analysts in December 2002 provide for further differentiation of the Quelle and Neckermann brands and continued organic growth and acquisitions within the specialogue division. In e-commerce, on top of developments with Thomas Cook and its now 60 e-shops, KarstadtQuelle purchased its own TV licence in July 2002 and started travel TV programming (Neckermann UrlaubsWelt TV) in November 2002 on Home Shopping Europe channel. In addition, a strategic alliance in the development of interactive television was announced with Sony.

Chapter 24

Modernization in Greek food retailing

Interview with Konstantinos Macheras, general manager, Alfa-Beta Vassilopoulos, SA

Alfa-Beta Vassilopoulos, 81 Spaton Avenue, PO Box 60011, 153-44 Gerekas, Attica, Greece
Tel.: +30 210 661 2501 9; Fax: +30 210 661 2675

Richard Bell

Alfa-Beta has become the second largest food retailer in Greece, since its acquisition of Trofo (the sixth largest food retailer in Greece in 2001). In 1992, Delhaize Group acquired control of Alfa-Beta Vassilopoulos. It currently owns 50.6 per cent of Alfa-Beta. The Greek operating company of Delhaize Group had 6,248 employees as of December 31, 2001, and was operating 104 stores. Alfa-Beta focuses on customers looking for competitive pricing as well as high quality products and services. In common with many southern European retailers, it has a strong fresh food offer which has implications for private-label penetration and supply chain management. In 2002, sales in the southern and central European operations of Delhaize Group (Greece, Czech Republic, Slovakia and Romania) grew by 6.9 per cent. In Greece, sales were strongly affected by the integration of Trofo, which generated more than 20 per cent comparable stores sales growth after their remodelling. The existing Alfa-Beta stores also continued to perform well resulting in a gain of market share. In this exclusive interview, Kostas Macheras discusses the ways in which the company has adapted to its new owners and how he sees the Greek food industry evolving to meet the demands of globalization.

The spur to internationalization

Restricted by physical distribution barriers and the need to maintain freshness, food retailers have historically tended to consolidate within national boundaries, with speed of expansion limited by the sophistication of the infrastructure. To expand their businesses, and generate scale economies, some have diversified into non-perishable food sectors, enabling them to increase their purchasing power and make improvements to the supply chain. These factors have been the basis for the creation of national chains. Each company has its own criteria and drivers for success, with the most successful companies tending to be those that have expanded outside their home market. In continental Europe, similarities in culture and consumer behaviour have facilitated expansion into neighbouring countries, creating international players. As retailers were expanding internationally, producers were organizing themselves globally via the development of global brands. Global thinking was a product of global communications manifest today in the Internet. As a result, retailers have been driven to develop global standards of performance, which have been reinforced by the homogenization of global culture, through the mass media.

Personally, I believe that the ground for global retailing in some countries is well prepared. Most retailers like to think on a global scale, but very few have actually been successful in pursuing globalization.

Globalization does not necessarily mean that every international retailer has to be active in every country or on every continent, but that their 'presence' is felt. I believe that around 10 retailers, depending on their channel, format and market, will dominate the awareness, but not the majority of the retail market. Medium-sized retailers will continue to play an important role in their local economy, the best examples of which are the US operators, in particular those active in the food market.

Costs and benefits of internationalization

Internationalization is likely to generate substantial savings – particularly in purchasing, logistics and communication systems – whilst the ultimate goal is to achieve process synergies that will result in greater employee motivation and customer satisfaction. Globalization will accelerate the pace of change and modernization of retailing in southeast Europe.

Wal-Mart is no different to many other retailers operating in Europe – it wants to be a dominant player. All of us are trying to develop low cost operating models that enable us to sell at relatively low prices. In Europe we have to improve our efficiencies within the constraints of an environment that is more tightly regulated than in the US.

Given the threat of Wal-Mart, I expect that European retailers will increase the number of their acquisition targets in order to achieve scale efficiencies – although it is difficult to centralize some functions across Europe, which in principle would generate both savings and greater purchasing strength. European retailers often operate different formats and product ranges in different countries. However, integration is within our grasp – a common European currency will create the opportunity to unify retailing in a similar manner to that which exists in the US.

Operating on a global scale creates higher sales volumes, operating experience, profits and shareholder value. Although this is good for the company as a whole, it is at the point of sale where the battle is really waged. This is where we have to fulfil shoppers' expectations, by offering new services and products, guaranteeing food safety and providing quality at every level of the organization.

It is far easier to have a global brand in a food product than in a retail concept, where stores and operations have to adapt to local legal regulations. This affects both the way in which decisions can be implemented and the speed at which they are carried out. Within the Delhaize Group, we have a common organizational framework that is adapted to the local environment.

Relationship with Delhaize 'Le Lion'

Alfa-Beta has benefited considerably from its relationship with parent company Delhaize Le Lion. In the first two years following the acquisition, the differences between the two companies were quite evident with the relevant historical, cultural, economic, social and political backgrounds.

The philosophy and strategy of the Delhaize management was, and still is, to develop a common policy in each country that it operates. This is also the case with Alfa-Beta. We determine the best practices and assemble multi-national teams to accelerate communication. The projects that we are implementing must add value throughout the group without jeopardising local relationships and local visibility to consumers. We have enhanced our assortments and developed new concepts that were previously unknown to our customers.

Through synergies, we have improved our efficiency and productivity and we have learnt a lot. We constantly question our performance with internal bench-marking. Delhaize has provided us with a technology platform that has enabled us to improve communication and decrease our operational expenses.

With respect to the level of influence that Delhaize exerts over our operations, it is important to bear in mind two key issues. As a quoted company on the Greek stock exchange we have a responsibility to follow local regulations with regarding the way we structure our finances. Secondly, we have to deliver a performance that is acceptable to the Greek financial market. However, in terms of the broad philosophy and general thinking of the company, we try to follow the objectives of the head office.

In terms of philosophy and guidelines, we do not differentiate ourselves from the parent company, because Delhaize, like us, thinks global and acts local. In this way, we belong to an international group, but act as a Greek retailer with regards to our clients and customers. Best practice is disseminated across the group via various committees and co-ordinators. Meetings are held across the world in person or are conducted via video conferencing with both the head office and our sister companies.

Delhaize is, and will always primarily be, a supermarket operator, specializing in food retailing. Centralized warehousing and delivery are key components of our strategy, with 80 per cent of sales from products that are distributed through our network of regional distribution centres.

Food retailing in Greece

Food retailing in Greece accounts for €17,800 million in value terms (food, drink and tobacco sales in 2001), of which some €5,700 million is purchased through supermarkets. The top five chains account for some €3,655 million in sales.

Greek shopping habits have changed little since the beginning of the 1990s, with high levels of shopping frequency, particularly in city centres. Planned purchasing (i.e. with a shopping list) is high amongst the younger generation, whilst 'mom and pop' stores still account for two-thirds of food spending. This is helped by the existence of 14,000 kiosks, 10,000 milk shops and 8,000 bakeries across the country which have all somehow been transformed into mini supermarkets.

Due to the strength of small stores in Greece, wholesalers have traditionally been key players in food distribution. However, more recently cash and carries have become more important with many small retailers preferring to buy their stock directly. The Greek Metro, Makro, and Trofou, now owned by Delhaize, are the key cash and carry players in the Athens area.

Changes within the food market

The role of the supermarket sector is likely to change, and we are going to see radical improvements driven by the growth of hypermarkets and discounters. Since their initial development in Greece at the beginning of the 1990s, hypermarkets have so far captured only a small proportion of the market, whilst the discount sector has been shaken up with the entrance of Lidl in 1999. Previously, Dia (Carrefour/Promodès) monopolized the market with 181 stores, however Lidl entered in 1999 and opened 34 outlets. It now has 50 outlets. Alfa-Beta has responded by stocking Netto brand discount products in its stores.

Competition

Our main competitor in the supermarket sector is Sklavenitis (no. 3) and Marinopoulos (a joint venture with Carrefour/Promodès), which is the market leader. In the next few years, we believe that the smaller food retailers will group together to form new buying groups or will join forces with strategically well placed, foreign partners. Some of them see the Athens stock exchange as a panacea to improve their cash flow. In other words we are likely to see further concentration in organized trade, with a resultant increase in the size of the total market. The majority of Greek retailers aim to be not only national players but also key players in the Balkans as a whole, with priority given to Bulgaria, Romania and FYROM.

Logistics and supply chain management

With regards to supply chain management, Greece remains very traditional. However, there are some changes afoot with modernization the key word for leading operators. Our operations are already highly centralized with 80 per cent of sales from products supplied by the central warehouse network. Although our competitors are not as advanced as this, they are gradually moving towards this level with EDI, PRICAT and WEBEDI becoming part of their everyday vocabulary.

However, we have a lot of ground to cover if we are to achieve the inventory levels of the supply chain in the UK: 11.7 days at the supplier, 9.7 days at the central warehouse and 7.2 days at the store (source: ECR Greece). In Greece, suppliers work on 40 days plus, most of the retailers keep a stock of more than 30 days at their warehouses, and about 20 days plus at their store level. Within Alfa-Beta we work on much tighter schedules than these averages.

In terms of stock replenishment, we operate a 16-hour service, reduced from two days initially. Fast turnaround is essential as the majority of our business is based on food (80 per cent of sales), 50 per cent of which is perishable. We are trying to reduce the turnaround time still further to 12 hours. Not only do shorter replenishment times give us more flexibility at the store level to minimize stocks, they are also more environmentally friendly. Previously, stores were receiving deliveries from around 52 trucks a day from various suppliers. On a 16 hour cycle, only three deliveries are needed per day.

As with other aspects of our operation, our warehouses are benchmarked to ensure that certain standards are met. In most functions the first comparison is Alfa-Beta to Alfa-Beta, and then we compare ourselves to Delhaize in various countries. Therefore, we have internal benchmarking in two ways, locally but also internationally in order to see where we are going.

Store development programme

There are no difficulties in developing on new sites in Greece, although land is very expensive, especially in city centres. It is easier and cheaper to build in the suburbs, although problems often arise with the municipality playing a protectionist role towards the local retailers by restricting opening hours. In terms of store sizes, there are no limits in municipalities with more than 100,000 people. In smaller towns and cities, stores sizes are restricted according to the size of the population.

Marketing strategy

Since the acquisition of Alfa-Beta by Delhaize, we have come to realize that micro marketing is of increasing effectiveness and mass marketing is of diminished effectiveness. This was something that as a local company we did not understand because we had no input from suppliers alerting us to this trend. Since every retailer offers roughly the same product assortment and similar promotions, we have had to differentiate our offer with a higher level of in-store service and a customer loyalty scheme.

Loyalty scheme

Customers accumulate points based on the value of the transaction and the products purchased. According to the number of points accumulated, they receive a cheque that can either be cashed at one of our POS terminals or exchanged against products of a higher value with a discount. We are trying to utilize the data collected from the loyalty card to help with marketing, however we have to act within the constraints of existing legislation to protect both ourselves and the privacy of our customers.

We are hoping to improve our marketing effectiveness by developing a category management programme and integrating it with our loyalty scheme. In the long term, we believe that micromarketing is going to bring us more revenue and be more efficient.

Pricing strategy

We are gradually moving our pricing strategy towards an everyday low price policy. However, there is currently a price war raging in Greece, started by Promodès and the hypermarkets. Some of the local players such as Sklaventis and Marinopoulos, who are part of the Carrefour-Promodès group, are also following this strategy. These retailers are selling below the net cost.

Although this is not legal, it is possible. To compete, we are trying to keep our prices competitive on at least 4,800 everyday products, out of a total of more than 16,000 products in our bigger stores. We are working with our suppliers to keep prices in line with the market and to drive costs out of the system. Over the last three years our operating expenses have reduced significantly.

Private label

Historically, private label was not an integral part of Alfa-Beta's culture. It is only since the acquisition by Delhaize that a new opportunity was opened up to us. We were able to select from a much broader base of products and we have developed a more aggressive pricing strategy which has been very successful. Sales of private label currently represent around 10 per cent of our turnover. This may sound relatively small, but it is important to bear in mind that 50 per cent of our sales are from perishables.

We have a differentiated private-label strategy with an economy range, marketed as Netto, which is priced in line with Dia and Lidl, and branded private-label ranges such as Loddi for snacks and Active for detergents, where the store name is the secondary or signature name. Private label is strongly associated with the corporate name, with the Delhaize logo (flame) used as well as the Alfa-Beta symbol.

Purchasing

The proximity of manufacture determines how we purchase any product. If it is locally produced then we buy it locally and can supply good prices for the parent company as well, such as for olive oil. However, if it is not produced locally we may buy it centrally through Delhaize.

Human resources

With regards to staff recruitment, there is a large pool of people to choose from although they are in need of intensive training. The concept of professional retailers does not yet exist as the retail sector is still largely in the hands of charismatic entrepreneurs.

Consumer behaviour

Consumer behaviour varies quite significantly between the more sophisticated, urban Athenians and those from the provinces. With the development of shopping centres in the provinces, we have seen a major change in consumers' purchasing habits and higher levels of demand for branded and international products especially in clothing and textiles. Women continue to be the key decision makers for household related purchases. Over the last three decades, there has been a one-way flow of Greeks towards Athens or abroad.

Chapter 25

Financial management at Sainsbury's

J Sainsbury plc, 33 Holborn, London, EC1 N2HT
Tel: +44 (0) 20 7695 6000; Fax: +44 (0) 20 7695 7610

Dmitry Dragun

The UK's second largest grocery retailer, Sainsbury's is a company with 180,000 employees, 470 stores of various formats (supermarkets, hypermarkets, convenience) and sales of £17.1 billion in the financial year 2001/2. The bulk of the company's sales (80 per cent) come from the home base in the UK (Sainsbury's Supermarkets); the US foodservice Shaw's accounts for the remaining 20 per cent. As one of the leading grocery providers in the UK, Sainsbury's runs an extensive supply chain network across the UK, as well as a number of supplementary operations such as the Internet-based fulfilment service sainsburystoyou.com, Sainsbury's Bank and the property development arm JS Developments. Renowned for the unmatched combination of quality and price, Sainsburys' held the number one position in the UK until 1994, when the price challenge by Tesco and Asda led to loss of the market share and severe erosion of profitability. Having spent the late 1990s recovering from the setback, by 2003 Sainsbury's has disposed of all peripheral businesses, scaled back non-core international undertakings, started sweeping modernization of the IT systems and supply chain infrastructure, streamlined organizational structure, instituted rigorous cost controls, and established the financial function at the forefront of decision making.

This slightly longer case study mirrors the more extensive chapter on financial management in Part II and similarly reflects the contemporary importance of this retail business function. It explores the critical role of financial management at Sainsbury's.

Sainsbury's Supermarkets

Financial management at Sainsbury's Supermarkets – the largest operating unit of the group – encompasses three major functions.

Financial operations

Financial operations (FO) is a back-office backbone of the company. FO deals with financial processing of all transactions occurring on a daily basis at Sainsbury's including invoicing, trade payments, payroll and other related tasks. With approximately £14 billion of sales for Sainsbury's Supermarkets alone, the FO group – spread across three locations in the UK (Streatham, Bromley and Sidcup) – is one of the largest transactional processing units for a single company in the UK. The major tasks of the FO are timely processing of the business transactions and supply of the high integrity information to the business.

The integrity of information is achieved via internal review processes whereby the information moves from one controlling system to another (invoicing – goods delivery – store transaction – cash receipt – payment to supplier) and is continually verified at each stage. Such information filter is an effective tool in facilitating early identification and timely elimination of gaps and inconsistencies in the flow of data.

Planning and budgeting

Planning and budgeting (P&B) is the second major function of financial management at Sainsbury's. This function focuses on the provision of support to the business through the formulation, discussion and communication of plans to the operating units (stores). Here, a major duty is to integrate the operating performance with the financial metrics in a way that sets a clear set of objectives for the operating units and facilitates achievement of the corporate financial targets.

One of the most interesting and challenging aspects of the P&B function is a sequential integration of business plans. As different business units form the operating forecasts and communicate them to the finance department, the corporate business plan evolves as an aggregate of projections for the business units. A commonplace challenge encountered by the large companies is that plans on the corporate level are by necessity more forward-looking (three years at Sainsbury's) than the activity plans of the business units which are often geared towards short-term performance targets (up to 12 months). An important role of the finance function is to overcome the mismatch between the long-term corporate aims and the short-term business objectives. At Sainsbury's, this is achieved by arranging the planning process as a single planning 'loop'.

Target setting is a task adjacent to P&B in that it utilizes inputs from the corporate activity plan (CAP) and translates them into the divisional goals. The CAP is collated and verified within the period of early January and mid-February of the upcoming financial year. After having balanced the plan among the competing requirements for growth, profitability and capital expenditure, the finance group cascades the corresponding targets to the divisional and store levels, at which point the CAP becomes the budget.

Investment budgeting and cost control

The third separate function of financial management at Sainsbury's is *investment budgeting and cost control* (IBCC). Retailing is a capital-intensive business. In order to deliver value to customers and shareholders, to meet competitive challenges, and to continue to innovate successfully, the retailers have to invest inordinate amounts of capital in new building, store refurbishments, and support systems such as supply chain and IT. In consequence, the capital expenditures (capex) of leading retailers sometimes reach astonishing levels. Widely perceived as under-investing in the main store formats, Sainsbury's has been active in pursuing the ambitious programme of the store development and enhancements from 2000 onwards. (The scale of the capex requirement at Sainsbury's is illustrated by Figure 25.1.)

Most recently (financial year 2001/2) Sainsbury's gross capital expenditure amounted to £1.1 billion, with the significant element of it going into renovation of existing stores and expansion of the store network. Going forward, the capex plan calls for spending of £1.5 billion over the next four years, including the investments in the supply chain and support infrastructure. The magnitude of the capex requirement necessitates ongoing communication and monitoring of the capex delivery targets against the financial performance objectives. This is an area where the major responsibility of the finance function lies.

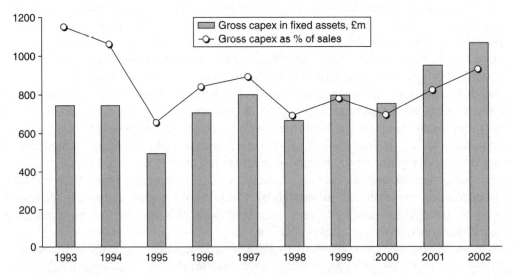

Figure 25.1 Gross capital expenditure, 1993–02
Source: company reports

Dictated in part by the scale of the financial outlays, financial control at Sainsbury's Supermarkets is tightly linked to managing the financial and operating performance. There is no split of the business goals between the financial and the operating sides as it is accepted that operating and financial performance are closely linked. This link results in a performance measurement framework (PMF) that permeates the entire company and provides a set of performance indicators for every business. The 'operating' performance is perceived as more customer-driven whereas financial performance, especially on the store level, is viewed as a natural outcome of operating decisions. In consequence, a lot of time and effort at Sainsbury's is put into measuring and examining the customer-related metrics such as satisfaction, quality, choice and availability.

In effect, for every financial measure there are a number of underlying operating metrics that are monitored and analysed on the continuous basis. For example, staff turnover is customarily used as a proxy for colleague satisfaction (although it could also reflect the location of the store). Changes in staff turnover have a direct and immediate impact on customer service, which in turn has an effect upon sales. Having to hire and to re-train personnel is an expensive proposition, hence turnover-induced expenditure will ultimately affect the cost base and, by extension, profitability. The PMF incorporates various factors of performance into a unified system of performance attribution for each business division. Sequentially, the PMF starts off with the economic profit for the entire business, by subtracting the cost of capital from the operating profit. It then breaks operating profit into components such as gross margin, operating costs, colleague commitment and supply service levels. Likewise, the gross margin can be split into two components: sales and cost of sales. The end result of such disaggregation is a set of fundamental, store-floor level factors that drive the business: number of lines, stock availability, product quality, stock loss and customer service. Importantly, all these 'micro'-factors have a direct relationship to – and are the drivers of – the crucial performance metrics at the group level – like-for-like sales, cost of sales, profits. Eventually, it is hoped that the PMF will link operating and financial performance to the share price.

The sheer extent of the capex requirements is a reason for why the budgeting and planning process at Sainsbury's Supermarkets, as indeed in many other retail companies, is mainly driven by the corporate centre. Such a 'top-down' approach is in contrast to the 'bottom-up' method of starting from the business units and going up to the corporate centre.

In order to achieve alignment of the business goals with the career aspirations of the colleagues, the budgeting process is closely linked to the individual performance evaluation. The device used at Sainsbury's for this purpose is a performance evaluation matrix (Figure 25.2).

There are nine boxes in the matrix, each corresponding to individual performance in accordance with a pre-specified set of criteria for a particular role. Regions in the matrix reflect four broad types of individual performance. The

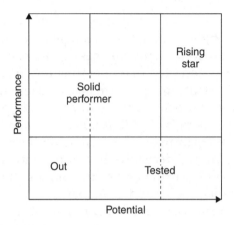

Figure 25.2 Performance evaluation matrix
Source: J Sainsbury

upper-right corner of the matrix, marked 'Rising star', is a position for aspiring, well-performing individuals on their way up in the organizational ladder. The left-hand region positioned roughly in the middle of the matrix and marked 'Solid performer' is reserved for people with proven performance credentials but limited (or doubtful) prospect of career progression. The right-hand lower region – labelled 'Tested' – comprises individuals who are perceived to have substantial performance potential but lag in actual performance. Finally, the lower left-hand box, denoted 'Out', is the least tolerable position from the company's standpoint: the individuals assigned to this box neither perform satisfactorily nor possess potential for improvement. Although by necessity a simplification of reality and an inexact performance guide, the matrix is nevertheless recognized and used as a useful tool for assessment and communication of individual performance. The finance function plays a central role in such individual evaluation because the structure of the process, communication and career-related decisions are always taken through the framework of financial assessment.

The group finance function

The top-down approach to financial planning and budgeting practiced at Sainsbury's Supermarkets is replicated at the group level, where the finance function is organized to deal with four main responsibilities:

- Financing of the group as a whole.
- Implementing the treasury and tax policies.
- Developing new business.
- Reporting and communication of financial performance.

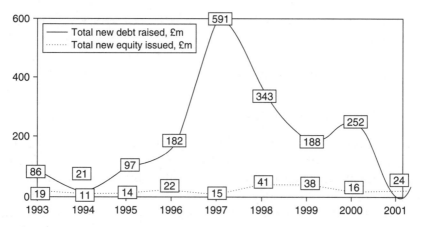

Figure 25.3 New debt and equity issues, 1993–02
Source: Datastream

Financing of the group as a whole

This task includes raising the long- and medium-term funds from the capital markets on favourable terms, as well as supporting the high credit rating of the company. Traditionally, Sainsbury's has preferred debt financing, with equity financing accounting for only a small proportion of the new funds (see Figure 25.3). Although arguably the cheaper method of funding, debt issuance has nevertheless led to a noticeable increase in the stock of accumulated debt and a subsequent rise in leverage (reflected in the 'Gross leverage' component of the DuPont model, see the following section).

Two interesting questions arise with respect to the company's preferred funding mode. The first is why, being a quoted company, does Sainsbury's not make use of the public equity markets? In part, the answer lies in the intention of the founding family to protect its stake – 38 per cent at the time of writing – from dilution. The other part of the answer is a relatively low valuation of the shares, traditionally traded at around 12–14 times earnings. In order to raise a meaningful amount of equity capital, the company would have to issue a significant number of new shares, which may have an adverse impact on the share price and cause a substantial change in equity structure.

The second question is what benefits does being a public company, as opposed to a privately-held concern, confer to Sainsbury's? The answer may be two-fold. First, the public status ensures the continuous visibility of the company in debt markets. Bonds issued by Sainsbury's are publicly held and – due to the company's size – are of considerable interest to institutional shareholders who traditionally account for the bulk of demand for the new issues. A high public profile helps raise finance quickly and inexpensively. Secondly, public companies – as opposed to private enterprises – are usually more forthcoming and efficient in disclosing the investor information, in part for statutory reasons. Such enhanced disclosure is an additional factor of comfort for investors, because it facilitates performance monitoring.

However, there is a price to pay for being a public company, for example strategic flexibility and the ability to act quickly, irrespective of any outside views that may be impaired. A private company can go ahead with what it believes is right in the long term, without the additional overhead of communication restriction.

Implementing the treasury and tax policies

This corporate duty ensures that short-term liquidity (cash reserves and short-term market instruments) is sufficient to meet the group's needs at all times. It also aims at optimizing the group's tax position, within allowable limits of the tax laws and regulations. Alongside the treasury and tax policy implementation – and a separate brief of the treasury and tax team – is management of the financial risks, including interest rate, currency, credit, and liquidity exposures. Although the treasury is also aware of the non-financial risks such as food contamination and competitive threats, they are mostly dealt with at the executive and board levels.

Developing new business

This area, although relatively small at present, has significant growth potential and is likely to grow in importance. As Jonny Mason, Director of Corporate Finance at J. Sainsbury's PLC, puts it:

> The corporate development area looks at what opportunities there might be to invest in other companies. It is not an area that Sainsbury's has been very active in over recent years as the focus has been on fixing the various businesses we own. But we look at the opportunities all the time and we hope to be active before too long. Most business development opportunities are managed within the subsidiaries. For example, in the UK supermarket business there are business development teams looking at ways of generating new revenues, such as selling financial services, mobile phone air-time, new concessions in our stores, new ranges of non-food products. At group level we are interested in larger transactions, typically anything involving publicly quoted companies. We are constantly monitoring our competitors and how we perform compared to them. We also look at the US and European markets for further lessons on growth opportunities.

Reporting and communication of financial performance

This is the major area of work for the group financial function:

> The area of most interest today is financial reporting. What happens in the group is that we take the plans, budgets or actual

results, and consolidate four operating companies into a Group
picture, adding corporate items like tax and finance and costs. We
report firstly to the Group executive committee and the Group
board, and then to the external audiences.

Jonny Mason

As the issues of transparency and responsibility have come to the fore amidst a spate of recent corporate mishaps, particular attention is being paid to speedy and informative communication with stakeholders. In addressing the issue, Sainsbury's finance function at the group level has a number of agreed policies for managing the news flow from the company to interested parties. These policies (and the corresponding operating procedures) serve as a reliable tool of professional communication with different audiences. Issues surrounding the area will be further explored in the following section.

External communication

As a publicly quoted concern, Sainsbury's maintains a multitude of external communication links. As the focus of this case study is financial management, the financial aspects of performance reporting and communication will mainly be considered.

In recent years, Sainsbury's has faced a number of challenges related to financial performance. As Table 25.1 and Figure 25.4 show, the year 1994 marked the watershed in the company's fortunes. In that year, the company lost the UK leading market share position to Tesco, failed to deliver the projected profits, and fell short

Table 25.1 Components of the extended DuPont model, 1993–02

Component	1993	1994	1995	1996	1997	1998	1999	2000	2001	2002
Operating profit	7.8%	3.7%	7.6%	6.2%	5.2%	5.7%	6.0%	3.8%	3.3%	4.1%
Total asset turnover	1.8	1.9	2.0	1.9	1.8	1.6	1.5	1.5	1.7	1.6
Interest expense rate	0.4%	0.4%	0.8%	1.0%	1.3%	1.1%	0.9%	1.0%	1.3%	1.2%
Gross leverage	1.7	1.8	1.8	1.9	2.0	2.2	2.2	2.2	2.1	2.3
Tax retention rate	75.5%	40.4%	72.7%	61.9%	66.2%	75.4%	65.2%	57.2%	61.3%	70.1%
ROE	18.3%	4.9%	17.9%	12.5%	11.0%	13.2%	11.6%	6.1%	5.4%	8.3%

Source: Datastream

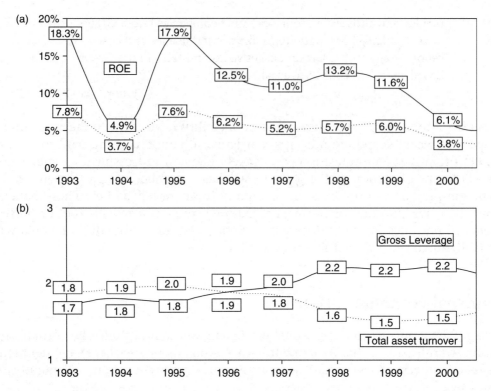

Figure 25.4 (a) Operating profit margin and ROE, 1993–2000. (b) Total asset turnover and gross leverage, 1993–2000
Source: Datastream

of the profit margin targets. As a result, Sainsbury's ROE in 1994 dropped precipitously to 4.9 per cent from 18.3 per cent in the previous year. Although the returns had recovered in the following year, the profitability decline had extended into the late 1990s. The company's dilemmas – price versus value positing, in-house update of IT infrastructure versus external outsource, international expansion versus domestic growth – were well documented at the time.

Strategic indecision has also contributed to the unfavourable analyst coverage and explained much of the adverse media publicity that the company received. Painful restructuring has been implemented in several waves, starting in 1996 and proceeding in the subsequent years. One of the results was the sharpening of the focus and reorganization of the group's financial function, especially with regard to external communication. In consequence, today's Sainsbury's is a retailer with an effective external communication function and a well-developed mode of dealing with the stockmarket community.

For example, it is now a matter of policy at Sainsbury's that every message coming out of the company to the external audiences must be coherent, consistent and supportive of the company's strategy. Such a communication task, never easy in the best of times, is particularly challenging in the midst of the operating turnaround engineered by the company. The overriding goal, therefore, is

> ... to ensure that we have total control over the processing of information and reporting of performance, especially the integrity bit of it. We have four main communication pieces. The statutory annual report goes to people who want detailed information. The operating and financial reviews, which highlight the sections of the annual report, have a wider audience. There are also periodic [annual and semi-annual] presentations. The whole release process needs a high degree of integration to ensure that we have total control over the information and reporting of performance.
>
> Jonny Mason

There are a number of performance parameters that are watched closely by stockmarket analysts: like-for-like (LFL) sales, profits and profit margin, capital expenditure and exceptional costs. Among these, LFL sales growth is the single most important performance indicator. Monitored and reported on a quarterly basis, LFL growth is viewed as a definitive signal as to whether the company is meeting, exceeding or missing targets. The LFL sales dynamic also contains important clues about the future direction of the entire retail sector, such as the seasonal acceleration of spending or changes in levels of consumers' confidence. In conveying these clues to the investor community, Sainsbury's faces the vexing dilemmas of language and interpretation.

> We try to anticipate the questions the market will have and provide answers in advance. The messages behind the numbers are as important as the numbers themselves. Markets hate surprises. We are constantly managing the messages to provide a clear idea of what is happening and where we are going.
>
> Jonny Mason

The future role of the finance function

Traditionally, the finance function in the retailing business has been highly centralized. Back-office processing operations, planning and budgeting, performance assessment, and reporting procedures are all conducted under the strict supervision of the corporate finance group. There is nothing particularly surprising or controversial about the practice. The controversy begins where the finance function starts interacting directly with the rest of the company. Operating divisions, in particular, have a vital stake in influencing the funding decisions taken at the corporate level. Infusion of extra capital and bigger cost allowances are great incentives for the operating divisions to treat the finance function as 'dotted', or subordinated to the business units. This 'dotted' configuration, one argument goes, allows for tight congruence of financial targets and operating objectives at the divisional level. However, the hidden flaw of such a structure is that the financial function could lose sight of corporate goals. This may happen if the operating divisions leverage their influence to extract capital budgeting or cost concessions from the finance department. The possibility of this occurring is perhaps less pronounced for retailers exhibiting significant influence from the founding families such as Sainsbury's than it is for widely held public companies. In order to avert internal conflicts, many retailers adopt a 'solid' dividing line for the finance function, whereby it retains complete independence from the operating units and exercises substantial procedural influence on the decision-making process.

In a business of such considerable operational complexity as retailing, it is finally always important for the finance function to stay focused on the internal 'value added' from its activities. Although value added continues to remain an elusive concept to grasp, let alone to implement, there is a consensus at Sainsbury's as to what it means for the finance department.

The future role of the finance function is evolving along three key dimensions. The operating and processing sides will become more effective and far more efficient in conveying information as needed. In the future, the processing part will function so smoothly that no one will realize it is there, and its presence will only be noticed when there is a problem. The finance department is likely to progress further in its role as an internal service provider, by filtering and collating information and providing professional support to the businesses.

Progressively, the finance group will become responsible for integration of the various business functions. The role of business integrator comes from the ability of finance to bring the disparate functional areas together. With the balanced scorecard, internal performance evaluation and external financial reporting, all businesses are already viewed as tightly integrated. Hence the finance division will continue to evolve towards comprehensive evaluation of the financial contribution from every business and individual, to ensure, ultimately, that the integrated performance picture emerges.

Part IV

Putting it all together

Chapter 26

An exercise in successful retailing: the case of Tesco

Tesco plc, Tesco House, Delamare Road, Cheshunt, Hertfordshire, EN8 9SL
Tel.: +44 (0)1992 632222; Fax: +44 (0)1992 644481

Jonathan Reynolds

The final part of this book begins with a set of integrative case studies based on the experiences of Tesco, the UK's leading grocery retailer and an increasingly significant international retail business. Tesco operated over 2,000 stores (including the recently acquired T&S convenience stores) within 10 markets in 2002, and employed more than 296,000 people. Group sales in 2002/3 were £28.6 billion (€41.75 billion) and pre-tax profits were £1.2 billion (€1.76 billion). The company's strategy is fourfold, to:

- deliver a strong UK core business – by continuing to grow and to build market share;
- develop non-food – with the goal to be as strong in non-food as food;
- develop retailing services – following the customer into new areas such as personal finance and on-line retailing;
- develop internationally – through a long term organic growth programme which has successfully aimed to account for 45 per cent of group space by 2002/3.

We bring three particular cases together in order to address three different aspects of the Tesco business, with the aim of putting across to the reader the multi-faceted and inter-related nature of retailing. The first two cases examine some of the underlying mechanisms, on the demand side and the supply side, that work to sustain Tesco's continuing profitability. The first case reviews the phenomenal success of Tesco's Clubcard in the UK. Through an interview with Clubcard director

Crawford Davidson, we examine the way in which Clubcard seeks to provide the tangible evidence of Tesco seeking its customers' lifetime loyalty. The second case explores the extent to which Tesco has been able to harness the developments in business-to-business exchanges to enhance the efficiency and effectiveness of its supply chain. Barry Knichel, supply chain divisional director at Tesco, claims that the company has achieved a fourfold return on its investment in exchanges so far, most of which has been directly passed on to the consumer in lower prices. The third case provides real insights into the final plank of Tesco's overall strategy – its international growth. The business is market leader in the first five markets which it has entered. The adopted business model delivers increasing operating profits and is beginning to more than cover the cost of funding new development (for example, businesses in Hungary and Thailand will be covering their capital expenditure from internally generated cash for the first time in 2003). In an interview with David Wild, European corporate development director, we look in detail at the progress of the company in its central European markets.

As with Part III, the cases here should be read in conjunction with the appropriate chapters in Part II. At the end of the third case, we provide a short series of review questions for the reader.

Chocolate on the cappuccino: the Tesco Clubcard

Interview with Crawford Davidson, director of Clubcard at Tesco

Richard Cuthbertson

Introduction

Clubcard was launched in February 1995. It is a programme for all Tesco customers. Essentially, it is a magnetic strip card, free to all customers, and for every £1 spent by the customer, we give one point, which is worth one penny. We have around 10 million account households and about 13 million accounts, which implies that some customers have more than one account. Clubcard covers about 80 per cent of Tesco sales. Customers earn points over 12 or 13 weeks, and we mail the customers with vouchers to the value of points accumulated, and additional coupons for redemption against specific products. We are thereby committed to mail customers four times a year, which is a large part of the investment. In the last 12 months, our customers have redeemed £200 million worth of Clubcard vouchers.

Funding

The programme is well funded. It is part of the absolute belief in creating value for customers because it supports a fundamental Tesco belief that we have to earn our customers' lifetime loyalty. In the UK market, customers have a great deal of choice. The typical customer has a choice of three supermarkets within a similar drive time. The average supermarket chain gets about 40 per cent of a customer's grocery spend, and so the main issue is consolidation. We think of loyalty as a blend of rational factors, as in share spend, and emotional factors, and we find that our most loyal customers exhibit a mixture of rational and emotional loyalty.

Focus on retention

The scheme is focused very much on retention rather than acquisition. When you consider the issue of acquisition versus retention, it is almost foolish to focus on acquisition. A focus on acquisition rather than retention becomes more expensive when you regain customers that you have lost, only to find that you have not fixed the reasons that they left in the first place. Therefore, the emphasis is on retention. Tesco has the highest share spend and our customers are loyal to Tesco. They do not lapse, and that constitutes value.

Another way to look at it is that typically, in general retailing, the top 20–25 per cent of customers will account for 50 per cent profit, and that is profit rather than sales. The top 40 per cent of customers usually work out at 90 per cent of the profit. Those customers at the bottom of the Pareto curve are not that loyal. In fact they are doing most of their spending elsewhere. If you like, the customer from whom Tesco gets about 10 per cent share of his or her spend may be a Sainsbury customer or a Wal-Mart customer who pop in to Tesco occasionally and use their Clubcard because they don't want to lose out.

Loyalty drivers

We have asked customers what creates their loyalty and they agree that firstly, the retailer needs to be efficient. If a customer cannot get into the car park or a shopping cart has wobbly wheels, he or she does not enjoy the shopping experience, their loyalty may disappear. If the retailer can satisfy those basic requirements and have the products that customers want, then we can move on to things that add value or provide a personal service. The retailer can offer to pack bags at the checkout but only when everything that comes before is right. Getting the basics right allows the retailer to add personal services and extra value. Tesco provides high quality, a great range and great value. It is only then that the loyalty scheme can start to amplify the benefits.

Using the analogy of a cappuccino, my role as Clubcard director is sprinkling the chocolate on top of the cappuccino. Marketing provides the froth of the milk. But both have to be based on the good, fresh, hot coffee below. 'Good coffee' is created by my retail colleagues. We are passionate about it. Tesco has spent in the region of £1.5 billion on cutting prices, and we have to create more value. Around Christmas 2002, we recruited 10,000 extra staff because we recognized that we had to give a better service. We halved the number of shop floor display stacks because customers told us the experience was too congested. We reduced the opportunity to sell by having less displays and we took higher costs by having more staff. This may seem contrary to normal retail practices but we had a fantastic Christmas; we grew well ahead of the market; customers voted Tesco across those six weeks because we had done the things that they prize.

Every little helps

When Clubcard was launched it was pioneering. It was the first major loyalty scheme in the UK. Famously, Lord Sainsbury compared the Clubcard to electronic green shield stamps, but in Tesco, the Clubcard was to say thank you, we care, we try harder, and to give you that little bit extra. The philosophy of 'every little helps' and 'no one tries harder' forms the basis from which we encourage loyalty. As we build a picture of our customers we can see which customers are more loyal and which are less loyal. This allows us to identify what we do well and what we have to change.

Most annual accounts have a cash-flow analysis and we have an internal customer flow analysis to monitor customer loyalty. It allows us to focus our investment. If a group of very loyal customers start to diminish, something is wrong. We can do much by simply analysing the frequency and monetary value of transactions before analysing the products bought by loyal customers. We can then move on to who is buying what, and why.

In the early days, Boots, for example, would often carry out quantitative surveys of customers. Most customers would claim they visited Boots weekly. The reality was less than twice a month. They felt they visited Boots weekly because they walked past it, and so the behaviour they reported was very different from actual behaviour. When you get authentic data from a customer visit, then it can be used to make effective changes. It allows the retailer to make huge leaps. The most powerful examples may be seen when creating a new fresh range. The whole dynamic of the range is about sustaining distribution and there is a huge waste bill because customers do not buy initially. It is a huge risk but if you can see which customers are buying in, you start to build a picture that includes identifying the early adopters and the laggards. That allows us to target the bigger prize, to persist and be more confident than others who might be brave enough to try. Even better, direct marketing can be used to attract customers to new products far quicker because those who would be interested have been identified.

Customer power

Whether to focus on customers who are loyal or on those that are not loyal is a real dilemma. Tesco is in no way like other retailers, who talk about 'good customers' and 'bad customers'. We turn that view on its head. There are no good and bad customers, just good and bad retailers. The customer has the power in this relationship. We believe in rewarding the behaviour we seek. We are proud that we spend more time and money on the customers who are most loyal than trying to win customers.

We really do worry about what we do, and we continue to reward loyalty in the future. We have designed the Clubcard as a mechanism of reward. In the quarterly statement, we send about £40 million in redemption value of coupons per year. We select coupons based on what customers have bought in the last eight weeks, and so we expect a very high redemption rate. In addition to the vouchers for the points accumulated, there are four coupons for a specific product included in each mailing. We track purchases and the more loyal a customer appears, the more likely it is that they receive a coupon for something they have bought within the last eight weeks. It is a deliberate attempt to thank the customer and reward loyalty. The more loyal a customer becomes, the greater the share of that £40 million investment. These customers clearly have the choice to redeem the coupons or not. That way the scheme is permission based. A further four coupons, which are quite clearly marked differently, are for products the customer might like to try. They are for products that it seems logical the customer might be interested to try and to inspire the customer to shop more broadly.

Emotion in the relationship

Thus the Clubcard programme provides a mixture of an unconditional gift for past behaviour, reward for continued behaviour, and enticements for future behaviour. In this way, Tesco is communicating an emotional commitment to the customer.

For some customers, it is a straightforward, rational decision – to save money on the family shopping bill. That is great, perhaps especially for those on low incomes, because being able to buy some clothes for the children or some extras at different times of year is incredibly important and there is enough emotion in that very straightforward relationship.

For customers who are more affluent, we can take it to another level. We invented several programmes of interesting and fun ways to spend points. One of these is 'Tesco free time'. Tesco free time allows customers to convert their Clubcard points into leisure days out or a holiday. The joy of getting a free holiday can last forever. For a customer spending £25 a week, the Clubcard points are doubled when they spend it through the scheme. If they are very loyal customers spending on average £60 a week, the value is multiplied by four. Around 90 per cent of the UK population can spend about £60 per week at Tesco, which means that the scheme is relatively inclusive. However, we are continuing to challenge ourselves by asking if it is inclusive enough. That is the way in which the Clubcard can amplify emotion, by realizing far more value in a way that is important to the individual customer.

We recently acquired Air Miles in the UK from one of our competitors, Sainsbury's. Air Miles is aimed at doing the same for a different group of customers. Many Tesco customers, perhaps with two salaries and no children, get their joy from independent travel. These customers are also likely to collect Air Miles with other retailers and so the Air Miles offer has the same effect as Tesco free time.

Customers who participate in these redemption programmes spend more each week than control groups in a way that justifies our investment. Tesco is a retailer. We look at costs and sales in everything we do. Whatever we invest, we expect increased sales that exceed our investment. However, we look at that in the short term and then in the long term.

The results of the first programmes were so successful that we have recently launched another called 'Tesco Me Time', which is aimed entirely at women. Seventy per cent of our shoppers are female. They shop for the family and they deserve a reward for themselves, so we have constructed an opportunity for these women to take their points and convert them into premium beauty and premium fashion, some of which are provided outside of Tesco. This is another example of the value we can add, and the more value customers receive, the more loyal they are.

Customer question time

Tesco have a programme to obtain vital customer feedback. Customer question time is ongoing and run through all our stores. Every time we make a change, a group of perhaps 40 customers sit in a room with a group of directors. Feedback suggests that customers typically want three things from a loyalty programme, and customers can grade Tesco on how well they think their desires are currently satisfied. First, they want more benefits. The most loyal will often want more because of their loyalty. Secondly, customers want to be able to use their loyalty points to do something special, to treat themselves or have something extra that they might not otherwise have. Finally, they do want mailings but only those that are relevant. Customers are aware that Tesco has all this knowledge and data about them, and want to see it used to their advantage.

In a Clubcard statement we mail 13 million people, and last year we sent out 9 million variations. We typically run five or six million variations. That includes variations of coupons and flashboxes. We used to write long letters but now we simply give people flash summary messages. Tesco customers are often people with little time. They do not want to take a great deal of time to read everything, so we use these mailings effectively to add value. We often find that our up-market customers will say they do not want mailings but then will phone our call centre and ask why it has not arrived. Although they might start with the prejudice that the mailings will be junk, they see their friends or family receive them and can see the value in being a participant. Relevance is best measured by customer behaviour. We monitor the way in which customers choose to respond, and in reacting to that response Tesco are satisfying more and more customers, more and more often.

By working with other retail partners, customers can get even more value, and that means they can reach their goal, for example, a holiday in Lanzarote, quicker. So we can bring value to our retail partners because of our huge customer base, and they can bring value because they can help the customer to get their dreams quicker. Together we can give the customers more reason to consider our brand by creating a retail village. Now, I think it's something like 7,000 places in the UK you can earn Clubcard points, and only 700 of those are Tesco.

Further segmentation

We have recognized that customers can have a greater say determining their own participation. Tesco have approximately 1.5 million self-selected customers participating in a number of different clubs focusing on different lifestyles, ranging from a Baby & Toddler Club to the World of Wine. There is a Healthy Living Club that is further segmented into, for example, eating healthily, giving up smoking and alternative health. The customer chooses to join and then gets four mailings a year containing information, entertainment and added value.

I am very proud of the Kids Club. We have just over 200,000 children as members. The parent enrols the child, and the mailing is addressed to the child with a pack inside for grown-ups. The Kids Club provides education and entertainment for the child, and the parent discovers the new foods that children are interested in and further information about what is happening in-store for kids. We find a tremendous emotional involvement with families in this manner.

Using the Tesco club and Clubcard data, Tesco have very powerful segmentations. The main segmentation we use is based on 'you are what you eat'. We give each product different attributes and return to the customer database to build a profile. There are approximately 15 segments, amalgamated to six high-level segments. That is great from a marketing standpoint, and a customer can be in a segment and still be different. For example, in the case of the finer foods segment, our customers tend to be quite wealthy. They buy more organic produce than any other group. There is a healthy living segment within a sub-segment of customers who buy large amounts of organic products but less of the finer foods. What they have in common is an interest in healthy living, but they are different.

The club effectively allows the customer to vote and this is what I am passionate about. Giving more information, more value and sharing our passion makes customers feel more loyal to Tesco. We always return to our need to earn loyalty from customers.

Lifetime loyalty

In Tesco, our whole organization is aligned around a different philosophy and a different set of rules from most other organizations. I have worked in many organizations and most would define their main objective to create shareholder value – earn the bottom line. Tesco is different. Tesco's core purpose is to earn our customers' lifetime loyalty. When you earn lifetime loyalty, the shareholder value comes as a consequence. We earn lifetime loyalty through a whole set of values, underpinned by our 'no one tries harder' for customers' philosophy, and that becomes our edge. We believe in being innovative, energetic, first for customers. We want to understand customers better than anyone else. We recognize that we have to use our strengths to deliver unbeatable value for customers, and that we have to look after our people so they can look after the customers, and that is expressed in 'every little helps'. 'Every little helps' is not only about prices or quality or range. It is not only about service or the shopping experience. It is all of these.

From a customer perspective, they have many requirements. A customer wants to be able to get everything on his or her shopping list. They want the aisles clear. They expect great value. They do not want to queue, and the staff need to be great. Tesco knows that when we get the basics right we get the 'wow factor'. The basics are very simple and easy to implement, and so Clubcard becomes a tool to amplify. It is even possible to identify when a store has become too busy though Clubcard data because if customers who normally shop broadly suddenly become quite narrow in their choices, it may be because they are trying to get out quickly. They are no longer comfortable. Then we have to decide a course of action. Perhaps it needs further investment in staff or property, or perhaps it is possible to persuade customers to shop at different times, because when customers start enjoying shopping less, pretty soon they will vote for someone else.

Tesco chief executive Terry Leahy and marketing director Tim Mason started the Tesco Clubcard, and so the commitment goes right to the top of the organization. They were there at the time of Ian MacLaurin, and together they created a philosophy that continues today. That created a culture that turns received wisdom on its head. Now we have to ask customers if we deserve their loyalty and if the answer is not yes, what do we have to do to earn your loyalty again? Most of our competitors seem to expect something from their customers, rather than the customers expecting something from them.

Suppliers

A focus on the customer might seem to suggest that we ignore the supplier. However, satisfying the customer requires good relationships with suppliers and changes in the retailer–supplier relationship are about becoming more open with suppliers at many levels. At the distribution level, Tesco is entirely transparent. At a sales level, we are entirely transparent in terms of the products supplied so that a supplier can see the level of sales at each store. In order to gain value from customer data, we have to know how to use the data. We make a promise to our customers that we will never pass on names and addresses to a third party. We will never pass their personal information on to anyone, so our relationship with our suppliers has been managed through dunnhumby, a data analysis bureau. We liked them so much that we bought the company. Dunnhumby are in a position to provide analysis to our suppliers. This can be of tremendous benefit to the supplier. For example, a supplier of yoghurt was able to identify some areas of under-distribution based on an analysis of repeat sales of similar products. We were able to make the change based on their understanding of sales in Tesco stores. In the cake market, our category champion has been in a position to suggest we reduce the range. In narrowing the range, however, it is essential to ensure that the candidates for reduction include those products that have the lowest customer loyalty or are most frequently substituted, and not simply those products with lowest sales and lowest profitability. Once again it is the customer data that allows us to reduce the impact of the reduction to the consumer.

Natural tension

In practice, the range and distribution of products is decided by collaboration. Sometimes the manufacturer, particularly a large manufacturer such as Procter & Gamble, will instigate a change and at other times we will suggest something, particularly to a smaller supplier. Tesco has a great belief that there will always be a natural tension between suppliers and Tesco. In fact, a natural tension exists within Tesco when we think of the tension between those who manage retail formats, those who focus on categories, those who focus on the marketing levers of price, quality, range and service. The balance is achieved with good insight, some really good underpinning values and a customer perspective. Although aspects of the business are in opposition, and although there will necessarily be conflict, those who manage the customers have no agenda other than the wishes of the customers.

It is the same in our relationship with suppliers. We allow the friction, allow the tension and great results often emerge because friction can produce heat but it can also produce light. That is often why we make great leaps and why we can be faster than most other organizations. We will take a jump and leave our competitors behind.

Performance measures

When you look at a loyalty programme, it is incredibly difficult to measure the results after you have launched it, and you end up with no control. You cannot go back to the start. Tesco has a passion and belief in Clubcard that is partly based on the period in which the launch took place. Around that time, Tesco overtook Sainsbury's as the UK's leading grocer. Tesco did not just overtake but lapped Sainsbury's; Tesco just rocketed ahead. Some of the real clarity of this success is based on the concentration of the impact four times a year. When we mail the £40 million worth of coupons, customers appear in store to redeem them, and that is concentrated into a few weeks. Therefore, it is very, very obvious what effect Clubcard has on the business. The ideal world is if you can breakeven from a customer that responds within say 12 weeks and then you've got all the long-term benefits for free. That's the way we look at it – break even very quickly and then measure the long-term loyalty by retention. If you can get that, you've given customers something they want, they voted with you, that's repaid you immediately, and in effect is where the profit comes from in the future. Largely that's how we balance everything out.

Tesco operate a balanced scorecard. When you look at the customer quadrant, it is about how many loyal customers do we have and how many are being retained. We just look at growing that, and keep growing it. Customers really do just vote with their feet and we define the loyalty for that measurement just simply based on spending frequency. It is not real loyalty but we know that the emotion actually almost mirrors the rational loyalty. For some customers, and I count my Mum as one of those, they can't spend enough to be described as a high spending customer, but you can see their loyalty because they come to our stores every week.

Exchanging best practice with Tesco

Interview with Barry Knichel, WWRE representative and supply chain divisional director, Tesco

Richard Cuthbertson

Introduction

There are a number of public and private Internet-based business-to-business (B2B) electronic exchanges operating within the retail sector today. These include the WorldWide Retail Exchange (WWRE), Transora (funded by 58 leading consumer products manufacturers), the GlobalNetXchange (GNX) and Wal-Mart's own private hub using Atlas Commerce. WWRE includes Royal Ahold, Tesco, Marks & Spencer, Kingfisher, Auchan, Casino, Albertson's, CVC Corp, Kmart, Safeway (US), Target, Walgreen's, Delhaize, Jusco, Best Buy and JC Penney among its founder members. In total, WWRE currently comprises 58 retailers and one supplier (SCA Hygiene); though it should be noted that membership has only just been opened up to include manufacturers and suppliers. Indeed, the WWRE aims to be a retail exchange, not a retailer exchange. According to the WWRE, the exchange was created 'with the fundamental purpose of reducing costs and improving efficiencies throughout the supply chain', and was designed to 'simplify trading between retailers, suppliers, partners and distributors'.[1] The exchange offers a range of value-adding or cost-saving, non-competitive, back-office services, in purchasing and supply chain management.

Currently, the electronic auction process between retailer and supplier has attracted most participation, though new services are being introduced on an ongoing basis, such as the WWRE Collaborative Planner. The WWRE Collaborative Planner employs the VICS-CPFR© methodology and enables retailers and suppliers 'to share information on strategic plans, sales and order forecasting and replenishment'. In many ways this represents the essence of B2B exchanges, providing software tools that allow information to be exchanged in a structured and timely manner.

According to Barry Knichel, Tesco supply chain divisional director, membership of the WWRE increases Tesco's ability to drive four key elements of successful supply chain management: 'scale, speed, cost and best practice'.

Scale

Much of the original thinking behind public retail exchanges focused on the collaborative auctioning of contracts for the supply of goods not for resale, such as office equipment, store fittings or stationery. The idea was that retailers would group together their individual requirements for such products and so leverage their combined scale to achieve greater value, such as lower prices or higher quality. However, this form of collaborative buying is only possible where everyone agrees on the product specification. The principle of buying A4 paper collaboratively may seem simple to implement. In practice, there are many variables in specification even with this basic product, such as the thickness of the paper or the recycling qualities of the paper. Thus, these specifications have to be negotiated and agreed before any collaborative auction can take place.

Greater benefits of WWRE may be delivered in the future through collaborative services, rather than collaborative product purchasing. For example, there may be scope for consolidating haulage or warehousing between members to reduce wasted transport and space. This may prove particularly useful in smoothing peaks or troughs in demand or supply. Similarly, there may be opportunities for the collaborative purchasing of virtual services, such as licences for software tools.

---

[1] WWRE (2001) Press release: WWRE progress exceeds members' expectations 23/10/01.

Thus, where appropriate, the WWRE may provide Tesco with increased scale, and hence improved purchasing power.

Speed

While the collaborative purchasing of goods not for resale has been slow to develop due to the difficulties in agreeing product specifications, the individual auctioning of supply contracts for goods for resale has expanded rapidly, particularly for staple private-label (own-brand) products. A retailer wishing to purchase a staple private-label product for resale, such as mature cheddar cheese, will generally purchase individually and not collaboratively for two major reasons. First, there may be important competitive issues in terms of a unique product specification. Secondly, collaborative purchasing of products for resale may infringe competition law where the collaborative market share is significant; this works against collaborative purchasing of manufacturer-branded products. Moreover, such auctions usually involve staple products due to the straightforward specifications. For a more complex and dynamic product, such as a ready meal, an electronic auction would probably not be appropriate due to the very high level of face-to-face retailer-supplier interaction required.

Where the electronic auction process provided by the WWRE is appropriate, it is not only quicker than a manual auction process but also makes it almost as quick and easy for a retailer to negotiate with 3 suppliers as 10 suppliers. Thus, the WWRE auction process provides Tesco with quicker supplier negotiations, as well as potentially providing a wider selection of suppliers than previously available through a manual process.

Cost

The results of the WWRE appear impressive. Products worth over US$1 billion (€1.1 billion) have been auctioned through the exchange providing substantial savings for members – claimed to be around US$200 million (€224 million) in total. Measurable results from the WWRE Collaborative Planner pilots are claimed to include 'reduced delivery time by 25%, a 33% decrease in safety stock, improvements in in-stock supply by 20–25%, and increased forecast accuracy by 30–35%'.[2]

For many members, these results represent an attractive return on investment. Reduced costs can then be invested elsewhere in the business or passed on to the consumer in the form of price cuts. For example, Barry Knichel claims that Tesco

---

[2] WWRE (2001) Press release: WWRE announces availability of CPRF solution to all members 10/04/01.

have achieved a fourfold return on their WWRE investment so far, most of w
has been directly passed on to the consumer in lower prices.

Thus, the WWRE provides Tesco with the tools to potentially reduce costs, as well as improve the overall functioning of the supply chain.

Best practice

The benefits of using an electronic exchange are not just based around clearly measurable costs and benefits. For example, the auction process provided by WWRE is primarily only an electronic version of the previous manual negotiations. However, because it is electronic, the auction process requires a disciplined approach that is not always evident in manual negotiations. Thus, there is a clear process for all participants to follow, resulting in clear requirements and responsibilities, with the aim of achieving standards of best practice. The potential downside to this approach is that it may not be flexible enough to be applicable in all circumstances; hence its lack of use, for example, for ready meals.

One of the advantages of having a public electronic exchange is that operational and technical standards are agreed through negotiation. There is still much debate as to who may ultimately decide on industry standards within the retail sector. Some commentators, such as Rubin and Charron (2001), argue that 'Wal-Mart will establish standards faster than any consortium could agree [them]', and by implication the retail industry will follow Wal-Mart's lead. The public exchanges may argue in response that it is better for standards to be agreed rather than imposed by a single retailer. In either case, there is general agreement that operational and technical standards will lead to a much more efficient supply chain.

Thus, the WWRE provides Tesco with a forum to influence standards of best practice and software tools to implement best practice, where appropriate.

Future developments

Internet-based electronic trading will continue to develop, both in technical terms and operationally. The retail sector will move towards established standards and common practice over time. There are clear benefits to be gained within the sector by sharing information in a structured and timely manner. What is not clear is the extent to which all participants will benefit. Collaboration and competition make uneasy bedfellows. Standards need to encourage best practice through collaboration while allowing for innovation through competition. A balance needs to be sought that fulfils the needs of all parties within the supply chain, including the consumer.

ket leadership in central Europe

:h David Wild, European corporate development
:sco

Introduction

Tesco is not only the leading food retailer in the UK, but is also a significant overseas player. In 1993 it started to develop abroad and now operates in nine overseas countries – Ireland, Hungary, Poland, Czech Republic, Slovakia, Thailand, Korea, Malaysia and Taiwan. In the year to February 2002, total international sales grew by 37 per cent to £3.9 billion (€5.69 billion) and contributed £119 million (€173.74 million) to group profits. When investing abroad it aims to be a major player in the market by pursuing growth through hypermarkets in emerging markets or acquiring existing businesses in developed markets. Furthermore, by competing with Europe's leading international retailers, it aims to strengthen its UK operation by bringing its learning experience back to its core UK business. In this interview, David Wild, European corporate development director, discusses the means by which Tesco is planning to be the market leader in central Europe. This interview has been supplemented with data from a September 2002 analysts' visit to Tesco's central European operation.

Entering the market

Tesco has been operating in central Europe since 1994, when it opened its first store in Hungary. What attracted the company to the region, and still holds true today, was the combination of an emergent economy, with the prospect of high growth, together with a very immature retail infrastructure.

Tesco penetrated the region by acquiring entry vehicle businesses – a convenience store chain in Hungary, a supermarket business in Poland and department store chains in the Czech Republic and Slovakia. This method of entry enabled the company to get its foot through the door and to understand the way that business was done in these markets.

The company rapidly decided that its primary development format would be hypermarkets. What it realized in central Europe, as in most emergent economies, is that the hypermarket, with its combination of wide range and the opportunity to sell at discount prices, is a very powerful and attractive vehicle for appealing to customers. Compared with smaller stores, sales densities in hypermarkets are comparable. Nevertheless, absolute sales are significantly higher and Tesco is in no doubt that the growth prospects of the hypermarket exceed the growth prospects of smaller stores and are much more resilient to competitor openings.

In the longer term, David Wild believes that there is room for four key types of food retailers in central Europe, similar to the situation in France – hypermarkets, infill supermarkets, discounters and convenience stores. However, for Tesco the priority is to get the hypermarkets up and running.

Pursuing a winning strategy

Although many retailers are entering the region, very few of them are building as large a presence as is Tesco through a significant number of stores. Auchan for example, opened its first hypermarket in Hungary about three years ago and now has only four. In comparison, Tesco has opened 26 stores since 1996 and is now the number one retailer in Hungary. David Wild explains:

> We are pursuing a far more aggressive opening strategy, whereas the competition is being much more pedestrian. Although there are a lot of companies who are active in the region, it is not an

Table 26.1 Hypermarket growth

Country	Number of hypermarkets 2002	Comments
Thailand	41	
South Korea	20	6–10 stores p.a. planned
Taiwan	3	Lack of scale to date
Malaysia	2	2 confirmed for 2003, 15–20 planned
Hungary	26	
Czech Republic	11	
Slovak Republic	12	
Poland	21	

Source: Tesco, 2002

Table 26.2 Financial performance data (typical store). All figures %

Country	Gross margin	Payroll	Retail/store expenses	Mall or other income	Store contribution
Thailand	16	(3)	(7)	3	9
South Korea	16.4	(3.5)	(5)	1.2	9.1
Central Europe	18	(5)	(4)	–	9

Source: Tesco, 2002

> easy market and we are winning. We're determined to be number
> one or two in every market in which we compete.

With regards to pricing, competition is fierce because of the number of international entrants and that is why it is important to have the right operation, employ the right people and look after your customers. The effect is increased efficiency, lower costs and higher levels of customer loyalty.

Growing the business

Tesco is in the fortunate position of having a core business with a very healthy operating cash flow, so generally speaking the financial constraints in terms of capital availability are less than they would be in other organizations. This is actually a source of the company's competitive advantage. In 2001/2, the company invested some £325 million (€474.5 million) in continental Europe, which very few retailers in the world could afford to spend on an organic growth programme. However, Tesco's ability to grow is constrained by two factors – people and the planning environment.

People

There is no point opening stores if there aren't the people to run them. This means people with the right skills to look after customers in the right way. Tesco spends a lot of time and money developing its people. Tesco is a great believer in using local talent, so local managers generally manage the stores, and wherever possible local nationals are used. In recruiting the right calibre managers, English language skills are important but not essential. In Hungary, the business has 12,000 employees, and the business team is 99.9 per cent Hungarian. Hungarian nationals direct the business in:

- finance,
- marketing and PR,
- personnel,
- information technology,
- site acquisition, and
- company secretarial roles.

David Wild describes the situation:

> In 2002, there were about 70 ex-pats in the region, which seems a
> lot but spread across four countries and given the scale of our
> growth, it is not that significant.

One of the fortunate things about acquiring local businesses when Tesco entered the region was that it gave them some store management expertise. This expertise has been utilized with many of the existing managers now running the company's hypermarkets. They have been trained in Tesco skills and techniques by ex-patriot regional management and have spent some time in the UK. In addition to people acquired from the legacy businesses, however, Tesco has also needed to recruit new people.

Some staff have been recruited from competitors and Tesco has also established a graduate trainee programme to develop the skills of younger people in the region. The programme has been running for six years with trainees spending some time in the UK prior to running stores in central Europe. English is always spoken in conjunction with the local language. As an international organization, graduates are also able to work in Tesco's other stores across the world. David Wild observes:

> As our priority is looking after our customers, store managers
> must be given the freedom to adjust their store to the needs of
> their customers. Provided they understand what they have to do,
> they will do the right thing. There is nothing wrong with store
> managers being independent provided it is in line with looking
> after customers and making money.

Planning environment

Across central Europe, Tesco has found many discrepancies in the planning environment, as the discussion in Part II suggested. Regulations can vary city by city and Wild feels that there is a slightly irrational approach to gaining development consent. One of the problems is that there isn't the same disciplined, transparent approach that Tesco is accustomed to in the UK.

A combination of people is used to identify and develop sites. This includes four or five ex-patriot site finders and site researchers, who utilize the skills and processes that the company uses in the UK, in order to assess the turnover potential of a particular location, negotiating permission to buy the land and converting the land to a permitted site. Tesco also has a much larger team of local nationals who, in addition to using the business's core site location skills, also understand the local environment, which is particularly important when applying to the local authority. The third element is developers and advisors, who help the company in specialized areas to ensure that the whole thing comes together.

Logistics and supply chain management

The vast majority of deliveries are direct to the store. Although Tesco chose not to invest in the supply chain, it does have some depots and it has deliberately developed retail systems that have the capability to operate on a centralized distribution basis. The company hasn't invested heavily in distribution because it wanted to invest most of its money in building stores and was uncertain as to what was the best format, and therefore supply system, to develop. The hypermarket is a new format and Tesco did not want to rush into developing a supply chain infrastructure until it knew more about what it would actually need. The company is now at this stage and undertook a major piece of work in Hungary, which is our lead country, looking at what the supply chain should be in the future. Tesco's 26 stores in Hungary in 2002 serve over 1 million customers per week and have a 13 per cent market share. Up until recently, the company has relied to some extent on suppliers' ability to deliver regularly and frequently to store. This has not until recently allowed Tesco to fully develop our private label business. Today, a 21,000 m^2 distribution centre at Herceghalom ships 700,000 cases per week and a dedicated 8,000 m^2 produce distribution centre ships 100,000 cases per week to Hungarian stores.

Developing the Tesco brand

David Wild observes:

> As we grow our presence in central Europe, I think we have a great opportunity to develop a true retail brand and be a clear brand leader. We are hoping to achieve this by investing heavily in marketing and developing our private-label lines. We have taken some initial steps in rolling out private label, with the Tesco Value range appearing in every store, which is a good place to start in an emerging market. We are also launching other Tesco brand products. Private label is a key part of our global capability, and I think Tesco is one of the best own-label developers of any retail business in the world. It is a real skill that we have and something we should use.

In Poland, Tesco has launched over 1200 private-label lines, comprising 600 Tesco Value and 600 Tesco brand lines. In Hungary, over 750 lines are now private label.

As far as loyalty cards are concerned some of Tesco's competitors have them, although the company has not chosen to introduce one at this stage. It will monitor the situation and bring one in if appropriate.

Consumer shopping habits

Central Europe is still very much a cash economy, with most customers preferring this payment option. However, credit cards are becoming increasingly widespread, whilst cheques are very rarely used. The frequency with which consumers shop very much depends on the store location. In the more densely populated parts of cities, shopping frequencies are relatively high at around two to three times per week.

However, Tesco have a growing number of stores on the edge of town, which is a more conventional location for hypermarkets, where the shopping frequency is once a week, or even once a month, if it serves a very wide catchment area.

Where necessary, Tesco provides public transport arrangements, but with an increase in car ownership in the region, it has some very successful stores where most of the customers travel by car.

Apart from an increase in car ownership, there have also been some changes in consumption habits which have increased the popularity of the hypermarket format. In the Czech Republic, for example, demand for microwaves is growing exceptionally fast. This requires Tesco to sell a range of foods suitable for the microwave.

Growth strategies

First, Tesco will gain leadership in the region by looking after its customers. It aims to win by better responding to its customers than its competitors, and by not looking over its shoulder. Secondly, Tesco is in the fortunate position of having a very focused international strategy. It claims not to be bothered about putting flags on maps, its aim rather is to invest heavily in markets in which it seeks to be the number one retailer, and this leads the company to a policy of depth within a market.

Some of Tesco's competitors are very proud of the long list of countries in which they are active, but they may only have three or four stores in each and are only opening one or two a year. What Tesco is doing is focusing on a much smaller number of markets and aiming to be number one or two in them. David Wild concludes:

> We are number one in the UK, Ireland, Northern Ireland, Poland and Hungary. We are investing to be number one in all the four markets of central Europe in which we trade, and we're probably number one, or close to it, in Thailand. We are investing heavily in Korea, which is a very diverse and large market; Malaysia also provides an exciting location for future growth. We are more about saying let's be the market leader by looking after customers and investing heavily in our strategy, than trying to have a presence in every country across the world.

Review questions

1 Do Tesco's central European markets provide opportunities to develop Clubcard? If so, why? If not, why not? How might you overcome any barriers to adoption? (See Part I, Chapter 2.)

2 Are Tesco's experiences with B2B exchanges likely to permit the company to 'break the mould' in a similar way to their experience in B2C electronic commerce? (See Part I, Chapter 6.)

3 Does the business model within Tesco's central European operations appear to be significantly different from that in the UK? What do your conclusions tell you about the challenges of retail internationalization in relation to grocery retailing? (See Part I, Chapter 5.)

Reference

Rubin, R. and Charron, C. (2001) 'Transora and WWRE: Unite and follow Wal-Mart'. Forrester Research Brief 31/10/01.

Chapter 27

Portents: strategic retail futures

Ten more years of change: looking back and looking forward

Elizabeth Howard

Knowing the future is impossible. We cannot forecast the form that retailing will take in another decade, nor what events and fashions will be shaping consumer interests. But in this section of the book, we are attempting to look forward towards the end of 2012. We do it not because we can see the future, but because the exercise of forecasting is itself worthwhile. It forces us to try to identify the factors that underlie the trends we can see and to make explicit our assumptions about the nature and direction of change. Often we do not quite realize what our assumptions are, and what they imply we should worry about in business planning, until we write them down or discuss them with others.

Each of the six contributions that makes up this final chapter of the book is different in character. Some are deliberately provocative. Some are from academics, some from retail chief executives.

Back to the future

Looking forward usually demands that we do a little looking backwards first, to find some perspective and to see the trends. So where were we in 1992, and what were the forecasts then for the next decade? The year 1992 was not just a date in Europe: it was a programme and perhaps an ideal. It represented the European Community's plan to complete the single market. The programme achieved huge amounts of de-regulation and harmonization, and in 1991 and 1992 there was much discussion of what change retailers could expect to flow from it. There was speculation that levels of concentration across Europe might be as high as they were in individual countries by the end of the century. Today, several major grocery retailers have gained top 5 ranking in more than one country, and six of them in three or more countries. None has, however, any very great share of the market at the European level. Looking around in 2002, we can see that the European Union, now of 15 rather than 12 countries, is far from a single retail market. Indeed Alan Giles, CEO of HMV Media, comments in his contribution that consumers may be becoming more, not less, distinct in different countries. Consumer interests, but also planning and development regulations, food standards and many other issues keep the markets somewhat separate.

New and expanding markets

Alongside the discussion about the EU in 1992, was the excitement about the opening up of eastern Europe. The Berlin Wall fell in 1989; by 1992 several companies were expanding fast towards the east. More was forecast. Expectations in this direction have, I suggest, been met. Retail re-structuring and growth in the former East Germany, Hungary, Poland and the Czech Republic have been striking. Hopes for substantial development in Russia have, however, not so far been realized. Interest today in international development focuses on eastern Europe and Asian emerging markets. John Dawson, professor of marketing at Edinburgh, in his contribution asks if Russia (or India, or Africa) might be on the agenda for the next decade.

Integration and concentration

Retail integration and concentration have progressed more slowly than perhaps most were forecasting within the EU; eastern Europe has opened more or less in the way anticipated. What has moved faster than we expected? E-commerce perhaps? In 1992 as I look back, there was little enthusiasm for it, and, though there was much discussion about communication between suppliers and retailers, we did not foresee the web-based B2B exchanges that are a reality today. We were hearing relatively little about B2C e-commerce either in 1992 (and of course we did not use the word: it was home shopping or tele-shopping then). The flurry of experiments and excitement of the 1980s had died away and the potential of the worldwide web had not dawned. Yet Jonathan Reynolds' story about future shopping is actually not so new – similar discussions appeared in the 1980s, though referring to different technologies. So what is the lesson here? First, I think that speed and timing are very difficult to predict, even if trends are not. Secondly, we need to focus on real consumer benefits, and real business models and opportunities, not technology, in forecasting change in e-commerce.

Transforming technology

Technology has transformed retailing in the past decade, but not through home shopping. In the last decade, the retail industry as a whole has become a technologically based, information-driven sector. That is something that was foreseen: the forecasts I have been re-reading look remarkably prescient. Information technology, starting with EPOS systems, has come to drive the supply chain, internal forecasting, ordering and logistics. Geodemographics was invented earlier, but in the 1990s planning and analysis packages were developed so that more scientific location and network planning has swept through the industry. Distributed computer power within organizations has given managers at all levels powerful information to use in controlling their businesses. We can see how far the industry has moved just by looking at the relatively low figures for the proportion of grocery turnover that was scanned through the checkout in 1992. In Germany it was still under 25 per cent, in Belgium 53 per cent, France 62 per cent and Great Britain 66 per cent (*source:* ACNielsen). Today, it is over 90 per cent in France, Britain and Belgium and over 75 per cent in Germany. Non-food retailers are moving in the same direction. The 1990s overall was the decade when control of very large retail organizations became possible. Going forward to 2012, we will see what size of organization might be possible.

Green gold

What else was forecast in 1992? Many things by many people, of course. I was struck by discussions of new formats, and the expectation of growth in Europe of discount formats, and in America of warehouse clubs – and the then new Wal-Mart Supercentres. We have seen each of these trends, but not quite so much of the related suggestion of the expansion of American companies in European countries. 'Green' was in the forecasting headlines too in 1992. Environmental concerns had risen dramatically in public opinion polls at the end of the 1980s, and by 1991 FMI's poll of European top executives' concerns also had the environment rising from bottom to fourth place. Green will be gold: consumers will drive retailers towards environmentally friendly products and practices, we were told. Indeed, today most big firms have a raft of environmental policies that did not exist a decade ago. But products promoted on environmental grounds? There are not so many. And overall, it is interesting that it has not been consumers who have directly led the change, but rather it has been regulation of one kind or another. Beyond that, there is a growing sense among retailers now of the need to think about ethical sourcing and fair-trading issues.

Corporate governance and national business regimes

Finally I want to return to the question of international expansion and concentration, and raise an issue that has not been much discussed in retail studies, so far. That is the question of corporate governance and national business regimes. One of the main shifts of the past decade has been for European retailing to become an activity of large, public corporations and modern co-operatives, replacing family firms, small firms and traditionally organized co-operatives. There were no retail companies in the Fortune 500 list of the largest firms at the beginning of the 1990s. The 2002 list will probably be headed by a retailer, Wal-Mart, and include more than 50 others. Public companies in particular are leading the drive for international scale. Shareholders are increasingly demanding growth from these companies and punishing those who do not expand.

One of the reasons pan-European retailing does not really exist yet is the difficulty of corporate merger and takeover in especially, but not only, Germany. The complex ownership of some firms with the lack of transparency in corporate and banking relationships, combined with financial regulation, make it difficult to use shares as currency for acquisitions, and make it difficult for others to acquire or merge with them. An organization like Metro AG, for instance, has found it necessary to change its corporate structure in order to better compete, to raise the capital it needs and so on. The European Commission has proposed harmonizing financial regulation, especially of take-over codes. So far the proposals are stalled. Surely they will progress: how can a European Union go forward with (at least) two different models of corporate governance? And if they progress, then I forecast we will at last see pan-European retailers.

The retail industry over the next ten years

Dr Hans-Joachim Körber, CEO, Metro AG, Germany

Dr Hans-Joachim Körber has been chairman of the management board of Metro AG since June 2001 and is responsible for investor relations, corporate communications, corporate development, management development, law, associations, environment and internal audit.

What will happen to the retail industry over the course of the next 10 years? It is always difficult to make predictions. With regard to the retail industry, one can observe current trends and anticipate where they will lead over the course of the coming years. The future of retailing in the industrialized countries will be affected by several key trends.

Changing consumers

The ageing populations will lead to an increase in the demand for services, although consumers in general will spend even less of their income in retailing compared to travel or entertainment.

At same time, consumers will become even more educated, which will lead to a rising group of 'smart shoppers'. Their behaviour will greatly differ from price-consciousness to a strong orientation towards lifestyle, a fact that retail companies will have to observe and analyse closely in order to better understand customers' needs.

Knowledge

The key to successful retailing in saturated markets truly lies in understanding what the customer really wants – data-based retailing will give retailers the information they need to have to provide for adequate customer orientation. It is knowledge about the customer that cannot be copied easily by competitors, whereas product assortments and the layout of stores can be duplicated within a few months.

E-commerce

What will happen with regard to e-commerce? Evaluations about the perspectives of e-commerce have become more realistic. Within the next 10 years, only a small number of online-retailers will prove that their business model does earn profits and they will gain a limited market share in the distribution of selected non-food products. Overall, retailing will remain a clearly 'bricks and mortar'-dominated business, with only niches left to be taken over by B2C-e-commerce. The big players from the 'old economy', with their long-standing expertise in logistics and with a solid financial backing, are in the best position to become the key players in e-commerce in the future.

Economies of scale

The necessity to achieve economies of scale together with a higher transparency due to the introduction of the euro will accelerate the ongoing consolidation in European retail. Thus, in a highly competitive environment we will see an increase of mergers and acquisitions, but no significant decline in selling space over the next few years.

Internationalization

It is also safe to say that the global trend to internationalization will continue. What makes me confident about this preposition? First, the past has proven and the present is showing again and again, that the home markets of established retailers in western Europe, the US and in Japan (Triade) are more or less saturated. In these regions, the global players have their operations running, using modern formats. At the same time, a varying percentage of traditional retailing, the 'mom and pop' stores, have weathered competition by occupying specific market niches.

Additional growth for modern formats can thus only be generated through predatory competition. As a consequence, the leading retail companies must expand into emerging markets, notably in eastern Europe and east Asia. We will see tough competition there, because each player will want to exploit windows of opportunity. However, internationalization in retailing will not lead to an end of local or traditional formats in the emerging countries. At the end of this decade, the top 10 retailers will have approximately 20 per cent market share, with sufficient potential for others to fill the gap.

Among the emerging countries, China will be the single most attractive market for retailing. With a population of more than 1.3 billion, an annual growth estimate of 7 per cent for the next few years and a national culture in which commerce and trading are in-born, China is positioned to play a major role in international retailing. The WTO entry in 2001, a high computer literacy and a prudent political leadership will add to China's importance, which in turn could trigger a long-awaited economic rise throughout east Asia, of which the retail industry should take advantage.

Thoughts on the future of grocery retailing

Richard Bell

Changes in the structure and nature of grocery retailing should be seen in the context of likely changes in food processing technology and in consumer lifestyles as well as anticipated developments in the efficiency of food distribution. In recent years the role of the distributor has expanded into areas of food production, and in turn has influenced patterns of consumption. The growth of private label, the shift to increased sales of fresh and chilled foods, and the reaction of the farming community are all a reflection of the retailers' expanded role. Retailers have made a new range of foods available to consumers. Marks & Spencer has developed into food retailing largely on the back of chilled, ready-to-eat meals.

The fundamental drivers of change in any society are demographics, technology and income levels (wealth). The fusion of these trends will shape consumer lifestyles. There are three specific trends that will shape the future of food retailing; time-poor consumers, mobile consumers, and the emergence of new technologies in food production.

Time-rationed society

More working women and the pursuit of leisure are among the causes of the move towards a time-rationed society. The consequence is to increase the responsibility of the food retailer for food preparation and processing. In the United States the average time spent cooking per day during the week had fallen to 20 minutes by the mid-1990s compared to three hours in the 1940s. The case of a US retailer, Ukrops, provides an interesting perspective. Ukrops seeks to provide meals that can be speedily completed at home. All the ingredients for a selected menu are prepared and sold together: preparation and assembly takes place in a centralized kitchen supplying all of Ukrop's stores. Ukrop's has, in effect, moved the domestic kitchen from downstream of the retail store to upstream. All that is required is a domestic re-heating facility, the microwave oven.

Increased mobility

The second trend is in the increased mobility of the population so that more feeding occasions occur away from home. It is not simply an access to transportation, but a social phenomenon. Today more people are going to more places, more often than ever before. This gives rise to additional – and more diverse – eating occasions. Event catering, for example, has become a major opportunity to feed consumers at events such as sporting occasions and exhibitions. The effect of this is to increase the market for the food service industry and reduce the potential market for food retailers.

Application of technology

The third trend is the application of technology to food processing which allows the location of food preparation to be separated from food consumption. The application of *sous vide* (under vacuum) now enables food to be prepared in a central kitchen, transported to the restaurant and re-heated. The skill of the restaurant is now in the presentation and garnishing of the food. Importantly, *sous vide* technology has been developed to improve both the quality and the range of the food available to restaurants. The technology allows many more restaurants to be created, increasing the opportunity for out-of-home consumption.

The growth in opportunity for preparers of food contrasts sharply with the reduction in the number of retail food outlets. Most significantly, a distinction is emerging between the location of food preparation and food consumption. No longer is the choice simply at-home or out-of-home: it now includes food eaten at home but prepared out-of-home. Two telling statistics emerge from the United States. By 1997 over half the food consumed was prepared out of home. The supermarkets were now supplying less than half of total food consumption. Second, of the food prepared out of home, a half was consumed at home. The take-away restaurant business was now as big as the in-house business. In Europe we can expect that food retailing will face increasing competition from restaurants to supply prepared meals to consumers for in-home consumption.

Conclusion

In summary, the shape of food retailing will be as much influenced by external forces as internal change. In this context, debates about store size and location, home delivery via the web, and retailer own brands will be as relevant as rearranging the deck chairs on the Titanic.

Speciality retailing over the next decade

Alan Giles, chief executive, HMV Media, UK

> Alan Giles was appointed to the board as joint chief executive of HMV Media in March 1998 and became sole chief executive in March 1999. He was managing director of Waterstone's from February 1993 to May 1999. He is a non-executive director of Somerfield plc and was a director of the board of WHSmith Group plc from November 1995 to March 1998.

Specialist retailers have been under sustained attack. Sentiment towards the sector was, until very recently, blighted by the short-lived belief that real-world shopping would succumb to perceived convenience and cost structure advantages of online retailers. A more enduring concern has been the 'Wal-Mart effect' – the potential for specialist retailers with high operational gearing to come under pressure from the scale advantages of mass-merchandisers who 'cream' their ranges.

Resilience of the specialists

However, as a breed, specialist retailers have proved remarkably resilient. Consumers worldwide enjoy shopping as a leisure activity. That emotional need is hard for Wal-Mart *et al.* to fulfil. Good specialists have exploited this with a whole array of innovations – coffee shops, interactive facilities, more comfortable quasi-domestic surroundings, interesting architecture and more. The best have realized that passionate enthusiasm for their product is a necessary but not sufficient condition for success. With some painful cultural change, and expensive systems investment, they have learned to be good retailers too.

Current trends

So what lies ahead? It's tempting, if somewhat unimaginative, to simply extrapolate the current trends:

- creation of 'flagship' stores that define the brand and complement a multi-channel offer;
- escalating investment in a relaxing yet stimulating store environment – 'retail as theatre';
- development of ever more sophisticated inventory and customer information management systems;
- globalization – the tenants on Chicago's North Michigan Avenue, London's Oxford Street, and Singapore's Orchard Road look pretty much the same.

Warning signs

However, there are warning signs that some of these concepts must be implemented with great care and sensitivity:

- The economics of retailing in a low-inflation competitive environment are harsh. Capital expenditure cannot be allowed to spiral upwards, so to achieve long-term success the relentless upgrading of the customer experience must be balanced by radical and imaginative cost engineering programmes.
- The standard UK institutional lease is hopelessly incompatible with the accelerating store format cycles prevalent in much of the specialist sector. Clearly the landlord's low-risk security that derives from 15, 20 and even 25 year leases with upward only reviews is 'priced in' to the rent. However, most specialist retailers find it difficult to predict the shape, size and location of their stores even five years out. Something has to change here to improve goal congruence and more equitably share the risks and rewards.
- Despite the homogenizing effect of pan-continental communication, there is some evidence that consumers in individual countries are becoming more, not less, distinct. For example, in most music markets worldwide the share of local artists is increasing at the expense of the huge international names.

Furthermore, there are new trends that are only in their embryonic stages. As it becomes tougher to differentiate their business on the obvious dimensions of brand, merchandise ranges and customer service, specialist retailers will need to reach for tools that are harder to use. For example, supply chain management is much less developed in this sector than, say, food retailing.

Complementary competitors

Despite the challenges, the prospects for specialist retailing are excellent. Proponents of one-stop shopping have consistently underestimated consumers' appetite for the authenticity, expertise and excitement of shopkeepers who show single-minded focus on a narrow category of product in which they can truly excel. Mail-order catalogues, department stores, supermarkets and e-tailers have all been heralded as the evolutionary threat to the specialist retailer. History proves that those business concepts have been viable, but complementary, competitors.

Consumers are in control

Peter Williams, chief executive, Selfridges, UK

Peter Williams has been CEO of Selfridges since December 2002. He had been Finance Director of Selfridges since 1991 and of the Company since March 1998. He qualified as a chartered accountant with Arthur Andersen and has worked for Andersen Consulting, Aiwa (a division of Sony) and Freemans PLC. He is chairman of the British Retail Consortium's working party reviewing the practical implications of the euro and is a member of its economics and research panel.

Meeting the challenge

Do we as retailers really meet the challenge of meeting future consumers' needs? There has never been so much merchandise available, so easily, to so many people. Those who have the money are prepared to pay £500 for the 'to die for' Louis Vuitton handbag rather than a cheaper alternative, and for some handbags there is even a waiting list. The consumer continues to raise the bar in the demands they place on retailers in terms of environment, the merchandise presentation and customer service. In fact, consumers are in control.

As retailers, we concentrate on merchandise. We go through periodic re-branding exercises because someone decides that the existing shopfit is now old hat. But is this enough? In Selfridges, we would like to do away with the name 'department store' because we no longer have departments dedicated to product categories such as coats and separates. We are deliberately diminishing space dedicated to traditional china and glass and oriental rugs, and we removed haberdashery and sewing machines several years ago. Well-being is now more important to the consumer than oriental rugs.

Flagship department stores, urban monuments in all major cities, with their grand scale of architecture and space, have the unparalleled opportunity to capture the senses, attention and imagination of the consumer.

Why do so many retailers provide a boring environment? Retailers concentrate on the product, with some cursory attention to the design of the store and possibly the music. At Selfridges we are looking to stimulate and arouse the senses that other retailers do not reach. The smell of the food hall and the coffee shop. The music that makes your hips sway or your feet tap because it is relevant to you and stirs a memory. The soft carpet that conveys luxury and seduction and the lighting that accentuates all the fantastic colours in the merchandise. Sales associates at Selfridges wear the product they sell, or dress in their own clothes to express individuality and style.

In our world of department stores, most of our competitors have removed their food halls. The accountants have taken over and said the contribution per square metre is not as good as the other product areas so we must stop selling food and provide yet more space for clothing and washing machines. But food is an everyday purchase and provides the reason for the consumer to make a visit to your store every day. She or he may not buy anything else on that particular day, but it doesn't matter. Food is the only product that unites all people, of all ages – it is a 'need' rather than a 'want'.

And product, generally, is oversupplied. Do I need another shirt? Do I need another tie? No. My wardrobe is full. So why do I buy another shirt and tie? Because I can afford to, because I see a colour combination that I like and because it gives me pleasure.

Learning from the big brands

The brands, of course, have recognized this for many years. The cosmetics and perfumery industry, amongst the most focused and successful companies in the consumer goods sector, has succeeded for years in promoting a product that nobody really needs, but everyone wants. For years they have projected a strong lifestyle image and created a desire. Now with the globalization of many fashion brands, this is also happening in apparel. Some want to be a member of the Prada or Versace tribes. Not me personally, but then I do like Boss Sport, Zegna, Oswald Boeteng and Richard James. Everyone is looking to create an image and their own sense of style.

The Selfridges experience

So how will Selfridges differentiate itself? We will do it by concentrating on the architecture externally and internally; building large space stores – size really does matter; having a range of brands and products that is accessible to all, whether it be Gucci or Levi's; creating atmosphere in the store through events such as Bollywood in May 2002 with film, fashion and glamour; using music, with gospel singers at

Christmas; and providing space for cafés, where people can watch other people, the sport most enjoyed and most played by everyone!

2012: a retail nightmare?

John Dawson, professor of marketing, University of Edinburgh

John Dawson has taught and researched retailing and marketing in universities in the UK, USA, Japan and Australia and has worked on projects with major retail and information technology companies in several countries. John Dawson holds the Chair of Marketing at Edinburgh and is a visiting professor at ESADE, Barcelona. He has spent periods as visiting professor at EUI Florence, UNISA Pretoria, UMDS Kobe and Boconni Milan. Current research is in five main areas: the nature of change and innovation in European retailing; international activity of retailers; e-retailing and information management in retailing; the measurement of performance in retailing and distribution; inter-relationships between European and Asian approaches to retail management. In the early 1970s whilst working in the University of Wales he was the founding editor of *Cambria* and in 1984 founded the *International Journal of Retailing*, which he edited until its merger with *Retail and Distribution Management*. He then established the *International Review of Retail, Distribution and Consumer Research*, which he now co-edits. He is the author of over 20 books and major government reports and around 200 papers in academic and professional journals.

Crystal ball gazing

In 1992 finding sushi in British supermarkets was difficult. Now it is easy. Will we find locust brochette and fried ants in the chill cabinet in 2012? In 1992 the banks and building societies provided our various bank accounts. Now large retailers do this. By 2012 what will retailers be providing that is presently provided by other sectors? Might they be providing healthcare, pre-school education, accounting services or hotel accommodation? In 1992 the privatization of central Europe and the launch of the European single market encouraged retailers to look at expansion opportunities in Europe. At the end of 2002 east Asia was the cynosure of retailers 'sparkling eyes'. In 2012 where will it be – India, Africa, Russia?

What is certain is that retailing will change more before 2012 than it has since 1992. Reaction time is getting faster. Retail processes throughout the value chain are operating at an ever-faster rate. Store development, buying, marketing, merchandising, logistics, staff training, product development, investment payback, all have to operate on ever faster schedules. This quickening trend even affects consumers with demands for shorter fashion cycles and more new products, customer demands for faster service, and consumers applying a fashion mentality to staple products.

To get a glimpse, perhaps, of what might be happening in 10 years we can look into the three crystal balls of strategy, structure and performance.

The crystal ball of strategy

Ten years is a long time in retailing strategy, particularly in the hyper-competitive oligopolistic retail markets of today, characterized by rapidly operating processes. But the essence of strategy is to have a vision. Over the next ten years:

- Scripted strategy will give way to a more creative and innovative approach. Presently the view is that strategy is designed, developed and implemented in a linear and sequential way – the so-called scripted approach. This will be too slow a process by 2012. Strategy will merge with innovation and become more immediate, but within the broad parameters of the company vision and culture.
- Porterian views of strategy through managing 'five forces' and trying to be lowest cost, or focused firms will become interesting but historic concepts – perhaps this has happened already. The retailers' value chains will change dramatically as the boundaries of retailing are expanded into new arenas of providing for consumer wants. A new body of strategic concepts will be used.
- The links amongst firms in the demand (not supply) chain of retailing will exhibit greater variety with firms existing in complex networks, not as discrete firms as at present. The increasing speed of processes will mean that firms contract-out more functions but also become service providers for other firms.
- Bigger will continue to be better. Scale economies at organizational level (not necessarily shop or delivery unit level) will continue to become more powerful as innovation and technology enable costs to be removed from the demand chain in scale related ways.

The crystal ball of structure

Retailers' attempts to create monopoly markets are not new. What has changed is the definition of relevant market. Having moved from a regional view in the 1970s to a national and continental view in the 1990s it is likely that a multi-continental view will have emerged by 2012. However, while we will measure Wal-Mart, Tesco, Ahold, Home Dept and others as operating within a global market, at the same time the need to dominate local markets will remain the essence of retail structure. Thus these same firms will seek local spatial monopolies – in exactly the same way as the Hudson Bay Company did 300 years ago. Therefore, within Europe smaller and smaller communities will become the focus of attention of the large firms.

A second big change in structure will be the multi-channel dimensions of retailers, both big and small – if any small firms survive that long. Yes, there will be micro-firms in retailing but fewer will grow into small and medium sized firms simply because they will not be able to accommodate the new speed of the processes in retailing. Retailers will be deliver retailing through multiple channels – fixed store, Internet, automated sales units, catalogues, maybe even interactive TV, and possibly others.

The crystal ball of performance

From a consumer perspective, retailer performance will improve dramatically before 2012 with low prices and high service being the standard positioning. In achieving this we are likely to see some or all of the following, and more:

- frantic attempts by retailers to halt the decreases in productivity of space;
- the death of ECR as it becomes defined as collusive activity by fair trade authorities;
- loyalty schemes that focus on retailer loyalty to customer rather than, as now, customer loyalty to retailer;
- automated space planning by store;
- widespread customer self-scanning;
- even more investment in retailer brand building;
- 'time of day'-driven merchandising and marketing;
- a major conversion, within the firm, of tacit knowledge to explicit knowledge.

Conclusion

The world's largest retailer presently has sales of about the size of all retail sales in Spain. By 2012 we can expect at least 20 retailers of this size with the largest retailer with sales of well over €500 billion, at current price levels, and with over two million employees. For these large firms the investment in technology at 1 per cent of sales will facilitate radical new forms of innovation. But, from recent evidence, at least 5 of the top 20 retailers will not exist – having been merged or acquired.

Much of retailing in 2012 will still be the same simple business as now – buying goods from manufacturers, adding a margin and selling them to customers. Looking into the crystal balls, by 2012 the only things to have changed will be the strategy, structure and performance of the sector and its firms – and maybe some of the products that are sold. The nightmare is not the vision of 2012 but the traumas of getting there!

Shopping 2012?

Jonathan Reynolds

Alex could see the red light blinking at him as he rolled Leo's pushchair up the hill. The village's Automated Service Dispenser was playing up again. As he got nearer, he could see the vivid display flashing 'Corrupt substring: Retry, Cancel,

Ignore' and playing the theme tune from an old '90s soap opera. He muttered under his breath – another virus had clearly got past the system and this was another of today's errands to be foiled by technology. Alex of course didn't really need to use the box – thanks to their combined incomes, from various sources, they were comfortably off and had most of the gadgets they needed with them or at home to ensure that they stayed pretty well connected to the net. But the ASM (or 'shop-in-a-box', as some villagers called it) had been installed five years ago with the closure of the village stores and post office. It had been originally designed to give those people without at-home access to online services a way of providing for themselves. Not everyone could afford one of the fully-fledged ambient packages around – and some didn't want them anyway. But Alex felt that he had to use the box occasionally, or it might go the same way as the shop – and in any case he had needed the exercise. But these publicly funded terminals were becoming less and less reliable as more people carried the net with them in their pockets or on their wrists. Some, like Alex's brother Elton, were even using wireless implants, although there'd been some recent health scares about metal fatigue. He carried on past the machine to the Millennium Village Hall and called in at the weekly fruit and vegetable market. Allotments were becoming very fashionable again – not least because of the continuing preoccupation with organic food and widespread resistance to commercially grown GMO crops – and a lot of the excess produce from weekends of hard work was redistributed amongst the locals. And anyway, it was a lot more fun than looking at pictures of carrots on the online grocer's service, if you had the time.

His partner Sophie was away on one of her short business trips, looking at new hard landscaping ideas in France for her garden design business. He had charge of Leo for the next couple of days and was also acting as Sophie's human PA (rather an antique concept, but quite fun to fool people) for the duration. His next tranche of fitness consultancy, which he ran from the home videosuite, wasn't due to kick in until the following week.

Getting back to the house, he lifted Leo back into his playpen and looked at the living room screen, which, as always, was left on permanently. After all, it didn't cost anything: in fact, some people made money out of watching professionally – they were paid for watching and responding to advertising. In the corner of the plasma display, a convincing imitation of Britney Spears murmured 'four messages for us, Alex'. The screen had come with Spears pre-programmed as a personal assistant and Alex had never got around to changing the settings – not least because the online manual was pretty incomprehensible. His wife wasn't too concerned – she had a younger version of Pierce Brosnan all to herself, whilst Leo, when he grew a bit older, would be able to choose from several well-known cartoon characters, some of whom were already being pressed into service by Alex to read Leo bedtime stories.

Alex checked the household messages. The first was the regular weekly vmail for Sophie from maybebaby.com, with its advice on the early stages of pregnancy and a downloadable holovideo of energetic antenatal exercises. Alex hurriedly moved on – Sophie could pick up the message herself from her pocket assistant later in the day. The second was an update from Britney herself. She'd been busy. She'd been bidding on Alex's behalf for one of the capsules from the London Eye on offer through bidsrus.com. The big wheel was being dismantled and Alex thought that a capsule would look great in the back garden. Britney was negotiating on his behalf and the latest was that she had beaten British Airways down to €9500 including delivery. She looked very pleased with herself – as far as an avatar ever could. The third message was from a well-known general merchandiser offering 15 per cent off gazebos this week. 'It hazda be Supa', read the message. A pop-up window hoved into view as a sales executive from the company sought to add some personal persuasion to the advertising. Alex looked outside as the rain began to fall and shouted 'Sin Bin, Britney', adding the retailer to his 'junk vmail' list. Some companies never learned. Finally, he turned to the last message. It was from Greenfields, the UK's biggest regional shopping centre, outside Bristol. They were having an Italian theme day on Saturday, with wine tasting, a fashion show from Versace, a performance by the two tenors (the third having sadly died the previous year) and (Alex noted with especial interest) free crèche time for under 5s for any parent wanting to test drive a Lamborghini. That might be worth a trip, he thought.

You had to go a long way these days to find a big collection of good quality shops. With the growth of online trading – even to only around 15 per cent of business – most bricks-and-mortar retailers tended to cluster together for warmth near the largest towns. The costs of doing something really spectacular to attract customers away from their screens meant that upscale retailers could only afford to do it in a few places and anyway, investors and developers were still very wary of putting money into marginal retail property. This was especially so, given the introduction of road-pricing the previous summer. The only exceptions were the big general merchandisers who were using cheap warehousing space on the edge of town, sharing the space with their online distribution and fulfilment centres. Retail parks, which had largely been offering bulky commodities, had been reinvented as sharespace enterprise parks for business start-ups. Smaller towns, which had something to offer in the way of historic attractions, were doing well; but other places had lots of shop-in-the-boxes, collection points, markets and temporary lets to discounters. If you weren't plugged-in in some way, thought Alex, you really lost out these days.

Alex heard the purr of an electric motor outside the house. It was the regular Value Alliance Network (VAN) delivery. They'd signed up for the service when Leo was born, because of the sheer difficulty in getting out of the house and it had become hard to do without. Run by a consortium of retailers, VAN charged €100 a week for a complete fulfilment service. Regular orders (beer, nappies, toilet tissue, milk, cereal) were dealt with automatically and adjusted in line with demand; other goods accumulated through scanning of used product barcodes and shopping lists which they dictated to Britney or Pierce during the day. But VAN also provided services – dry cleaning, prescription fulfilment and the like. The driver keyed the code to get access to the family's secure storage unit and fridge/freezer – provided by the Network. It was like having a regular housekeeper – but considerably cheaper, given today's hourly rates. It was unusual for Alex to be around when the order came through – VAN didn't of course require the householder to be in to make the delivery. Alex enjoyed going to nearby Felpersham to Enrico's Emporium to pick up (and sample) the odd deli item – the service was wonderfully old-fashioned – but had given up long ago on the regular weekly shop. He was in no hurry to go back to the old ways.

With Sophie back at the weekend, the family decided to make the trip to the mall. It was another opportunity for Alex to try out his new fifth generation pocket assistant, which had been a freebie as a result of taking out a subscription to the Bloomberg Personal News Jockey. The News Jockey was a neat hologram, which popped up to keep him up-to-date with his personal business news agenda. 5G-PAs were otherwise prohibitively expensive, since they involved portable holographic imaging, still at the trial stage. He'd heard about Greenfields' new Golden Touch service, which tempted consumers by calling in exclusive offers and showing a short holo or video of the product on offer. The mall server identified him as his PA Bluetooth module switched in. Thanks to the integral global positioning chip, the mall knew exactly where Alex was until he left the car park. The server also had access to all of the family's previous shopping experiences at Greenfields, his credit rating, psychographic profile and his current interests. (Although it has had to pay him for the privilege: the days of consumers providing free marketing information were long over.) Even as they moved towards the atrium with its fountains and mock-Tuscan architecture, vendors were vying for Alex's disposable income. Sitting with Sophie at the fashion show, his PA vibrated gently. Through his earpiece he heard a cultured Italian voice offering him a personal discount of 15 per cent on the price of a delicately crafted Gucci leather briefcase. The briefcase appeared in miniature, but solidly and expensively above the holoscreen, being carried nonchalantly by a tiny, dapper figure that bore a suspicious resemblance to Alex. 'Transmit your sig now to reserve this item for two hours at this price. Come and see us soon, Mr Bond.' Alex sneaked a look at Sophie; she was engrossed in the commentary to the fashion show being played through her tiny headset; on her flat screen PA, options and prices for the items being displayed were flashing up. She hesitated and pounced on one particularly fetching evening gown. The item would be made within three days to her stored measurements and delivered with the next VAN consignment. Sophie sighed: 'not quite the same as picking it off the rail, but they probably wouldn't have had my size in stock anyway . . .'

Peter and Louise, Alex's parents, lived in Felpersham. Although Peter had been a software engineer in the '80s, since his retirement he had increasingly lost touch with technology. Indeed, if he was honest, what was happening to the net had left him behind (along with the company that used to employ him) quite a while ago. Like everyone else, he had dutifully replaced his old analogue TV with an integrated digital model and subscribed to a reasonable range of services. But he'd baulked at Alex's suggestion that they get themselves a wall-sized screen and personal assistant a few years ago. Peter and Louise were comfortable with their 'walled garden', seen through a modestly sized screen. Not for them the jungle of the unregulated nets. In an era of uncertainty, they desperately needed the security of trustworthy brands and the comfort of the everyday rituals of buying. Louise thumbed the remote control and accessed Supa's food store. They only needed a few more points to get favoured customer status and she was determined that today was the day. FCS would allow her to use the store at any time during the day or night and have the services of a personal shopper. She saw that there was a gazebo on offer with a 5 per cent discount for Golden Gardeners. (She and Peter had joined the Golden Gardeners scheme a few months ago and they had picked up quite a few bargains.) The gazebo attracted 2500 points. She aimed her 'magic mouse' (as she like to call it) at the screen and just managed to hit the flashing 'Buy Me!' logo with the infrared. She'd tried using the voice-operated screen at Alex and Sophie's, but she was frightened of being embarrassed by the thing misunderstanding her. Anyway, she'd never liked Pierce Brosnan. At least you knew where you were when you pressed a button.

Only in one area had they really moved with the times. Both Peter and Louise enjoyed their food and Alex, Sophie and Leo were coming to dinner that evening. Slipping into the kitchen, Louise consulted the fridge. It was suggesting an Italian meal – something to do with Euro 2010. It had most of what it needed already. It was proposing to order some oregano and dried porcini mushrooms. It was also recommending what it described as 'a rather saucy valpolicella' to accompany the meal. Louise touched the screen and the fridge transmitted the order to Enrico's Same Day Direct. It also played a short review by Oz Clarke of her wine choice. Enrico's van would be up that afternoon to drop it off at the local box and Peter would pop up to collect it. Things That Think (TTTs) had been a feature of the early part of the decade; just about everything that could be had been linked to the net. But some TTTs were more useful than others. She noticed that the fridge had changed the upcoming order for butter to low fat spread; and it had deleted the streaky bacon – Peter's automatic cholesterol monitor in the bathroom had clearly been telling tales again.

An earlier version of this scenario appeared in Retailing 2010, *published by the National Foresight Programme.*

Index